A Handbook for Office Professionals

HOW 10

James L. Clark

Professor, Business Department, Pasadena City College

Lyn R. Clark

Chair, Computer Applications and Office Technologies Department
Los Angeles Pierce College

THOMSON
™
SOUTH-WESTERN

Australia · Canada · Mexico · Singapore · Spain · United Kingdom · United States

THOMSON

SOUTH-WESTERN

HOW 10: A Handbook for Office Professionals, 10e

James L. Clark and Lyn R. Clark

Editorial Director:
Jack W. Calhoun

Editor-in-Chief:
George Werthman

Acquisitions Editor:
Jennifer Codner

Developmental Editor:
Taney H. Wilkins

Marketing Manager:
Larry Qualls

**Senior Production
Editor:**
Kara ZumBahlen

Media Technology Editor:
Jim Rice

**Media Developmental
Editor:**
Josh Fendley

Media Production Editor:
Kelly Reid

**Manufacturing
Coordinator:**
Diane Lohman

**Production House/
Compositor:**
Bay Island Books/
John Richards

Printer:
QuebecorWorld, Taunton, MA

Internal Designer:
John Robb, Robb &
Associates

Cover Designer:
John Robb, Robb &
Associates

Cover Photo Source:
PhotoDisc, Inc.

Library of Congress Control
Number: 2002116182

ISBN: 0-324-17882-4

Contents

Preface

HOW 10: A Handbook for Office Professionals, tenth edition, has been designed for the Internet Age to provide assistance in the preparation of all types of written business communications. Its content and style focus upon the needs of students, office personnel, business writers, and other business professionals to produce suitable documents for success in a highly competitive, fast-paced global economy.

HOW 10 presents detailed and precise information for writing, formatting, and transmitting business documents. It serves as a reference book to answer specific questions regarding language conventions, business formats, and document transmission as they relate to the preparation of E-mail messages, business letters, memorandums, reports, manuscripts, proposals, bulletins, résumés, faxes, agendas, itineraries, press releases, and meeting minutes.

A Comprehensive Reference Manual for Business

HOW 10 is succinct, yet comprehensive. It covers thoroughly the principles of grammar, punctuation, capitalization, number usage, word hyphenation and division, and abbreviation format in simple, easy-to-understand language. Each rule is illustrated with examples or example sentences related to business circumstances or conditions. In addition, nearly 200 word confusions—ones such as *affect/effect, ensure/insure*, and *principal/principle*—are differentiated by simple definitions and discriminating examples.

Content and formats for various business documents are covered thoroughly in *HOW 10*. All the major parts of a business letter, forms of address for domestic and foreign correspondence, and commonly used letter styles are discussed and illustrated, along with the basic formats for writing memorandums. Report writers will find helpful the up-to-date guidelines for citing sources, preparing visuals, setting up listings, providing main and text headings, compiling preliminary pages and bibliographies, and formatting a report in general.

Instructions and examples for preparing E-mail messages, itineraries, agendas, and meeting minutes further enhance the usability of this book as a business writer's resource. To assist readers with the entire document processing cycle, *HOW 10* provides detailed procedures for preparing business documents on computer-based equipment and accessing the Internet to collect information.

New to *HOW 10*

The following information has been added to *HOW 10*:

- *New and expanded information* on connecting to the Internet, accessing the World Wide Web, using search sites to locate information, and evaluating Web sites (see Chapter 9).

- *New and expanded information* on E-mail messaging—purpose and function, features, templates, procedures, message preparation, and E-mail netiquette (see Chapter 10).
- *New section* on proofreading and editing documents created with voice-recognition software (see Chapter 8).
- *New perspectives* on accessing and using Internet career centers as well as specific instructions and examples for preparing résumés to be placed on-line (see Chapter 13).
- *New and expanded listings* of relevant Internet sites—reference, news, business, government, directory, career center, and travel (see Chapter 15).
- *New information* on organizing and managing computer files and folders in Windows XP (see Chapter 16).
- *Expanded glossary* of commonly used computer and Internet terms (see Glossary B).

Special Features

Several features, besides the Contents and the extensive Index, increase the functionality of *HOW 10* as a reference book:

1. **Solution Finders**—comprehensive topic indexes at the beginning of each chapter enable readers to locate easily solutions to their problems.
2. **Two-color format**—rules are printed in red and examples are printed in black so that principles may be located, read, and understood quickly.
3. **Example headings**—boldfaced headings differentiate aspects of each rule so that specific examples and applications may be located immediately.
4. **Spiral binding**—the lie-flat feature of spiral binding permits readers to compare readily their problems with the examples.
5. **Glossary of grammatical terms**—a listing with definitions and examples of all the grammatical terms used in this book may be accessed for further clarification of any language principle.

Finding Solutions to Problems

Information you need may be located easily and quickly in *HOW 10* by using a four-step process:

1. Find the chapter you need by turning to the list of contents shown on the back cover.
2. Turn to the Solution Finder at the beginning of that chapter by using the page-edge chapter divider tab.
3. Locate the information you need in the Solution Finder. Each main topic is listed alphabetically followed by subsections of that topic and their corresponding section numbers.
4. Turn to the appropriate section within the chapter by referring to the page-guide references (the section numbers shown at the top right corner of the odd-numbered pages).

If information cannot be located through surveying the contents listed on the back cover, use *HOW's* comprehensive Index at the end of the book to find the appropriate section.

Supplementary Materials

HOW 10 may be employed as a classroom text or supplement for instructing potential office employees, administrative assistants, business writers, and managers—anyone who deals with the preparation of written business documents.

The *Workbook for HOW 10* (ISBN 0-324-17884-0) provides reinforcement for the major principles contained in the reference manual. This 364-page supplement contains exercises that are coordinated specifically with sections in *HOW 10* and are designed to provide students with realistic learning applications, not just isolated sentence exercises.

Workbook exercises enable students to apply the rules governing punctuation, capitalization, number usage and applications, grammar, word confusions, abbreviations, spelling, proofreading, and editing. In addition, students receive practice in locating reference sources on the Internet, composing E-mail messages, using correct address formats, formatting business letters and memorandums, and indexing names for filing.

The *Instructor's Manual and Key* print version (ISBN 0-324-17883-2) includes keys to all the exercises in the *Workbook for HOW 10*. In addition, this teaching tool supplies more than 120 instructional transparency masters that contain the major punctuation, grammar, capitalization, and number-usage principles in *HOW 10* and correspond directly with the exercise applications in the workbook. Other teaching materials in the instructor's manual include a familiarization exercise and a series of business letter and memorandum applications.

The *Instructor's Manual and Key* CD-ROM version (ISBN 0-324-19058-1) includes PowerPoint presentations for the major language principles and communication concepts covered in *HOW 10*. All information contained in the print version also appears on the CD-ROM version of the *Instructor's Manual and Key*. Please visit the *HOW 10* support Web site at http://how.swlearning.com for downloadable instructor's material and other useful resources.

User Profile

HOW 10 may be used by students in word processing, keyboarding, business English, business communication, voice-recognition, transcription, legal office, medical office, and office procedures courses—all courses that require the processing of written words. It functions as a resource for class assignments—answering questions on language applications, punctuation, document framework, and document format. Use of the handbook enables students to produce more nearly correct business documents. This reference book continues to be a valuable resource as students enter the business environment and encounter actual assignments in business writing and document preparation.

Leaders of seminars designed to improve communication proficiency will find *HOW 10* a useful tool for assisting participants in improving their language competence, mechanics of expression, and knowledge of document framework and formats.

HOW 10 serves as a reference for all persons in business who are responsible for communicating through the written word. Similar to the indispensable dictionary, this handbook compresses other essential reference information into a single source for producing effective business documents. It is targeted for use in businesses by managers, administrative assistants, secretaries, word processors, and all others who have responsibility for producing effective written communications. Persons in all fields of business, education, government, law, and medicine will benefit from using *HOW 10* as a reference in preparing written documents for their professional position and their personal business circumstances.

Acknowledgments

We thank the following reviewers for their assistance in the preparation of this reference book:

Dawna Andrea, North Idaho College
Dr. Carole Bennett, Santa Rosa Junior College
Dr. Judy High Diffley, Washburn University
Ron Kapper, College of DuPage
Dr. E. Rebecca Limback, Central Missouri State University
Diana S. McKowen, Indiana University
Virginia Melvin, CPS, Southwest Tennessee Community College
Cathy Peck, Chippewa Valley Technical College
Dr. Kristina Sheeler, Indiana University
Dana H. Swensen, Utah State University

James and Lyn Clark
E-mail: ClarksHOW@aol.com

1

Punctuation

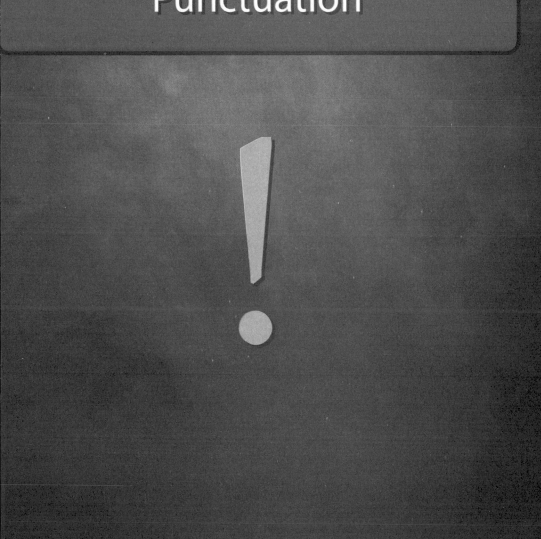

Punctuation Solution Finder

Punctuation Solution Finder *(continued)*

Punctuation (left sidebar tab)

Punctuation Solution Finder *(continued)*

Period

Abbreviations   1-35a
Decimals   1-37
Ellipses   1-38, 1-52
Emphasis in advertising   1-38
End of independent phrase   1-34
End of sentence   1-33
Initials   1-35
Omissions in quotations   1-38, 1-52
Outlines   1-36
Period format and use with other
   punctuation marks   1-39
Polite requests   1-33, 1-41e

Question Mark

Direct questions   1-40
Expressions of doubt   1-42
Indirect questions   1-41d
Polite requests   1-41e
Question mark format and use with
   other punctuation marks   1-44
Series of questions   1-43
Statements meant as questions
   1-41c
Statements with questions   1-41a, b

Quotation Marks

Capitalization with quotation marks
   1-53
Definitions of words and expressions
   1-49b
Direct quotations   1-47
Ellipses   1-52
Literary and artistic titles   1-50

Long quotations   1-48
Omissions in quoted material   1-52
Quotation mark with other punctua-
   tion marks   1-54
Quotations within quotations   1-51
Short expressions requiring emphasis
   1-49
Short quotations   1-47
Titles of literary and artistic works
   1-50
Words *marked, labeled, stamped,* or
   signed   1-49c

Semicolon

Enumerations   1-21
Explanations   1-21
Independent clauses with coordinat-
   ing conjunctions   1-18
Independent clauses with transitional
   expressions   1-19
Independent clauses without coordi-
   nating conjunctions   1-17
Semicolon use with other punctua-
   tion marks   1-22
Series containing complete thoughts
   1-20
Series containing internal commas
   1-20

Underscore

Underscore format and use with
   other punctuation marks   1-66
Use of the underscore   1-4e, 1-49b,
   1-50, 1-66

Comma

1-1 **Series**

a. A series appearing in a sentence consists of three or more parts— equally ranked words, phrases, or short clauses. The last part in the series is connected by a conjunction (*and, or,* or *nor*). Place a comma after each part in the series except the last one. Be sure to use a comma before the conjunction (*and, or, nor*).[1]

words

Four popular Internet search sites are Yahoo!, AltaVista, Lycos, and Excite.

As a bonus on our luncheon special, you may select soup, salad, or dessert.

We accept only cash—neither checks, bankcards, nor purchase orders are accepted for payment.

Next year's budget will permit our department to hire an accountant, a network administrator, and an additional administrative assistant.

phrases

A consultant was hired to improve customer service, computerize our accounting system, and implement cost-effective procedures.

short clauses

Dana Girard made the sale, I approved the contract, and Chris Lopez authorized the shipment yesterday.

b. Commas are not used when the parts of a series are all joined by conjunctions.

words

You must present a passport **or** a driver's license **or** a state-issued picture identification card.

Your monthly phone plan includes a message service **and** call waiting **and** call forwarding.

phrases

For the past year we have contracted with A-Z Building Services to clean the offices nightly **and** manicure the grounds weekly **and** provide general repairs as needed.

c. Although generally avoided, *etc.* is sometimes used to indicate "and so forth" at the end of a series. If used, *etc.* is set off by commas; it is not preceded by the word *and*.

---

[1]Some periodicals and literary writers prefer to omit the comma before the conjunction in a series. For business writing, however, use the comma before the conjunction to promote ease of reading and clarity.

within a sentence

Checking accounts, savings accounts, money market accounts, **etc.,** are available through our Internet banking service.

end of a sentence

We plan to visit all our branch offices this year—Dallas, Los Angeles, Chicago, London, Paris, Rome, **etc.**

d. **A comma is not used before an ampersand (&) in an organizational name unless the organization uses the comma in its official name.**

no comma

Jones, Hill **&** Howard will move into its new offices on May 1.

comma

Our company has retained Duncan, Phelan, Liggett, **&** Phelan to perform an internal audit.

1-2 Parenthetical Expressions

a. **Transitional words and expressions that are considered unnecessary for the grammatical completeness of a sentence and that *interrupt its natural flow* are set off with commas. A partial list of such parenthetical expressions follows:**

according to our records	however	no doubt
accordingly	in addition	obviously
after all	incidentally	of course
all in all	in conclusion	on the contrary
all things considered	indeed	on the other hand
also	in effect	on the whole
as a matter of fact	in essence	otherwise
as a result	in fact	perhaps
as a rule	in general	periodically
at any rate	in my opinion	secondly
at the same time	in other words	so
besides	instead	that is
between you and me	in summary	then
by the way	in the first place	therefore
consequently	in the meantime	thus
even so	likewise	too
finally	moreover	under the circumstances
for example	namely	unfortunately
fortunately	needless to say	what is more
furthermore	nevertheless	without a doubt
hence	no	yes

beginning of a sentence

Needless to say, our company continues to update its Web site regularly.

end of a sentence

Your order will arrive in time for your Labor Day weekend sale, **without a doubt**.

within a sentence

A large crowd, **nevertheless,** remained until the football game ended.

b. Sometimes words and phrases used as parenthetical expressions *do not interrupt* the flow of a sentence. In such cases no commas are used with the expression.

beginning of a sentence

Perhaps you would prefer receiving information about our new 300 PDA series.

end of a sentence

Our manager is planning to visit Boston **too**.

within a sentence

She was **indeed** concerned about the error in the financial report.

c. An exclamation at the beginning of a sentence is a parenthetical expression that requires a comma.

Oh, what a surprise to see Ms. Lexington in court again!

Ah, we did not expect the price of our stock to drop to this level!

d. Enumerations or explanations used as parenthetical expressions *within a sentence* are set off by commas, dashes, or parentheses. Use commas when the enumerated or explanatory information has no internal commas, dashes when the information contains commas within it, or parentheses when the information is considered to be only incidental to the rest of the sentence.

commas

Only one company, **namely, Empire Plumbing,** bid on the contract.

dashes

This client reported income from several sources—**namely, salary, interest, dividends, and rentals**—on his last income tax return.

parentheses

Our vice president toured several Ohio cities **(Cleveland, Columbus, and Toledo)** to locate a suitable plant site.

e. A parenthetical expression that introduces an enumeration or explanation *after a complete thought* may be set off with either (1) commas or (2) a semicolon and a comma. If the enumeration or explanation itself is a complete thought or contains internal commas, use a semicolon and a comma. Otherwise, use commas.

7

commas

Next week we are expecting large shipments from two major computer manufacturers, **namely,** Compaq and Toshiba.

There are several ways we can cut expenses during the next quarter, **for example,** by reducing our advertising and convention budgets.

semicolon and comma

Remodeling a kitchen generally entails purchasing new appliances; **namely,** a stove, an oven, a dishwasher, and a refrigerator.

f. Short introductory prepositional phrases essential to the meaning of a sentence should not be mistaken for parenthetical expressions. These phrases answer specifically questions such as *when, where, why,* or *how.*

Introductory prepositional phrases containing fewer than five words (but not containing a verb form) generally flow smoothly into the sentence and are *not* followed by a comma.

when?

In the future you may wish to make your airline reservations through the Internet.

At your convenience please stop by our showroom to see this year's new Lexon models.

where?

At this conference we met agents from all parts of the United States, Canada, and Mexico.

In this case we obtained a large tax refund for the client.

why?

For that reason your account has been turned over to a collection agency.

On this basis we decided to expand our operations to Central and South America.

how?

In this way you will be able to cut your travel costs significantly.

With this software you can easily capture text and images from the Internet.

g. Parenthetical expressions that are used as adverbs do not require commas.

However brilliant his work may be, Mr. Rogers will not be promoted until his disposition improves.

Obviously concerned about the drop in sales, our manager called a meeting of all sales personnel.

1-3 Direct Address

In written documents use commas to set off the name, title, or affiliation of a person when addressing that person directly. Speaking directly to individuals or groups in written works by using their names requires that you set off their names by commas. For words used in direct address within a sentence, capitalize only (1) proper nouns and (2) personal and professional titles.

beginning of a sentence

Ladies and gentlemen, congratulations on your achievements!

Ms. Crane, you have been promoted to vice president of operations.

within a sentence

Will you please, **Mr. Flanagan,** send us your check for $185.40 by April 30.

The book you ordered, **Professor,** will be shipped to the bookstore tomorrow.

Please examine, **ladies and gentlemen,** how this proposal will affect you and other residents in your neighborhood.

You, **fellow golfer,** will now be able to cut strokes from your game with this new Leading Edge driver.

end of a sentence

Please place your application in my mailbox, **Ms. LaGrasta-Sundy**.

You also should be concerned about this issue, **fellow American**.

1-4 Appositives

a. Appositives are word groups that rename, describe, or explain the nouns or pronouns they follow. These descriptive words usually add extra information and are set off by commas. (See 1-4b and 1-4c for exceptions.)

within a sentence

All expense claims must be submitted to Ms. Wells, **our sales manager,** for approval.

Our vice president, **Mr. Voddon,** will be in Belgium all next week.

end of a sentence

Yesterday we contacted a representative in your nearest branch office, **the Hillsdale office**.

You have reservations on the 6:45 p.m. flight, **the last flight to Portland today**.

b. Restrictive appositives—word groups that are *needed to identify* a person or thing described further—are not set off by commas.

These descriptive word groups tell *which one* or *which ones* and are essential to the meaning of the sentence.

necessary for identification—tells which one or which ones

The book **Web Site Design and Development** has been ordered for your course.

Your student **Vladimir Paransky** has requested an appointment to see you.

We **board members** are responsible for ensuring that each child in our community receives a quality education.

unnecessary for identification

Their latest book, **Cyberstyle! The Writer's Complete Desk Reference,** is available through most on-line bookstores.

Your best student, **Sandra Dubin,** made an appointment to see you.

c. Closely related one-word appositives or those forming parts of proper names do not require commas.

closely related one-word appositives

My sister **Stephanie** received two promotions within the last year.

I **myself** plan to attend the organizational meeting in Memphis.

State legislation in this area sets forth guidelines for us **teachers**.

proper name

His last two novels dealt with the lives of Alexander **the Great** and Richard **the Lionhearted**.

d. College degrees and abbreviations written after individuals' names are set off by commas; the abbreviations *Jr.* and *Sr.* and Roman numerals, however, are not set off by commas unless the individual chooses to include them.

An abbreviation such as *Inc.* or *Ltd.* that appears after a company name is also set off by commas if the particular company elects to include them.

commas with college degree or abbreviation after name of individual

Marilyn Drengson, **Doctor of Divinity,** will deliver the main graduation address.

Please schedule an appointment with Neal F. Kirby, **D.D.S., M.D.,** to have your wisdom teeth extracted.

The author of *Executive Decision Making* is Caroline R. Ryan, **Ph.D.**

Our firm has retained Alan Moskley, **Esq.**[2]

---

[2]Courtesy or professional titles are not used with the abbreviation *Esq. Esq.* may be used after the name of a lawyer. It replaces the courtesy title (*Mr., Mrs.,* or *Ms.*) and the professional title *Attorney-at-Law.*

no commas with Jr., Sr., or Roman numeral after name of individual

Our new sales representative in South Africa will be Mr. Lowell T. Harrison **Jr.**

Please send copies of the contract to David Warburton **Sr.**

Donald J. Ellington **III** has just been appointed secretary of state.

commas with abbreviations after company names

A. G. Edwards & Sons, **Inc.,** has moved its offices to Wilshire Boulevard.

One of the largest jobbers on the West Coast is Clothiers, **Ltd.**

no commas with abbreviations after company names

We have contracted with Ricon MED **Inc.** to install wheelchair lifts in our new hospital vans.

Most of the stocks in this estate are held by PaineWebber **Inc.**

Your crystal order from Cash & Co. **Ltd.** will be shipped from Ireland within the next week.

e. Words or expressions referred to simply as words or expressions should be written in italics rather than set off by commas. If an italic font is not available, underscore or place in quotation marks the words or expressions.

italics

Too many writers use **insure** when they should use **ensure**.

underscored

The word **convenience** is often misspelled in business documents.

quotation marks

The phrase **"Thanking you in advance"** is an outdated expression that should not be used in business documents.

1-5 Dates and Time Zones

a. Dates containing combinations of weekday, calendar date, and year require commas. Place a comma *after each element* used unless, of course, the element concludes a sentence. Remember *always* to place a comma *after* the year when a calendar date and year appear within the sentence.

Commas are not used with a calendar date expressed alone.

calendar date expressed alone

On **June 28** the Internal Revenue Service audited our books.

calendar date and year

On **June 28, 2004,** the Internal Revenue Service audited our books.

weekday and calendar date

On **Tuesday, June 28,** the Internal Revenue Service audited our books.

weekday, calendar date, and year

On **Tuesday, June 28, 2004,** the Internal Revenue Service audited our books.

b. **Expressions of month and year are written without commas.**

The Internal Revenue Service audited our books in **June 2004**.

In **March 2006** we will release our new line of products.

c. **Set off by commas any time zones used with clock times.**

Our flight will leave Denver at 9:35 a.m., **MST,** and arrive in New York City at 3:18 p.m., **EST.**

We received your fax from Japan at 10:40 a.m., **PDT.**

1-6 Addresses

a. **Separate by commas parts of an address that are written in sentence form.**

name and complete address

Please send the check to Ms. Donna-Mae Villanueva, Manager, Accounting Department, American Paper Company, 2996 Grandview Avenue, N.E., Suite 312, Atlanta, Georgia 30305-3245, by May 1.

complete address only

Mr. Buckley may be reached at 625 Hilgard Avenue, Apt. 5, Los Angeles, California 90025.

b. **Use commas to set off a state following the name of a city. Likewise, use commas to set off a country following the name of a city. Remember to use the second comma after the state or country name when it appears in the middle of a sentence.**

within a sentence

Our main office will be relocated to Kansas City, **Missouri,** next year.

Please confirm this order from Frankfurt, **Germany,** at the company's E-mail address.

end of a sentence

This inquiry came from a client in Boston, **Massachusetts**.

Our tour is also scheduled to visit Brisbane, **Australia**.

1-7 Coordinating Conjunctions

a. **The words *and, but, or,* and *nor* are coordinating conjunctions. Place a comma before any of these words that separate two**

independent clauses (complete thought units) in a compound sentence. No comma is used if both clauses are not totally independent and could not stand alone as separate sentences. (See Section 1-18 for use of a semicolon instead of a comma.)

two independent clauses

Most of our sales staff should reach their annual goal, **and** they will then be eligible to receive an end-of-the-year bonus.

Thirty-seven orders still remain unfilled, **but** we will close for vacation as scheduled.

You may have the interest added to your account, **or** we can send you a monthly check for the interest earned.

We have not purchased any appliances from this distributor within the past three months, **nor** have we requested an extension of our credit line.

You may, Mr. Villano, obtain up-to-date flight schedules from our Web site on the Internet, **and** you can make your reservations at the same time.

no second independent clause

The committee plans to have this data collected by March 10 but cannot promise to have the report completed before March 25.

Our marketing director is aware of the sales potential in the Detroit area and that an additional salesperson should be assigned to this territory.

b. In imperative sentences (command statements), the subject *you* is understood. Separate with a comma two independent clauses, whether one or both are in the imperative form.

Ship the books to me at North Valley Occupational Center, **but** send the invoice to the business manager at our district offices.

Please call Dr. Greenberg's office tomorrow morning, **and** his nurse will let you know what time the doctor is expected to finish surgery.

c. When a simple adverb, an introductory phrase, or a dependent clause precedes and applies equally to two clauses, the second clause is not a totally separate thought unit. Consequently, no comma is placed before the conjunction.

simple adverb

Please call the doctor's office tomorrow morning and arrange to have your appointment rescheduled for next week. (The adverb *please* refers to both *call* and *arrange*. Therefore, the second clause is not an independent thought unit and a comma is not required.)

introductory phrase

During the next month several board members will visit selected sites in Memphis and they will choose one on which to build a branch office. (*During the next month* applies equally to both clauses. Consequently, the second clause is not an independent thought unit and a comma is not required.)

dependent clauses

When Mr. Anderson arrives, ask him for his new address and give him 100 copies of our revised sales brochures. (Subject *you* is understood in both clauses. *When Mr. Anderson arrives* applies to both clauses. Therefore, the second clause is not an independent thought unit and no punctuation mark is required.)

As soon as we receive your E-mail response, we will notify our distributor and he will ship your order the next day. (In this case *As soon as we receive your E-mail response* applies to both clauses; therefore, no punctuation mark is needed before the conjunction *and*.)

d. Omit the comma in short compound sentences connected by *and*. For simplicity, "short" in these cases *may be* interpreted as those compound sentences containing up to 12 or 13 words.

Format five floppy disks **and** use them to back up this subdirectory.

John wrote the letter **and** his supervisor signed it.

We received the inquiry yesterday **and** my assistant responded to the client immediately.

1-8 Independent Adjectives

Use commas to separate two or more independent adjectives that modify a noun. No commas are needed, though, when the first adjective modifies the second adjective and the noun as a unit.

To identify independent adjectives, (1) reverse the adjectives, (2) read the adjectives independently, and (3) read the sentence with the word *and* between the adjectives. If the sentence makes sense and means the same thing with the adjectives read in these ways, then commas should be placed between them.

independent adjectives

Be sure to enclose a **stamped, addressed** envelope with your inquiry.

The president had surrounded herself with **efficient, intelligent** assistants.

Just as many businesses are conducted on a **global, 24-hour, 7-day** basis, so is education moving toward **anywhere, anytime** scheduling with on-line classes.

first adjective modifies second adjective and noun

The posters were lettered in **large bold print**.

He received several **attractive business offers**.

The room contained **old local newspapers** dating back to the 1970s.

Does the press release describe Liza's **dazzling blue evening gown**?

1-9 Introductory Clauses

a. Introductory clauses begin a sentence, contain a subject and a verb, and usually start with one of the following words:

as	after	provided	until
if } are most common	although	since	whenever
when	because	so	while
	before	unless	

Place a comma after an introductory clause.

After Steve received his inheritance, he invested $50,000 in mutual funds.

So that we may reach a decision by July 15, please fax us your bid within the next two days.

b. Occasionally an introductory clause may contain an implied verb and/or subject. This shortened form is treated the same as any other introductory clause. Place a comma after the shortened form.

If so, delivery of these manuals may be delayed. (If that is so, ... *or* If this is so, ...)

As agreed, we will offer the contract to the lowest qualified bidder. (As we agreed, ...)

c. Occasionally an introductory clause may follow another introductory word group. In such cases place a comma only after the introductory clause.

Our credit manager indicated that **if these overdue accounts are paid,** we will reinstate their credit privileges.

I suggest that **before you file your income tax return,** you check with our tax attorney on this issue.

d. When an introductory clause is followed by two main clauses, place a comma only after the introductory clause.

When Jack addresses prospective clients, he explains clearly all our investment options and he answers all questions patiently and courteously.

If you wish employment with our company, visit our Web site at www.remco.com and complete our on-line application form.

e. When a sentence contains two introductory clauses, place a comma only after the second clause.

If you decide to purchase this network server and **after you obtain the vice president's authorization,** please submit all the specifications on our standard purchase order form.

1–10 Introductory Phrases

a. An introductory infinitive phrase begins a sentence and starts with the word *To,* which is followed immediately by a verb. Place a comma after an introductory infinitive phrase.

To arrive at an immediate decision, the Board of Directors called an emergency meeting.

To meet the contract deadline, Ms. Morris hired two additional employees.

b. An introductory participial phrase begins a sentence and starts with a verb form ending in *ing* or *ed.* Place a comma after an introductory participial phrase.

Starting in late 1998, networks in selected cities across the United States began to deliver digital television (DTV) broadcasts in addition to all existing analog broadcasts.

Interested in learning how e-commerce might increase sales, Jordan plans to attend the E-COM convention next month in Philadelphia.

c. An introductory prepositional phrase begins a sentence; it starts with a preposition and ends with an object. A partial list of prepositions occurring in introductory prepositional phrases follows:

about	among	behind	during	on	until
above	around	below	for	over	up
after	at	between	from	through	upon
along	before	by	in	under	with

Place a comma after an introductory prepositional phrase if it contains a verb form *or* consists of five or more words.[3] After an introductory prepositional phrase that contains no verb form and fewer than five words, use a comma only if it is necessary for clarity.

verb form

Upon *receiving* **your authorization,** I notified Swift & Company that our firm would handle its suit against its former parent company.

After *reviewing* **the case,** the judge ruled in favor of the plaintiff.

By *enrolling* **today,** you are assured of receiving a place in the class that begins on March 1.

---

[3]Some authorities suggest four words.

After *calling* you, I notified the other committee members of the new meeting date.

five words or more

During the past few days of litigation, both sides have made significant concessions.

Between July 1 and August 31, all our stores will be closed on Monday.

Within the next few days, you should receive a written confirmation from the Sunset Village Hotel.

no verb form and fewer than five words

About three months ago our laboratory released to the press information about several new medical breakthroughs.

Through your efforts we have been able to locate new customers for our towel and linen service.

For two weeks our offices have been without air-conditioning.

On September 30 we will open our new branch office in London.

comma necessary for clarity

After the class, discussion on this issue will continue until 3 p.m. in Conference Room 14.

In my office, files dating back to 1995 are stored in three of the cabinets.

Until next Monday, morning deliveries will be accepted only between 8:30 and 10 a.m.; afternoon deliveries, between 3 and 5 p.m.

d. **An introductory phrase that follows another introductory word group is treated as if the opening introductory word group were not included. In other words, mentally omit the opening expression, and punctuate the introductory phrase according to the rules in Section 1-10a–c.**

infinitive phrase

Mr. Matson explained that **to meet our production deadline,** we would need to work overtime for the remainder of the week.

participial phrase

Ms. Winston expressed concern over the poor handling of complaints by our customer service representatives; and **speaking calmly and empathetically,** she demonstrated how they should handle irate customers.

prepositional phrase containing a verb form

Our plant manager believes that **by using new technologies,** the company will be able to reduce its production costs.

17

prepositional phrase, five or more words

I hope that **in view of the urgency of the situation,** we will obtain full cooperation from our staff.

We expect that **during this rapid growth period,** many investors will attempt to acquire our successful e-commerce enterprise.

prepositional phrase, fewer than five words

We were notified that **by next month** our union and the company management will have reached a contract agreement.

We assure you that **within the next week** we will call you.

e.   A phrase that begins a sentence and acts as the subject is not followed by a comma. Likewise, an opening phrase that is part of the predicate is not followed by a comma.

beginning phrase that acts as a subject

To answer your question would require several days' research.

Helping his employees prepare for advancement does not rank high among Mr. Green's management attributes.

beginning phrase that is part of the predicate

From the intensive police investigation came some new evidence that led to the apprehension of the suspected arsonists.

Among the group of dignitaries from Seattle were a number of school children and their parents.

1-11   Restrictive and Nonrestrictive Phrases and Clauses

Restrictive phrases and clauses modify and contribute substantially to the main idea of a sentence and are essential to its meaning. They tell *who, what,* or *which one* and are not set off with commas.

Nonrestrictive phrases and clauses add an additional idea and do not significantly change or contribute to the main idea of a sentence. They are nonessential word groups; that is, they are not needed by the main clause to tell *who, what,* or *which one.* Set off nonrestrictive phrases and clauses from the rest of the sentence with commas. Notice that phrases and clauses directly following proper nouns are nonrestrictive.

a.   Relative clauses (those beginning with *who, whose, whom, which,* or *that*) are either restrictive (no comma) or nonrestrictive (comma required).

restrictive and essential to meaning

Business applicants **who are able to use all components of Microsoft Office** can obtain well-paying jobs. (Tells *which kind* of business applicants.)

nonrestrictive and not essential to meaning

Ms. Kennedy, **who readily uses all components of Microsoft Office,** can obtain a well-paying job. (Provides additional idea. Clause following a proper noun.)

In the first example the clause "who are able to use all components of Microsoft Office" limits the type of business applicants who "can easily obtain well-paying jobs." In the second example "who readily uses all components of Microsoft Office" is of no assistance in *identifying* Ms. Kennedy but is merely an additional idea. Therefore, this example is a nonrestrictive clause that is set off by commas.

restrictive and essential to meaning

All employees **who have been employed by the company longer than six months** are eligible to participate in its retirement program. (Tells *which* employees.)

nonrestrictive and not essential to meaning

Joseph, **who has been employed by the company longer than six months,** is eligible to participate in its retirement program. (Provides additional idea. Clause following a proper noun.)

b. Careful writers will use *that* for restrictive clauses (no comma) and *which* for nonrestrictive clauses (comma required).

restrictive

The DVD movie **that you requested us to rent yesterday** was not available at All-Star Videos. (Tells *which* movie.)

All our insurance programs **that appeal to young adults** should be featured in this new brochure. (Tells *which* insurance programs.)

nonrestrictive

Unlike HTML (hypertext markup language), **which is a fairly rigid set of standards,** XML (extensible markup language) is designed for flexibility. (Provides additional idea.)

We have canceled our winter sales meeting, **which was scheduled from December 11–13 in Miami.** (Provides additional idea.)

c. Dependent adverbial clauses (clauses beginning with words such as *if, as, when, since, because,* etc.) that follow the main clause may be restrictive (no comma) or nonrestrictive (comma required). Restrictive clauses (1) answer such questions as *when, why, how,* or *whether* or (2) limit the main idea of the sentence. Nonrestrictive clauses add an additional idea that does not, however, alter the meaning of the main clause.

restrictive and essential to meaning

We will deliver a new laptop to your office **as soon as our shipment of Compaq computers arrives**. (Tells *when*.)

Our monthly sales have increased significantly **since the advertising campaign began**. (Tells *when*.)

Please send us this information by March 1 **so that we may update our records**. (Tells *why*.)

Our company will discontinue the manufacture of VCRs next month **because DVD will soon become the industry standard**. (Tells *why*.)

You can have 5,000 bonus miles added to your frequent flyer account **if you answer our on-line questionnaire**. (Tells *how*.)

We can still promise you the discount price **if we receive your order on or before July 15**. (Tells *whether*.)

We cannot install the additional equipment you requested **unless we receive authorization from your main office**. (Limits main idea.)

You may order these sale items from our Web site **as long as our current supply of merchandise lasts**. (Limits main idea.)

nonrestrictive and not essential to meaning

Our agent bid on this commercial property, **although he felt his bid would not be accepted**. (Provides additional idea.)

We will continue with our plans to introduce upgrades for our speech-recognition software, **whatever the competition might be**. (Provides additional idea.)

Next week our Board of Directors will tour our new South Haven plant site, **where we will be hiring several hundred new employees**. (Provides additional idea.)

d. A dependent clause or a short independent clause used to provide an extra idea within a sentence is nonrestrictive. Set off such clauses with commas (or dashes for emphasis).

interrupting dependent clause

On Monday, **when you arrive for your first appointment,** please give your completed health history form to the receptionist.

I can, **if you wish me to do so,** give you a list of Internet service providers in your area that provide a connection to the Internet.

This year's line of holiday greeting cards—**although the cards are larger and more exquisite**—is less expensive than last year's.

interrupting short independent clause

Ms. Lee is, **I believe,** the only applicant who resides in Utah.

We will, **I hope,** be able to obtain this information by July 1.

e. Participial, infinitive, or prepositional phrases appearing within a sentence may be restrictive (no comma) or nonrestrictive (comma required), depending upon whether or not they tell *who, what, what kind,* or *which one.* Phrases that answer these questions are restrictive (no comma).

participial restrictive

All current employees **planning to participate in the company stock option program** must sign up by September 1. (Tells *which ones.*)

participial nonrestrictive

Mr. Fletcher, **planning to participate in the company stock option program,** has signed up to attend the August 10 seminar on stock options. (Provides additional idea. Phrase following a proper noun.)

infinitive restrictive

We plan **to sign up for the program** by September 1. (Tells *what.*)

infinitive nonrestrictive

Hill & Hill's stock option program offers employees an excellent investment opportunity, **to mention only one company fringe benefit**. (Provides additional idea.)

prepositional restrictive

The advertising brochures **for our August sale** will be ready June 30. (Tells *which ones.*)

Manufacturers **like us** find themselves in financial difficulty today. (Tells *what kind.*)

Clients **like the Atkinsons** make the real estate business a pleasure. (Tells *what kind.*)

Companies **such as IBM and General Electric** offer low-risk investment opportunities. (Tells *what kind.*)

Words **such as *cite*, *site*, and *sight*** are often confused in business writing. (Tells *what kind.*)

prepositional nonrestrictive

We are planning, **in response to numerous requests,** to open our city ticketing agencies on Sundays as well. (Provides additional idea.)

Upstart Internet e-commerce companies, **like us,** are in financial difficulty today. (Provides additional idea.)

Small tool manufacturing companies, **such as Belmont Tools and Lindgren Tool Manufacturers,** are having difficulty showing a profit in this tight economy. (Provides additional idea.)

Large, worldwide hotel chains—**such as Marriott, Hilton, and Hyatt**—provide toll-free numbers for guests to book reservations. (Provides additional idea.)

1-12 Contrasting, Limiting, and Contingent Expressions

Contrasting, limiting, or contingent expressions are set off with commas. Words often used to introduce contrasting and limiting expressions include *not, never, but, seldom,* and *yet.*

contrasting expression

Our company has found on-line surveys, **not telephone interviews,** to be the most effective means for assessing customer satisfaction.

limiting expression

The realtors' association will give us four tickets, **but only for members of our sales staff**.

contingent expression

The sooner you are able to determine which property you prefer, **the sooner** we will be able to enter escrow.

The more money you invest, **the greater the return** you can expect.

The more lines of resolution a monitor can display, **the sharper the detail** you will observe in the picture.

1-13 Omitted Words

Commas are often used to indicate the omission of words when the context of the sentence makes the omitted words clearly understood.

Three new sales associates were hired by the Oxnard store; two, by the Ventura store. (Two *new sales associates were hired* by the Ventura store.)

Last week I used speech-recognition software to prepare four long reports; this week, two long reports. (This week *I used speech-recognition software to prepare* two long reports.)

Our B-124 contract expired on June 14; the B-127 contract, June 16; and the B-132, June 21. (The B-127 contract *expired on* June 16, and the B-132 *contract expired on* June 21.)

1-14 Punctuation for Clarity

a. Separate by a comma two identical verbs that appear together in a sentence.

Whoever **wins, wins** an all-expense paid vacation to Hawaii for two.

Whatever irregularities **occurred, occurred** without my knowledge.

b. Separate by a comma words repeated for emphasis.

Many, many years ago this company was founded by Bernard Harris.

The vice president has not visited our branch for a **long, long** time.

c. Set off by a comma a word or phrase at the beginning of a sentence that could be read incorrectly with the words that follow.

Ever since, she has been employed by Disney Studios in Burbank.

The month before, the corporation expanded its operations to Brazil.

In our business, letters are written primarily to sell goods and services and to collect money.

d. Place a comma between the last name and the first name of a name written in inverted form.

Irwin, Carl   Luers, Barbara R.

1-15 **Short Quotations**

a. Set off a short quoted sentence from the rest of the sentence by a comma. When the quoted sentence is broken into two parts, commas are required before and after the interjected thought.

beginning quotation
"All employees will receive two days' paid vacation after the contract is completed," said Mr. Adams.

interrupted quotation
"All employees will receive two days' paid vacation," said Mr. Adams, "after the contract is completed."

ending quotation

Mr. Adams said, "All employees will receive two days' paid vacation after the contract is completed."

b. Unless a beginning quotation is interrupted, omit any separating commas when the quoted sentence is a question or an exclamation.

question
"When will the bids for this contract be opened?" asked Ms. Snow.

interrupted question
"When," asked Ms. Snow, "will the bids for this contract be opened?"

exclamation
"What a wonderful opportunity you have given our staff!" exclaimed Mr. Stevens.

interrupted exclamation
"What a wonderful opportunity," exclaimed Mr. Stevens, "you have given our staff!"

c. No comma is needed to set off a quotation or part of a quotation that is woven into a complete sentence or one that is not a complete thought.

23

woven into sentence

The chairperson operated on the premise that **"a stitch in time saves nine."**

John is reported to have said that **" . . . no vacancies will be filled."**

incomplete sentence

Please mark the top of this package **"This Side Up."**

The human resources manager advised me to **"e-mail your résumé as soon as possible."**

He merely answered **"yes"** to all the questions.

d. **When a comma and a quotation mark fall at the same point in a sentence,** *always* **place the comma inside the closing quotation mark. Periods, too, are** *always* **placed inside the closing quotation mark.**

"We intend to give customers access to our services over wireless," reported Dawn Chambers, E-Trade's chief information officer.

Her last article, "Western Travel," appeared in *Automotive Digest.*

John said, "Be sure to e-mail your response by June 11."

e. **For placement of question marks and exclamation marks with closing quotation marks, see Sections 1-44a and 1-46c.**

1-16 **Numerals**

a. **Expressed in United States format, numerals of more than three digits require commas.**

1,320   63,481   963,481   1,293,070   23,092,946   450,500,000

b. **Separate by a comma two independent figures that appear consecutively in a sentence.**

Do not separate by a comma two consecutive numbers that function as adjectives to describe the same noun. Instead, write the first number in words and the second one in figures. If the first number cannot be expressed in *one or two words*, **place it in figures also.**

independent figures

Of this **$213,000, $187,000** is secured by real property.

During **2003, $1,876,000** in sales were financed through our credit card program.

By May **1, 43** people had submitted on-line résumés for this position.

two numbers modifying a noun, word-figure form

Please purchase **thirty 13-gallon** wastebaskets for our offices.

Each package contains **twelve 2-inch** nails.

Please order **twenty-four 100-watt** bulbs for the reception-area lamps.

two numbers modifying a noun, figure-figure form

While you are at the post office, please buy **125 37-cent** stamps.

The prescription was for **250 10-milligram** tablets.

When the carton fell, **127 40-watt** bulbs were broken.

c. Commas are omitted in years, house numbers, zip codes, telephone or fax numbers, decimal fractions, metric measurements, and any label-numeral combinations. In metric measurements use a space to separate all numerals containing more than four digits.

year

1856   1992   2005

house number

6201 Corbin Avenue   18564 Washington Boulevard

zip code

Northridge, CA 91325   Bothell, WA 98041-3011

telephone or fax number

(212) 555-9768, Ext. 4412   *or*   212-555-9768, Ext. 4412

decimal fraction

0.4769

metric measurement

1400 kilometers   12 600 kilometers

label-numeral combination

Serial No. 9226263   page 1072   Room 3210   Invoice 43798

d. Volume numbers and page references are separated by commas.

Please refer to Volume XII, page 119.

The article appeared in Volume VII, August 2002, page 87.

e. Measurements (such as weights, capacities, dimensions, etc.) are treated as single units and are not interrupted by commas.

weight

The Carsons' new baby weighed **8 pounds 7 ounces** at birth.

dimension

The patient is **5 feet 10 inches** tall.

Our reception area is **21 feet 8 inches** by **18 feet 6 inches**.

time period

Is our flight time still estimated to be **3 hours 15 minutes**?

Semicolon

1-17 Independent Clauses Without Coordinating Conjunctions

a. Place a semicolon between two or more closely related independent clauses (complete thoughts that could stand alone as separate sentences) that are not connected with a coordinating conjunction (*and, but, or, nor*).

two independent clauses

Last month too many orders were delayed leaving the Milwaukee office; Ms. Lee will check into our shipping procedures there.

Plan to attend the next meeting of the American Management Association International; you will find this organization to be well worth your time.

three independent clauses

Mr. Horowitz drafted the contract specifications last week; Ms. Ames consulted the firm's attorneys on Monday; Mr. Dotson signed and mailed the company's offer on Wednesday.

b. Short and closely related independent clauses may be separated by commas.

two short independent clauses

Pittsburgh Bank issued the checks, TSI mailed them to the clients.

three short independent clauses

The monitor flashed, it emitted sparks, it went blank.

He came in, he looked around, he left.

1-18 Independent Clauses With Coordinating Conjunctions

Two independent clauses linked by a coordinating conjunction (*and, but, or, nor*) are generally separated with a comma. Lengthy, complicated sentences containing internal commas in either or both clauses, however, may be punctuated with a semicolon between the two clauses.

clauses separated with a comma

She had planned to attend the Chicago meeting, **but** several important clients needed her immediate assistance.

We were pleased with the results of the survey, **and** you will, of course, receive a copy of the summary.

Yes, you may mail in your payment, **or** you may take it to one of the fast, convenient express registers located throughout our stores.

clauses separated with a semicolon

Several large orders were recently placed and filled through the new Dayton office; **and** Ms. Baca, our national sales manager, commended the sales staff for its diligent efforts in making such rapid progress.

You, of course, need not attend the committee meeting scheduled for June 4; **but** I believe, Mr. Newton, you will find reading the minutes helpful before you address the Board of Directors next week.

1-19 Independent Clauses With Transitional Expressions

Two independent clauses (complete thoughts) separated by a transitional expression require a semicolon. A partial list of common transitional expressions follows. In addition, those words and phrases listed in Section 1-2a may be considered transitional expressions when they separate two closely related complete thoughts.

accordingly	however	moreover	otherwise
besides	indeed	nevertheless	so
consequently	in fact	notwithstanding	then
furthermore	in other words	on the contrary	therefore
hence	likewise	on the other hand	yet

Place a comma after a transitional expression of more than one syllable or where a strong pause is needed after a one-syllable expression.

transitional expression with one syllable

All departments will have difficulty obtaining any budget increases this year; **thus** members of your staff should not plan to receive all the equipment and supplies requested.

transitional expression containing more than one syllable

Stellar's recent promotion of its satellite communications network has induced a large number of television viewers to switch to satellite reception; **consequently,** companies providing cable reception have experienced a sudden decline in revenues.

1-20 Series Containing Internal Commas or Complete Thoughts

a. Items in a series are usually separated by commas. However, when one or more of the parts contain internal commas, use semicolons to separate the items.

Our on-line courses serve nontraditional adult students; provide flexible, convenient learning options; and satisfy students' needs for continual lifelong learning.

Managers from Hartford, Connecticut; San Francisco, California; and Little Rock, Arkansas, were unable to attend the sales conference.

b. **Three or more independent clauses (complete thoughts) comprising a series are separated by semicolons. Only very short clauses may be separated by commas.**

series of independent clauses

Nearly 7,000 circulars were mailed to prospective clients in 1997; more than 15,000 circulars were mailed in 2002; and next year we plan to mail more than 10,000 new brochures as well as 20,000 circulars.

series of independent clauses with internal commas

John Harris, our company president, will welcome the stockholders at 10 a.m.; Olga Williams, one of our vice presidents, will report on the past year's sales at 10:30 a.m.; and Carol Watson, our company treasurer, will provide a complete financial picture at 11 a.m. using PowerPoint slides.

series of short independent clauses

The tenant called yesterday, we investigated his complaint immediately, and the air-conditioning will be serviced this afternoon.

1–21 **Enumerations and Explanations**

a. **Certain words and phrases are used to introduce enumerations or explanations that follow an independent clause (complete thought). Some common introductory expressions follow:**

for example (e.g.)   for instance   that is (i.e.)   namely (viz.)

If the enumeration or explanation following the introductory expression *contains commas* or *forms another complete thought*, use a semicolon after the opening independent clause and a comma after the introductory expression.

enumeration containing commas

Many factors have contributed to the sharp increase in production costs during the past three months; **namely,** price increases in raw materials, wage increases for electrical workers, and overtime payments to supervisors.

explanation forming another complete thought

To open its Syracuse plant, Caldwell Industries advertised for a number of new employees; **that is to say,** not all its employees were willing to transfer to the new location.

b. **Some independent clauses followed by expressions that introduce enumerations or explanations require a comma, not a semicolon, after the independent clause. If the enumeration or explanation that follows the introductory expression does *not* contain commas or form another complete thought, use commas after the independent clause and the introductory expression.**

enumeration without internal commas

As a member of our user group, you are eligible to purchase additional computer peripherals through our discount program, **for instance,** a scanner or a CD-RW (Compact Disk-Rewritable) drive.

explanation forming an incomplete thought

You may wish to call Ms. Hendrix for further advice, **for example,** to inquire what accounting software would be best suited for your office.

c. Enumerations or explanations used as parenthetical expressions within a sentence are not set off by semicolons. Use commas when the enumerated or explanatory information has no internal commas; use dashes or parentheses when the information contains internal commas.

commas

Your accounting procedures, **for example, posting customer deposits,** can be streamlined with our software.

dashes

Because of current economic conditions, we must find new sources for purchasing multimedia equipment—**e.g., digital video cameras, digital still cameras, and portable data projectors**—to stay within our budget allocations.

parentheses

Your recommendations **(namely, downsizing our human resources staff, scanning all incoming résumés, and computerizing our testing program)** were approved unanimously by the board.

d. Complete thoughts that introduce enumerations or explanations without an introductory expression are followed by a colon, not a semicolon.

Several new software concepts for workplace access are being developed by our company: retina scanners, fingerprint scanners, and face-recognition systems.

The following staff members have requested vacation time in July: Roberta Adams, Horace Brubaker, Phillip Haledon, and Susan McCloskey.

Only 82 teachers attended the ARTA state conference: apparently many of our members did not receive their brochures in time to plan for this event.

1-22 Semicolon Placement

Always place the semicolon outside closing quotation marks and parentheses.

29

quotation marks

Last month Mr. Hale promised, "I will mail you a check the 1st of next month"; but we have received no money or explanation from him.

parentheses

Our accounting supervisor was ill last week (with the flu); consequently, our end-of-month reports will reach the home office a week late.

Colon

1-23 **Formally Enumerated or Listed Items**

a. Use a colon after an independent clause (complete thought) that introduces a formal listing or an enumeration of items. Words commonly used in introductory independent clauses include *the following, as follows, these,* and *thus.* Sometimes, however, the introduction is implied rather than stated directly. Use a colon following both direct and implied introductions.

direct introduction

The office manager requested that we order the following new furniture and equipment: two computer stations, two secretarial chairs, one sofa, two desktop computers, and one color laser printer.

These rules should be observed for a successful job interview:

1. Dress appropriately.
2. Obtain information beforehand about the company.
3. Appear interested in the company and the job.
4. Answer questions courteously.
5. Thank the interviewers for their time.

implied introduction

Several kinds of laptop computers were on display: Compaq, Dell, Hewlett-Packard, IBM, Sony, and Toshiba.

In determining whether to use a colon or a semicolon for introducing enumerated items, use the colon when the enumeration is not preceded by a transitional introductory expression such as *namely, for example, e.g., that is,* or *i.e.* If an introductory expression immediately precedes the listing, use a semicolon before the expression and a comma after it. (See Section 1-21a for examples.)

b. The colon is *not* used to introduce listings in the following situations: (1) an intervening sentence separates the introductory sentence and the listing; (2) the items follow a "being" verb or are the object of a verb; (3) the items are the object of a preposition; and (4) the listing is preceded immediately by an enumerating expression.

no colon: intervening sentence

The following new stemware patterns will be available January 1. They will be introduced to our dealers next month.

1. Fantasia
2. Sunburst
3. Apollo
4. Moonglow

no colon: following a "being" verb or acting as the object of a verb

The words most commonly misspelled **were** *convenience, occasionally, commodity, consequently,* and *accommodate.* (Not: "... were: *convenience,* . . . .")

Examples of popular Web browsers **include** Netscape Navigator, Microsoft Internet Explorer, and America Online. (Not: "... include: Netscape . . . .")

no colon: object of a preposition

The first lessons introduce the new Microsoft Word user **to** the Menu Bar, the Standard Toolbar, and the Formatting Toolbar. (Not: "... to: the Menu . . . .")

Departmental meetings are scheduled **for** January 3, February 4, March 7, and April 9. (Not: "... for: January 3, ...")

no colon: listing after enumerating expression

Please order some additional supplies; **namely,** 8½- by 11-inch white laser printer paper, legal-size envelopes, and letter-size manila file folders.

1-24 Explanatory Sentences

Separate two sentences with a colon when the second sentence explains, illustrates, or supplements the first.

explanation

During the next three months, we will gross approximately 50 percent of our annual sales: major toy purchases occur during September, October, and November.

illustration

Our new advertising campaign will be directed toward buyers of economy cars: we will stress efficient gas mileage, low maintenance costs, and reliability.

supplement

Several new customers complained about the delay in receiving their charge cards: they wished to have them in time to complete their holiday shopping.

1-25 Long Quotations

Long one-sentence quotations and quotations of two or more sentences are introduced by a colon.

For a quotation containing two or more sentences (and usually more than three lines), omit the quotation marks and format it as a separate paragraph. Indent the left and right margins, and separate the quotation from the main text by single blank lines before and after the quotation.

long one-sentence quotation

Ms. Judy Dolan, human resources manager of Hartnell Corporation, reported in her annual summary: "Graduates from the University of Southern California's School of Business have been placed in a number of our divisions, and they have risen to middle-management positions within a three-year period."

long quotation of two or more sentences

New developments in navigating the Internet are apparent from the report released by our Research Department on February 12:

> A new standard—Speech Applications Language Tags (SALT)—will extend existing markup languages such as HTML, XHTML, and XML. This new platform will permit multimodal and telephony-enabled access to information, applications, and Web services from PCs, telephones, tablet PCs, and wireless personal digital assistants (PDAs). Users will be able to input data using speech, a keyboard, a keypad, and a mouse/stylus, employing these modes independently or concurrently.

According to the report issued by our Research Department, SALT will be available within the next six months for developers to incorporate into . . . .

1-26 Special-Purpose Uses for the Colon

a. **In business letters a colon is placed after the salutation when the mixed punctuation format is used (see Section 12–22).**

Dear Bill: Dear Ms. Madison: Gentlemen:

b. **Use the colon to separate hours and minutes in expressions of time.**

The meeting has been scheduled for **8:30 a.m.** on Thursday, October 9, in Room 2216.

At **12:15 p.m.** Ms. Hardesty is scheduled to address the Compton Chamber of Commerce.

c. In expressing ratios, use the colon to represent the word *to*.

The label instructions recommend proportions of **4:1**.

The council members voted **2:1** against the proposed zoning change.

d. The colon is often used to separate elements in literary references.

between title and subtitle

Dr. Susan Cornner's latest book, *Business Communication: Theory and Applications*, 4th ed., is now in stock at our college bookstore.

between place of publication and publisher in footnotes and bibliographies

Clark, James L., and Lyn R. Clark. *HOW 10: A Handbook for Office Professionals*. 10th ed. Mason, Ohio: South-Western Publishing, 2004. (bibliography)

between volume and page number in footnotes and bibliographies

10Marian D. Barron and Robert C. Scott, "Developing Company Web Sites: A Framework for Making Yours 'User Friendly,'" *The Bulletin for the Association of Webmasters* 8 (April 2003): 42–45. (footnote)

biblical citation

The minister quoted Isaiah **24:1** (Chapter 24, verse 1).

1-27 Colon Format and Use With Other Punctuation Marks

a. In computer-generated (or typewritten) copy, space once or twice after a colon. Placing two spaces after a colon in business documents promotes ease of reading.

Please send me copies of the following documents: the rental agreement, the returned check, and the 30-day notice to move.

b. Place the colon outside closing quotation marks and parentheses.

closing quotation mark

I distributed to the following staff members copies of Lynn Haile's latest article, "Closing the Sale Effectively": Mina Balejian, Charles Ballesteros, Paul Kellogg, and Kyung Kim.

closing parenthesis

Several contractors are being considered for the new project (Mountain Hills): Wyeth & Sons, Burnside Developers, and Hartman and Associates.

c. In vertical listings introduced by a colon, conclude each item in the listing with a period only if the items are complete sentences.

Single-space the items in a vertical listing. If any item in the listing occupies more than one line, double-space between the items. If all the items in the listing consist of a single line, you may *either* leave one blank line between each item *or* just single-space the listing. Always place one blank line before and after a listing.

In business letters and memorandums, vertical listings may be indented from the left and right margins *or* may assume the margins of the main text.[4] Items in a listing may be numbered, bulleted, or untagged.

complete sentences, numbered items, standard margins

We have discontinued manufacturing our Model 1040A microwave oven for the following reasons:

1. The popularity of our smaller ovens has decreased continually during the past eighteen months.

2. Manufacturing costs and prices differ only slightly from those for our standard-size ovens.

3. Two other models smaller than our standard-size ones have been more popular.

incomplete sentences, bulleted items, indented margins

A computer may be connected to the Internet through one of the following:

- Modem and telephone line
- DSL
- Cable modem
- T line

incomplete sentences, unnumbered items, indented left and right margins

Effective July 1 new premium rates will be in force for the following types of policies:

Jewelry riders on home owners' policies
Liability coverage for drivers under 25
Earthquake riders on all casualty policies
Term life insurance for males 65 and older

1-28 Capitalization With Colons

a. When a colon is used to introduce a horizontal listing of items, the first letter after the colon is not capitalized unless it begins a proper noun. Capitalize the first letter of each item in a vertical listing.

---

[4]See Section 13–9 for guidelines governing the format and preparation of horizontal and vertical listings in reports and manuscripts as well as in business letters and memorandums.

lowercase letter in horizontal listing

Place the following items in the tray: **t**he original invoice, the duplicate invoice, and the shipping copy.

proper noun capitalized

Four employees were promoted last week: Teresa Caruana, Sue Rigby, Lloyd Bartholome, and Arthur Rubin.

capitalized letters in vertical listing

You may pay for your Empress Vacation Time-Share package in a number of ways:

Personal check
Credit card—VISA, MasterCard, or American Express
Eighteen monthly installments of $637.50

Do not miss the opportunity to get in on the ground floor of this ....

b. **Do not capitalize the first letter after a colon when the second sentence explains or supplements the first unless the letter begins a proper noun.**

lowercase letter begins second sentence

Your account has been frozen temporarily: **o**utstanding bills for $938.44 still remain unpaid.

proper noun capitalized

The $1,000 award was given to Andrew Schultz: **Dr.** Schultz's Web site was judged by a panel of three experts to be the best in Web page design.

c. **Capitalize the first word after a colon when the colon introduces a formal rule or principle stated as a complete sentence.**

Format your E-mail messages properly: **A**lways use a subject line to identify the content of your message.

Mr. Redmond emphasized the importance of adhering to the following policy: **I**n case of absence an employee must notify his or her immediate supervisor by 8:30 a.m. that day.

d. **When two or more sentences follow a colon, capitalize the first letter of each sentence.**

Several suggestions emerged from the discussion: **T**o begin with, an engineering firm should be retained to determine the extent of damage to the building. **T**hen several contractors should be contacted to provide estimates for repairing the damage. **F**inally, lending resources should be investigated to determine the best means for financing the repairs.

e. Capitalize the first letter of sentences or phrases introduced by words such as *Note, Attention, Warning, Caution,* or *For Sale*.

Warning: All cars parked illegally will be towed away at vehicle owner's expense.

Caution: Please hold children by hand.

For Rent: Large three-bedroom home with family room, fireplace, air-conditioning, and pool. Phone (617) 555-3542.

f. Capitalize the first word of a quotation that follows a colon.

Mr. Rosen informed the board about expansion plans for this year: "Since the property on Tampa Avenue has already been purchased, construction of our new branch office will begin early this spring so that we can open this office in September."

Dash

1-29 **Parenthetical Expressions, Appositives, and Summaries**

a. Parenthetical expressions and appositives are usually set off from the rest of the sentence by commas. When the parenthetical expression or appositive contains internal commas, however, substitute dashes (or parentheses) for the separating commas.

Where possible, use an em dash—a character that appears as a solid line and is twice the length of a hyphen. If access to an em dash is unavailable through an extended character set,[5] form the dash by typing two hyphens with no space before, between, or after (see Section 1-32).

parenthetical expression with internal commas
Last month Ms. Callaway—with the hope of increasing sales, recruiting new employees, and establishing additional sources of supply—made several trips to the Middle East.

appositive with internal commas
A number of Internet sites—for example, Amazon.com, Schwab.com, and eToys.com—have set the precedent for a revolutionary pattern in American purchasing trends.

b. Use a dash to set off a brief summary from the rest of the sentence.

Thanksgiving Day, Christmas Day, and New Year's Day—these are the only holidays our stores will be closed.

Black, navy, and bone—the Sling purse is available in these colors.

---

[5]Word processing programs provide access to extended character sets. Extended characters are letters, number styles, symbols, and foreign language characters that are not on the standard keyboard but are needed to produce documents.

c. To achieve greater separation, use dashes instead of commas to set off abrupt parenthetical expressions or those requiring emphasis. Appositives requiring emphasis may also be separated from the rest of the sentence with dashes instead of commas.

abrupt parenthetical expression

Her main interest—notwithstanding job security—was to obtain employment in an organization with opportunities for advancement.

emphatic parenthetical element

Several orders were rerouted to the Boise office—not to the Salt Lake City office.

emphatic appositive

We will need some heavy-duty equipment—bulldozers and graders—to complete the first phase of the project according to schedule.

d. For emphasis use a dash in place of a comma or a semicolon to introduce an example or explanation.

example requiring emphasis

Insurance coverage adequate five years ago may no longer fulfill the purpose for which it was designed—for example, if current inflationary trends continue, fire and theft insurance may not cover the replacement costs of the insured properties.

explanation requiring emphasis

Our sales of multimedia software have increased 25 percent since 2002—namely, from $1 million to $1.25 million.

e. Afterthoughts or side thoughts generated from the text, but not necessarily part of it, may be separated from the rest of the sentence by a dash or a pair of dashes.

afterthought

Mrs. Lopez will install our new accounting software this afternoon—at least John thinks she has planned to do so then.

side thought

Several items from our new product line—I do not know which ones—will be featured at our exhibit in New Orleans next month.

1-30 Hesitations in Verbal Reports

Use dashes to indicate hesitations, faltering, or stammering in reports of conversations, testimonies, or speeches.

Ms. Phillips: Yes, Mr. President—we expect perhaps oh—a—35 percent increase in sales during the next year.

1-31 Source of Quotations

Place a dash before the source of a quotation when the source is listed after the quotation.

"We can expect a great decrease in our unemployment rate during the next ten months."

—H. J. Scott

"The difference between the right word and the almost right word is the difference between lightning and the lightning bug."

—Mark Twain

1-32 Format and Placement of Dash

a. **For printed documents and documents prepared with desktop publishing or word processing software, use an *em* dash (not a hyphen or an *en* dash) to form the dash. The *em* dash is the length of two hyphens and may be accessed through the extended character set of most word processing programs.[6] Leave no space before or after the *em* dash.**

Form the dash with a typewriter by typing two hyphens consecutively; leave no space before, between, or after the hyphens.

A dash may not begin a new line, but it may appear at the end of a line.

em dash

Several influential community organizations—the Kiwanis Club, the Chamber of Commerce, and the Rotary Club—sponsored Courtney R. Delgado for the vacant seat on the city council.

typewritten dash

```
Three cities--Atlanta, New Orleans, and Fort
Worth--are still under consideration for our new
plant site.
```

end of line

Contract negotiations—after reaching an impasse on December 20— were resumed on January 5.

b. **Only one punctuation mark may precede an opening dash—a period in an abbreviation. Closing dashes may be preceded by a period in an abbreviation, a question mark, or an exclamation mark.**

opening dash after abbreviation

As you requested, we will ship your order c.o.d.—merchandise and shipping costs amount to $110.84.

---

[6]Extended characters are letters, number styles, symbols, and foreign language characters that are not on the standard keyboard but are needed to produce documents.

closing dash after question mark

Electronics Magazine—are you familiar with this magazine?—has rated the Milton surround-sound system as "No. 1."

Period

1-33 **End of Sentence**

Place a period at the end of a declarative sentence, an imperative statement or command, an indirect question, and a polite request.

Polite requests end with a period, even though they may appear to have the format of a question. A polite request (1) asks the reader to *perform a specific action* and (2) is *answered only* by the reader's doing or not doing what the writer has requested. (See Section 1-41e for additional information and examples.)

declarative sentence

We have received free introductory offers for an Internet connection from America Online, MSN, and EarthLink.

Two new products were introduced at the July 1 stockholders' meeting.

imperative statement

Be sure to mail your income tax return by or before April 15.

Please lock all entrances and engage the security system before you leave the store.

indirect question

Jay asked who was responsible for approving overtime hours.

Many customers have asked when our summer sale will begin.

polite request

Will you please send us your check for $283.76 by November 1.

May I have your fax number so that we can fax you your prescription today.

1-34 **End of Independent Phrase**

Conclude independent phrases with a period. An independent phrase implies a complete thought and is not connected directly to the following sentence.

Now, to the point. Until we are able to pinpoint the reasons for the continual sales decline in the South Bend area, we will be subject to sustaining increasing losses.

Yes, for the most part. Our salespeople have increased their sales since the new incentive program was established.

1-35 Abbreviations and Initials

a. Abbreviated words are usually followed by a period. (See Section 1-39a for spacing following the period.)

However, abbreviated forms for business and governmental organizations, associations, radio and television stations, federal agencies, and certain professional designations (*CLU, CPA, CPS, PLS*), do not contain periods.

period after abbreviation

Stern, Hart, and Company **Inc.** has been handling our investment portfolio.

periods after abbreviations

The furniture is being shipped **f.o.b.** from Charleston, South Carolina.

Most of these products were manufactured in the **U.S.A.**

no periods with certain abbreviations

Will the educational project director for **NASA** be able to address our national convention?

Almost all new computers sold today have **AOL** trial version software loaded on their hard drives.

b. Place a period after an initial. Leave one space between the period and the next word or another initial.

Ms. Angela **K.** Wells has accepted our invitation to be the keynote speaker.

We have tried for several days to contact **A. F.** Elliot.

1-36 Outlines

a. The outline feature of word processors supplies automatically sequencing characters before each item in an outline. The software offers several outline models from which to choose. The setup and amount of space between the sequencing character and the item are determined by the kind and location of tabs set in the document.

Use periods after letters and numbers in alphanumeric outlines, except those enclosed in parentheses. Leave the equivalent of two blank spaces before beginning the contents of the item.

Use periods after whole numbers in decimal outlines. Leave the equivalent of two blank spaces after the last typed character before beginning the contents of the item.

alphanumeric outline

I. Xxxxxx
   A. Xxxxxx
   B. Xxxxxx
      1. Xxxxxx
      2. Xxxxxx
         a. Xxxxxx
         b. Xxxxxx
            (1) Xxxxxx
            (2) Xxxxxx
               (a) Xxxxxx
               (b) Xxxxxx
                  1) Xxxxxx
                  2) Xxxxxx
                     a) Xxxxxx
                     b) Xxxxxx
II. Xxxxxx
III. Xxxxxx
IV. Xxxxxx

decimal outline

1. Xxxxxx
   1.1 Xxxxxx
   1.2 Xxxxxx
      1.21 Xxxxxx
      1.22 Xxxxxx
         1.221 Xxxxxx
         1.222 Xxxxxx
            1.2221 Xxxxxx
            1.2222 Xxxxxx
               1.22221 Xxxxxx
               1.22222 Xxxxxx
                  1.222221 Xxxxxx
                  1.222222 Xxxxxx
2. Xxxxxx

b. No punctuation mark is placed after an incomplete thought in out-lines and listings. Use periods only after complete sentences.

no periods—incomplete sentences

A. Two types of digital broadcasts
   1. HDTV (high-definition television)
      a. Offers extremely high resolution
      b. Shows film-like pictures
      c. Provides CD-quality sound
      d. Uses a wide-screen format
   2. SDTV (standard-definition television)
      a. Offers good quality digital pictures
      b. Provides CD-quality sound

periods—complete sentences

A. Two new processes were developed as a result of the experiments.
   1. Lamination of fiberglass to wooden surfaces contributes to vessel buoyancy.
   2. Sealing of surfaces prevents excessive moisture absorption.

1-37 Decimals

Use periods to signify decimals.

Only **24.6** percent of the customers responding to our survey rated our service as "Excellent."

Last year Mr. Phoenix paid $120 for the 2,000 sale announcements; this year he paid **$175.50** for the same kind and number.

1-38 Ellipses

An ellipsis (a series of three periods with a space before, between, and after the series) is used for emphasis in advertising material or for showing omissions in quoted material. In showing omissions, indicate the completion of a thought with an additional period or other closing punctuation mark. (See Section 1-52 for further information on the use of ellipses.)

emphasis

Place your order today . . . for relief from tension headaches . . . for ending miserable aches and pains . . . for a happier, tension-free you.

omission

The president read from the consulting company's report: "Basically, operations for the next year should be conducted according to the attached plan . . . . Several of your current operations personnel should . . . implement the recommended procedures."

1-39 Period Format

a. **No space is placed between a decimal point and a number or after a period within an abbreviation. However, within a sentence one space follows an initial or the concluding period in an abbreviation. In copy prepared on a word processor, allow one or two spaces after a period at the end of a sentence.[7] Always allow two spaces in typewritten copy.**

---

[7]For desktop publishing some authorities recommend one space after a period that concludes a sentence. To promote ease of reading in documents written for business, others use two spaces after a period that concludes a sentence. Spacing after a concluding period is discretionary, and word processing software can be defaulted to permit one or two spaces.

decimal—no space

All these price increases may be attributed to the **21.5** percent increase in the cost of manufacturing materials since 2002.

period within abbreviation—no space

Be sure to quote all furniture prices **f.o.b.**

initial—one space

Cameron **T.** Miller has been promoted to national sales manager.

abbreviation within sentence—one space

Dr. Sussman has scheduled **Mrs.** Hoffman for surgery at 8 **a.m.** on April 17 in Encino Hospital.

end of sentence—one space

Please submit proof that the property taxes have been **paid.** As soon as we receive copies of your canceled check, we can close escrow.

end of sentence—two spaces

Please submit proof that the property taxes have been **paid.** As soon as we receive copies of your canceled check, we can close escrow.

b. **Use only one period to end a sentence, even though the sentence may end with an abbreviation.**

A courier is scheduled to deliver the contracts between 9 and 10 a.m.

Mr. Kirk's mail will be forwarded to him in Washington, D.C.

c. **Always place a period inside the closing quotation mark.**

Ms. Allison promptly replied, "No funding requests will be honored after June 30."

Our editor was pleased with your magazine article, "New Ideas for Home Builders."

d. **Place a period inside the closing parenthesis when the words in parentheses are a complete sentence. When the words in parentheses are not a complete thought and are part of another sentence, place the period outside the closing parenthesis.**

complete sentence in parentheses

A large number of employees left the company after the merger. (They were disappointed with the new leadership.)

incomplete sentence in parentheses

Two major marketing strategies were implemented after Dylan Consulting completed its analysis (last August).

Question Mark

1-40 Direct Questions

Conclude a direct question that requires an answer with a question mark.

How many times have you tried to contact Mrs. Shannon?

Of the 115 employees attending the board meeting, how many would you estimate were disappointed with the salary proposal?

1-41 Statements With Questions

a. When a sentence contains a statement followed by a direct question, conclude the sentence with a question mark. Separate the statement from the question with a comma, dash, or colon, depending upon the nature of the statement.

question mark with comma

I recommend that we contact at least three other vendors before selecting a permanent source of supply, wouldn't you agree?

question mark with dash

The committee members were pleased with the findings of the survey—weren't they?

question mark with colon

Each of us should consider the following question: what can we do to improve the profit picture for next year?

b. Conclude a statement that contains a short, direct question with a question mark.

You have filed your income tax return, have you not, for the last taxable year?

Our rental payments are current—aren't they—for the leased offices in the Bradley building?

c. Conclude with a question mark a statement that is meant as a question.

You have already finished reconciling last week's receipts?

The conference has been delayed until April?

d. Place a period, rather than a question mark, after an indirect question.

Mr. Joyner asked when we expected our Albany office to release the information.

Ms. Casavilca inquired about placing several of her students in our Accounting Department as trainees in an internship program.

e. Polite requests phrased as questions are followed by periods rather than question marks because they are considered to be commands or "please do" statements. A polite request (1) asks the reader to perform a specific action and (2) is answered by having the reader either complete or ignore the action requested instead of responding with "yes" or "no." Both components *must* be present for a period to be used; otherwise, a question mark is correct.

polite request requiring period

Will you please send us a copy of your medical insurance card.

May I please have this information by July 31.

Won't you take five minutes now to fill out the questionnaire and return it in the enclosed envelope.

May we count on your support with a "yes" vote on Proposition A.

direct question requiring question mark

Would you be willing to sponsor a runner (with a small financial contribution) in the San Diego Marathon to fight against leukemia? (Specific action that requires a "yes" or "no" response.)

May we call on you within the next two weeks for a demonstration of our Ultra 780 data projector? (Specific action that requires a "yes" or "no" response.)

Wouldn't you like to be the proud owner of a new Supra 28 laptop computer? (Does not require reader to return a "yes" or "no" response; however, no *specific* action is requested.)

May we have your support in the future? (Does not require reader to return a "yes" or "no" response; however, no *specific* action is requested.)

May I compliment you on your outstanding performance in meeting this year's sales quota? (No "yes" or "no" response is required; however, no *specific* action is requested.)

1-42 Expressions of Doubt

Signify doubt in expressing factual statements by enclosing a question mark in parentheses.

The national sales manager's last visit to the South was in 2001 **(?)**.

Our administrative assistant earns $3,760 **(?)** a month.

1-43 Series of Questions

When a sentence contains a series of questions, place a question mark at the end of each question. Only the first letter of the sentence is capitalized unless a question in the series begins with a proper noun or is a complete thought. Leave one space after a question mark that appears within a sentence; leave one or two spaces after the concluding question mark (depending upon the style used throughout the document).[8]

series of incomplete questions

What are the primary responsibilities of the president? the executive vice president? the treasurer?

Who requested copies of the police report—the judge? the insurance company? the plaintiff's attorney?

series of proper noun questions

Will the new flight route stop in San Diego? Los Angeles? San Francisco?

series of independent questions

Several important issues were discussed at the conference last week: What style trends will be popular during the next decade? What comfort demands will the public make on furniture manufacturers? How much will price influence consumer furniture purchases?

1-44 Question Mark Placement and Format

a. Question marks may be placed either inside or outside the closing quotation mark or parenthesis.

When a complete question is contained within the quotation or parenthetical remark, place the question mark inside the closing quotation mark or parenthesis. If the entire sentence—not just the quotation or parenthetical remark—comprises the question, place the question mark outside the closing quotation mark or parenthesis.

Use only one concluding punctuation mark at the end of a sentence.

complete question contained in quotation marks

"Will the entire original New York cast be present for the opening night in Philadelphia?" asked a local reporter.

The governor then inquired, **"Who authorized these payments?"**

complete question contained in parentheses

We received official notification yesterday **(did your notice arrive yet?)** that all tenants must vacate the building by the 1st of February.

Today one of our employees informed me that Wilson Edwards has been appointed manager of the New Haven office. **(Has the Board of Directors already announced its decision?)**

---

[8]Some desktop publishing authorities recommend only one space after the concluding punctuation mark; others use two spaces to promote ease of reading in business documents. The use of one or two spaces after a concluding punctuation mark is governed by the preference of the document originator.

question encompasses entire sentence

Have you finished reading the article "Investment Opportunities Abroad"?

Will you be able to ship this order by May 15 (earlier if possible)?

b. If an entire sentence and a quotation within the sentence are both questions, use only the first question mark—the one appearing inside the closing quotation mark.

Did the president ask, "When will the directors hold their next meeting?"

c. In word processing copy leave one space after a question mark that appears within a sentence and one or two spaces after a question mark that appears at the end of a sentence.[9] In typewritten copy leave two spaces after a question mark at the end of a sentence.

one space after questions within sentence

Should I place these supplies on the desk? in the cabinet? in the storeroom?

one space after ending question mark

When is your flight scheduled to depart? What time should we leave for the airport? What time do you expect to arrive in Washington, D.C.? May I please have answers to these questions today.

two spaces after ending question mark

When is your flight scheduled to depart? What time should we leave for the airport? What time do you expect to arrive in Washington, D.C.? May I please have answers to these questions today.

Exclamation Mark

1-45 **Use of Exclamation Mark**

To express a high degree of emotion, use an exclamation mark after a word, phrase, clause, or sentence.

word

What! You mean the new software will not arrive until next week?

phrase

How beautiful! The designer certainly used a great deal of color and imagination in creating this pattern.

---

[9]Some desktop publishing authorities suggest using only one space after a concluding punctuation mark; others use two spaces in business documents to promote ease of reading. The choice of one or two spaces remains with the document originator, and word processing software may be defaulted to implement this choice.

clause

If he attends! He'd better attend, or Mr. Ray will get a new assistant.

sentence

Yes, Dillon finally received an opportunity for an interview!

1-46 Exclamation Mark Placement and Format

a. In word processing copy leave one or two spaces after the exclamation mark before beginning the next word.[10] In typewritten copy use two spaces after the exclamation mark.

b. Exclamation marks should be used sparingly in business documents. Placing exclamation marks at the end of two consecutive sentences or thought units should be avoided. Instead, use commas, periods, or question marks to complete an exclamatory thought.

exclamation with comma

Oh, I don't see how we can possibly meet the contract deadline without working overtime!

exclamation with period

What a surprise! I did not know that Martin had resigned.

exclamation with question mark

Impossible! Do you really believe the network has a virus?

c. Exclamation marks may be placed either inside or outside the closing quotation mark or parenthesis.

When a complete exclamatory remark is a quotation or is enclosed in parentheses, place the exclamation mark inside the closing quotation mark or parenthesis. If the entire sentence, not just the quotation or parenthetical element, comprises the exclamatory expression, place the exclamation mark outside the closing quotation mark or parenthesis.

Use only one concluding punctuation mark at the end of a sentence.

complete exclamatory expression in quotation marks

At the time of the emergency, one of the employees shouted, **"Break down the door!"**

complete exclamatory expression in parentheses

He obtained the help of several advisors **(what a mistake that was!)** to assist him in selecting the project subcontractors.

---

[10]Some desktop publishing authorities recommend only one space after an ending punctuation mark; others use two spaces to foster reading ease. Document originators may use either style as long as they are consistent throughout the document.

Management was surprised by the employees' reactions to the new procedures. **(Only 14 percent welcomed the change!)**

exclamatory expression encompasses entire sentence

I cannot believe the mayor's statement, **"Only two members of the city council voted in favor of a rapid transit system for our city"**!

If you wish to take advantage of the convention hotel rates, you will have to act immediately **(before the block of rooms is sold out)!**

Quotation Marks

1-47 Direct Quotations

Direct quotations contain the exact wording used by a writer or speaker. In business documents place one-sentence quotations and short two-sentence quotations within quotation marks.

Use commas to introduce most one-sentence quotations. Long one-sentence quotations and quotations of two sentences or more are introduced by a colon.

Quotation marks are not used for indirect quotations, which do not use the exact wording of the source.

direct quotation

"The economy should begin to recover early next year," said Dr. Roger Watson, a renowned economist.

"Although this stock has split three times since 1987," explained Ms. Mooneyhan, **"you cannot anticipate that it will continue to do so."**

The reporter shouted, **"Look out! The scaffold is collapsing."**

Mr. Collins recommended the following in his report: **"Because interest rates are declining and property prices are rising steadily, we should investigate the possibility of refinancing our building. One of our managers should contact several mortgage brokers to see if such a plan would be to our economic advantage."**

indirect quotation

Perry Goldman, our production manager, forecasts that costs will increase 20 percent unless we update our manufacturing process.

1-48 Long Quotations

In business documents quotations of two or more sentences (usually three or more lines) are written without quotation marks, single-spaced, and formatted as separate paragraphs. They are indented from the left and right margins (0.5 inch) and separated from the main text by single blank lines at the beginning and the end.

The speaker also brought out the importance of effective management communication when she made the following statement:

> To exercise the function of leadership, there must be effective communication. If a leader cannot communicate, there is no leader because information cannot pass between the two groups. For instance, in management one cannot delegate duties and authority without effective communication.

Effective communication is paramount to effective leadership in . . . .

1–49 Short Expressions

a. When short expressions such as jargon, words used in humor or irony, technical words used in a nontechnical way, coined expressions, or slang words are used in a document, they are placed in quotation marks.

words used in irony

The FCC (Federal Communications Commission) has set 2006 as a **"reasonable date"** for broadcasters to give back their analog channels.

slang words

Mr. Rhodes has difficulty working with others on the production team because he always wants to be **"in the driver's seat."**

technical words used in a nontechnical way

Mr. Rollins announced that **"all systems are go"** for the new golf course and condominium project in Scottsdale.

b. Place in quotation marks the definitions of words or expressions. Italicize (or underscore if italics are not available) the word or expression defined.

defined word

According to some economists, a *recession* is actually a **"little depression."**

defined expression

The French term *faux pas* means **"a social blunder."**

c. References to the words *marked, labeled, stamped,* or *signed* are placed in quotation marks.

Please mark all cartons **"Glass—Handle With Care."**

Stamp the envelope **"Addressee Unknown, Return to Sender."**

The letter was signed **"Sean Drexel"** but contained no return address on either the letter or the envelope.

1-50 Literary Titles

Titles of various kinds of literary or artistic works such as magazine or newspaper articles, chapters of books or pamphlets, unpublished manuscripts, episodes in television series, acts in plays or musicals, short poems, lectures, songs, and themes are placed within quotation marks.

Names of books, magazines, pamphlets, newspapers, and other complete published or artistic works that contain subdivisions, however, are placed in italics (or underscored if italics are not accessible). (See Section 3-6 for further information and examples of titles placed in italics or underscored.)

book and chapter title

The chapter **"Webmaster Responsibilities"** contained in *Web Site Design and Maintenance* was helpful in specifying the duties and responsibilities of our Webmaster.

musical and song title

Of all the songs from the musical production *Man of La Mancha*, **"The Impossible Dream"** is probably the most well recognized.

episode in television series

For the past four years, **"To Serve Man"** has been aired on our network's Thanksgiving Day marathon of selected episodes from the *Twilight Zone*.

lecture title

The last lecture, **"How to Reduce Your Mortgage Payment,"** attracted a larger audience than any other lecture in the series.

1-51 Quotations Within Quotations

Use single quotation marks to signify a quotation within a quotation. If your software does not support single quotation marks, use the apostrophe key.

For quoted material within single quotation marks, return to using double quotation marks.

quotation within a quotation

The report stated, "According to the U.S. Chamber of Commerce, **'The problem of air and water pollution must be solved within the next decade if our cities are to survive.'** "

quotation within single quotation marks

The newspaper article quoted the defendant's attorney as saying, "When I asked my client, 'Did you endorse the check **"Robert S. Parry"** and then proceed to cash it?' he replied, 'No, I did not.' "

1-52 Ellipses

An ellipsis (a series of three periods with a space before, between, and after each period) is used to show an intentional omission of quoted material:

(1) If the omission begins the quoted sentence, use an ellipsis to begin the quotation.

(2) If the omission occurs within a sentence, use an ellipsis to substitute for the omitted words.

(3) If the omission occurs at the end of a sentence, use an ellipsis and then add the closing punctuation mark for the sentence.

(4) If one or more sentences have been omitted after the quoted sentence or sentences, first conclude the last sentence with the appropriate punctuation mark and then follow with an ellipsis to show the omission.

omission at beginning of quotation

The instructions stated, " . . . and turn knob in clockwise direction." (Remember to leave one space between the opening quotation mark and the first period in the ellipsis, one space between the periods, and one space after the closing period in the ellipsis.)

omission within sentence

The sign warns nonresidents about parking in this private lot: "Violators will be towed . . . cars will be released only upon payment of a $500 fine."

end-of-sentence omission

According to the guarantee, "All repairs not under warranty will be made at manufacturer's costs . . . ."

The new director inquired, "How often do we visit our various branch offices; i.e., Houston, Fort Worth, Oklahoma City, . . . ?"

one or more sentences omitted

The directive stated specifically: "Please ship our international orders by July 1. . . . Our European distributors must have their merchandise by August 1." (Close the sentence with a period. Place one space before each period in the ellipsis; place one or two spaces after the final period in the ellipsis before beginning the next sentence.)

The marketing manager wrote in her September 1 memo, "Will you be able to attend the conference in Baltimore? . . . We will need to set up our display booths on October 9." (Use a closing punctuation mark followed by an ellipsis with a space before, between, and after each period. Place one or two spaces after the final period in the ellipsis before beginning the next sentence.)

1-53 Capitalization With Quotation Marks

a. **Capitalize the first word of a complete sentence enclosed in quotation marks.**

"You may obtain more information at our Web site," replied Mrs. Edwards.

Kevin asked, "When will our area receive high-speed Internet access?"

b. **Capitalize incomplete thoughts enclosed in quotation marks only if the quoted words themselves are capitalized. First, last, and main words[11] in quoted expressions preceded by *stamped* or *marked* are usually capitalized.**

capitalized

His check was returned from the bank marked **"Insufficient Funds."**

"Handle With Care" was stamped on the package.

Did you mark the invoice **"Paid in Full"**?

not capitalized

Ms. Farrow asked us to spend **"as little time as possible"** to complete this project.

1-54 Quotation Mark Placement

a. **Commas and periods are always placed inside the closing quotation mark; semicolons and colons, outside the closing quotation mark.**

period

The purchase requisition stipulates, "Cancel this order if the merchandise cannot be delivered by the 1st of July."

comma

"We must find ways to lower our operating costs," said Mr. Collins.

semicolon

The consultant's report stated, "A thorough analysis of the company's data and information processing system should be undertaken"; however, no steps have been taken to initiate such an analysis.

colon

Mrs. Cox asked that the following vacation policy be adopted "unless a better one can be formulated": (1) Employees should select their vacation time based on seniority and (2) conflicts should be resolved by the employees themselves, whenever possible.

---

[11]*Main* words are all words EXCEPT (1) the articles *a, an,* and *the;* (2) the coordinating conjunctions *and, but, or,* and *nor;* (3) the word *to* in an infinitive (*to* write); and (4) prepositions with three or fewer letters (e.g., *of, for, in, on, by*).

b. When a complete question or exclamation is contained within the quotation, place the question mark or exclamation mark inside the closing quotation mark. If the entire sentence comprises the question or exclamation, then place the appropriate mark outside the closing quotation mark. If both the quotation and the entire sentence are questions, use only the first question mark.

complete question within quotation

The accountant asked, **"Where are the receipts for these expenditures?"**

entire sentence comprises question

Which issue of *Business Today* contained the article "Speech Technology Revolutionizes Internet Strategies"?

complete exclamation within quotation

"Do not," exclaimed Mr. Rey, **"leave the lights burning all night!"**

entire sentence comprises exclamation

Our new sales manager is a real "go-getter"!

question within a question

Did Mark inquire, "Who is responsible for engaging the security system next week?"

Apostrophe

1-55 **Possessives**

a. When a noun, singular or plural, does not end with a pronounced *s*, add an apostrophe and *s* (*'s*) to form the possessive case.

singular noun

Yes, I located the purchase requisition on my **assistant's** desk.

Lisa's appointment has been rescheduled for November 23.

Most of the **company's** profits were earned during the first quarter of this year.

plural noun

Women's fashions will be moved to the third floor next week.

Most of our discounted **children's** toys have already been sold.

These sweaters are made from 100 percent **sheep's** wool.

b. When a noun, singular or plural, ends with a pronounced *s*, add an apostrophe (*'*) to form the possessive case. However, an apostrophe and *s* (*'s*) may be added to singular nouns if an *additional s* sound is pronounced.

singular noun—add ' only

Ms. Simons' income and credit rating qualifies her to purchase this residence.

Most of these museum pieces were found among **Athens'** ruins.

plural noun—add ' only

Our staff reviews **customers'** accounts every 90 days.

Yesterday one of our agents listed the **Lopezes'** home.

singular noun with additional s sound—add 's

We have been invited to our **boss's** home for dinner on April 27.

Your **class's** scores on this state examination were very high.

Ask **Mr. Jones's** assistant for a copy of the report.

Were you present in court during the **witness's** testimony?

c. Use an apostrophe to show possession with (1) nouns that represent people, animals, and other living entities (animate objects) or (2) nouns related to time, distance, value, or celestial bodies. For other types of nouns (inanimate objects), use an *of* phrase to show possession.

animate possessive

Ask the **employees'** representative to meet with me on July 15.

Were the **horse's** hooves lacerated during the race?

Preserve your **hair's** color and luster with Canterbury's Protein+ conditioning shampoo.

Can you ensure that the **tree's** roots will not crack the swimming pool?

Our **company's** steadily declining profits led to the replacement of its executive officers. (The word *company* is animate because it is composed of animate objects—people.)

time possessive

This past **year's** profit and loss statement showed a gain of nearly 9 percent.

Six **months'** interest on your bankcard alone amounted to $1,218.60.

Yesterday's mail was still lying unopened on her desk when this **morning's** mail arrived.

distance possessive

The Kingston Hotel is just a **stone's** throw from the airport.

Although the suspect rushed by within **arm's** length, we were unable to supply a description to the police.

value possessive

Our office manager ordered several thousand **dollars'** worth of supplies and equipment.

We owe the customer 50 **cents'** change.

celestial possessive

During the summer months the **sun's** rays can be extremely harmful.

Is **Mars'** atmosphere suitable for human survival?

inanimate possessive

The **terms of the loan** were extended six months. (Not *loan's terms*)

Who broke the **base of the pot**? (Not *pot's base*)

d. **Form the possessive of compound nouns by having the last word show possession.**

Ms. Hollis was appointed her **father-in-law's** custodian by the courts.

Our meeting will be held at the **chairman of the board's** home.

My two **sisters-in-law's** business is doing well.

e. **When two or more nouns have joint ownership (own one thing together), only the last noun shows possession. When the nouns represent individual ownership (each owns something separately), however, each noun must show possession.**

joint possession

Bill and Sheryl's new assistant has worked at ABCO Corporation for three years. (Bill and Sheryl share the same assistant—joint possession.)

The Harrises and the Bradys' new boat was damaged in the storm. (The Harrises and the Bradys own the same boat—joint possession.)

individual possession

Natalie's and Jack's offices have been relocated to the new wing of our building. (Natalie and Jack have different offices—individual possession.)

The Schaeffers' and the Gonzalezes' houses are on the same street. (The Schaeffers and the Gonzalezes live in different houses—individual possession.)

f. **Express the possessive form of indefinite pronouns such as *anyone, everyone, someone, anybody, everybody, somebody,* and *nobody* by using the same rules that apply to possessive nouns.**

Anyone's car that is parked illegally in a handicapped space will be towed away.

Somebody's keys were left on the front counter this morning.

g. The possessive forms of personal or relative pronouns (such as *its, yours, hers, theirs,* or *whose*) do not include apostrophes. These pronouns are often confused with verb contractions, all of which contain apostrophes.

possessive pronoun

Although the company had **its** greatest sales volume last year, it still did not show a profit.

The bill was introduced by Senator Adams, **whose** term will end this December.

contraction

It's (It is) one of our most profitable lines.

We met with Taney, **who's (who is)** the developmental editor for this project.

h. Express the possessive form of abbreviations by using the same rules that apply to possessive nouns (Sections 1-55a and 1-55b).

abbreviation not ending with pronounced s

The **CPA's** report was short, yet comprehensive.

NASA's new space project is scheduled for a 2007 launching.

abbreviation ending with pronounced s

Barker Bros.' annual sale has been extended for another week.

All **R.N.s'** and **L.V.N.s'** identification badges are reissued annually.

You should visit the **IRS's** Web site to obtain more information about this issue. (Use *'s* instead of just an apostrophe because of the extra pronounced *s* sound.)

i. Use the possessive form of a noun or a pronoun before a gerund (an *-ing* verb used as a noun).

noun

Joshua's suggesting that we expand our operations to Europe and Asia has proved to be profitable.

pronoun

We would appreciate **your returning** the enclosed form by March 31.

j. When a possessive noun is followed by an explanatory expression (an appositive), use an apostrophe only in the explanatory expression. When this form of writing sounds awkward, as it does in most cases, show possession by using an *of* phrase.

apostrophe

Ms. Norton, **our advertising manager's**, office is being renovated.

of *phrase*

The office **of our advertising manager,** Ms. Norton, is being renovated.

k. **Many organizations with plural possessives in their names have omitted the apostrophe; organizations with singular possessives have tended to retain the apostrophe. Use an apostrophe in an organizational name only if the organization itself does so.**

plural possessive

Your loan approval from **Farmers** Bank and Trust arrived this morning.

singular possessive

The contract was issued to **Linton's** Manufacturing Company.

l. **Sometimes the possessed item is not stated explicitly in a sentence; instead, it is understood or implied clearly. In such cases the ownership word still requires an apostrophe to show possession.**

This month our stock club will meet at **Steve's.**

Be sure to arrive at the **doctor's** by 2 p.m.

The wallet found in the corridor was **Mr. Lopez's.**

Deliver this floral arrangement to the **Briggses'** before noon.

This month's sales are considerably higher than last **month's.**

1-56 **Additional Uses of the Apostrophe**

a. **Use the apostrophe to form contractions.**

single-word contraction

| acknowledged | **ack'd** | national | **nat'l** | cannot | **can't** |

two-word contraction

| you would | **you'd** | is not | **isn't** | I have | **I've** |

b. **The apostrophe is used for clarity to form the plural of all isolated lowercase letters and the single capital letters *A, I, M,* and *U.***

plural of lowercase letter

Be sure to dot your *i's* and cross your *t's*.

How many times must you be reminded to watch your *p's* and *q's*?

plural of capital letters A, I, M, *and* U

Sandra received three *A's* in business classes this semester.

Avoid using too many *I's* in the business documents you write.

c. **The apostrophe may be used for the single quotation mark to signify a quotation within a quotation.**

Terry reported, "The president opened the forum with **'We're going to drive QuickWrite's sales back up to and beyond its former high!'**"

d. **Use the apostrophe to signify the omission of figures in expressing a year.**

Job prospects for the class of **'05** look favorable—especially in the computer industry.

e. **In technical material the apostrophe may be used as a symbol for *feet*.**

12' x 15' (room)   5' 3" (height)   80' x 110' (area)

Parentheses

1-57 **Nonessential Expressions**

Parentheses are used to set off and subordinate nonessential expressions that would otherwise confuse the reader because (1) they give supplementary information that has no direct bearing on the main idea or (2) they call for an abrupt change in thought. References and instructions are two examples of expressions that are often enclosed in parentheses.

abrupt change in thought
I wrote to Mr. Furstman **(I tried to call him, but there was no answer)** and asked him to contact us before October 4.

reference
All purchases over $5,000 must be approved by the vice president of business services. **(See Bulletin 8 dated March 2.)**

instructions
Please mail 200 copies of our annual report to each of our European offices. **(Send them by Airmail M-bags service.)**

1-58 **Numerals**

Numerals in legal, business, and professional documents are often shown in parentheses to confirm a spelled-out figure.

All repair work is guaranteed for ninety **(90)** days.

Compensation for services rendered will not exceed three thousand dollars **($3,000)**.

The committee may not consider any bid over nine thousand nine hundred ninety-nine dollars **($9,999)**.

On March 4 our client received a check for two thousand eight hundred forty-three dollars and seventy-five cents **($2,843.75)**.

1-59 Enumerated Items

Enclose in parentheses numbers or letters used to enumerate lists of items within a sentence.

See Section 1-36a for the use of parentheses with alphanumeric outlines.

numbers

Please supply me with the following information for the current year: the number of **(1)** new hires, **(2)** retirements, **(3)** voluntary resignations, and **(4)** terminations by the company.

letters

This report supplies the following current information for Marengo County: **(a)** salary trends, **(b)** unemployment statistics, and **(c)** placement requests.

1-60 Parentheses With Other Punctuation Marks

a. Words, phrases, and clauses enclosed in parentheses in the middle of a sentence function as part of the sentence in applying rules of punctuation and capitalization.

word

We will fly to Fort Lauderdale **(Florida)** for our annual convention.

phrase

Ms. Haven will gross nearly $800,000 **(as compared to a $500,000 average)** in sales this year.

clause

Our new manager **(several members of our staff met him last week)** will conduct a communications seminar in the spring.

b. When an incomplete thought enclosed in parentheses ends a sentence that requires a period, place the period outside the closing parenthesis.

According to our legal counsel, this procedure violates laws in only two states **(Minnesota and Wyoming).**

c. When a complete thought enclosed in parentheses follows a sentence that requires a period, the two parts are treated separately. Place a period at the end of each sentence, with the final period appearing inside the closing parenthesis.

Yes, your order was shipped on April 17. **(You should receive it within five or six working days.)**

Several members of our staff attended the ATLW conference this year. **(This year's conference was held in Honolulu.)**

d. If an interrupting word, phrase, or clause shown in parentheses requires a question mark or exclamation mark, use such a mark of punctuation only if the sentence ends with a different mark.

parenthetical question

Our new vice president **(do you know Colleen Madison?)** will arrive in Los Angeles tomorrow.

When will our new price list **(has your copy arrived)** become effective?

parenthetical exclamation

Have you heard about the recent enormous price increases **(I can't believe them!)** in single-family dwellings?

Living conditions **(you can scarcely call them that)** are absolutely deplorable in this section of the city!

e. Place commas, semicolons, and colons outside the closing parenthesis.

comma

If you plan to attend the president's retirement banquet (on May 16**)**, please send your reservations to Terry Thomsen by Monday, May 12.

semicolon

His report deals primarily with the importance of our country's major transportation systems (railroads, inland waterways, motor trucks, pipelines, and air transportation**)**; therefore, little emphasis was given to rising transportation costs.

colon

On February 15 Ms. Haddad will introduce two new product lines (for women's fashion departments**)**: the Sportswoman Series and the Sun and Surf Coordinates.

Brackets

1-61 **Use of Brackets**

a. Use brackets to insert an explanation, a correction, or a comment in quoted material.

To show that an error in quoted material appeared in the original document, enclose the term *sic* (meaning "so" or "this is the way it was") in brackets.

Mr. Morton stated in his report: "With new equipment to speed up the production process **[he did not specify what new equipment was needed]**, substantial reductions can be realised **[sic]** in both labor and overhead costs."

b. **Brackets may be used within parentheses to indicate yet another subordinate idea.**

The auction of Rita Rothchild's possessions (including jewelry, furs, furniture, movie costumes **[from 1950 through 1980]**, china, silverware, and other memorabilia) is scheduled for July 17 and 18.

1-62 Use of Angle Brackets

In footnotes or bibliographical citations, some authorities use angle brackets to enclose the addresses (URLs) of Internet sites.

5Ellen Neuborne, "Time for Retailers to Face Their Web 'Terror,'" *BusinessWeek Online: BusinessWeek e.biz*, 5 July 2002, <http://www. businessweek.com/ebiz/index.html> (5 July 2002).

1-63 Brackets With Other Punctuation Marks

The placement of other punctuation marks with brackets follows the same principles outlined for parentheses in Section 1-60.

Asterisk

1-64 Use of Asterisk

Asterisks may be used to call the reader's attention to footnotes in a document when they appear infrequently and occur at widely spaced intervals. The asterisk follows other punctuation marks— except the dash, closing parenthesis, or closing bracket.

after most punctuation marks

A recent government report states, "Air traffic is expected to double within the next decade."*

before dash, closing parenthesis, or closing bracket

We are studying the works of Ray Bradbury*—one of our leading contemporary science fiction writers.

Companies that have hired outside consultants to develop cost-cutting procedures have reported successful results. (Several articles supporting the effectiveness of outside consultants have recently appeared in leading professional journals.*)

A number of prominent national magazines (such as *Time, Newsweek,* and *BusinessWeek* [May and June issues*]) have published informative, interesting articles on issues regarding the Internet.

Diagonal

1-65 **Use of Diagonal**

Use a diagonal (also called a "solidus," "slash," or "virgule") between (1) letters in some abbreviations, (2) numerals in fractions, and (3) the expression *and/or* to show that the terms are interchangeable. No space appears before or after the diagonal.

abbreviation

Please send the package to Mrs. Monica Sullivan, **c/o** Mr. George Martin, Display Manager, Wilson Paper Company, 1141 Western Avenue, Los Angeles, California 90024.

fraction

Our state sales tax will increase **½** percent on January 1.

To reupholster the reception room sofa will require **12 5/8** yards of fabric.

and/or

Authorization for future purchases may be obtained from Ms. Jorgensen **and/or** Mr. Kline.

Underscore

1-66 **Use of the Underscore**

The underscore is generally not used in computer-generated or printed copy. Other font attributes—italics, bolding, bolded italics, and varying font sizes—substitute for the underscore.

In typewritten copy the underscore is used to emphasize such items as headings; words that would normally be italicized; and titles of books, magazines, newspapers, pamphlets, and various other published or artistic works (see Section 3-6). Continuous lines, with no spacing between words, are used for underscoring. Except for periods with abbreviations, punctuation marks immediately following underscored material are not underscored.

italicized word

He always misspells the word **convenience**.

magazine title

According to an article in **BusinessWeek**, most movies are currently being filmed outside the United States.

television show with subdivision

"Jack the Ripper" was the first episode on this season's television series **Unsolved Mysteries**.

abbreviation

Be sure to place **a.m.** in lowercase letters.

punctuation mark following standard underscored material

Did the bookstore order sufficient copies of **Merriam-Webster's Collegiate Dictionary**?

Ampersand

1–67 **Use of the Ampersand**

a. The ampersand (&), a symbol that represents the word *and*, is used primarily to express the official name of some business organizations.

ampersand in company name

Johnson **&** Johnson was the subcontractor for the project.

A. G. Edwards **&** Sons, Inc., is handling the sale of this new stock issue.

use of **and** *in company name*

All merger talks with Merritt **and** Sons have been delayed until the end of our fiscal period.

b. When an ampersand appears in a series, use a comma before the ampersand only if the organization does so in its official name.

no comma before the ampersand

The law offices of Levitt, Myers **&** Cohen represented the plaintiff in this case.

comma before the ampersand

Fall fashions from Liz, Lee**,** **&** Co. should arrive in our store by the middle of July.

2

Hyphenating and Dividing Words

Hyphenating and Dividing Words Solution Finder

Hyphenating Words

2-1 **Compound Nouns and Verbs**

Often two or more words act as a single idea. Nouns and verbs in this class may be written as separate words, written as single words, or hyphenated. Consult an up-to-date dictionary to determine the exact form of compound nouns and verbs.[1]

separate words, nouns

income tax	editor in chief	life insurance	charge account
data processing	air conditioner	time sheet	voice mail

single words, nouns

checkbook	workforce	salesperson	paycheck
spreadsheet	database	stepfather	moneymaker

hyphenated words, nouns

sister-in-law	attorney-at-law	by-product	self-confidence
double-talk	face-lift	log-in	air-conditioning

separate words, verbs

to set up	to mark down	to step down	to call in
to stand out	to trade in	to slip up	to double up

single words, verbs

to upgrade	to keyboard	to downsize	to landscape
to videotape	to download	to handpick	to mastermind

hyphenated words, verbs

to tape-record	to air-condition	to triple-space	to cross-examine
to ill-treat	to e-mail	to double-check	to piece-dye

2-2 **Compound Adjectives**

When two or more words appearing together act as a single idea to describe a noun or pronoun, these words function as a compound adjective. In many cases compound adjectives are hyphenated; in other cases they are not. Use the following guidelines to determine whether a compound adjective should be hyphenated.

a. A number of compound adjectives are listed and shown hyphenated in the dictionary. These adjectives may be considered *permanent* compounds. They are hyphenated whenever they are used as adjectives in a sentence, no matter where they appear in the sentence—before or after the nouns or pronouns they modify.

---

[1]All spellings and hyphenations used in this manual are based upon *Merriam-Webster's Collegiate Dictionary,* 10th ed. (Springfield, Mass.: Merriam-Webster, Incorporated, 2002). For a complete, up-to-date on-line Internet resource, visit Merriam-Webster at www.m-w.com (no fees or registration required).

permanent compound adjective before a noun or pronoun

up-to-date	**up-to-date** records
well-known	**well-known** personalities
part-time	**part-time** employees
snow-white	**snow-white** mountains
small-scale	**small-scale** investments
hands-off	**hands-off** policy
machine-readable	**machine-readable** text
no-fault	**no-fault** insurance
public-spirited	**public-spirited** citizens

permanent compound adjective following noun or pronoun

Because we installed new accounting software, all our accounts receivable records are **up-to-date**.

Our line of clothing is **well-known** throughout the world.

Since your position is **part-time**, you are not eligible for health insurance benefits.

Mailing addresses on all envelopes from our company are **machine-readable**.

The majority of families in this community are **public-spirited**.

b. Sometimes compound nouns are used as single-thought adjectives to describe other nouns or pronouns. When these combinations are shown as *open compounds* (not hyphenated) in the dictionary, they are not hyphenated when they are used as compound adjectives.

compound noun	compound noun used as compound adjective
stock market	**stock market** information
life insurance	**life insurance** premiums
savings account	**savings account** passbook
human resources	**human resources** management
finance company	**finance company** records
charge account	**charge account** customer
high school	**high school** principal
word processing	**word processing** software
income tax	**income tax** forms
department store	**department store** personnel
real estate	**real estate** office

c. Many single-thought word groups that function as compound adjectives are not shown in the dictionary. Such word groups are known as *temporary compounds*. These temporary compounds are hyphenated and written in singular form (where applicable) when they appear *before* the nouns or pronouns they describe. They are not hyphenated, however, when they appear after the words they modify.

temporary compound before noun or pronoun—hyphenated

We have already installed **speech-recognition** software in most of our computers.

All **city-owned** property is exempt from these county taxes.

We retained a **well-established** legal firm to represent our interests.

Capture that **never-to-be-forgotten** event with pictures taken by ProPhotographers!

The mayor's **not-too-cordial** attitude toward the press was evident.

temporary compound in singular form before noun or pronoun— hyphenated

The **160-foot** driveway leading up to the house will need to be paved before our clients will purchase the property.

Most of our clients are interested in purchasing a **four-bedroom** home in a quiet, residential neighborhood.

The Butlers' **6-pound-11-ounce** daughter was born on April 5.

The state highway patrol enforces strictly the **65-mile-an-hour** speed limit on this highway.

temporary compound following noun or pronoun

All the software programs on this list are **speech recognition**.

None of the properties in this area are **city owned**.

Cox & Cox has been **well established** in Austin for thirty years.

Your wedding should be a day that is **never to be forgotten**.

Mr. Winters' greetings this morning were certainly **not too cordial**.

The driveway leading up to the house is **160 feet** long.

The Holtzes' new home has **four bedrooms**.

At birth the Butlers' baby weighed **6 pounds 11 ounces**.

The speed limit on this highway is **65 miles an hour**.

d. When *two separate* proper nouns or *two separate* common nouns are combined to form single-thought adjectives before other nouns or pronouns, hyphenate these compounds.

separate proper nouns used as an adjective

This morning's issue of *The Wall Street Journal* carried several articles on **Chinese-American** relations.

Your **New York-London** flight has been delayed for three hours.

separate common nouns used as an adjective

All the applicants have experience in **union-management** relations.

Classes may not exceed a 15:1 **student-teacher** ratio.

e. **Two or more words that represent a *single* proper noun are not hyphenated when they are used as an adjective.**

Our company has been negotiating with a **Middle Eastern** firm for the past six months.

How many **University of Florida** alumni have you been able to locate in Salt Lake City?

f. **Adverbs ending in *ly* that are combined with adjectives to form a single modifier are not hyphenated.**

Your session sparked the most **hotly debated** issues at the conference.

Dr. Matsuyama is an **exceptionally gifted** nuclear physicist.

g. **Two separate colors stated in a compound modifier are hyphenated. Other adjectives, however, used in conjunction with colors are not hyphenated unless the combination is a permanent compound shown in the dictionary.**

two separate colors

We selected a **blue-green** fabric to reupholster the chairs in the reception area.

Albert Hayes used **red-orange** hues effectively to portray the Hawaiian sunset in these paintings.

adjective combined with color

In this tank the **bluish green** water magnifies the colorful fish.

Women's clothing this season is featuring **bright red** accessories.

Ask all our sales representatives to wear **dark gray** or black suits to the exhibition.

The **emerald green** cover of your new book definitely sets it apart from your competitors' books.

Place these artists' prints against a **snow-white** background to accentuate their deep color contrasts. (The adjective *snow-white* is shown hyphenated in the dictionary.[2])

h. **When a series of hyphenated adjectives has a common ending, use suspending hyphens.**

Have these announcements printed on **8½- by 11-inch** bond paper.

Please order a supply of **1⁄16- and 1⁄8-inch** drill bits.

These awards are for **eleventh- and twelfth-grade** students.

All construction bids for this hillside development are based on **one-, two-, and three-level** family dwellings.

---

[2]*Merriam-Webster's Collegiate Dictionary,* 10th ed. (Springfield, Mass.: Merriam-Webster, Incorporated, 2002), 1109.

i. Amounts in the millions and billions, percentages, and words used with numerals or letters are *not* hyphenated when they function as compound adjectives.

amounts in the millions and billions

How does the president propose to deal with the projected **$1.2 billion** decline in the Gross Domestic Product?

Over **210 million** people worldwide use the Internet; **64 million** people in the United States alone use the Internet regularly.

percentages

Between July 1 and July 31, you will receive a **10 percent** discount on all orders placed through our Web site.

We will experience a ½ **percent** increase in our state sales tax effective May 1.

words used with numerals or letters

Cynthia will be rated in as a **Grade 1** administrative assistant.

How many **vitamin C** tablets are in each container?

We will receive these Paramount **Model 17G** PDAs by June 1.

j. Simple fractions are hyphenated *only* when they are used as compound adjectives.[3]

compound adjective

John sold his **one-fourth** ownership in the company for $1,560,000.

Amendments to the bylaws require a **two-thirds** majority approval.

simple fraction as noun

Only **one third** of the stockholders responded to the questionnaire.

The Board of Directors voted to reinvest **one half** of this year's profits in additional research and development projects.

2-3 Prefixes

a. Words beginning with *ex* (meaning "former") and *self* are hyphenated; those beginning with *pre*, *re*,[4] and *non* are generally not hyphenated. Words beginning with *co* and *vice* may or may not be hyphenated. Use your dictionary to check the hyphenation of words with either of these beginnings.

---

[3]"Table of Numbers," Footnote 5, *Merriam-Webster's Collegiate Dictionary*, 10th ed. Springfield, Mass.: Merriam-Webster, Incorporated, 2002), 796.

[4]The words *re-collect* meaning "to collect again," *re-cover* meaning "to cover anew," *re-create* meaning "to create again," *re-lease* meaning "to lease again," *re-present* meaning "to present again," *re-press* meaning "to press again," *re-sign* meaning "to sign again," *re-sort* meaning "to sort again," and *re-tread* meaning "to tread again" are exceptions to this rule. Note that without the hyphens these words would have completely different meanings.

ex *and* self

Bill Rullo, the **ex-mayor** of Hampton, is now a financial adviser.

The **ex-chairperson** of our committee still has all last year's records.

Successful salespeople usually project **self-confidence**.

Employee **self-satisfaction** contributes to raising productivity.

pre, re, *and* non

All the floppy disks we purchase have been **preformatted**.

When will the **preemployment** interviews be held?

Please **recheck** all the receipts from our Corona store carefully.

The tires on this truck are in need of **realignment**.

Tuition **reimbursements** are unavailable for classes taken at **nonaccredited** educational institutions.

Do you wish to initiate legal proceedings against Fox One-Hour Photo for **nonpayment** of its account?

co

co-edition   coauthor
co-owner   codefendant
co-occurrence   coinsurance

vice

vice-chancellor   vice admiral
vice-consul   vice president

b. **When a prefix is added to a proper noun, place a hyphen between the prefix and the proper noun.**

We found that many firms operating in the South today date back to **pre-Civil War** times.

If you cannot promise a **mid-August** delivery date, cancel the order.

For some a 4th of July without fireworks would be **un-American**.

2-4 **Numbers**

a. **Compound numbers from *21* to *99* are hyphenated when they appear in word form.**

Ninety-six of our agents responded to the questionnaire, but we are still awaiting replies from **twenty-four** more.

b. **In numbers over *99* expressed in word form, components other than compound numbers are not hyphenated. Begin each number with a capital letter in formal legal documents.**

The lessee shall pay a sum of **Two Thousand Eight Hundred Seventy-five Dollars and Twenty-four Cents** ($2,875.24) to the lessor.

c. Simple fractions not used with units of measure are expressed in word form. Hyphenate these fractions *only* when they function as compound adjectives.

simple fraction used as noun

Over **two thirds** of our employees voted to accept the new contract.

Approximately **three fourths** of our company cars are now equipped with cellular phones.

simple fraction used as compound adjective

Westfield, Inc., has purchased a **one-half** interest in the Topanga Canyon Shopping Mall.

A **two-thirds** majority vote is needed to pass this proposition, which will appear on the November ballot.

d. When a number-word combination functions as a *single unit* to describe a noun (a compound adjective), (1) express the word part of the compound adjective in singular form and (2) separate the parts of the compound adjective with a hyphen. Only in percentages, amounts in the millions and billions, and capitalized word-numeral combinations are the hyphens omitted.

hyphen—number-word compound adjective

Our **three-year** lease for these offices will expire on August 31.

Major highways in our state have a **65-mile-an-hour** speed limit.

Drivers along this turnpike are charged **50-cent** tolls.

One of our students just started a **$3,200-a-month** job.

The Joneses' **7-pound-8-ounce** baby girl was born on December 25.

no hyphen—percentage

Your division experienced a **15 percent** sales increase during the last quarter.

no hyphen—amount in the millions

Ridgewood Inc. announced a **$3 million** profit for the current year.

no hyphen—capitalized word-numeral combination

Your Evansdale **Model 380** curio cabinet should arrive in our store within the next three weeks.

e. In word processing copy use an *en* dash (if possible) to represent the terms *to* or *through* between two numerals. In typewritten copy, though, use the hyphen to replace these terms.

As you requested, your vacation this year has been scheduled from July **3–18**.

Refer to pages **70–75** for further instructions.

End-of-Line Word and Word-Group Divisions

Where possible, avoid dividing words at the end of a computer-generated or typewritten line because complete words are easier to read, easier to understand, and neater in appearance. Sometimes, however, word divisions at the end of a line are necessary to avoid overly uneven line lengths or, in justified copy, awkward-appearing lines with large spaces between words.

Observe the following rules to divide words and certain word groups correctly at the end of a line. Some of these rules should be followed strictly; others are flexible in their application, especially in desktop-published copy. The following sections address (1) words and word groups *never* to be divided; (2) word divisions to be avoided, if possible; and (3) rules and guidelines for proper end-of-line word and word-group divisions.

2-5 Words and Word Groups Never to Be Divided

Some words and certain word groups may not be divided under any circumstances:

a. Do not divide one-syllable words, including those that end in *ed*.

one-syllable words

freight   straight   threats   thought   through   bread

one-syllable ed *words*

called   changed   weighed   planned   striped   shipped

b. Do not set off a single-letter syllable at either the beginning or the end of a word.

beginning of a word

i tinerary   a warded   e nough   o mitted   u niform

end of a word

radi o   bacteri a   health y   photocop y   criteri a   rati o

c. Do not set off a two-letter syllable at the end of a word. At least three characters of a divided word must appear on the next line.

present ed	compa ny	month ly
build er	week ly	debt or

d. Do not divide abbreviations unless a hyphen already appears within the abbreviation. Hyphenated abbreviations may be divided after the hyphen.

not divided

UNESCO	AMSLAN	U.S.A.	AOL	UCLA	Ph.D.
Ed.D.	B.A.	Sept.	bdrm.	c.o.d.	equiv.

may be divided

AFL-CIO   KMET-TV   NBEA-WBITE

e. Do not divide month and day; *a.m., p.m., noon,* or *midnight* from clock time; percentages from the word *percent*; page numbers from page references; or other such closely related word-and-numeral combinations.

If you are using a word processor, place a nonbreaking space between the components of the combination to keep all parts on the same line.

month and day

April 8   October 27   September 30

a.m., p.m., noon, *or* **midnight** *with clock time*

9 a.m.   7:30 a.m.   1 p.m.
4:05 p.m.   12 midnight   12 noon

percentage with the word **percent**

0.5 percent   1 percent   8.25 percent
63.5 percent   100 percent

page number with page reference

page iv   page 87   page 283   page 1176

other word-and-numeral combinations

9 ounces   Room 310   Model 56A   No. 628179
Check 419   8 inches   483 miles   16 yards
34 cents   Suite 600   Chapter 12   size 14

f. Do not divide contractions or numerals.

contractions

wouldn't   doesn't   haven't
won't   you're   o'clock

numerals

$15,487   1,240,500   3 billion   4,500 $2.5 million

g. Do not divide the last word in more than two consecutive lines.

h. Do not divide the last word in a paragraph or the last word on a page.

2-6 Words to Avoid Dividing, If Possible

Observing the following rules is certainly desirable, but situations may occur where end-of-line word divisions are unavoidable. Apply these rules—unless doing so would result in an extremely ragged right margin.

a. Avoid dividing words that contain six letters or fewer.

forget   person   better   number   listen   filter

b. Avoid dividing a word after a two-letter prefix.

en large   re warding   im portant
de pendent   un necessary

2–7 Rules and Guidelines for Dividing Words

Divide words *only* between syllables. Use an up-to-date dictionary or a word-division manual to locate the correct syllabication of words to be divided. All word divisions shown in this reference manual are based on the syllabication shown in *Merriam-Webster's Collegiate Dictionary*, 10th ed., the 2002 printing, published by Merriam-Webster, Incorporated.

Words containing several syllables often require forethought to determine the appropriate place to separate the word. Use the following guidelines to determine where to divide a word:

a. Divide hyphenated and single-word compounds at their natural breaks.

hyphenated compound

vice-/chancellor[5]   self-/esteem   Governor-/elect   brother-/in-/law

single-word compound

common/place   hand/made   break/down   sales/person

b. Where possible, divide words after a prefix or before a suffix.

prefix

anti/body   super/intendent   mis/fortune   sub/stantiate

suffix

evasive/ness   corpora/tion   employ/ment   conscien/tious

c. Divide words between double letters *except* when the root word itself ends with the double letters and is followed by a suffix.

divided between double letters

bul/letin   accom/modate   neces/sarily
vacil/late   mil/len/nium

divided after double letters

business/like   fulfill/ment   helpless/ness   install/ing

d. Divide words between two vowels pronounced separately.

---

[5] The slash (/) as used here and in the following sections of this chapter signifies appropriate places for dividing words at the end of a line.

continu/ation	experi/ence	gradu/ation	influ/ential

e. Divide words *after*, not before, a single vowel pronounced as a syllable except when the vowel is part of a suffix.

single vowel

clari/fication	apolo/gize	congratu/lations	bene/ficial

suffix vowel

accept/able	allow/able	collaps/ible	forc/ible

2-8 Guidelines for Dividing Word Groups

Certain word groups are preferably divided in specific places. Use the following guidelines to separate dates, names of individuals, addresses, numbered items, copy containing dashes, and copy containing ellipses. If you are using word processing software, place a nonbreaking space between any parts in the word group that should appear on the same line.

a. Divide dates between the day and the year, but *not* between the month and the day.

October 21, /2002	*not*	October /21, 2002
February 7, /2006	*not*	February /7, 2006

b. Full names of individuals are ideally divided directly before the last name, but they may be divided before a middle name. Do not, however, divide a name after a courtesy title, before a middle initial, or before an abbreviation.

Names preceded by long professional titles *may also be* divided between the title and the first name or between words in the title.

divided before last name

Ms. Bernadine /Lancaster	*not*	Ms. /Bernadine Lancaster
Dr. Beverly K. /Gelobedian	*not*	Dr. /Beverly K. Gelobedian
		Dr. Beverly /K. Gelobedian
Mr. Jason /Montgomery Jr.	*not*	Mr. /Jason Montgomery Jr.
		Mr. Jason Montgomery /Jr.

divided before middle name or last name

Lorraine /Hoover /Clark   Jordan /Christopher /Savage

divided after long title or between words in a long title

Associate /Professor /Alice H. /Duffy

Lieutenant /Colonel /Daniel /Ritzkowski

c. Avoid, where possible, dividing a street address directly after the house or building number. Street addresses are preferably divided between the street name and the street type (*Street, Avenue, Boulevard, Lane,* etc.). If the street name contains more than one word, the street address may also be divided between words in the street name.

division of single-word street name

1571 Charleston / Avenue   One Blythe / Drive

20 Wilshire / Boulevard   4810 36th / Street

division possibilities of street name containing more than one word

4300 Coldwater / Canyon / Avenue   817 East / Jersey / Street

17325 San / Fernando / Mission / Boulevard

3624 West / 59th / Place

d. City and state lines in addresses may be divided between (1) the city and state and (2) the state and zip code. They may also be divided between words in those cities and states containing more than one word.

Dubuque, / Iowa / 52001   San / Diego, / California / 92109-2134

Poughkeepsie, / New / York / 12601-1032

e. A numbered or lettered horizontal listing may be divided directly before the number or letter, but not directly after.

An affirmative action officer offered these three reasons: (1) fewer openings in the teaching profession, (2) enrollment declines, and (3) no mandatory retirement age for teachers.

f. A sentence with a dash may be broken after the dash, but not directly before it.

The vice president agrees that your recommendation is excellent— a step in the right direction.

When our peak sales subside at the end of the year—in December— we plan to move our offices to San Francisco.

g. A sentence may be divided directly after an ellipsis, not directly before. At least one word of the sentence must appear on the same line before the ellipsis.

If you are using word processing software, place a nonbreaking space before and between the periods in an ellipsis to prevent the periods from word wrapping incorrectly to the next line.

As the article stated, "The mayor's campaign issues focus on . . . crime prevention in our city."

According to the *Newsweek* article, "As the number of Internet access providers continues to grow, prices for these services will drop. . . . Such factors will result in substantially fewer providers."

3

Capitalization

Solution Finder for Capitalization

Solution Finder for Capitalization *(continued)*

3

Capitalization

3-1 **Beginning Words**

a. Capitalize the beginning words of sentences, quoted sentences, independent phrases, lines of poetry, and items in an outline.

sentence

Sign up today for our free on-line bill-paying service.

quoted sentence

According to the warranty, **"Defective** parts will be replaced free of charge within 60 days from the date of purchase."

independent phrase

Now, for the most important consideration.

poetry

By the rude bridge that arched the flood,
Their flag to the April's breeze unfurled,
Here once the embattled farmers stood,
And fired the shot heard round the world.

　　　　　　　　　　　　　—Emerson

outline

1. **Specific** instructions
　　a. **Type** of product
　　b. **Tools** needed for assembly
　　c. **Diagrams** illustrating assembly

b. The first word of an incomplete quoted thought that is woven in with the rest of the sentence is not capitalized unless it is (1) a proper noun, (2) introduced by an identifying term such as *marked* or *stamped*, or (3) capitalized because of another rule of capitalization.

lowercase

Mr. Reyes was directed to **"take** care of this situation immediately."

proper noun

Our stock analyst's response was simply **"General** Motors common stock."

*introduced by identifying term **marked** or **stamped***

The client's check was returned by the bank marked **"Insufficient Funds."**

Request our Shipping Department to stamp all these packages **"Fragile—Handle With Care."**

another rule of capitalization

Remind students that these forms are machine-readable and that the instructions say to use **"No. 2** pencils only."

c. In business letters addressed to specific individuals, groups of individuals, or companies, capitalize the first word and any nouns contained in the salutation. For letters directed to undetermined individuals, capitalize the first word and all main words[1] in the salutation.

Capitalize only the first word of a complimentary close.

standard salutation—first word and all nouns

Dear Mr. Mikus: Gentlemen: My dear Friend:

Dear fellow American: Ladies and Gentlemen:

salutation to undetermined individual—first word and all main words

To Whom It May Concern:

To Stockholders of Record on May 1, 2004:

complimentary close

Sincerely yours,   Cordially yours,   Yours very truly,

d. The first word following a colon is generally not capitalized. Capitalize the first word, however, when the following words (1) begin with a proper noun, (2) consist of two or more sentences, (3) begin a vertical listing, (4) present a rule, or (5) require emphasis.

first word not capitalized

To finish landscaping the model homes, our crew will require the following supplies: **lawn** seed, liquid fertilizer, and insect spray.

Our supplier is experiencing a two months' delay in its production schedule: **the** warehouse fire set back the company considerably.

proper noun following colon

Three colleges are involved in the project: **DeKalb** Community College, MiraCosta College, and the City College of New York.

two or more sentences following colon

Here are two important questions to consider: **Will** enlarging our facilities at this time be economically feasible? **Is** the current market able to assimilate any increased production?

vertical listing following colon

Please send us copies of the following items:

1. **Lease** agreement with Property Management Associates
2. **Statement** of income and expenses for 2004
3. **Budget** of projected income and expenses for 2005

---

[1]*Main* words are all words except the articles *a, and, the;* the conjunctions *and, but, or, nor;* the word *to* used with an infinitive; and prepositions containing two or three letters (*of, for, on,* etc.).

formal rule following colon

Use the following style to prepare all correspondence for our company: **Format** letters in modified block style with blocked paragraphs and mixed punctuation.

item of special emphasis following colon

Note: **Several** of our employees consistently access nonwork-related Web sites during working hours.

Wanted: **Full-time** salesperson to work weekdays 8 a.m. until 5 p.m.

e. The first word of a complete thought contained in parentheses *within a sentence* is not capitalized—unless the word is a proper noun. A complete thought contained in parentheses appearing immediately after a sentence is treated as a separate unit, and the first word is capitalized.

first word not capitalized within sentence

Several minor changes (**these** were recommended by Mr. Lorenzo) will be made in the final draft.

parentheses within sentence—proper noun capitalized

Your suggestions (**Ms.** Watson approved all of them) will be incorporated into the marketing survey.

parentheses after end of sentence—first word capitalized

A group of marketing students wishes to tour our main plant in Atlanta. (**The** students are seniors from Georgia State University.)

3-2 Proper Nouns and Adjectives[2]

a. Proper nouns (words that name a particular person, place, or thing) and adjectives derived from proper nouns are capitalized. Capitalize the names of persons, cities, states, countries, rivers, mountains, streets, parks, colleges, buildings, shopping centers, malls, developments, organizations, ships, airplanes, specific events, and other such entities.

proper noun

Our field representative for your area is located in **Austin, Texas**.

I invite you to visit our offices in the **Atlantic Richfield Building** on **Fifth Street**.

The **Ventura County Fair** will be held in **Viking Park** this year.

We flew to **Florida** on a **Boeing 757** to meet our cruise ship, the **Song of Norway**.

---

[2]The capitalization principles that follow are based primarily on those suggested by *The Chicago Manual of Style*, 14th ed. (Chicago: The University of Chicago Press, 1993).

When will the **Brownsville Shopping Mall** be ready for occupancy?

Next month **Gordon** and **Allison** will take a raft down the **Colorado River**.

How much is the toll for the **Golden Gate Bridge**, which crosses **San Francisco Bay**?

adjective derived from proper noun[3]

Football, basketball, and baseball are typical **American** sports enjoyed by both children and adults.

Be sure to order **Roquefort** dressing and grated **Swiss** cheese for the salad bar.

Where can I find a listing of **Internet** access providers for our area code?

How many **Canadian** dollars do you anticipate we will need while we are on this tour?

Our decorator showroom, The Gallery, always carries an extensive line of **Victorian** furniture.

b. **When well-known descriptive terms, such as nicknames, are used in place of proper nouns, they are capitalized.**

My territory includes all sales districts west of the **Rockies**. (Rocky Mountains)

Most of his recent business trips have been to the **Windy City** and to the **Big Easy**. (Chicago and New Orleans)

Old Hickory was particularly popular with the frontiersmen. (Andrew Jackson)

Several managers from the **Big Apple** will attend the convention. (New York City)

c. **Sometimes proper nouns, such as the names of widely used commercial products, become common nouns through popular usage.[4] As a result, they are not capitalized. Always capitalize, however, specific brand or trade names of products. Any words that describe a type or kind of product (such as *refrigerator, vacuum cleaner, television, computer,* or *printer*) are not capitalized unless they represent a coined derivative that is considered part of the trade name.**

---

[3]The capitalization of all adjectives derived from proper nouns is based upon entries shown in *Merriam-Webster Collegiate Dictionary*, 10th ed. (Springfield, Mass.: Merriam-Webster, Incorporated, 2002).

[4]Check an up-to-date dictionary to determine which proper nouns have become common nouns and are no longer capitalized. The examples shown here are based on entries from *Merriam Webster's Collegiate Dictionary*, 10th ed. (Springfield, Mass.: Merriam-Webster, Incorporated, 2002).

3 Capitalization

common noun meaning

Addresses without a **zip code** on this mailing list are undeliverable as bulk mail.

Before computer-aided design software became available, these drawings were all done in **india** ink.

Our restaurant serves **french** fries with all its sandwiches.

Copies of the **braille** alphabet may be obtained from the Foundation for the Junior Blind.

Reproductions of this statue can be made from plaster of **paris**.

How many **china** patterns does Regency carry in its line?

You will find dining at Adagio's Ristorante an **epicurean** delight.

The demand for our cars with **diesel** engines is declining steadily.

brand or trade name with common noun product

Should we purchase a **Sony flat-screen television** for the reception area?

Our new **Frigidaire side-by-side stainless steel refrigerator** was delivered today.

Please install a tape backup system in this **Compaq computer** for our client.

This **Xerox copier** produces photographic-like colored images.

Our store no longer carries **Kleenex facial tissues** exclusively.

product name part of trade name

Your **Amana Classic Radarange** (microwave oven) will give you many years of service.

Please process this purchase order for the **Sony MICROMV Handycam** (camcorder) by June 30.

Almost every day for lunch Mr. Campbell orders either a **Filet-O-Fish** or **Chicken McNuggets** from McDonald's.

3-3 Abbreviations

Most abbreviations are capitalized only if the words they represent are capitalized. Exceptions to this rule are the abbreviations of academic degrees and certain coined business expressions. Refer to Section 6-11 for the proper format of abbreviations commonly used in business.

lowercase words represented by lowercase abbreviations

Please send the 4 **doz.** three-ring binders **c.o.d.** (*dozen* and *collect on delivery*)

Our office is open weekdays until 5:30 **p.m.** (*post meridiem*)

capitalized words represented by capitalized abbreviations

Lippett & Associates hires only applicants who have passed the **CPA** examination. (*Certified Professional Accountant*)

Ms. Chin was awarded a bachelor of arts degree from **UCLA** in 1999. (*University of California, Los Angeles*)

exceptions

Our university offers **B.S.** and **M.S.** degrees in psychology through the College of Letters, Arts, and Sciences. (*bachelor of science* and *master of science*)

On this application form please include any other names by which you may be known and precede them with the initials *AKA*. (*also known as*)

3-4 **Numbered or Lettered Items**

Capitalize word-numeral and word-letter combinations except in reference to pages, paragraphs, lines, sizes, vitamins, and verses.

The word *number* is abbreviated except when it appears at the beginning of a sentence.

capitalized word-numeral and word-letter combinations

Your electronic ticket is for **Flight 1413** to Philadelphia on May 2.

Please check **Invoice 187324** to verify that all the items have been received.

Did you receive our order for your **Model D** china case?

The class is scheduled to be held in **Room 132** of the Barnard Business Building.

lowercase word-numeral and word-letter combinations

Refer to **page** 6, **paragraph** 2, of the contract for the schedule of project completion.

We are sold out of **size** XL in our Style 483 blazer.

the word number abbreviated within a sentence

Have you had an opportunity to restock our supply of **No.** 10 white envelopes?

My home owner's policy, **No.** HO387092, has covered this loss.

Your Invoice **No.** F23146 was paid with our Check **No.** 871 dated February 14.

the word number written out at the beginning of a sentence

Number 982-RC stock should arrive from the manufacturer within the next week.

3-5 Personal and Professional Titles[5]

a. Capitalize the courtesy titles *Mr., Ms., Mrs., Miss, Master*, and *Dr.* when they precede and are used in conjunction with persons' names.

Capitalize also a title representing a person's profession, company position, military rank, service rank, religious station, or political office when it precedes and is used directly with a person's name *in place of a courtesy title*.

A title representing family relationship or nobility is capitalized when it appears before the name of an individual and is used directly with the name.

courtesy title

Two board members, **Mr.** Joshua Logan and **Dr.** Scot Ober, are unable to attend the March 4 meeting.

Both **Ms.** Bergstrom and **Mrs.** Scher-Padilla have agreed to serve on the selection committee for this position.

Please inform **Master** Todd Jaffarian that he has been selected as one of the finalists in the "eight-year-old" category of our children's contest.

professional title

The manuscript will be critiqued by **Professor** Donna Anderson.

title indicating company position

Although **President** Newton attended the stockholders' meeting, he asked **Vice President** Eleanor Chu from our Minneapolis branch to present last year's earnings report.

military or service rank title

Major Michael Zimmerman has requested a transfer to Edwards Air Force Base.

Police matters of this type are under **Captain** Murillo's jurisdiction.

religious title

Please ensure that **Archbishop** Lucatorto receives copies of these district reports.

The **Reverend** William Gillespie will be the guest minister for next Sunday's services.

Marvin and Stephanie have requested that **Rabbi** Cogan perform the marriage ceremony.

---

[5]The principles presented here are based upon those contained in *The Chicago Manual of Style*, 14th ed. (Chicago: The University of Chicago Press, 1993), 240–244.

political title

Mayor Charles Bowshier will meet with the city council on Monday.

As soon as **Senator** Rhodes authorizes payment of this invoice, we will issue you a check.

When will **Governor** Forrester release a statement to the press about this crisis?

title showing family relationship

As soon as **Aunt** Mabel's house is sold, her attorney will establish a trust fund.

These U.S. Savings Bonds were given to the children by **Grandpa** Peterson.

title of nobility

Several recent magazine articles have dealt with the life of **Prince** Charles.

This furniture style dates back to the era of **Queen** Victoria.

b. A person's title—professional, business, military, service, religious, political, family, or one pertaining to nobility—is not capitalized when it is followed by the person's name used as an appositive.

She consulted her **doctor, Linda Montgomery,** after the accident.

You will need to obtain approval from the **executive vice president, F. Ross Byrd**.

Please consult the **captain, John Blakely,** before recommending any changes in this precinct's boundaries.

Such decisions are made solely by the **governor, Paul Whalen**.

Rebecca Dentino inherited the property in Denton, Texas, from her **uncle, Mitchell Marcus**.

c. In running text do not capitalize a title that appears after a person's name.[6]

political title

Tonight at 8 p.m., EST, George Bush, **president** of the United States, will appear on national television.

Max Cleland, **senator** from Georgia, has received another award for outstanding service.

This new bill is awaiting only the signature of Gray Davis, **governor** of California.

---

[6]The principles presented here are based upon those contained in *The Chicago Manual of Style*, 14th ed. (Chicago: The University of Chicago Press, 1993), 240–244. Some organizations, however, choose to capitalize the titles of their high-ranking company officials.

military title

Marie Stewart's manuscript deals with the life of Ulysses S. Grant, **commander in chief** of the Union army.

Captain Harrison, our **company commander**, has been alerted that our unit may be placed on active duty next month.

business title

You may wish to invite Janet Horne, **president** of AMCO Products, to address the convention participants on May 11.

Carl Irwin, **director of marketing**, has developed several innovative ideas for advertising our G_{six} Home Care System.

professional title

You will need to address this inquiry to Michael Cornner, **dean of academic affairs**.

If you wish additional information, please contact Laura Jeffreys, **professor of business**, at Simpson Community College.

religious title

Pastor Ellis Jones, **minister** of Ascension Lutheran Church, will deliver the graduation address at Concordia College.

Did Dr. David Schultz, **rabbi** of Temple Beth Torah, accept our invitation to give the invocation at the opening banquet?

d. When a person's title is used in place of his or her name, the title is generally not capitalized. However, in cases of family relationships and direct address, capitalize the title if it *replaces the name*.

Do not capitalize common nouns such as *sir, madam, ladies,* or *gentlemen* used in direct address.

title used in place of name—not capitalized

Has the **president** announced who will fill the vacancy left by the **secretary of state**?

Since the **governor** will be in Washington, D.C., the **lieutenant governor** will open the bicentennial celebration to honor the founding of our city.

The **president** directed her **executive assistant** to inform all the department managers that the **director of marketing** has resigned.

family title used in place of name—capitalized

I believe **Grandpa** is eligible for these veteran's benefits.

Do you think **Mother** has a copy of my birth certificate?

family title used as common noun—not capitalized

Both my **mother** and my **father** have personal Web sites on the Internet.

title capitalized in direct address

When will final grades for this course be available, **Professor**?

Yes, **Doctor**, we have confirmed your flight reservation for August 3.

If you wish to change your schedule, **Captain**, please notify me.

common noun not capitalized in direct address

I believe, **ladies and gentlemen**, that all our sales personnel will meet their quotas this year.

e. **In business correspondence always capitalize a person's title when it appears in an inside address, a signature line, or an envelope address.**

Mrs. Delieu Scopesi, **Director of Human Resources**

Dr. Thomas Rinnander, **Chancellor**

f. **When the title of an executive officer is used in that organization's formal minutes, bylaws, or rules, it is capitalized. Also capitalize the title of a high-ranking government official when it is used in a formal context (an introduction or acknowledgment).**

The **Treasurer's** report was read and approved.

The **President** is responsible for negotiating all labor contracts.

We gratefully acknowledge the contribution of Tony Knowles, **Governor** of Alaska, to promoting research in the conservation of our natural resources.

g. **Descriptive terms such as *ex, elect, late,* and *former* are not capitalized when they are combined with a title.**

ex

Since **ex**-President Devon J. Morandi has become chairman of the board, our company has prospered.

elect

Councilman-**elect** Norman Rittgers will be sworn in on January 2.

late

The **late** President Eisenhower was an avid golfer.

former

Last month **former** President Clinton addressed a student group at Harvard University.

3-6 **Published and Artistic Works Containing Subdivisions**

Capitalize the first letter of the principal words in the title of a published or artistic work. Articles (*a, an, the*), conjunctions (*and, but, or, nor*), and prepositions with three or fewer letters (*of, in, on, to,*

for, etc.) are not capitalized unless they appear as the first or last words of the title or as the first word of a subtitle following a colon. The *to* in infinitives (*to write, to exercise, to study*) is also not capitalized unless it appears as the first word in the title or subtitle.

Italicize (or underline if an italics font is not available) the titles of complete published and artistic works that contain subdivisions. Use italics for the titles of books, magazines, newspapers, booklets, pamphlets, compact discs, plays, musicals, operas, musical albums, Web sites, and other similar works that contain subdivisions such as chapters, articles, columns, acts, episodes, songs, or links.

Italicize or underline also the titles of movies and television shows.

book

Your copy of *The Random House Dictionary of the English Language* arrived yesterday.

DuPont, the Autobiography of American Enterprise is available at your local bookstore.

A new edition of <u>Resources on the Internet</u> will be released in May.

book with subtitle

This topic is addressed on page 32 of *HOW 10: A Handbook for Office Professionals*, 10th edition.

magazine

Use the enclosed coupon to renew your subscription to the *Journal of Higher Education.*

Did you receive the July issue of <u>Better Homes and Gardens</u>?

newspaper

An article in *The Wall Street Journal* yesterday discussed sales trends in the consumer electronics industry.

Our hospital will place an advertisement in the <u>Los Angeles Times</u> for nurses and nurses' assistants.

pamphlet or booklet

Distribute copies of *How to Write Effective E-mail Messages* to all members of our administrative staff.

A copy of *Your Attitude Is Showing* will be given to all new employees.

Print at least 5,000 copies of our employee pamphlet, <u>Employee Programs and Benefits</u>, for distribution worldwide to our employees.

compact disc

Esta Lancome, as part of its February gift-with-purchase promotion, has included a free CD entitled *How to Keep It Natural.*

play or musical

Neil Simon's play, *Jake's Women*, was originally performed at the Stevens Center of the North Carolina School of the Arts.

Yesterday we saw the last performance of *Les Miserables*; next month *Phantom of the Opera* will open.

The Los Angeles production of <u>The Lion King</u> continues to attract theatergoers in an unprecedented run at the Pantages Theater.

movie title

The latest remake of *Father of the Bride* stars Steve Martin.

Next month local theaters will schedule children's matinees for showings of Disney's *Snow White and the Seven Dwarfs*.

The movie <u>Twelve Angry Men</u> is considered to be a classic among American films.

television show

Weekly episodes of *Frasier* still attract millions of television viewers.

Web site

Have you tried to locate this information through *The Internet Public Library*?

3-7 Subdivisions of Published and Artistic Works

a. Capitalize the main words[7] and place in quotation marks the titles of individual chapters, sections, articles, columns, acts, episodes, or songs contained in complete published and artistic works such as books, magazines, booklets, pamphlets, newspapers, compact discs, plays, musicals, operas, television series, and musical albums.

chapter in a book

The last chapter, "Information Systems and Applications," has contributed greatly to the success of *Contemporary Office Management.*

section in pamphlet

Please review the section "Submitting Your Application On-Line" before you apply for a job through the Internet.

article in a magazine

Did you read "Successful Ideas for the Indoor Gardener" in last month's issue of *Ladies' Home Journal*?

---

[7]*Main* words are all words except the articles *a, an, the;* the conjunctions *and, but, or, nor;* prepositions containing fewer than four letters (*of, for, in, on,* etc.), and the word *to* in infinitives (*to say, to enter, to look,* etc.).

column in a newspaper

Potter's "Financial Outlook" predicted yesterday that investors will see a rising stock market during the next quarter.

section in a compact disc

More detailed information about the big bang theory may be found in "Cosmology" in Microsoft's *Encarta '02.*

act in a play or musical

During the second act, "Homecoming," many people in the audience were tearful.

episode in a television series

"Holiday in London," next week's scheduled broadcast of *Worldwide Travels,* has been postponed.

Rerun marathons of the *Twilight Zone* usually include the popular episode "To Serve Man."

link in a Web site

Just click the "Biz Research" link in *CEO Express* at www.ceoexpress.com to obtain current information on data resources.

b. In a published work capitalize the first letter of subdivisions such as *preface, contents, glossary, appendix*, and *index* when they refer to a specific work.

specific work

All rules of punctuation are contained in the Appendix.

Consult the Index to find the page on which the explanation of molecular theory begins.

general reference

The index follows any appendixes that may be included in a book.

3-8 Published and Artistic Works Without Subdivisions

Capitalize the first letter of the principal words in any title. (See Section 3-6 for an explanation of *principal words*.)

Place in quotation marks the titles of radio programs, poems, songs, paintings, sculptures, and essays—any such published or artistic works that do not contain subdivisions with subtitles.

radio program

Our new talk show, "Opinion—From the Queen City," has been well received by Cincinnati radio listeners.

poem

Jennifer Durand's poem "A Mother's Love" has been published in poster format.

song

For his audition Malcolm chose to sing "Why Can't the English?"

3-9 Unpublished Works

a. **Place the titles of unpublished essays, manuscripts, reports, theses, and dissertations in quotation marks. Capitalize the first letter of the principal words[8] in the title.**

title of a report

Copies of "Progress Report on Street Maintenance and Repair" will be distributed to city council members next week.

title of a thesis or dissertation

Casey Wong's thesis, "Differences in Accounting Practices of Three Major Accounting Firms As Compared With Accounting Theory Taught in the Three Leading Accounting Textbooks," was approved by the committee last week.

b. **Capitalize the main words and place in quotation marks the titles of lectures and sermons.**

Capitalize the main words and place the subject lines of memorandums and E-mail messages in quotation marks when they are referred to in textual material.

lectures and sermons

Dr. Strozer's last presentation, "Religion, Politics, and Education," concluded with a challenge the audience could not overlook.

subject line of memorandums or E-mail messages

According to John Baudry's July 28 E-mail, "Production Schedule Time Line," the Model 690 scanners should be ready for shipment to retail outlets by September 1.

3-10 Headings and Text Headings

a. **In all published or unpublished written works, capitalize the principal words in main headings, secondary headings, centered text headings, and side (or margin) text headings. (See Section 3-6 for an explanation of *principal words*.)**

The Age of the Universe	Origins of Communication
The Big Bang Theory	Communication Through the Ages
Time Is Money	Document Creation With Voice Input
Evolution of the Computer	Developments on the Horizon

---

[8]*Principal* or *main* words are all words except the articles *a, an, the;* the conjunctions *and, but, or, nor;* prepositions containing three or fewer letters (*of, for, on, in,* etc.); and the word *to* in infinitives (*to purchase, to sign, to negotiate,* etc.).

b. In published and unpublished written works, capitalize only the first word and any proper nouns in paragraph text headings.

> **Investment in Europe and other foreign markets**. During the past year the company has established offices in Frankfurt, London, Paris, Mexico City, and Tokyo. With an overseas staff of 23 and a home office staff of 6 dedicated to enlarging our foreign markets, we expect to . . . .

3-11 Computer Software Program Titles

Capitalize the main words in computer software program titles. Note that in some cases main words are capitalized and written without an intervening space. Follow the format used by the manufacturer. (See Section 3-6 for an explanation of *principal* or *main words*.)

software title written as separate words

Did you use **Microsoft Word** to prepare this manuscript?

Our company uses **Quattro Pro** as its spreadsheet program.

software title written without spaces

What version of **WordPerfect** is your law office presently using?

My administrative assistant used **FrontPage** to construct our company Web site.

3-12 Punctuation Format for Literary and Artistic Titles

a. Titles of literary and artistic works are often used in appositive expressions; that is, they are used to rename a previously mentioned noun. In cases where the title is not needed to identify the work, set it off from the rest of the sentence with commas. Where the title is needed for identification, no commas are used.

title unnecessary to determine which article

Mark's latest article, "Marketing Strategies in the Automotive Industry," recommended a startling departure from current practices.

title necessary to determine which book

The book *Escape to Riches* should soon make the best-seller list.

b. Always place periods and commas *before* the closing quotation mark; always place semicolons and colons *after* the closing quotation mark.

period and comma before closing quotation mark

Hawaii is the location of our new episode, "Mousetrap."

Your March 13 report to the Board of Directors, "Computerized Accounting Procedures in the Banking Industry," has been helpful to me in planning our new system.

semicolon and colon after closing quotation mark

A number of our clients have requested reprints of your article "Increasing the Value of Your Portfolio"; the reprints will be mailed tomorrow.

These newscasters may be heard nightly on "Kansas City Reports": Rob McCoy, Elsa Newcomb, Steve Markham, and Lisa Darnell.

c. Question or exclamation marks appearing with and at the end of quoted titles are placed before the closing quotation mark. If the question or exclamation mark in a title appears at the end of the sentence, no other form of punctuation is required. However, if the sentence, not the title, is a question or exclamation, place the ending punctuation mark outside the closing quotation mark.

quoted title phrased as question in middle of sentence

Your article "Are You Earning the Most From Your Investment Dollars?" will appear in next month's newsletter to our banking customers.

Have you read the article "Are You Earning the Most From Your Investment Dollars?" that appeared in last month's newsletter?

statement with quoted title phrased as question at end of sentence

This week's feature article was entitled "What Is Earthquake Readiness?"

question with quoted title phrased as question at end of sentence

Have you read this week's feature article, "What Is Earthquake Readiness?"

quoted title separate from question

What percent of our subscribers read "Talk of the Town"?

3-13 Academic Courses and Subjects

a. Capitalize the names of numbered courses and specific course titles.

names of numbered courses

Professor Dunn's section of **Computer Science** 101 has 14 students on the waiting list.

To earn an associate in arts degree, you must satisfactorily complete **Psychology** 182, **Anthropology** 1, and **Music** 30.

specific course title

You are scheduled to teach two sections of **Introduction to the Internet** next semester.

Last semester Christina took **Speech 125, Introduction to Public Debate**.

b. Capitalize only proper nouns in the names of academic subject areas.

subject area

May I suggest, Sally, that you take an **accounting** class next semester.

Our community college offers more than 20 different **history** courses.

subject area containing proper noun

How many students earned an *A* in your **business English** class?

Before you leave for Paris, you may wish to take a course in **conversational French**.

3-14 Academic Degrees

a. References to academic degrees are generally not capitalized unless they are used after and in conjunction with the name of an individual.

general reference

Don Allison will be awarded a **bachelor of science** degree this June.

She earned her **master's** last summer.

after person's name

Ann Drew, **Doctor of Divinity**, will deliver the opening address.

b. Capitalize abbreviations of academic degrees appearing after a person's name. Remember, though, that the *h* in *Ph.D.* appears in lowercase form.

Make your check payable to Lawrence W. Erickson, **M.D.**

Marcia McKenzie, **Ph.D.**, will join our clinic as a staff psychologist.

James Bennett, **D.D.S.**, **M.D.**, is an excellent oral surgeon.

We have asked Pauline Newton, **D.B.A.**, to be our guest speaker.

3-15 Organizations

a. Principal words in the names of all organizations—business, civic, educational, governmental, labor, military, philanthropic, political, professional, religious, and social—are capitalized. Articles (*a, an, the*), conjunctions (*and, but, or, nor*), and prepositions with three or fewer letters (*of, in, on, to, for,* etc.) are not capitalized.

Boston Chamber of Commerce	National Council of Churches
Los Angeles Board of Education	Tactical Air Command
Arizona Department of Motor Vehicles	American Cancer Society
	Illinois Bar Association
Twenty-third Congressional District	DreamWorks
United States Department of Defense	Metro-Goldwyn-Mayer

b. When the word *the* precedes the organizational name and is officially part of the name, it must be capitalized.

Our client is insured by **The** Prudential Insurance Company of America.

c. When the common noun element of an organization's name is used in place of the full name, it is generally not capitalized. In formal documents and in specific references to national government bodies, however, capitalize the shortened form.

general communication

Full-time employees of the **company** are entitled to ten days' paid sick leave each year.

The **board of education** convened for a special meeting yesterday to consider the budget crisis.

Two members from our local **chamber** received special recognition from the state senate for outstanding community service.

How many members of the **city council** will support our proposal for low-cost housing in the inner city?

formal communication

As executive director of the **Association**, I am authorized to sign the convention contracts.

On July 1, 2004, the **Company** acquired Western Mutual Bank, which has 23 branches throughout the state.

national government bodies

John Johnson, our former mayor, has been elected to the **House**. (United States House of Representatives)

The president still needs to appoint two additional **Cabinet** members. (President's Cabinet)

Congress will reconvene next week. (United States Congress)

Who is presently majority leader of the **Senate**? (United States Senate)

This issue is now before the **Supreme Court**. (United States Supreme Court)

d. Government terms such as *federal, government*, and *nation* are often used in place of their respective full names. Because they are used so often and are considered terms of general classification, they are not capitalized.

federal

Security measures have been heightened in all **federal** buildings.

government

Since the **government** is concerned about inflation and its effect on the economy, it often uses economic measures to control pricing.

Student loans such as these are fully guaranteed by the **federal government**.

nation

Through the strength and courage of its people, the **nation** has been able to overcome a number of crises.

e. **Principal words in the official name of a division or department within a business organization are capitalized. When a division or department is referred to by its function because the official or specific name is unknown, do not capitalize this reference.**

Always capitalize main words in a division or department name used in a return address, an inside address, a signature block, or an envelope address.

official or specific name

Please notify the **Department of Human Resources** by 8 a.m. if you will be absent from work that day.

All contracts in excess of $25,000 must be approved by the **Board of Directors**.

Last month three members of our **Accounting Department** retired.

We will send a copy of our findings to your **Department of Research and Development**.

Our department needs a technician from the **Information Technology Department** to solve our network problem.

official or specific name unknown

The efficiency of your **accounting department** can be increased by using our new computer software.

Ask a member of your **advertising department** to contact one of our account executives so that your company can take advantage of this rare opportunity.

return address, inside address, signature block, or envelope address

Mr. Arthur Chu, Manager, Credit Department

f. **Capitalize the principal words in the names of departments, bureaus, divisions, offices, and agencies in government organizations.**

We will forward your application to the **Department of Health and Human Services** within the next week.

Please contact the **Bureau of Indian Affairs** for further information.

This case is under investigation by the **Office of Internal Affairs**.

Copies of the proposed freeway route are available from the **Division of Highways**.

g. Capitalize the main words in the names of specific departments, divisions, and offices within educational institutions. Main words in the names of schools or colleges within universities are also capitalized.

educational departments, divisions, or offices

This year LaCosta Community College's music festival, sponsored by the **Music Department**, will be held from April 27–29.

Does Professor Joyce Arntson teach in the **Social Science Division**?

Departmental budgets for the next academic year must be submitted to the **Office of Business Services** by April 30.

university schools or colleges

I have been admitted to the M.B.A. program in the **School of Business and Economics** at Kentview State University.

The major in which you are interested is offered in the **College of Letters, Arts, and Sciences**.

3-16 Geographical Locations

a. The names of places—for example, specific continents, countries, islands, states, cities, streets, mountains, valleys, parks, oceans, lakes, rivers, canals, bays, and harbors—are capitalized. When a geographical term (such as *city, street, bay*, or *island*) appears directly after a place name, it is considered part of the name and is capitalized. Terms used in this way are capitalized in both singular and plural forms.

A geographical term appearing before the name of a place is generally not capitalized. Capitalize the term only if (1) it is part of the official name or (2) it is used by the governing bodies of that place as part of an official name.

specific place

Our products are distributed throughout **North America**.

Which airline has a direct flight from **Los Angeles** to **Philadelphia**?

Clients residing in the **Hawaiian Islands** will soon be serviced by our new branch office in **Honolulu**.

The article dealt with recreational facilities on the **Colorado River**.

We sponsor tours for visitors to **Yellowstone National Park**.

Many of our shipments are routed here through the **Panama Canal**.

Property taxes in **Ventura County** have risen steadily during the past five years.

specific places—geographical term in plural form

The excursion will include river boat rides on both the **Mississippi and Missouri Rivers**.

Most of the new earthquake faults have been discovered in the **San Bernardino and San Gorgonio Mountains**.

The Westgate Shopping Mall is located on the corner of **59th and State Streets**.

geographical term appearing before specific place—not capitalized

Most of our business is conducted within the **state** of Utah.

The **city** of Los Angeles was selected as the site for our next convention.

The estimated 2005 population for the **county** of Ventura is 953,609.

geographical term appearing before specific place—capitalized

Our regional warehouse is located in the **City of Industry**. (Geographical term part of city name.)

The **City of Los Angeles** has approved a new budget plan. (Geographical term used by governing body as part of its official name.)

Did the **State of California** adopt a new automobile insurance plan for low-risk drivers? (Geographical term used by governing body as part of official name.)

b. **Capitalize nicknames of geographical locations and names of regional areas that have evolved as a result of usage.**

geographical nicknames

The **Aloha State** attracts tourists from all over the world. (Hawaii)

When were the Olympics held in the **City of Angels**? (Los Angeles)

How many times each year must you travel to the **Big Apple**? (New York City)

This year our convention will be held in the **Windy City**. (Chicago)

regional names emerging from usage

Many of our clients are from **Upstate New York**.

Police reports indicate that the **Lower East Side** has the highest crime rate in our city.

Merchants from the **Greater Los Angeles Area** have banded together to support this worthwhile project.

Many residents of the **Bay Area** are concerned about the pollution occurring in San Francisco Bay.

c. Points of the compass are capitalized when they are used as simple or compound nouns to designate *specific regions*. Points of the compass are not capitalized, however, when they are used to indicate *direction* or *general localities*.

specific regions

Firms connected with the aerospace industry are heavily concentrated in the **West** and **Southwest**.

Most of the granite sold and installed by our company is imported from the **Middle East**.

The parade and festival are scheduled to be held in **East Los Angeles**.

Sales in our **Southern Region** have increased 15 percent during the past year.

Within the next month we will expand our operations into **East Texas**.

directions

Your new territory, as regional manager, will include all states **east** of the Mississippi River.

The consultant's report recommended that our new plant be located directly **northwest** of Baltimore.

To avoid the harsh winter weather, many retirees travel **south** or **west** during the snow season.

By taking the **eastbound** on-ramp, you will be able to drive to the downtown area of Madison.

general localities

The **southern** section of our state is suffering a severe drought.

Our delivery service is restricted to the **east** side of Miami.

Customers from the **northwest** sector of the city have registered more complaints than customers from any other sector.

Our analysis revealed that most of our sales were from customers in the **western** states.

This new weather stripping is guaranteed to protect you against the severity of **northern** winters.

d. Words derived from simple or compound nouns representing *specific* regions are capitalized.

A number of **Midwesterners** have inquired about our Mexi-Pepper franchises.

Southern Californians are known for their casual lifestyle.

Our most recent survey solicited responses only from **Easterners**.

Atlanta is known for its **Southern** hospitality.

3-17 **Dates, Time Periods, and Events**

Capitalize days of the week, months of the year, holidays (including religious days), specific special events, and specific historical events or periods.

The names of seasons, decades, and centuries are generally not capitalized. If, however, a season is combined with a year, capitalize the season.

day of week and month

Our committee will meet the first **Monday** in **March**, **June**, **September**, and **December**.

holiday

Will our store be closed on **New Year's Day** this year?

Each year **Veterans Day** is observed on a different date.

specific special event

Our company will celebrate its **Silver Anniversary** next year.

National Secretaries' Week is traditionally observed during the latter part of April.

This year the **Pomona County Fair** will be held from September 4 through September 27.

How many of your staff members will be attending the **ABC Convention** this year?

historical event or period

In this **Information Age** the Internet has emerged as a major communication medium and information source.

The stock market crash of 1929 brought the **Roaring Twenties** to a dismal end and catapulted our country into the **Great Depression**.

During the **Industrial Revolution** children were often forced to work long hours under intolerable conditions.

season

Our most popular sales item during this **spring** season has been the Model 650 patio set.

None of the **winter** coats we ordered have arrived yet.

If you wish to enroll for the **fall** semester, please submit your application by August 15.

We have received your application for admission for the **Winter 2005** quarter.

decade

This company was founded in the early **fifties** by Jonathan Hunt.

During the past year a number of movies portraying life in the **sixties** have been released.

century

Technological developments during the **twentieth century** have advanced the human race further than all other developments during our previous history.

Many of Mr. Donovan's employees believe that he operates his business on **nineteenth-century** management principles.

3-18 Ethnic and Religious References

a. Ethnic-related terms (references to a particular language, race, or culture) are capitalized. Generic terms such as *black, white*, and *brown* when used in reference to race are generally not capitalized.

language

A knowledge of both **German** and **English** is required for this job opening in Frankfurt.

race

The 2000 census indicated that this area is highly populated by **Asians**.

Courses in **African-American** history and culture are taught in many major colleges and universities throughout the United States.

Several **black** leaders have asked to address the city council on this issue.

culture

Cinco de Mayo is observed with many festivities in the **Mexican-American** community.

The predominant native language of **Hispanics** is Spanish, but a significant number claim Portuguese as their native tongue.

b. Capitalize references to specific religious groups.

Massive opposition from **Catholic**, **Protestant**, and **Jewish** clergy led to the defeat of this proposed legislation.

A **Mormon** temple will be built on this site in 2007.

3-19 Celestial Bodies

Capitalize the names of celestial bodies—planets, planet satellites, stars, constellations, and asteroids. Do not capitalize the terms *earth, sun*, and *moon*, however, unless they are used as the names of specific bodies in the solar system.

capitalized

We have been studying the orbital paths of **Mars** and **Earth**.

Can you pick out the **North Star** or the **Big Dipper** among the many stars in the sky?

When will **Earth** next pass between the **Sun** and the **Moon**?

The background of the scene embraces a darkened sky highlighted only by an array of stars and **Saturn** with its bright rings.

lowercase

Television broadcasts of the first **moon** landing were viewed by millions of Americans.

None of the pieces from the satellite found their way back into the **earth's** atmosphere.

Rays from the **sun** can damage your skin and subsequently cause skin cancer.

4

Number Formats
and Applications

$$0.2 \, / \, {}^2\!/_{10} \, / \, 20\%$$

Solution Finder for Number Formats and Applications

(side tab) Numbers 4

General Format

4-1 General Rules for Numbers

a. A number that begins a sentence *must* be expressed in word form. When the number cannot be written in one or two words, however, change the word order of the sentence so that the number does not begin the sentence. Then write the number in figures. This number rule takes precedence over all others.

number written in words

Twenty-four qualified applicants responded to our Internet job posting for a senior accountant.

sentence order rearranged for figure form

The questionnaire was returned by **260** people who had purchased goods or services on-line. (Not: *Two hundred sixty* [or *260*] people ... returned the questionnaire.)

b. Numbers *one* through *ten* used in general references[1] are written in words. Write numbers above *ten* in figures, except those used to begin a sentence (see Section 4-1a). This rule applies only to those numbers not governed by any other number-usage rule.

number **ten** *or below*

Please order **four** copies of this speech-recognition program.

number above **ten**

During the past month we have received **14** letters of complaint about service in our Santa Rosa office.

Twenty-seven of our present employees will not be moving with us to our new location.

c. Approximations above *ten* that can be expressed in one or two words may be written in either figures or words. Keep in mind that figures are more emphatic and conform to the conventions established for expressing general numbers.

approximation written in figures

Nearly **900** people sent letters or faxes to the governor to protest the proposed sales tax increase.

approximation written in words

We had expected that more than **fifty** people would be interested in attending this seminar.

---

[1]*General references* in this manual refers to numbers that are not governed by any other number-usage convention. Percentages, money amounts, weights and measures, addresses, and telephone numbers are among the kinds of numbers not considered to be "general references" because they are governed by separate usage protocols.

d. Numbers below *100* that are written in word form are hyphenated if they are written as two words; that is, compound numbers *21* through *99* are hyphenated if they are spelled out.

Seventy-nine homes remain unsold in the Park Shore Development.

e. Round numbers in the millions or billions are expressed in a combination of figures and words. Only *one million* used as an approximation is usually written in all word form; otherwise, it is written *1 million*.

round number
Captain Maez has flown **2 million** miles since he earned his wings.

round number with fraction
Our company manufactured more than **3½ billion** pens for worldwide distribution last year.

round number with decimal
By 2005 the population of this valley will exceed **1.7 million** people.

one million *as an approximation*
Look to establish additional locations in cities with populations of more than **one million**.

1 million *as an exact figure*
The company will recover all its research and development costs once it has sold **1 million** of these hand-held, voice-activated computers.

4-2 Related Numbers

a. Numbers used in a comparable or corresponding manner in the same document are considered related numbers and should be expressed in the same form. Therefore, write numbers *one* through *ten* in figures when they are used with related numbers above *ten*.

Of the **130** items inspected, only **2** were found to be defective.

Tomorrow you will receive the **24** reams of laser paper, **8** boxes of envelopes, and **2** file trays that were back ordered for you. (Note that items appearing in a series are always considered to be related.)

b. Round numbers in the millions or billions are expressed in figures when they are used with related numbers below a million or with related numbers that cannot be expressed in a combination of words and figures.

combined with number below 1 million
Our production of digital television sets rose from **970,000** last year to more than **2,000,000** this year.

combined with number over **1 million** *written in figures*

During the past two years, our circulation has risen from nearly **3,000,000** copies to **3,875,500** copies.

c. **Unrelated numbers used in the same sentence are considered individually to determine whether they should be expressed in words or figures.**

unrelated numbers in same sentence

Please distribute these **18** color printers equally among the **six** departments located in our home office.

To accommodate **120** people for this banquet, set up **15** tables with **eight** place settings at each table.

combination of related and unrelated numbers in same sentence

Our warehouse inventory of **22** dishwashers, **17** refrigerators, and **8** washing machines must be distributed among our **three** stores. (*Items in a series are always related.*)

These new packing boxes hold **four** cartons that contain **12** bottles each whereas the old boxes held **six** cartons that contained **6** bottles each. (*Cartons* is related to *cartons*; *bottles* is related to *bottles*.)

4-3 Number Format

a. **Numbers expressed as figures are separated by commas into groups of three digits. Exceptions include years, house numbers, telephone numbers, fax numbers, zip codes, serial numbers, page numbers, decimal fractions, and metric measurements. Metric measurements of five or more digits are separated into groups of three with spaces.**

commas in figures with more than three digits

| 3,221 | 15,931 | 485,921 | 3,247,500 | 1,680,921,900 |

no commas in certain figures

| page 1214 | Serial No. 3321987-BF | 1430 Hill Street |
| 0.5325 | Evansville, IN 47701-1957 | 1500 kilometers |

space in metric measures with five or more digits

We deliver more than **18 000** liters of bottled water daily to stores.

b. **When two independent figures appear consecutively (one directly after the other) in a sentence, separate the figures with a comma.**

Between 2002 and **2004, 12** new office buildings were built in our city.

Of the **18, 13** dining room sets were damaged in transit.

c. **Two consecutive numbers that act as adjectives modifying the same noun are *not* separated by a comma. Instead, write the first** number in words and the second one in figures. If the first number cannot be expressed in *one or two words*, place it in figures also.

two numbers modifying a noun, word-figure form

Your order for **twelve 42-inch** glass tabletops was processed today.

When did you place the order for **seventy 60-watt** bulbs?

Each box contains **twelve 6-pack** cartons of Pepsi.

Our contract is for **three 25-second** commercials daily.

Each package contains **twenty-four 3-inch** nails.

The contractor will build **thirty-six 5-bedroom** homes in this tract.

two numbers modifying a noun, figure-figure form

Please purchase **150 37-cent** stamps from the post office.

Security Bank has approved your loan to purchase a **2002 40-foot** mobile home.

Your prescription is for **175 50-milligram** tablets.

d. Separate volume numbers from page references with commas.

This information is contained in **Volume VII, page 326**.

e. Weights, capacities, and measures that consist of several words are treated as single units and are not separated by commas.

weight as a single unit

The Nelsons' newborn weighed **6 pounds 9 ounces** at birth.

capacity as a single unit

This ceramic pitcher holds **3 quarts 1 cup**.

measure as a single unit

New carpeting has been ordered for the hotel ballroom, which measures **122 feet 8 inches** by **58 feet 10 inches**.

Your flight time from New York to Phoenix is **4 hours 20 minutes**.

f. The plural of a figure is formed by adding *s.*

There is one too many **4s** in this serial number.

The **1900s** will be noted for man's first successes in space travel.

Numbers Expressed in Figure Form

4-4 Money

a. Amounts of money *$1 or more* are expressed in figures. Omit the decimal and zeros in expressing whole dollar amounts, even if they appear with mixed dollar amounts.

money expressed in figures

With a one-year subscription to Air-Touch, you can own this new Microlite cellular phone for only **$59.95**.

omission of decimal and zeros

Purchases included items for **$3**, $6.50, $79.45, **$200**, and **$265**.

b. Amounts of money *less than $1* are expressed in figures combined with the word *cents* unless they are used in conjunction with related amounts of *$1 or more*. Unrelated amounts of money appearing in the same sentence, however, are treated separately.

amounts less than $1

The transit company increased bus fares from **60 cents** to **75 cents**.

related amounts of money

To mail the three reports, I paid **$.85, $1.40**, and **$2** in postage.

unrelated amounts of money

The tax on this **$8** item was **64 cents**.

c. Round amounts of money in millions or billions of dollars are expressed in combined figure and word form except when they are used with related dollar figures below a million or related amounts that can be expressed in figures only.

round amount

Cost estimates for the new technology building are **$12½ million**.

Nearly **$3.5 billion** in assets provides the customer confidence that makes Liberty Mutual the largest federal savings bank in the country.

related to amount less than $1 million

We estimate that **$850,000** will be needed to retool the Wilmington plant and **$2,000,000** will be needed for the Van Nuys plant.

related to amount that can be expressed in figures only

Our domestic sales decreased from **$12,458,000** last year to less than **$12,000,000** this year.

d. Amounts of money in formal legal documents are expressed in words followed by the figure amount contained in parentheses. The word *and* is used only to introduce cents included in money amounts written in word form.

round dollar amounts

The Company shall pay up to **Five Thousand Dollars ($5,000)** within 30 days upon receipt of a valid release statement.

The amount of indebtedness incurred by the defendant was **Ten Thousand Five Hundred Eighty-three Dollars ($10,583)**.

dollar amount with cents

A check for **Two Thousand Four Hundred Sixty-one Dollars and Forty-eight Cents ($2,461.48)** was received from Westin Industries on May 3.

4–5 Decimals and Percentages

a. Numbers containing decimals are expressed in figures. To prevent misreading, place a zero before a decimal that does not contain a whole number or begin with a zero.

decimal with whole number

Most of our trucks average **15.63** miles per gallon of gasoline.

decimal beginning with 0

According to our government contract, this part must be manufactured within **.004** inch of specifications.

decimal not containing whole number or beginning with 0

Only **0.3** percent of all items manufactured this year were rejected because of defective workmanship.

b. Write percentages in figures followed by the word *percent.* The percent symbol (%) is used only for statistical or technical tables or forms.

percent *used in sentence format*

Last month our company was able to decrease its energy consumption by **7 percent**.

This year's travel expenses have increased only **1 percent** over last year's.

A **12½ percent** pay increase will be granted to all office employees, effective July 1.

Our state legislature is expected to levy a **0.5 percent** increase in sales tax this year—from **7 percent** to **7.5 percent**.

% used in statistical tables or forms

| 47.5% | 60% | 99.9% | 5.63% | 7% | 0.8% |

4–6 U.S. Standard Weights and Measures

a. For quick comprehension express in figures the amount something weighs or measures. Weights and measures (inches, feet, yards, miles, ounces, pounds, tons, pints, quarts, gallons, each, dozen, gross, reams, pecks, bushels, degrees, acres, etc.), however, are written out fully in words. Abbreviations or symbols representing these units are limited to use in business forms or statistical materials.

general use

This carton is **4 pounds 3 ounces** in excess of the U.S. Postal Service weight limitation.

Nearly **3 tons** of cement and gravel will be needed for this project.

According to *The Weather Channel* at www.weather.com, **98 degrees** is the forecasted high for Las Vegas on Tuesday.

The decorator estimates that **120 square yards** of carpeting will be needed for our office suite.

Use **2-inch** screws for this job.

use for forms and statistical materials

5 doz.   10 yd.   92°   4#   8 ft.   75 lb.   12 ea.

b. Standard measures of length may be expressed in mils, inches, feet, yards, rods, furlongs, miles, and leagues. Standard weights may be expressed in grains, drams, ounces, pounds, hundredweights, and tons. Standard capacities may be expressed in teaspoons, tablespoons, ounces, cups, pints, quarts, gallons, pecks, and bushels. The following tables provide equivalents for various standard measures of length, weight, and capacity:

standard measures of length

1 mil	=	0.001 inch
1 inch	=	1,000 mils
12 inches	=	1 foot
3 feet	=	1 yard
16.5 feet	=	1 rod
40 rods	=	1 furlong
8 furlongs or 5,280 feet	=	1 mile
3 miles	=	1 league (land)

standard measures of weight

1 grain	=	0.036 drams
1 dram	=	27.34 grains
16 drams or 437.5 grains	=	1 ounce
16 ounces or 7,000 grains	=	1 pound
100 pounds	=	1 hundredweight
2,000 pounds	=	1 ton

standard measures of capacity

3 teaspoons or 0.5 ounce	=	1 tablespoon
2 tablespoons	=	1 ounce
16 tablespoons or 8 ounces	=	1 cup
2 cups or 16 ounces	=	1 pint
2 pints, 4 cups, or 32 ounces	=	1 quart
4 quarts or 128 ounces	=	1 gallon
8 quarts	=	1 peck
4 pecks	=	1 bushel

4

Numbers

115

4-7 Metric Weights and Measures

a. The most common metric measurements are based on meters, grams, and liters. Prefixes indicating fractions and multiples of these quantities follow:

fractions

deci (1/10)　　　centi (1/100)　　　milli (1/1000)

multiples

deka (x 10)　　　hecto (x 100)　　　kilo (x 1000)

b. Express metric measurements in figures. For general correspondence spell out the units of measure.

Use a space to separate numbers of five or more digits into groups of three. No space or comma is used with four-digit figures.

regular metric measures

When will the company begin using **1.75-liter** bottles for its large-size fruit juices?

Our new package of pie crust sticks weighs 11 ounces, which equals **312 grams** or **3.12 hectograms**.

You will need at least twenty-four **4-centimeter** screws to assemble this computer station.

four-digit figures

The distance from Memphis to Boston is more than **2000 kilometers**.

Please request Central Supply to order **1800 kilograms** of flour and **1500 kilograms** of sugar for delivery to our bakeries throughout the state.

five-digit figures

His 5-acre parcel of land is equal to approximately 2 hectares, that is, approximately **20 000 square meters**.

c. Although units of measure are spelled out in general correspondence, they may be abbreviated in technical writing, medical reports, or any kind of forms.

general correspondence

12 millimeters　　　6 liters　　　90 kilometers

technical writing, medical reports, or forms

50 mm　　　500 mg　　　32 km　　　100 cc

d. The following tables show equivalents for metric and standard measures of length, weight, and capacity:

equivalents for measures of length

Metric to Standard	Standard to Metric
1 kilometer = 0.6214 (5/8) mile	1 mile = 1.609 kilometers
1 meter = 1.0936 yards	1 yard = 0.9144 meter (exact)
1 meter = 39.37 inches	1 foot = 0.3048 meter (exact)
1 centimeter = 0.3937 (2/5) inch	1 inch = 2.54 centimeters (exact)

equivalents for measures of weight

Metric to Standard	Standard to Metric
1 ton (or tonne) = 1.1023 tons	1 ton = 0.90721 ton (or tonne)
1 kilogram = 2.2046 pounds	1 pound = 453.592 grams
1 kilogram = 35 ounces	1 ounce = 28.35 grams
1 gram = 0.035 ounce	

equivalents for measures of capacity

Metric to Standard	Standard to Metric
1 hectoliter (hl) = 2.838 bushels	1 bushel = 35.239 liters
1 liter (L) = 0.264 liquid gallon	1 liquid gallon = 3.785 liters
1 liter (L) = 1.057 liquid quarts	1 liquid quart = 0.946 liter
1 liter (L) = 0.908 dry quart	1 dry quart = 1.101 liters
1 milliliter (ml) ⎱ = 0.034 fluid ounce 1 cubic centimeter (cc) ⎰	1 fluid ounce = 29.537 milliliters

e. Two common scales measure temperature: Fahrenheit and Celsius. In Fahrenheit 32 degrees is the point at which water freezes and 212 degrees is the point at which water boils. In Celsius water freezes at 0-degree temperature and boils at 100 degrees.

To convert Celsius temperatures to Fahrenheit, apply the following formula: (Celsius temperature × 1.8) + 32. To convert Fahrenheit temperatures to Celsius, use this formula: (Fahrenheit temperature − 32) ÷ 1.8. The following table illustrates some common conversions:

Fahrenheit to Celsius		Celsius to Fahrenheit	
32	0	0	32
40	4	5	41
45	7	10	50
50	10	15	59
55	13	20	68
60	16	25	77
65	18	30	86
70	21	35	95
75	24	40	104
80	27	45	113
85	29	50	122
90	32	100	212
95	35		
100	38		
212	100		

4

Numbers

Normal body temperature is **98.6 degrees Fahrenheit** or **37 degrees Celsius**.

The high temperature yesterday in Madrid was **31°C**—or **88°F**.

4-8 Numbers Used With Words, Abbreviations, and Symbols

a. Numbers used directly with words are placed in figures. Page numbers, model numbers, policy numbers, and serial numbers are just a few of the instances in which numerals are used with words. The words preceding the numerals are usually capitalized except for page, paragraph, line, size, and verse references. (See Section 3-4 for capitalization format.)

model number

We are considering the purchase of your **Model 620D** laser printer for our Accounting Department.

Our **Model No. 87** videocassette recorder has been discontinued.

policy and serial numbers

You will need to fill in the insured's policy number, **Policy 1284691D**, on the claim form.

Our old IBM desktop computer, **Serial No. A32-74603552**, has been replaced by a new, more powerful one.

page number

The Elton scanner is pictured on **page 56** of the enclosed catalog.

b. Capitalize and abbreviate the word *number* when it introduces a number. Use figures to express the number. When the word *number* begins a sentence, however, do not abbreviate it.

word number *capitalized and abbreviated*

We will replace our camera equipment with your **No. 550** series.

The following checks were returned by your bank: **Nos. 321, 323, and 326**.

word number *at beginning of sentence*

Number 42 is the table at which we normally seat parties of eight or ten.

Numbers 392, 972, and 1041 were the winning raffle ticket numbers.

c. The use of symbols is generally avoided in business writing. However, for preparing forms (such as invoices and orders), charts, tables, and other documents where space is limited, symbols are used liberally. Numbers expressed with symbols are written in figures.

2/10, N/30   8%   #455

Time

4-9 Dates

a. When the day is written after the month, use cardinal figures (*1, 2, 3,* etc.). Ordinal figures (*1st, 2nd, 3rd,* etc.) are used for expressing days that appear before the month or that stand alone.

month followed by day

January 15, 2006, is the deadline for filing your application.

Your **April 15** payment is now 90 days past due.

day appearing before month

Payment must be made in full by or before the **30th of June**.

Our new offices will be ready for occupancy by the **3rd of April**.

day used alone

Your reservations at the Atlas Hotel for the **9th** through the **15th** have been confirmed.

Rental payments on this office are due by the **1st** of each month.

b. Dates in most domestic business correspondence are expressed in terms of month, day, and year. A comma separates the day and the year. In military and international correspondence, dates are generally written day, month, and year without an intervening comma.

domestic business correspondence

December 4, 2005

military or international correspondence

4 December 2005

4-10 Clock Time

a. Figures are used with *a.m., p.m., noon,* or *midnight* to express clock time. Omit the colon and zeros with even times, even if they appear with times expressed in hours and minutes.

The terms *noon* and *midnight* may be used with or without the figure *12*. When these terms are used with other clock times containing *a.m.* and/or *p.m.,* however, include the figure *12*. Never use *a.m.* or *p.m.* following *12, noon,* or *midnight.*

a.m., p.m., noon, midnight *with figures*

Our plane was scheduled to depart at **8 p.m.**, but it did not leave until **11:30 p.m.**

The museum tour begins at **10:45 a.m.** and ends at **12 noon**.

Afternoon shifts are scheduled from **4 p.m.** until **12 midnight**.

4

Numbers

noon *and* midnight *with the figure* 12

All our luncheon guests are expected to arrive by **12 noon**.

Present job openings are available only for the night shift, which begins at **12 midnight**.

The Northridge branch of the U.S. Postal Service is open Saturdays from **8 a.m.** until **12 noon**.

Burger Roundup is open daily from **8 a.m.** until **12 midnight**.

noon *and* midnight *without the figure* 12

May we please have your answer before **noon** on July 30.

All envelopes containing federal income tax payments must be postmarked before **midnight**, April 15.

b. **Either word or figure form may be used with *o'clock*.**

We must leave the office by **eight o'clock** [or **8 o'clock**] if we are to arrive at the airport on time.

c. **When even clock hours of the day are expressed without *a.m., p.m.,* or *o'clock,* use word form. Either word or figure form may be used, however, when both hours and minutes are expressed.**

exact hour

The last performance of *Mama Mia* is scheduled to begin at **seven** on Sunday night.

hour and minutes

The committee meeting finally adjourned at **6:30** [or **six-thirty**].

The power shut down at **9:05** [or **five after nine**] this morning, but it was restored shortly before **10:30** [or **ten-thirty**].

d. **Phrases such as "in the morning," "in the afternoon," or "at night" may follow clock times expressed alone or with *o'clock,* but these phrases may not be used with clock times expressed with *a.m.* or *p.m.***

Coffee breaks are scheduled at **ten in the morning** and at **three in the afternoon**.

By **2 (or two) o'clock in the afternoon**, our campus is almost empty; but by **7 (or seven) o'clock in the evening**, it is filled with students attending night classes.

4-11 **Periods of Time**

a. **General periods of time specifying seconds, minutes, hours, days, weeks, months, and years are treated the same as any other general number. Numbers *ten* and below are written in word form, and numbers above *ten* are written in figure form.**

general references to clock time

Each candidate's response in this television debate is limited to **two minutes**.

We offer **24-hour** plumbing service to all residents in Bixby County.

general time period—days, weeks, months, or years

During the past **six months**, we have shown a slight increase in profits.

We have been in this location for **23 years**.

The auto workers' strike lasted **112 days**.

b. Time-period data related to specific loan lengths, discount rates, interest rates, payment terms, credit terms, or other such information dealing with business contracts or terms are expressed in figures.

Such loans must be paid in full within **90 days**.

All invoices paid within **10 days** of the invoice date are eligible for a 1 percent discount.

You have been granted a 9 percent loan for **6 months**.

4-12 Ages and Anniversaries

Ages and anniversaries that can be expressed in one or two words are generally written in word form; those that require more than two words are written in figures. Figures are also used when an age (1) appears directly after a person's name; (2) is used in a legal or technical sense; or (3) is expressed in terms of years, months, and sometimes days. Note that no commas are used to separate the years, months, and days in the expression of ages.

general expression of ages and anniversaries

Kevin will be **thirty-one** on June 30; his son will be **two** the same day.

Mrs. Wong retired the day after her **sixty-fifth** birthday.

Next month we will celebrate our manager's **twenty-fifth** anniversary with the company.

Our city will celebrate its **150th** anniversary in 2007.

age after name

Ms. Bergstrom, **52**, was promoted to vice president last week.

age used in technical or legal sense

Teachers are no longer required to retire at the age of **65**.

The legal voting age is **18**.

At **25** you will be eligible for these reduced insurance rates.

age in years, months, and days

According to our records, the insured was **42** years **7** months and **16** days of age upon cancellation of the policy.

Addresses and Telephone Numbers

4-13 **Addresses**

a. House numbers are expressed in figures except for the house number *One*. No commas are used to separate digits in house numbers.

One Alpha Street	**4** Headquarters Plaza North
2432 East Broward Boulevard	**16524** Gardenia Street

b. Street names that are numbered *ten* or below are expressed in word form with ordinal numbers (*First, Second, Third,* etc.). Street names numbered above *ten* are written in ordinal figures (*st, nd, rd, th*).

street name ten *or below*

All visitors to New York City must stroll down **Fifth** Avenue.

Mail your payment to our office at 360 East **Third** Street, Winston-Salem, North Carolina 27101-4036

street name above ten

Please send this order to 960 **37th** Street, Denver, Colorado 80205-2145.

His former address is listed as 3624 West **59th** Place.

c. Apartment numbers, suite numbers, box numbers, and route numbers are expressed in figure form.

2193 Gerald Avenue, Apt. **12**	Post Office Box **1320**
Tower Financial Building, Suite **300**	Rural Route **2**

d. Zip codes are expressed in figures (without commas) and typed a single space after the state. Address lines containing zip + 4 are written in the same manner as those containing five-digit zip codes. Separate the extra four digits from the first five digits with a hyphen.

sentence format

Redirect this order to Fairfield Electronics, 1586 North Cicero Avenue, Chicago, Illinois **60651.**

Ms. Foster requested that the books be sent to her at Pasadena City College, 1570 East Colorado Boulevard, Pasadena, California **91106-2003**.

inside address or envelope address

Mrs. Sidney Harrington
7820½ South Ninth Avenue
Moonachie, NJ **07074**

Mr. Arthur M. Manuel
1073 23rd Street, Apt. 2
Inglewood, CA **90305-1004**

Ms. Eleanor Chu, Vice President
Parke-Dunn Pharmaceutical Company
74 West Michigan Mall, Suite 300
Battle Creek, Michigan **49017-3606**

4-14 Telephone and Facsimile (Fax) Numbers

Telephone and facsimile (fax) numbers are expressed in figures. When the area code is included, place it in parentheses before the number. As an alternate format you may omit the parentheses and separate the area code from the telephone or fax number with a hyphen.

An extension number is introduced by the abbreviation *Ext.* and follows the telephone number. If an extension number ends a sentence, use a single comma to separate it from the telephone number. However, if an extension number interrupts a sentence, place a comma before and after it.

telephone or facsimile (fax) number

For further information just call our local state employment office at **892-4240**.

Please ask Dr. Wagner to fax the prescription for this prosthesis to **363-6534**.

area code with telephone or facsimile (fax) number

Please fax a copy of this proposal to me at **(427) 555-7821**.

Call our toll-free number, **800-885-3322**, to place your order.

area code, telephone number, extension

You may reach me any weekday at **(617) 555-7139, Ext. 3712**.

Ask Jill to call **(213) 347-0551, Ext. 244**, for an appointment.

Special Forms

4-15 Fractions

a. Simple fractions that can be expressed in two words are written in word form. Fractions written in word form are not hyphenated unless they are used as compound adjectives.[2]

---

[2]"Table of Numbers," footnote 5, *Merriam-Webster's Collegiate Dictionary*, 10th ed. (Springfield, Mass.: Merriam-Webster, Incorporated, 2002), p. 796.

simple fraction used as a noun

The sales staff has already met **three fourths** of its quota for this year.

Only **one third** of our clients returned the questionnaire by the deadline date.

simple fraction used as a compound adjective

A **two-thirds** majority vote is needed to ratify the union contract.

Our investment syndicate wishes to purchase a **one-fourth** interest in the proposed new financial center.

b. Use figures to express (1) long and awkward fractions, (2) fractions combined with whole numbers, or (3) fractions used for technical purposes.

long and awkward fraction

Our study indicated that $21/200$ of a second is needed for the average person to begin reacting in emergency situations.

fraction combined with whole number

Allston's new plant and warehouse is located **5½** miles from the center of Seattle.

fraction for technical use

The Maintenance Department is temporarily out of stock of ⅝-inch roundhead metal screws.

c. Use the extended character set of your word processing program to key fractions that are written in figures. Those commonly found are ½, ¼, ¾, ⅓, ⅔, ⅛, ⅜, ⅝, and ⅞.

Fractions written in figures that are not found in extended character sets of word processing programs are formed by using the diagonal to separate the two parts. Format the first number for superscript in a smaller font. Format the second number at the normal position on the line in the same smaller size.

In mixed numbers constructed by extended character sets or other font attributes, leave no space between the fraction and any whole number used with the fraction.

On typewriters and with simple word processors, key all fractions in normal type size using the diagonal construction. In mixed numbers leave one space between the whole number and the fraction.

fraction keyed through an extended character set

Our supply of ¾-inch nails is running low.

mixed number keyed through an extended character set

Food King Markets ordered **9⅜** tons of beef last week.

Our employees averaged **37½** hours of sick leave last year as compared with **27¼** hours this past year.

fraction keyed using a diagonal

These **15/16**-inch screws have been designed especially for assembling the Model 462 computer desks.

All these parts must be manufactured within **1/100** inch of specifications.

mixed number keyed using a diagonal

To be reupholstered, each dining chair in our restaurant will require **2⁵/6** yards of fabric.

These panels are exactly **35 11/16** inches wide.

4-16 Ordinals

a.   **Ordinal numbers (*first, second, third,* etc.) that can be written in one or two words are generally expressed in word form except those appearing in (1) dates before the month or standing alone and (2) numbered street names above *ten*.**

general use

Mr. Woo was elected to represent the **Sixty-third** Congressional District.

Mrs. Lang was criticized for managing the company according to **nineteenth**-century practices.

dates

Our next audit is scheduled for the **1st** of September.

Your order will be shipped by the **15th** of this month.

Please submit your report by the **1st** of the year.

numbered streets

We will be moving our store to 960 West **Fourth** Avenue during the last week of October.

I plan to meet Mr. Silverman at noon on the corner of Maple and **52nd** Streets.

b.   **Ordinals expressed in figure form end in *st, nd, rd,* or *th*.**

The note on this hillside property is due the **1st** of June.

May we have your response by the **22nd** of November.

This year marks the **123rd** anniversary of our city.

Our new offices are located at 1560 **12th** Avenue.

4-17 Roman Numerals

a. When keying Roman numerals for chapter or outline divisions, use capital letters to form the numbers. In using word processing programs with an outline feature, adjust the tab settings so that the periods align for Roman numerals as well as for other divisions in the outline.

Use capital letters for expressing years written in Roman numerals.

table of Roman numerals

Arabic Numeral	Roman Numeral	Arabic Numeral	Roman Numeral
1	I	16	XVI
2	II	17	XVII
3	III	18	XVIII
4	IV	19	XIX
5	V	20	XX
6	VI	30	XXX
7	VII	40	XL
8	VIII	50	L
9	IX	60	LX
10	X	70	LXX
11	XI	80	LXXX
12	XII	90	XC
13	XIII	100	C
14	XIV	500	D
15	XV	1,000	M

chapter divisions

When will you be able to complete the review of **Chapter VIII**?

divisions in an outline

  I. Hardware requirements
  II. Network capabilities
 III. Software requirements
 IV. Training programs

year expressed in Roman numerals

Chiseled at the top of the archway was the year the old stone church had been built—**MDCLXXXVI**. (1686)

b. The preliminary sections of a report (such as the transmittal letter, the table of contents, and the list of tables) are numbered with lowercase Roman numerals. Number the pages consecutively using *i, ii, iii, iv, v,* etc.

Business Calculations

4-18 Rounding Numbers

When answers to arithmetic calculations contain a number of digits after the decimal, they may be rounded for ease of understanding. For example, amounts of money in business calculations are commonly rounded to the nearest cent.

Use the following three-step process to round numbers:

(1) Identify the number of digits needed to the right of the decimal.

(2) Increase the last digit by one if the number to its right is *5* or greater.

(3) Eliminate the extra digits.

figure rounded to three decimal places

$45.6667 = $45.666|7 = $45.667   5.125463% = 5.125|463% = 5.125%

figure rounded to two decimal places

$45.6667 = $45.66|67 = $45.67   5.125463% = 5.12|5463% = 5.13%

figure rounded to one decimal place

$45.6667 = $45.6|667 = $45.7   5.125463% = 5.1|25463% = 5.1%

figure rounded to whole number

$45.6667 = $45.|6667 = $46   5.125463% = 5.|125463% = 5%

4-19 Converting Fractions to Decimals

To convert fractions to decimal form, divide the numerator (top or first number) by the denominator (bottom or second number).

$\frac{1}{2} = 1 \div 2 = 0.5$ $\frac{2}{3} = 2 \div 3 = 0.667$

$\frac{3}{4} = 3 \div 4 = 0.75$ $\frac{7}{8} = 7 \div 8 = 0.875$

$\frac{5}{6} = 5 \div 6 = 0.8333$ $\frac{11}{16} = 11 \div 16 = 0.6875$

4-20 Converting Decimals to Percents

To convert decimal numbers to percent form, move the decimal two places to the right and add a percent sign. If an additional digit is needed, add *0*.

0.2 = 20%   0.65 = 65%

0.7152 = 71.52%   1.1582 = 115.82%

4-21 Converting Percents to Decimals

To convert percentages to decimal form, move the decimal two places to the left. Omit any *0*s at the end. For decimal forms without whole numbers, place a *0* before the decimal to avoid misreading.

185.25% = 1.8525   150% = 1.50 = 1.5

65% = 0.65   32.62% = 0.3262

Decimal equivalents and percentages for common fractions are shown in the following table:

Fraction	Decimal	Percent	Fraction	Decimal	Percent
1/3	.3333	33.33%	1/12	.0833	8.33%
2/3	.6667	66.67%	2/12 (⅙)	.1667	16.67%
1/4	.25	25%	3/12 (¼)	.25	25%
2/4 (½)	.50	50%	4/12 (⅓)	.3333	33.33%
3/4	.75	75%	5/12	.4167	41.67%
1/5	.20	20%	6/12 (½)	.50	50%
2/5	.40	40%	7/12	.5833	58.33%
3/5	.60	60%	8/12 (⅔)	.6667	66.67%
4/5	.80	80%	9/12 (¾)	.75	75%
1/6	.1667	16.67%	10/12 (⅚)	.8333	83.33%
2/6 (⅓)	.3333	33.33%	11/12	.9167	91.67%
3/6 (½)	.50	50%	1/16	.0625	6.25%
4/6 (⅔)	.6667	66.67%	3/16	.1875	18.75%
5/6	.8333	83.33%	5/16	.3125	31.25%
1/8	.125	12.5%	7/16	.4375	43.75%
2/8 (¼)	.25	25%	9/16	.5625	56.25%
3/8	.375	37.5%	11/16	.6875	68.75%
4/8 (½)	.50	50%	13/16	.8125	81.25%
5/8	.625	62.5%	15/16	.9375	93.75%
6/8 (¾)	.75	75%	1/20	.05	5%
7/8	.875	87.5%	1/25	.04	4%

4-22 Determining the Percent of a Total

To determine the percent an amount represents of a total, divide the amount by the total.

Percentage of Department Sales

Dept.	Sales	Calculation	Decimal	Percent
A	$42,875	$42,875 ÷ $122,200	0.351	35.1%
B	$22,900	$22,900 ÷ $122,200	0.187	18.7%
C	$56,425	$56,425 ÷ $122,200	0.462	46.2%
Total	$122,200		1.000	100.0%

4-23 Computing Sales Tax

Calculate sales tax by multiplying the purchase amount by the sales tax percentage. Convert the sales tax percentage to a decimal equivalent to perform the calculation.

State and Local Sales Taxes

Amount of Sale	Sales Tax	Calculation	Amount of Sales Tax	Total Amount
$72.35	5%	$72.35 × .05	$3.62	$75.97
$145.80	7½%	$145.80 × .075	$10.94	$156.74
$890.50	8¼%	$890.50 × .0825	$73.47	$963.97

4-24 Determining Mileage Expense

Individuals who use their vehicles for business purposes are usually reimbursed for the expenses they have incurred. Reimbursement often takes the form of paying the individual a set amount of money for each mile driven on the employer's behalf. This reimbursement is known as *mileage expense.*

Use the following procedures to determine mileage expense:

(1) Subtract the beginning miles from the ending miles on the odometer to obtain the total miles traveled.

(2) Multiply the total miles traveled by the amount of money (usually cents) allowed per mile.

Mileage Expense Calculations

Trip	Ending Mileage	(−)	Beginning Mileage	(=)	Total Miles Traveled	(×)	Mileage Allowance	(=)	Total Expense
A	23,735		23,481		254		$.35		$88.90
B	42,804		41,775		1,029		$.28		$288.12
C	53,777		50,099		3,678		$.22		$809.16

4-25 Calculating Simple Discounts

Simple discounts are often given for quantity purchases and on sale merchandise. These discounts are usually stated as a percentage decrease of a regular price.

Use the following procedures to calculate the dollar amount of the discount and the cost of the purchase:

(1) Convert the percent of discount to its decimal equivalent.

(2) Multiply the regular price by the decimal equivalent of the discount to obtain the discount amount.

(3) Subtract the discount amount from the regular price to find the cost of the purchase.

Simple Discount Calculations

Regular Price	Discount	Calculation (Decimal Equivalent)	Amount of Discount	Cost of Purchase
$120.40	30%	$120.40 × .30	$36.12	$84.28
$885.90	45%	$885.90 × .45	$398.66	$487.24
$2,570.50	12%	$2,570.50 × .12	$308.46	$2,262.04

4-26 **Determining Percent of Increase or Percent of Markup**

Annual sales for a year may be greater than the previous year (the base year). Owners may wish to know by what percent these sales increased over the base year.

Business people purchase goods at a certain price (the base price) and sell them at a higher price. These people may wish to know their percent of markup over the base price.

Percent of increase and markup are the same; they are calculated identically. Use the following procedures to calculate percent of increase and percent of markup:

(1) Subtract the base figure (sales, price, etc.) from the more recent or higher figure to obtain the difference.

(2) Divide the difference by the base figure.

(3) Convert the resulting decimal to a percentage.

Percent of Increase

2004 Sales	2003 Sales (Base Year)	Amount of Increase	Increase ÷ Base Year	Percent of Increase
$987,695	$765,782	$221,913	0.290	29.0%
$87,843	$76,289	$11,554	0.151	15.1%
$6,841,980	$6,543,902	$298,078	0.046	4.6%

Percent of Markup

Selling Price	Cost (Base Price)	Amount of Markup	Markup ÷ Base Price	Percent of Markup
$18.98	$12.43	$6.55	0.527	52.7%
$49.99	$25.70	$24.29	0.945	94.5%
$149.50	$62.00	$87.50	1.411	141.1%

4-27 **Determining Percent of Decrease or Percent of Markdown**

Annual sales for a year may be less than the previous year (the base year). Owners may wish to know by what percent these sales decreased from the base year.

Business people price goods at a certain price (the base price) and then sometimes later sell them at a lower price. These people may wish to know their percent of markdown from the base price.

Percent of decrease and markdown are the same; they are calculated identically. Use the following procedures to calculate percent of decrease and percent of markdown:

(1) Subtract from the base figure (sales, price, etc.) the more recent or lower figure to obtain the difference.

(2) Divide the difference by the base figure.

(3) Convert the resulting decimal to a percentage.

Percent of Decrease

2003 Sales (Base Year)	2004 Sales	Amount of Decrease	Decrease ÷ Base Year	Percent of Decrease
$764,950	$583,415	$181,535	0.237	23.7%
$53,966	$46,630	$7,366	0.136	13.6%
$2,980,655	$2,743,062	$237,593	0.080	8.0%

Percent of Markdown

Original Price (Base Price)	Discounted Price	Amount of Markdown	Markdown ÷ Base Price	Percent of Markdown
$15.98	$10.50	$5.48	0.343	34.3%
$69.99	$49.99	$20.00	0.286	28.6%
$125.00	$109.00	$16.00	0.128	12.8%

4-28 Finding the Amount of Simple Interest

Simple interest is calculated (1) by multiplying the amount borrowed (principal) (2) by the rate of interest charged (3) by the years (time) for which the principal was borrowed. For loan periods less than a year, time is calculated on either a 365-day year (exact interest) or a 360-day year (ordinary interest).

Simple Interest Calculations

Amount Borrowed	Rate	Time	Calculation (Amount × Rate × Years)	Interest
$4,500	5%	2 years	$4,500 × .05 × 2	$450.00
$12,600	8½%	42 months	$12,600 × .085 × (42/12)	$3,748.50
$20,200	12%	90 days	$20,200 × .12 × (90/365)	$597.70

4-29 Determining Averages

a. The range in a group of numbers represents the spread between the highest and the lowest number. Determine the *mode* of a range by identifying the most frequently occurring number within the spread.

range

57 59 63 67 67 68 72 74 74 74 76 76 80 82 86 86 89 90 92 94 96 97

mode

74

b. The *median* is the middle value in a range of values. Therefore, half the values are greater than the median, and half the values are less than it.

range

57 59 63 67 67 68 72 74 74 74 76 76 80 82 86 86 89 90 92 94 96 97

median

76

c. **The *mean* is the arithmetic average of a range. Calculate the mean by summing the values in the range and dividing by the number of values in the range. The mean ($\bar{x}$) is the sum (Σ) of the values (x) divided by the number of values (n).**

Mean ($\bar{x}$) = $\frac{\Sigma x}{n}$

range

57 59 63 67 67 68 72 74 74 74 76 76 80 82 86 86 89 90 92 94 96 97

mean

Sum of values = 1,719   Number of values = 22

Sum (1,719) ÷ Number (22) = 78.1

5

Grammar and Usage

noun

Grammar and Usage Solution Finder

Grammar and Usage Solution Finder *(continued)*

5

Grammar and Usage

Sentences

5-1 Complete Sentences

a. Use complete sentences to express ideas. A complete sentence (1) contains a verb (a word showing action or describing a condition), (2) has a subject (a noun or pronoun that interacts with the verb), and (3) makes sense (comes to a closure). A complete sentence is an independent clause.

Verbs appear by themselves or in a verb phrase. The last verb in a verb phrase is considered to be the main verb.

Subjects are either simple or compound. *Simple subjects* consist of a single noun or pronoun whereas *compound subjects* contain two or more nouns or pronouns linked by *and, or,* or *nor.*

statements

(simple subject)
Last week several **employees** in our Manufacturing Department
(verb)
increased their standard output by 12 percent. (Makes sense)

(compound subject)
Robin and Tyler, as a result of their excellent forecasts,
(verb phrase)
have been promoted to senior analysts. (Makes sense)

(subject)   (verb)
This latest **proposal** by Kym Freeman **is** excellent. (Makes sense)

questions

When **may I expect** your reply? (Simple subject, *I*; verb phrase, *may expect;* makes sense)

How many **members** of your staff **plan** to attend the convention? (Simple subject, *members*; verb, *plan*; makes sense)

requests or commands

Please **return** the enclosed questionnaire by April 30. (Simple subject, *you* is understood; verb, *return*; makes sense)

Do not litter in the parks or on the highways. (Simple subject, *you* is understood; verb, *do (not =* adverb) *litter*; makes sense)

b. Simple sentences consist of a single independent clause that contains a subject and a verb or verb phrase. They express only one complete thought.

The **manager** of our Fairfield branch **has been employed** by the company for seven years. (Simple subject, *manager*; verb phrase, *has been employed*; makes sense)

Partnerships and corporations in this state **are** not eligible for this tax deduction. (Compound subject, *partnerships and corporations*; verb, *are*; makes sense)

c. Compound sentences contain two independent clauses (each with a subject and a verb or verb phrase) that are usually separated by a coordinating conjunction — *and, but, or,* or *nor*.

Our regional **representative will be** at Macy's next week, **and she will demonstrate** our new line of Creative Illusions cosmetics. (Simple subjects, *representative* and *she*; verb phrases, *will be* and *will demonstrate*; coordinating conjunction, *and*)

Neither of our vice presidents **will be** in the office this week, **but** our **general manager** for East Coast operations **is** available to answer your questions. (Subjects, *neither* and *general manager*; verb phrase and verb, *will be* and *is*; coordinating conjunction, *but*)

d. Other compound sentences contain two independent clauses (each with a subject and a verb or verb phrase) that are joined by either (1) a semicolon or (2) a semicolon combined with a transitional expression such as *therefore, however, for example,* or *of course.*

joined by a semicolon

The **loan** on your home **has been transferred** to American Home Finance Corporation; **you should receive** a new payment booklet from this lender within the next week. (Simple subjects, *loan* and *you;* verb phrases, *has been transferred* and *should receive*)

joined by a semicolon and a transitional expression

Professors and administrators at our college **are covered** under the same retirement program; therefore, **administrators**, too, **are** eligible for retirement at age 55. (Compound and simple subjects, *professors and administrators* and *administrators*; verb phrase and verb, *are covered* and *are*; transitional expression, *therefore*)

e. Complex sentences include an independent clause and a dependent clause, each of which contains both a subject and a verb or verb phrase. The independent clause can stand alone as a complete sentence because it makes sense, but the dependent clause cannot.

Dependent clauses begin with (1) relative pronouns such as *who, whom, that,* or *which* or (2) subordinating conjunctions such as *if, when, as, since, because, although, while,* and *whereas.* The dependent clause may begin, interrupt, or conclude the sentence.

complex sentence with a relative pronoun clause

Mr. Tanner asked me **who designed our Web site**.

None of the people **whom we interviewed** were willing to accept the position at the salary offered.

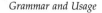

The software **that you recommended** is no longer available on-line.

Kevin is frequently late, **which may be the reason for his dismissal.**

complex sentence with a subordinating conjunction

As soon as we receive your check, we will process your application for admittance.

In the future you may, **if you wish**, pay your bills on-line at our secure Web site.

Our sales have increased substantially **since the new television ads have aired**.

f. **Compound-complex sentences contain two independent clauses and one dependent clause.**

We have discontinued our line of Pillow-Touch mattresses **because deliveries from the manufacturer to our customers have been slow**, but we plan to replace this line with one of equal or better quality.

We received more than 30 applications for this opening; but **after I read all the résumés**, I realized that not one of the candidates was qualified for the position.

5-2 Sentence Fragments

a. **Use only sentence fragments that *represent* a complete thought, and confine their use to informal business writing.**

And now to the point.

If only I had known!

What a relief!

b. **For the most part, use concluding punctuation marks (periods, question marks, and exclamation marks) only after complete sentences. You may, however, in informal writing use these marks after sentence fragments that represent a complete thought (Section 5-2a).**

Not: In the near future.

But: **In the near future** we will expand our international operations.

Not: Although the present contract has expired.

But: **Although the present contract has expired**, both management and the union are governed by its provisions until a new contract is negotiated.

Not: The biggest money-saving event of the year.

But: Be sure to take advantage of our annual clearance sale, **the biggest money-saving event of the year**.

Nouns

5-3 Nouns[1]

a. Nouns are words that name something—for example, persons, animals, places, things, objects, time, feelings, qualities, actions, concepts, measures, and states of being.

person

Please have your **doctor** fax us his diagnosis.

Did you refer this **client** to me?

animal

Are you interested in purchasing another **horse?**

This **fish** is too old to eat.

place

The new **park** will be located in our **county**.

When do you plan to visit our **city**?

thing

All this **information** is stored on the **network**.

Have the **company** and the **union** reached an **agreement**?

object

Did you find your **book**?

Place the **computer** on this **desk**.

time

Although we signed the contract yesterday, it will not become effective for 30 **days**.

Your last car payment is due next **month**.

feeling

Everyone in the room perceived Mr. Smith's **anger** as he spoke.

We can certainly sympathize with the family's **sorrow** and **grief**.

quality

I appreciate your **thoughtfulness** and **generosity**.

Such **irresponsibility** must be reported to the supervising physician.

---

[1]The rules and spellings in this chapter are based on *Merriam Webster's Collegiate Dictionary,* 10th ed. (Springfield, Mass.: Merriam-Webster, Incorporated, 2002). For a complete, up-to-date on-line Internet resource, visit Merriam-Webster <http://www.m-w.com> (no fees or registration required).

action

Do you enjoy **swimming** in our new Olympic-size pool?

Golfing is an individual sport.

concept

Our country was founded on **freedom** of **expression**.

Please report any **progress** you have made in locating the heirs.

measure

Johnson Industries' assets total more than **$700 million**.

Three **yards** of fabric will be needed to re-cover each chair.

state of being

Her **illness** has not yet been properly diagnosed.

Complacency in this rapidly changing industry could easily lead to **bankruptcy**.

b. Any noun that names a particular entity is capitalized. These capitalized nouns are known as *proper nouns*. Nouns that do not name specific entities are known as *common nouns*, and they are not capitalized.

proper nouns

Yesterday the **Fort Lauderdale City Council** approved an 8 percent increase in bus fares.

Repairs on the **Golden Gate Bridge** are still in progress.

You will have our decision by **November** 1.

Much of this information is available through the **Internet**.

common nouns

Yesterday the **city council** approved an 8 percent increase in bus fares.

Repairs on the **bridge** are still in progress.

You will have our decision by the **1st** of next **month**.

Most of this information is available through on-line **resources**.

c. Although most common nouns consist of single words, many contain two or even three words. These *compound nouns* appear as regular entries in the dictionary and are defined as nouns. Some are hyphenated, but most are separate words without hyphens (*open compounds*).

hyphenated compound nouns

This business is operated by the mayor's **brother-in-law**.

The **vice-chancellor** must approve all faculty appointments.

open compound nouns

Please have the **vice president** sign this purchase order.

Our local **high school** is sponsoring this event.

 Noun Plurals²

a. Most nouns form their plurals by adding *s*. However, nouns ending in *s, sh, ch, x,* or *z* form their plurals by adding *es*.

nouns adding s

account	accounts	executive	executives
letter	letters	message	messages

nouns adding es

bus	buses	branch	branches
business	businesses	tax	taxes
wish	wishes	waltz	waltzes

b. Common nouns ending in *y* form the plural in one of two ways. If the letter preceding the *y* is a vowel, just add *s*. However, if the letter preceding the *y* is a consonant, drop the *y* and add *ies*.

y preceded by a vowel

attorney	attorneys	money	moneys
delay	delays	valley	valleys

y preceded by a consonant

company	companies	reply	replies
policy	policies	photocopy	photocopies

c. Most musical terms ending in *o* form the plural by adding *s*. Other common nouns ending in *o* may form the plural by adding *s* or *es;* the correct plural forms are shown in the dictionary after the singular forms of the words.

musical terms

pianos   solos   sopranos   altos   librettos

common nouns ending in os

dynamos   mementos   portfolios   ratios   zeros

common nouns ending in oes

cargoes   tomatoes   heroes   potatoes   embargoes

d. Nouns ending in *ff* form the plural by adding *s*. Nouns ending in just *f* or *fe* may add *s*, or they may drop the *f* or *fe* and add *ves*. The

---

²Noun plurals, other than those regular ones ending in *s* or *es*, are shown in the dictionary immediately after the singular form of the word. For a complete, up-to-date on-line Internet resource, visit Merriam-Webster <http://www.m-w.com>.

plurals of those nouns taking the irregular form by adding *ves* are shown in the dictionary. If the dictionary does not show the plural form, just add *s*.

plural nouns ending in **ffs**

bailiff	bailiffs	plaintiff	plaintiffs
cliff	cliffs	sheriff	sheriffs

plural nouns ending in **fs** *or* **fes**

belief	beliefs	roof	roofs
chief	chiefs	safe	safes
proof	proofs	strife	strifes

plural nouns ending in **ves**

half	halves	shelf	shelves
knife	knives	thief	thieves
self	selves	wife	wives

e. The plurals of proper nouns are formed by adding *s* or *es*. Those proper nouns ending in *s*, *sh*, *ch*, *x*, or *z* form the plural by adding *es*. All others form the plural by adding *s*.

proper noun adding **es** *for plural form*

Bendix	the Bendixes	Rodriguez	the Rodriguezes
Bush	the Bushes	Ross	the Rosses
Finch	the Finches	Winters	the Winterses

proper noun adding **s** *for plural form*

Dixon	the Dixons	Kelly	the Kellys
Griffin	the Griffins	Russo	the Russos
Halby	the Halbys	Wolf	the Wolfs

f. Many nouns of foreign origin have both an English plural and a foreign plural. Consult your dictionary and use the form that appears first.

foreign-derived nouns with preferred English plurals[3]

appendix	appendixes	hors d'oeuvre	hors d'oeuvres
auditorium	auditoriums	index	indexes (book)
bureau	bureaus	memorandum	memorandums
formula	formulas	plateau	plateaus
gymnasium	gymnasiums	ultimatum	ultimatums

---

[3]Preferences for English and foreign noun plurals are based upon entries shown in *Merriam-Webster's Collegiate Dictionary*, 10th ed. (Springfield, Mass.: Merriam-Webster, Incorporated, 2002). For a complete, up-to-date on-line Internet resource, visit Merriam-Webster <http://www.m-w.com> (no fees or registration required).

foreign-derived nouns with preferred foreign-derived plurals

alumna	alumnae	emphasis	emphases
alumnus	alumni	medium	media
analysis	analyses	parenthesis	parentheses
basis	bases	phenomenon	phenomena
crisis	crises	stimulus	stimuli
criterion	criteria	syllabus	syllabi
curriculum	curricula	synopsis	synopses
datum	data	synthesis	syntheses
diagnosis	diagnoses	terminus	termini
ellipsis	ellipses	thesis	theses

g. Some nouns form their plurals by changing letters within the word or adding letters other than *s* or *es*. These irregular plurals are shown in the dictionary in the same entry with their singular form.

child	children	mouse	mice
foot	feet	tooth	teeth
man	men	woman	women

h. Some nouns have the same form in both the singular and the plural. Other nouns are used only with singular verbs while still others are used solely with plural verbs. These irregular constructions are explained in the dictionary entry that defines the word.

nouns with the same singular and plural forms

Chinese	gross	mumps	series
cod	headquarters	odds	sheep
corps	Japanese	politics	species
deer	measles	salmon	vermin
fish	moose	scissors	Vietnamese

nouns always used with singular verbs

aeronautics	genetics	news
economics (course)	mathematics	statistics (course)

nouns always used with plural verbs

belongings	earnings	premises	thanks
credentials	goods	proceeds	winnings

i. Hyphenated or open compound nouns containing a main word form their plural on the main word. Those hyphenated compounds not containing a main word and compound nouns consisting of only one word form the plural at the end.

plural formed on main word

attorneys-at-law	grants-in-aid	notaries public
bills of sale	graphic designs	personnel managers
co-owners	leaves of absence	sisters-in-law
goings-over	lieutenant colonels	vice-chancellors

5 Grammar and Usage

plural formed at end

bookshel**ves**	get-together**s**	stockholder**s**
come-on**s**	go-between**s**	teaspoonful**s**
database**s**	printout**s**	trade-in**s**
follow-up**s**	stand-in**s**	workm**en**

j. The plurals of numerals, most capital letters, words referred to as words, and abbreviations composed of initials are formed by adding *s* or *es*. For clarity, though, all isolated lowercase letters and the capital letters *A, I, M,* and *U* are made plural by adding an apostrophe before the *s*. For those plural numerals, letters, abbreviations, and words referred to as such, italicize only the singular form—not the plural ending.

plural formed with s or es

Please request our receptionist to write her *1***s** and *7***s** more legibly, since I often have difficulty distinguishing between them.

If you receive too many more *C***s** during the next two semesters, you may have difficulty entering our graduate program.

Ms. Graham, our new copy editor, does not use her *which***es** and *that***s** correctly.

On the last ballot did the *no***es** outnumber the *yes***es**?

Mr. Matthews wants this assignment completed without any further **ifs**, **ands**, or **buts**.

Make a list of **dos** and **don'ts** for the care of these scanners.

There are two vacancies for **R.N.s** on our team.

How many members of your accounting staff are **CPAs**?

Please ensure that these **c.o.d.s** are sent out by the end of the week.

Always express *a.m.***s** and *p.m.***s** with clock time in lowercase letters.

plural formed with an apostrophe and s

All of us were careful to mind our *p***'s** and *q***'s** while the government officials were touring the facilities.

To ensure that your writing is legible, be sure to dot your *i***'s** and cross your *t***'s**.

Your son received three *A***'s** on his last grade report.

Why do the *M***'s** appear smudged on this document?

k. When referring to two or more individuals with the same name and title, make either the name or the title plural, but never both.

the **Messrs.** Johnson	*or*	the Mr. **Johnsons**
the **Drs.** Clark	*or*	the Dr. **Clarks**
the **Mses.** Smith	*or*	the Ms. **Smiths**

the **Mesdames** Jones   *or*   the Mrs. **Joneses**

the **Misses** Fry   *or*   the Miss **Frys**

5-5 Noun Possessives[4]

a. **All nouns *not* ending with a pronounced *s*, whether singular or plural, form the possessive by adding *'s*.**

office of the **attorney**	**attorney's** office
toys belonging to the **children**	**children's** toys
books belonging to **Judy**	**Judy's** books
lounge for **women**	**women's** lounge
state tax of **Illinois**	**Illinois's** state tax
countryside of **Des Moines**	**Des Moines's** countryside
paycheck of **Ms. DuBois**	**Ms. DuBois's** paycheck
restaurant belonging to **Francois**	**Francois's** restaurant

(Note: The final *s* in words such as *Illinois, Des Moines, DuBois,* and *Francois* is not pronounced; therefore, *'s* is used with these possessive forms.)

b. **Nouns ending with a pronounced *s* form the possessive by simply adding an apostrophe unless an additional syllable is pronounced in the possessive form. In the latter case, *'s* is added.**

no extra pronounced syllable

clothing for **girls**	**girls'** clothing
the efforts of two **cities**	two **cities'** efforts
the home belonging to the **Foxes**	the **Foxes'** home
the pen belonging to **Mr. Simons**	**Mr. Simons'** pen

extra pronounced syllable

grades of the **class**	the **class's** grades
the briefcase belonging to **Mr. Harris**	**Mr. Harris's** briefcase
testimony of the **witness**	the **witness's** testimony

c. **In cases of joint ownership, show possession only on the last noun. Where individual ownership exists, show possession on each noun.**

joint ownership

Courtney and **Taylor's** office has been moved to the new building.

The Rodriguezes and the **Martinsons'** store is located on Sixth Avenue.

Our law firm is still working on drawing up Mr. Simms and **Ms. Ross's** partnership agreement.

Clark and **Clark's** handbook is required for this class.

---

[4]See Section 1-55 for additional examples.

individual ownership

All my **mother's** and **father's** clothes were damaged during the fire in their apartment building.

Tom's and **Dave's** payroll checks were drawn for incorrect amounts.

Mr. Granados' and **Ms. Stone's** applications for admission to our graduate program have been accepted.

All the **accountants'** and **administrative assistants'** desks have been moved into the new offices.

d. **The possessive form of compound nouns is shown at the end.**

investments of my **father-in-law**	my **father-in-law's** investments
the report for **stockholders**	the **stockholders'** report
convention of **attorneys-at-law**	**attorneys-at-law's** convention
report of the **systems manager**	**systems manager's** report

e. **Use the possessive form before a gerund.**

Lisa's assisting us with this project will ensure that it will be completed by the deadline date.

There is no record of the **witness's answering** these questions under oath.

f. **Use an apostrophe with the possessives of nouns that refer to time—minutes, hours, days, weeks, months, and years.**

time nouns—singular

peace for a **minute**	a **minute's** peace
work for a **day**	a **day's** work
delay for a **week**	a **week's** delay
notice of a **month**	a **month's** notice
mail from this **morning**	this **morning's** mail
calendar for **tomorrow**	**tomorrow's** calendar

time nouns—plural

work for four **hours**	four **hours'** work
interest for two **weeks**	two **weeks'** interest
trial for three **months**	three **months'** trial
experience for five **years**	five **years'** experience

g. **Use an apostrophe with the possessives of nouns that refer to distance.**

He lives just a **stone's** throw from the office.

The truck missed hitting our car by just an **arm's** length.

h. **Do not use an apostrophe to form possessives for inanimate (non-living) things or objects, except for time or distance. Instead, use a simple adjective or an *of* phrase.**

Words such as *company, team, organization, association, herd, flock,* and *committee* are not considered inanimate because they are composed of people or other living entities.

adjective

The **car seat** straps are too fragile. (Not: The car seat's straps are too fragile.)

The **computer** monitor was damaged in transit. (Not: The computer's monitor was damaged in transit.)

of phrase

The door **of the supply cabinet** is jammed. (Not: The supply cabinet's door is jammed.)

The stipulations **of the will** were presented by the attorney. (Not: The will's stipulations were presented by the attorney.)

group composed of people or another living entity

Most of the **company's** profits in 2003 were from Internet e-commerce.

The **college's** offerings have expanded significantly during the past few years.

Nearly 100 acres of the **herd's** grazing lands were destroyed by the floods.

i. In some possessive constructions the item or items owned do not directly follow the ownership word or are not named. The ownership word, however, still shows possession with an apostrophe.

item owned does not directly follow the ownership word

The only desk to be replaced is **Mary's.** (Mary's desk)

On Monday we will meet at the **Culleys'** to list their condominium for sale. (The Culleys' condominium)

item owned not named

Mr. Ardigo left the **attorney's** over an hour ago. (The attorney's office)

Did you leave your cellular phone at the **Gallaghers'**? (The Gallaghers' home)

Pronouns

 Pronouns

a. Pronouns are noun substitutes; they take the place of nouns. Business writers use pronouns to add variety and interest to their writing.

sentence without pronouns

When you see Mr. Lee, please ask Mr. Lee to sign Mr. Lee's time card for this week.

sentence with pronouns

When you see Mr. Lee, please ask **him** to sign **his** time card for this week.

b. Pronouns perform one of four functions: they may (1) substitute for a person or thing, (2) refer back to a noun used previously in the sentence, (3) substitute for an unspecific person or thing, or (4) act as an adjective by modifying a noun.

substitute for a person or thing (personal pronoun)

Michael has been ill for three days; **he** should schedule an appointment to see Dr. Morgan.

Because **Mrs. Scher-Padilla** is in charge of this program, please give your expense forms to **her**.

The board **members** can only blame **themselves** for this error.

Our **company** has opened stores in bordering states. However, **it** has been unable to show any profit from these new operations.

reference to a noun named previously in the sentence (relative pronoun)

Please send me the **book that** Tony recommended.

Brian interviewed three **students** from Japan **who** are interested in attending our college.

substitute for an unspecific person or thing (indefinite pronoun)

Do you know **anyone** who might be interested in this employment opportunity in Buenos Aires?

Neither of these plans is acceptable to the committee.

personal pronoun used as an adjective

His computer has only one floppy disk drive.

This savings account is **hers**.

5-7 **Personal Pronouns**

a. Personal pronouns may be expressed in three ways; these ways are referred to as *case forms.* The three case forms for personal pronouns are the *subjective,* the *objective,* and the *possessive.*

b. The subjective case[5] personal pronouns follow:

I	she	we	who
he	you	they	it

---

[5]The subjective case is also known as the *nominative case.*

Use a subjective case pronoun (1) for the subject of a verb, (2) for the complement of a "being" verb (*am, is, are, was, were, be, been*), and (3) after the infinitive "to be" when this verb does not have a subject (a noun or pronoun) directly preceding it.

subject of a verb

She *has been promoted* three times within the past six years.

They *will arrive* from Montreal at 10 a.m. on Wednesday and *return* the following Wednesday.

Mark, Erin, and **I** *have been appointed* to the committee.

complement of a being verb

The person who answered the telephone *was* not **I**.

"This *is* **she**," is the appropriate response when a telephone caller asks for you by name.

The visitors could have *been* **they**.

infinitive to be without a subject

Deanna is often thought *to be* **I**.

The doctor on duty during that shift is certain *to be* **he**.

c. The objective case personal pronouns are the following:

me	her	us	whom
him	you	them	it

The objective case is used when the pronoun is (1) the direct or indirect object of a verb, (2) the object of a preposition, (3) the subject of any infinitive, (4) the object of the infinitive *to be* when it has a subject, and (5) the object of any other infinitive.

direct object of a verb

Mr. Shaw *will meet* **her** at the airport tomorrow.

Please *ask* **him** to supply this information.

Ms. Orsini *asked* Ken and **me** to serve as judges on the selection committee.

indirect object of a verb

Please *fax* **me** *a receipt* as soon as possible.

We *will send* Natalie or **him** *these copies* before Friday.

object of a preposition

When was the shipment sent *to* **us**?

Two of the customers asked *for* **her**.

Between **you** and **me**, I do not believe the renovation will be completed by May 1.

subject of an infinitive

Our department manager expects **her** *to complete* the audit by June 30.

We thought **them** *to be* somewhat overconfident about their being awarded the contract.

object of to be with a subject

I wanted the **candidate** *to be* **her**.

Ms. Stevenson thought **them** *to be* **us**.

They expected **Maria** *to be* **me**.

object of an infinitive other than to be

Our office will not be able *to mail* **them** until Monday.

We asked her *to help* **us** with the decorations for the banquet.

d. **The possessive case personal pronouns are the following:**

my	mine	their	theirs
his, her	his, hers	its	its
your	yours	whose	
our	ours		

All pronoun possessive case forms are written without apostrophes. They should not be confused with contractions.

possessive pronouns—no apostrophes

Its wrapping had been torn before the package was delivered.

Is this **your** signature on the check?

The idea to sell our products on-line was **theirs**.

Whose briefcase was left in the conference room?

contractions—apostrophes

It's (It is) still raining very heavily here on the West Coast.

Let us know if **you're** (you are) going to the convention.

If **there's** (there is) a logical reason for the delay, please inform the passengers.

Who's (Who is) in charge of ordering supplies for our computers?

e. **Use the possessive case immediately before a gerund.**

His leaving the company was quite a surprise.

We would appreciate **your returning** the enclosed card by Friday, March 18.

f. **A pronoun after *than* or *as* may be expressed in either the subjective or objective case, depending on whether the pronoun is the subject or object of the following stated or implied verb.**

subjective case

Are you as concerned about our manager's decision as **I am**? (Stated verb *am*)

He has been with the company two years longer than **I**. (Implied verb *have*)

objective case

Our supervisor compliments Brandon more than he compliments **me**. (Stated subject and verb *he compliments*)

She works for Mr. Reece more often than **me**. (Implied subject, verb, and preposition *she works for; . . . than she works for* me.)

g. **Pronouns used in apposition take the same case as those nouns or pronouns with which they are in apposition.**

We, Barbara and **I**, have been subpoenaed for jury duty.

Larry told Karen to submit her expenses to one of our accounting **supervisors**, John or **me**.

h. **Pronouns followed by an identifying noun (such as *we employees* or *us employees*) are treated as if the noun were not there in determining the proper case form. Therefore, mentally omit the noun in such pronoun-noun combinations (restrictive appositives) to select the correct form.**

subjective case

Within the next week **we** ~~employees~~ must decide whether or not we will move with the company to Columbus. (Subject of verb phrase *must decide*)

The persons filing the petition in this case are **we** ~~students~~. (Complement of "being" verb *are*)

objective case

Dalton Industries has offered **us** ~~employees~~ the opportunity to purchase company stock at prices below the market value. (Indirect object of verb *offered*)

None of **us** ~~students~~ have received enrollment information for next semester. (Object of preposition *of*)

i. **Pronouns ending in *self* or *selves* emphasize or reflect a noun or pronoun used previously. They should not be used in place of objective case pronouns.**

emphasizes previous noun or pronoun

Wendy herself was not pleased with the results of the advertising campaign.

They themselves could not justify their exorbitant budget requests.

5 Grammar and Usage

reflects a previous noun or pronoun

Ken addressed the envelope to **himself**.

The **state legislature** voted **themselves** a salary increase of $6,000.

objective case pronoun used correctly

All these packages are for **me**. (Not: All these packages are for *myself.*)

The FedEx envelope containing the contract was addressed directly to **you**. (Not: The FedEx envelope containing the contract was addressed directly to *yourself.*)

j. The same rules apply to the pronouns *who, whoever, whom, whomever,* and *whose* as apply to the other personal pronouns. *Who* and *whoever* are used for the subjective case; *whom* and *whomever,* for the objective case; and *whose,* for the possessive case.

To distinguish easily whether to use *who* or *whom,* use the following procedure. See how the model sentence leads to the correct choice. The model sentence for this example is *John is the person [who, whom] I believe Ms. Wilkes will hire.*

(1) Isolate the clause in which the pronoun appears. (*[who, whom] I believe Ms. Wilkes will hire*)

(2) Eliminate any extra clauses. (– *I believe*) (= *[who, whom] Ms. Wilkes will hire*)

(3) Place the clause in subject-verb order if it does not already appear so. (*Ms. Wilkes will hire [who, whom]*)

(4) Apply the rules outlined for the subjective and objective case pronouns in Sections 5–7b and c. Mentally substitute *he* for *who* and *him* for *whom* to help you distinguish between the subjective and objective cases. (*Ms. Wilkes will hire him.* Thus the correct choice for the example sentence is *whom: John is the person whom I believe Ms. Wilkes will hire.*)

subjective case—who or whoever

Who removed this accounting software from our network? (Subject of verb—*[he]* removed)

Please give me a list of **who** will attend our committee meeting. (Subject of verb—*[he]* will attend)

I do not know **who** the caller may have been. (Place clause in subject-verb order.) (Complement of "being" verb *been*—the caller may have been *[he]*)

Please let me know **who** the winner is. (Place clause in subject-verb order.) (Complement of "being" verb *is*—the winner is *[he]*)

Who do you think will be elected to the board? (Omit extra clause *do you think.*) (Subject of verb phrase—*[he]* will be elected)

The city council must approve the appointment of **whoever** is nominated. (Subject of verb phrase—*[he]* is nominated)

The vice president will allow you to select **whoever** you think is qualified. (Omit extra clause *you think*.) (Subject of verb—*[he]* is qualified)

objective case—whom or whomever

Whom did Mr. Zimmerman recommend for promotion? (Place clause in subject-verb order.) (Direct object—Mr. Zimmerman did recommend *[him]*)

He is a person with **whom** we have had business dealings for more than 25 years. (Place clause in subject-verb order.) (Object of preposition—we have had business dealings with *[him]*)

Ask Mr. Worley **whom** he selected to replace José. (Place clause in subject-verb order.) (Direct object—he selected *[him]*)

We do not know **whom** to award the contract. (Place clause in subject-verb order.) (Object of an infinitive—to award *[him]* the contract)

Whom do you think the Detroit Spitfires will hire as its new manager? (Omit extra clause *do you think*.) (Place clause in subject-verb order.) (Direct object—the Detroit Spitfires will hire *[him]*)

The board will allow you to select **whomever** you wish to assist you. (Place clause in subject-verb order.) (Direct object—you wish *[him]* to assist you)

The president will need to interview **whomever** you recommend for this position. (Place clause in subject-verb order.) (Direct object—you recommend *[him]*)

possessive case—whose

Whose sales reports have not yet been received by the home office?

We do not know **whose** recommendations will be adopted to implement our new cost-savings plan.

k. **Pronouns must agree in gender and number with any nouns or other pronouns they represent.**[6]

A **customer** must first register **his** or **her** complaint with an assistant manager.

Both **Ms. Greer** and **Mr. Baty** received **their** orders yesterday.

The **puppy** caught **its** tail in the door.

The **company** will conduct **its** annual inventory next week.

---

[6]Refer to Section 5-18 for additional information on principles of agreement.

5-8 Relative Pronouns

a. Relative pronouns introduce dependent clauses that refer back (relate) to a noun in the main clause of the sentence. Relative pronoun forms are *who, whom, that,* and *which*.

b. Use *who* and *whom* to refer to a person or persons. To distinguish between *who* and *whom*, apply the procedures outlined in Section 5–7j.

subjective case—who

Mr. Vasquez is the *applicant* **who** was selected for the position. (Refers back to *applicant*) (Subject of verb—*[he]* was selected)

The *person* **who** served as chair of the committee was Ms. Bell. (Refers back to *person*) (Subject of verb—*[she]* served)

Peter is the *sales representative* **who** I believe is the best candidate to replace Mark as district sales manager. (Refers back to *sales representative*) (Omit extra clause *I believe.*) (Subject of verb—*[he]* is the best candidate)

Next month our *advertising manager,* **who** has held this position for more than twenty years, will retire. (Refers back to *advertising manager*) (Subject of verb—*[he]* has held)

objective case—whom

Mr. Vasquez is the *applicant* **whom** Ms. Jones selected for the position. (Refers back to *applicant*) (Direct object of verb—Ms. Jones selected *[him]*)

Our new *college president,* **whom** the board appointed just yesterday, has already called a meeting of campus administrators. (Refers back to *president*) (Direct object of verb—the board appointed *[him]*)

You are a *person* **whom** I know Ms. Ferraro would be pleased to hire. (Refers back to *person*) (Omit extra clause *I know.*) (Object of infinitive—Ms. Ferraro would be pleased to hire *[him]*)

c. Use *that* or *which* to introduce a dependent clause that refers back to a thing or things in the main clause—any noun that does not represent a person or persons. Careful writers use *that* to introduce restrictive dependent clauses and *which* to introduce nonrestrictive dependent clauses.

Restrictive dependent clauses provide essential ideas that refine the information contained in the main clause; that is, they specify *which one.* Nonrestrictive dependent clauses provide extra information that does not alter the substance of the main clause; in other words, the information is not needed to identify *which one.* Nonrestrictive clauses are separated from the main clause with a comma or a pair of commas.

restrictive dependent clause requiring that

Be sure to include on the order form the catalog number of each *item* **that** you order. (Refers back to *item*) (Specifies only items that are ordered)

The *prices* **that** are listed in this catalog are guaranteed until June 30. (Refers back to *prices*) (Specifies which prices—the ones listed in this catalog)

nonrestrictive dependent clause requiring which

The Model No. 431 noise-canceling microphone, **which** you ordered last week, has been replaced by the Model No. 642. (Refers back to *microphone*) (Clause not needed to identify which microphone— provides extra idea)

Please credit our account for the three Toshiba laptop computers, **which** were charged to our account in error. (Refers back to *computers*) (Clause not needed to identify which computers— provides additional information)

5-9 Indefinite Pronouns

a. Indefinite pronouns are pronouns that do not represent a specific person, place, or thing.

b. Simple indefinite pronouns include the following words used as subjects or objects:

each   every   either   neither

c. Compound indefinite pronouns end with *-body, -one,* or *-thing.*

____body	____one	____thing
anybody	anyone	anything
everybody	everyone	everything
nobody	no one	nothing
somebody	someone	something

d. Indefinite pronouns used as subjects require singular verbs.

simple indefinite pronoun as subject

Each of the candidates **has** been given an equal opportunity to address television audiences.

Neither of the applicants **is** qualified for the position.

compound indefinite pronoun as subject

Nearly **everybody was** late for the meeting because of the unexpected snowstorm.

Everything on these invoices **has** been paid.

5 Grammar and Usage

e. Any other pronouns representing an indefinite pronoun must agree in number and gender with the indefinite pronoun.

Neither of the winners has claimed **his** or **her** prize.

Would **everyone** please return **his** or **her** evaluation form by May 15.

Verbs

 Verbs

a. Verbs are often described as the motor of a sentence—they make a sentence "go." Verbs show action or describe a state of being at a certain point in time. Examples of action verbs are *run, swim, talk,* and *write.*

Nonaction verbs, those that describe a state of being, include words such as *seem, feel,* and *smell.* The most commonly used non-action verbs, however, are derived from the verb *be—am, is, are, was, were,* and *been.*

b. In their infinitive form, verbs are preceded by the preposition *to.*

action verbs	nonaction verbs
to go	to be
to demonstrate	to appear
to apply	to taste

c. Verbs appear alone or in phrases with helpers. The last word in a verb phrase is the main verb. Word groups must contain a verb or a verb phrase to be complete sentences.

verb in sentence

Darryl **checks** his E-mail messages at least twice daily.

Please **return** these defective hard drives to the vendor.

Vista Industries **is** one of our best customers.

verb phrase in sentence

We **have received** several contracts from Gourmet Cookery.

Our company **has been involved** in two lawsuits during the past year.

Our office staff **is** presently **processing** your order.

How much money **did** your company **invest** in this condominium project?

d. Verbs require varied forms to signify tenses, that is, points in time. The principal forms or parts of a verb used to construct tenses include the present part, the past part, the past participle, and the present participle.

5-11 Formation of Parts for Regular Verbs

Most verbs, regular verbs, form their parts in the same way:

(1) The present part has the infinitive form without the accompanying *to*.

(2) The past part adds *ed* to the present form.

(3) The past participle uses the past part with at least one verb helper.

(4) The present participle adds *ing* to the present form and uses at least one verb helper.

infinitive	present	past
to ask	ask	asked
to collect	collect	collected
to interview	interview	interviewed

past participle	present participle
(have, was) asked	(was, has been) asking
(has, had been) collected	(am, have been) collecting
(were, have been) interviewed	(are, will be) interviewing

sentence examples

You will need **to collect** more evidence before we can present this case to the district attorney's office. (Infinitive)

Jeff **collects** stamps from countries all over the world. (Present part)

The courier **collected** all our mail for overnight delivery about an hour ago. (Past part)

My assistant **has collected** prospectuses from seven major suppliers of health insurance programs. (Past participle with a helping verb)

Our Research Department **is collecting** additional information from consumers. (Present participle with a helping verb)

5-12 Formation of Parts for Irregular Verbs

a. Many verbs do not form their past part, past participle, and present participle in the usual manner. *All such irregular verb forms are shown in the dictionary; they are listed directly after the present form of the verb.* Verbs without such a listing are regular verbs, and their parts are formed in the regular way described in Section 5–11.

b. A number of irregular verbs form their parts in the same way. Most verbs ending in *e* form their past part and past participle by adding *d*. These same verbs form the present participle by dropping the *e* and adding *ing*.

Another group of verbs double the final consonant before adding the regular endings to the past part, past participle, and present participle.

verbs ending in e

Infinitive:	to change	to enclose	to complete
Present part:	change	enclose	complete
Past part:	changed	enclosed	completed
Past participle:	(has) changed	(have) enclosed	(have) completed
Present participle:	(is) changing	(are) enclosing	(is) completing

verbs that double the final consonant

Infinitive:	to trim	to stir	to clip
Present part:	trim	stir	clip
Past part:	trimmed	stirred	clipped
Past participle:	(has) trimmed	(has) stirred	(have) clipped
Present participle:	(is) trimming	(are) stirring	(is) clipping

c. **Some irregular verb forms do not follow a particular pattern in forming the past part and the past participle. A list of parts for some such commonly used irregular verbs follows:**

Present Part	Past Part	Past Participle	Present Participle
am	was	been	being
arise	arose	arisen	arising
become	became	become	becoming
begin	began	begun	beginning
bite	bit	bitten	biting
blow	blew	blown	blowing
break	broke	broken	breaking
bring	brought	brought	bringing
burst	burst	burst	bursting
buy	bought	bought	buying
catch	caught	caught	catching
choose	chose	chosen	choosing
come	came	come	coming
dig	dug	dug	digging
do	did	done	doing
draw	drew	drawn	drawing
drink	drank	drunk	drinking
drive	drove	driven	driving
eat	ate	eaten	eating
fall	fell	fallen	falling
fight	fought	fought	fighting
fly	flew	flown	flying
forget	forgot	forgotten	forgetting
forgive	forgave	forgiven	forgiving
freeze	froze	frozen	freezing
get	got	got	getting
give	gave	given	giving
go	went	gone	going
grow	grew	grown	growing
hang (an object)	hung	hung	hanging
hang (a person)	hanged	hanged	hanging

Present Part	Past Part	Past Participle	Present Participle
hide	hid	hidden	hiding
know	knew	known	knowing
lay	laid	laid	laying
lead	led	led	leading
leave	left	left	leaving
lend	lent	lent	lending
lie (to recline)	lay	lain	lying
lie (to tell an untruth)	lied	lied	lying
lose	lost	lost	losing
make	made	made	making
pay	paid	paid	paying
ride	rode	ridden	riding
ring	rang	rung	ringing
rise	rose	risen	rising
run	ran	run	running
see	saw	seen	seeing
set	set	set	setting
shake	shook	shaken	shaking
shrink	shrank	shrunk	shrinking
sing	sang	sung	singing
sink	sank	sunk	sinking
sit	sat	sat	sitting
speak	spoke	spoken	speaking
spring	sprang	sprung	springing
steal	stole	stolen	stealing
strike	struck	struck	striking
swear	swore	sworn	swearing
swim	swam	swum	swimming
take	took	taken	taking
tear	tore	torn	tearing
throw	threw	thrown	throwing
wear	wore	worn	wearing
write	wrote	written	writing

sentence examples

Our spring clearance sale **begins** June 1.

We **began** work on this construction project early last March.

Orders, as a result of our national television campaign, **have begun** to flood our telephone lines.

These stocks **are beginning** to pay substantial dividends.

5-13 Simple Tenses

Verb parts are used to form tenses that place an action or a condition in a time frame. The verb part itself may express tense, or a verb part with helpers (a verb phrase) may be needed to specify the time frame. The most commonly used tenses are the simple tenses—the *present*, the *past*, and the *future.*

a. The present tense is used to indicate an ongoing action or a currently existing condition. Use the present part or a conjugation (changes in spelling to accommodate person) of the present part to form this tense.

Place an *s* at the end of the present part when it is used with any singular subject except *I* and *you.* For verbs ending in *s, sh, ch, x,* and *z,* add *es* instead of *s.*[7]

present tense formations for most verbs

to eat	**to provide**	**to sit**
I eat	I provide	I sit
you eat	you provide	you sit
he eats	he provides	he sits
John eats	John provides	John sits
she eats	she provides	she sits
Mary eats	Mary provides	Mary sits
it eats	it provides	it sits
the cat eats	the company provides	the cat sits
we eat	we provide	we sit
you eat (pl.)	you provide (pl.)	you sit (pl.)
they eat	they provide	they sit
the children eat	the parents provide	the patients sit

present tense formations for verbs ending in s, sh, ch, x, and z

to wish	**to teach**	**to relax**
I wish	I teach	I relax
you wish	you teach	you relax
he wishes	he teaches	he relaxes
John wishes	John teaches	John relaxes
she wishes	she teaches	she relaxes
Mary wishes	Mary teaches	Mary relaxes
it wishes	it teaches	it relaxes
the board wishes	the program teaches	the cat relaxes
we wish	we teach	we relax
you wish (pl.)	you teach (pl.)	you relax (pl.)
they wish	they teach	they relax
the children wish	the schools teach	the travelers relax

---

[7]The verbs *do* and *go* add *es* also; i.e., the singular form of *do* for *he, she,* and *it* is *does.* The corresponding form for *go* is *goes.*

use of present tense

Our purchasing agent **buys** our software from local vendors.

Elton Electronics **establishes** offices in all countries in which it **conducts** business.

The All-Clean cleaning crew **waxes** these floors weekly.

He **goes** to the doctor regularly for checkups.

b. The *past tense* describes a single past action or event. Simply use the past part of a verb to express the past tense.

Dr. Williams **selected** gray carpeting for his new offices.

The attorney **received** your signed documents yesterday.

Our purchasing agent **bought** this equipment from an Internet site.

c. The *future tense* describes expected or anticipated occurrences. To form the future tense, use the present part with the helping verb *will*.

I **will call** you tomorrow to confirm our appointment.

The committee **will review** your proposal by March 1, and Mr. Rosen **will notify** you of the committee's decision by March 8.

Our company **will** not **participate** in the bidding for this contract.

5-14 Perfect Tenses

The perfect tenses—the present, past, and future—use the past participle of the verb along with a helping verb formed from *have*.

a. The *present perfect tense* describes an action or a condition that began in the past and has continued until and including the present. This tense is formed by using *has* or *have* with the past participle of the verb.

Mr. Randolf **has worked** for our company since July 1994.

We **have sent** you three reminders about your past-due account.

The company **has** already **paid** heavy fines for environmental-impact violations.

b. The *past perfect tense* describes a past action that occurred before another past action. Use *had* as a helping verb with the past participle of the main verb to form this tense.

Our client **had signed** this will just three days before he **died**.

We **accepted** Hadley Enterprises' offer only after we **had contacted** three other vendors.

Although we **had paid** for the merchandise, the manufacturer **did** not **ship** it in time for our summer sale.

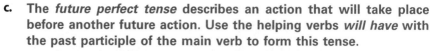

c. The *future perfect tense* describes an action that will take place before another future action. Use the helping verbs *will have* with the past participle of the main verb to form this tense.

By the time we publish this book, we **will have spent** more than $50,000 in fees to freelance writers.

If allowed to continue, this project at its conclusion **will have cost** United States taxpayers more than $3 billion.

5-15 Progressive Tenses

The progressive tenses show action in progress during the present, past, and future. Use the present participle of the verb along with a "being" verb helper—*am, is, are, was, were,* or *be.*

a. The *present progressive tense* describes an ongoing action during the present time. The being verb helpers *am, is,* and *are* are used with the present participle to form this tense.

I **am taking** several classes at Pepperdine University this semester.

Our company **is sponsoring** the 10k run scheduled for May 8.

Several of our employees **are relocating** to our main office in Boston.

b. The *past progressive tense* relates an ongoing action that occurred in the past. The being verb helpers *was* and *were* with the present participle of a verb are used to form this tense.

I **was discussing** this problem with the vice president when her administrative assistant interrupted us with an emergency message from the president.

Until the end of last year, we **were** still **selling** more copies of the sixth edition than the seventh edition.

c. The *future progressive tense* forecasts an ongoing future action. To form this tense, use the helping verbs *will* and *be* with the present participle of the verb.

We **will be hiring** employees for this new restaurant location approximately three weeks before construction is completed.

Our auditors **will be reviewing** Price Investment Corporation's books for at least another two months.

5-16 Passive Voice Constructions

Unlike other verb constructions, the passive voice does not necessarily identify who does what. Instead, the person or thing performing the action may be cloaked in ambiguity.

In business communications the passive voice is often used to soften the impact of a negative idea or to avoid placing blame for an oversight or error. It is also used simply to provide variety in sentence construction. Although grammar checkers (software programs) flag passive voice constructions, they are not grammar errors.

To form a passive voice construction, use the past participle of the verb with one of the following "being" verb helpers: *is, are, was, were, be,* or *been*.

Each on-line order **is acknowledged** by a message to the customer's E-mail account when it arrives at our site.

Our products **are sold** only through franchised retailers.

Unfortunately, the shipment **was damaged** in transit.

These eviction notices **were mailed** to the tenants on September 1.

The new medical office complex **will be completed** by the end of the year.

All depositors **have been notified** that the insured deposits of Universal Savings **have been assumed** by First Arizona Savings.

Use of *Lay* and *Lie*

a. Broadly defined, the verb *lay* means "to place or put" and the verb *lie* means "to recline." Forms of these two verbs are often confused in usage. The principal parts of *lie* and *lay* follow:

Present Part	Past Part	Past Participle	Present Participle
lie	lay	lain	lying
lay	laid	laid	laying

b. Use a form of *lie* when the subject of the verb is performing the action, that is, the subject is what is lying. Otherwise, if the subject of the sentence is not the person or thing doing the lying, use a form of *lay*.[8]

Always use a form of *lay* when the past participle appears with a "being" verb helper (*is, are, was, were, be, been*).

subject is performing the action—is lying

The new *shopping mall* **lies** at the base of the LaCrescenta Foothills.

Bob **lay** unconscious for nearly half an hour before the ambulance arrived.

Our *mainframe computer* **has lain** idle for nearly six hours.

Your *packages* **are lying** on the bottom shelf of the cupboard.

---

[8]Use of the verb *lay* with three of its parts—*lay, laid,* and (*has, have,* or *had*) *laid*—is often easily identified by substituting a form of the verb *put.* If *put* or one of its forms makes sense, then the use of *lay* or one of its forms is correct. Otherwise, a form of *lie* is more than likely to be correct.

163

subject of verb is not lying

Jennifer **lays** all new magazines on tables in the reception area. (*new magazines* are lying on tables—not subject of verb, *Jennifer*)

Before leaving the office, Sam **laid** the contracts on your desk. (*contracts* are lying on the desk—not subject of verb, *Sam*)

Our shipping clerks **have** always **laid** these booklets horizontally in their packing boxes. (*booklets* are lying in packing boxes—not subject of verb, *shipping clerks*)

Retail stores throughout the country **are laying** plans to capture their share of holiday purchases. (*retail stores*, not *plans*, is the subject of the sentence)

always a form of lay *("being" verb + past participle)*

Sandbags have **been laid** along the riverbed because of impending flood damage.

The carpeting **was laid** yesterday in our new offices.

5–18 **Principles of Agreement**

a. **The verb of a sentence must agree in person and number with the subject. To identify a subject, omit any prepositional phrases that separate the subject and the verb.**

Two **legs** of the table **were damaged** in transit. (Omit prepositional phrase *of the table*.)

The **stock** of cartridges for our Hewlett-Packard and Epson printers **is running** low. (Omit prepositional phrases *of cartridges* and *for our Hewlett-Packard and Epson printers*.)

b. **A pronoun that represents the subject must agree in number and gender with the subject.**

Mr. Donovan submitted **his** March expense report yesterday.

Remind **every student** to submit **his** or **her** class schedule by January 30.

Candace and **Mark** have already submitted **their** home loan application to Eastern Bank.

The **company** filed bankruptcy because **it** was unable to meet **its** obligations.

c. **Compound subjects joined by** *and* **generally require the use of a plural verb. When compound subjects are joined by** *or* **or** *nor*, **the form of the verb is determined by the part of the subject that is closer to the verb. If one part is plural and the other is singular, place the plural part, where possible, closer to the verb.**

***compound joined by* and**

My **son and daughter-in-law receive** monthly issues of *Business Forecast.*

Outgoing **letters and packages leave** our office on a regularly scheduled basis.

Mr. Lopez and his two assistants were requested to attend the board meeting.

***compound joined by* or *or* nor**

Neither Sharon nor **John was** available to meet with the client on Monday.

Either Aaron or **I am** responsible for opening the store on weekdays.

Ms. Binder or her **assistants are** reviewing the manuscript.

Candy or **flowers are** typically given on Valentine's Day.
(Not: Flowers or *candy is* typically given on Valentine's Day.)

d. Subjects joined by *and* take singular verbs in only two cases: (1) when the parts separated by *and* constitute a single person or thing and (2) when the compound is preceded by *each, every,* or *many a (an).*

single person or thing

Our **accountant and tax attorney has** prepared all the reports requested by the Internal Revenue Service.

Her **nurse and companion works** six days a week.

Bacon and eggs is served in our restaurant until 11 a.m. each day.

Luckily the **horse and carriage was** stolen after the movie scene had been shot.

***compound preceded by* each, every, *or* many a (an)**

Each home and condominium was inspected by the general contractor before it was released for occupancy.

Every man, woman, and child is responsible for carrying his or her belongings during the tour.

Many a student and instructor has requested additional tickets to our Drama Department's production of *Picnic.*

e. Indefinite pronouns such as *each, every, everyone, everything, somebody, anybody, either,* and *neither* take singular verbs.

Each of these books **has** been autographed by the author.

Everyone was pleased with the hotel accommodations.

Everything in these files **needs** to be transferred to microfiche.

Neither of them **was** present at the meeting.

f. When the word *there* precedes the verb, select the singular or plural verb form based on the number of the noun that follows. If the noun is singular, then use a singular verb; if it is plural, use a plural verb.

The same rule applies to those words such as *some, all, none, most, a majority, one fourth,* and *part* that indicate portions. When they function as subjects, the number of the noun that follows governs whether a singular or plural verb is correct.

there *preceding a singular verb form*

There **is** one **person** on the mailing list you may wish to call.

There **appears** to be only one **reason** why our bid was rejected.

there *preceding a plural verb form*

There **are** three **people** on the waiting list.

There **appear** to be several **reasons** why our bid was not accepted.

portion preceding a singular verb form

Some of the **money has** been invested in U.S. Savings Bonds.

Part of your **order has** been shipped.

One third of our **clerical staff needs** in-service training.

portion preceding a plural verb form

All the **materials were** shipped to you yesterday.

So far only **one half** of the **apartments have** been inspected.

A majority of our **employees receive** extra benefits from our incentive plan.

g. The words *a number* used as a subject require a plural verb. *The number* used as a subject requires a singular verb. Keep in mind that descriptive adverbs and adjectives may separate the article *a* or *the* from the word *number.*

a number *subject, plural verb*

A number of our customers **are** requesting a full refund.

A surprisingly small **number** of our students **have** registered late this semester.

the number *subject, singular verb*

The number of employees selecting MDA medical insurance **has** increased substantially since 2000.

The large **number** of customer inquiries received from our recent advertising campaign **was** far greater than we had anticipated.

h. To express the subjunctive mood (a situation or condition that is untrue or highly unlikely), use *were* instead of *was* after *if, as if, as* *though,* or *wish.* The verb *was* is used only if the situation after *if, as if,* or *as though* could be true.

use of were instead of was

If I **were** you, I would update my application before the deadline date. (A condition that is untrue—I cannot be you.)

Mr. Greeley took charge **as though** he **were** the owner of the store. (But Mr. Greeley is not the owner of the store.)

I **wish** I **were** able to answer that question for you. (But I cannot answer the question.)

use of was

If Sally **was** here, she did not submit her weekly time sheet. (Sally could have been there.)

The customer acted **as though** he **was** irritated with our credit policies. (The customer may have been irritated.)

i. **Avoid splitting an infinitive, that is, placing any words between *to* and the verb form.**

Unfortunately, I was unable **to follow logically** the technician's explanation. (Not *to logically follow*)

None of us seemed **to understand fully** the reasons for the policy change. (Not *to fully understand*)

j. **Collective nouns such as *committee, jury, audience, group, team, class, board, crowd,* and *council* may take either singular or plural verbs, depending upon the situation in which the noun is used. If the individual members of the collective noun are operating as a unit, use a singular verb; if the individual members are acting separately, use a plural verb.**

In most cases the use of a plural verb with a collective noun results in an awkward-sounding construction. To avoid such situations, restructure the sentence to use a plural-noun subject.

elements of collective noun acting as a unit

When an **audience gives** a speaker a standing ovation, you may be sure that he or she has delivered an exceptional address.

Has the standards **committee** finished its report?

elements of collective noun acting separately

The **jury were** arguing loudly. (Alternative: The jury members were arguing loudly.)

The **board are** still discussing various outcomes that may affect their decision. (Alternative: The board members are still discussing various outcomes that may affect their decision.)

restructured sentence with plural-noun subject

Unfortunately, the **members** of the council **do** not agree on the purpose of the newly formed committee.

After the game the team **members were** seen arguing with one another on national television.

k. A relative pronoun clause (a clause commonly beginning with *who* or *that*) must agree in gender and number with the noun or pronoun it modifies.

Ms. Silvers is a **person** who **is** concerned about maintaining **her** good health.

Our manager is the kind of **man** who **is** always considerate of **his** subordinates.

All **children** who **attend** this school are required to maintain **their** grade average at or above the *C* level.

Have you listened to all the **messages** that **have** accumulated in your message center during the past three days?

Our committee **meeting**, which **was** scheduled for January 7, has been postponed until next week.

l. Relative pronoun clauses (*who* and *that* clauses) preceded by such phrases as "one of those doctors" or "one of the doctors" generally agree with the plural noun—in this case, *doctors*. Phrases such as *one of those* (or *the*) *executives, one of those* (or *the*) *books*, and *one of those* (or *the*) *assistants* are in the same category. The entire group is described by the clause; therefore, plural forms must be used.

In sentences in which "one of those _____" or "one of the _____" is limited by the word *only*, the relative clause does not refer to the entire group. Singular forms are correct in these instances.

"one of those _____"—plural forms

Laura is one of those business **executives** who **travel** extensively in **their** jobs.

He is one of the **salespersons** who regularly **visit** all **their** customers.

Top of the Mountain is one of those **books** that **have** a surprise ending.

She is one of the **employees** who **work** in our Chicago office.

"one of those _____" limited by only—singular forms

Laura is the **only one** of the business executives who **travels** extensively in **her** job.

He is the **only one** of those salespersons who regularly **visits** all **his** customers.

Top of the Mountain is the **only one** of those books that **has** a surprise ending.

She is the **only one** of the employees who **works** in our Chicago office.

Adjectives

5-19 Adjectives Modify Nouns

Adjectives modify nouns or pronouns. They answer such questions as what kind? how many? which one?

what kind?

damaged merchandise   **laser** printers   **stylish** fashions

how many?

three salespersons   **several** years   **two dozen** pens

which one?

Karen's computer   **those** flight attendants   **your** idea

5-20 Use of the Articles *A* and *An*

Use the article *a* before a word that begins with a consonant sound, a long *u* sound, or an *h* that is pronounced. Use *an* before words that begin with a pronounced vowel sound (except long *u*) or before words that begin with a silent *h*.

use of **a**

a newspaper   a uniform   a hillside
a restaurant   a union   a history class
a large undertaking   a usual occurrence   a hidden entry

use of **an**

an answer   an unusual request   an hour
an opportunity   an upper floor   an heir
an effective solution   an ultimate goal   an honest person

5-21 Adjective Comparison

a. Adjectives may be used to compare two or more nouns or pronouns. Use the comparative form (-*er* or *more, less*) to compare two persons or things and the superlative form (-*est* or *most, least*) to compare three or more.

b. Most one-syllable adjectives ending in *e* add *r* for the comparative and *st* for the superlative.

5 Grammar and Usage

169

Most one-syllable adjectives ending in consonants add *er* for the comparative and *est* for the superlative, but some double the final consonant before adding *er* or *est*.[9]

most one-syllable adjectives ending in e

He has a **large** high-definition television screen.

He has a **larger** high-definition television screen than I have.

He has the **largest** high-definition television screen offered for sale in today's market.

simple	comparative	superlative
nice	nicer	nicest
fine	finer	finest
tame	tamer	tamest

most one-syllable adjectives ending in a consonant

This is a **short** report.

This report is **shorter** than the one you prepared last week.

This is the **shortest** report you have prepared this month.

simple	comparative	superlative
sweet	sweeter	sweetest
mild	milder	mildest
proud	prouder	proudest

some one-syllable adjectives ending in a consonant

Do you expect to make a **big** profit on this stock?

Which of these stocks do you think will yield a **bigger** profit?

Mr. Doble's **biggest** profit on investments this year came from Internet stocks.

simple	comparative	superlative
sad	sadder	saddest
trim	trimmer	trimmest
drab	drabber	drabbest

c. Most two-syllable adjectives and all adjectives containing three or more syllables use *more* or *less* and *most* or *least* to construct comparative and superlative forms. Forms for those two-syllable adjectives that do not follow this pattern are shown in the dictionary after their simple form. These words include *costly, friendly, happy, healthy, kindly, merry, lovely, pretty*—all ending in *y*.

two-syllable adjective with more, most, less, *or* least

Boston has a number of **superb** restaurants.

---

[9]Single-syllable adjectives that end in *e* or that double the final consonant before adding *er* (comparative form) or *est* (superlative form) are considered irregular. Therefore, these irregular forms are shown in the dictionary after the simple form.

Boston has **more superb** restaurants than the last city we visited.

Of all the cities I visited, Paris has the **most superb** restaurants.

simple	comparative	superlative
useful	more useful	most useful
	less useful	least useful
suitable	more suitable	most suitable
	less suitable	least suitable

three-syllable adjective with **more, most, less,** *or* **least**

We purchased an **expensive** scanner yesterday.

This copier is **less expensive** than the one we saw yesterday.

The Evans line is the **least expensive** grade of linens we carry.

simple	comparative	superlative
comprehensive	more comprehensive	most comprehensive
	less comprehensive	least comprehensive
practical	more practical	most practical
	less practical	least practical

two-syllable adjective using **er** *or* **est**

Our state initiated a **costly** accounting program last year.

Our state's highway program is **costlier** than its conservation program.

Our state's welfare program is the **costliest** one in the nation.

simple	comparative	superlative
lonely	lonelier	loneliest
heavy	heavier	heaviest

d. Irregular forms for adjective comparison appear in the dictionary. They are listed after the simple forms. A list of commonly used irregular adjective forms follows:

simple	comparative	superlative
bad, ill	worse	worst
good, well	better	best
far	farther, further	farthest, furthest
little	littler, less	littlest, least
many, much	more	most

e. Use *other* or *else* when comparing one person or object with the other members of the group to which it belongs.

Our London office earns more revenue than any of our **other** international branch offices. (Not *any of our international branch offices*)

Andrew is more diligent than anyone **else** in the class. (Not *anyone in the class*)

f. **Some adjectives cannot be compared in the regular sense because they are absolute. A partial list of such adjectives follows:**

alive	finished	round
complete	full	straight
dead	perfect	unique

Absolute adjectives may show comparison by use of the forms "more nearly" or "most nearly."

The water cooler in the employees' lounge is **full**.

The water cooler in your office is **more nearly full** (not *fuller*) than the one in ours.

The water cooler in the Office of Human Resources is the **most nearly full** (not *fullest*) one on this floor.

The police report is **accurate**.

The *Daily News'* report of the robbery was **more nearly accurate** (not *more accurate*) than the one appearing in the *Tribune*.

The *Daily News'* report of the robbery was the **most nearly accurate** (not *most accurate*) one that appeared in the media.

5-22 Independent Adjectives[10]

When two or more adjectives appearing before a noun independently modify the noun, separate these adjectives with commas.

His **direct**, **practical** approach to problem solving has created a high degree of respect for him among his staff.

We returned that **boring**, **poorly written** manuscript to its author last week.

Donna-Mae handled the problem in a **sure**, **calm**, **decisive** manner.

5-23 Adjectives With Linking Verbs

Use adjectives, not adverbs, after linking (nonaction) verbs. Common linking verbs include *feel, look, smell, sound,* and *taste*.

I **feel bad** that you did not receive this well-deserved promotion. (Not *badly*)

Cakes from Federico's Bakery always **taste delicious**. (Not *deliciously*)

The adjoining rooms **smelled terrible** after the reception room fire. (Not *terribly*)

---

[10]See Section 1-8 for a detailed explanation of the use of the comma with independent adjectives.

5-24 **Compound Adjectives**[11]

a. Adjectives containing two or more words that are shown hyphenated in the dictionary are known as *permanent compounds*.[12] These words are always hyphenated when they are used as adjectives.

Your **up-to-date** files have been very helpful in compiling this data.

My present job is only **part-time**, but I will begin looking for a **full-time** job in September.

As one of the oldest players in the league, Steve doesn't seem to know when he is **well-off**.

b. When two or more words appearing before a noun function as a single-thought modifier, place hyphens between the words, even though these words do not appear hyphenated in the dictionary. These compound adjectives are temporary compounds and are hyphenated only when they appear before the noun or pronoun they modify.

temporary compound adjective before the modified noun

Upon reading your **well-documented** report, the city council voted to establish a new community center.

Very little of the **high-priced** merchandise was sold during our clearance sale.

Do not exceed the **65-mile-an-hour** speed limit.

You may advertise this opening as a **$42,000-a-year** position.

temporary compound adjective following the modified noun

Your report is certainly **well documented**.

This merchandise is too **high priced** for our store.

The speed limit on this freeway is **65 miles an hour**.

Our manager's salary is at least **$42,000 a year**.

Adverbs

5-25 **Functions and Forms of Adverbs**

Adverbs modify verbs, adjectives, or other adverbs. They answer such questions as when? where? why? how? to what degree?

---

[11]See Section 2-2 for detailed rules regarding the formation of compound adjectives.

[12]All hyphenations for compound adjectives in this reference manual are based on those shown in *Merriam-Webster's Collegiate Dictionary*, 10th ed. (Springfield, Mass.: Merriam-Webster, Incorporated, 2002.) Entries for *Merriam-Webster's Collegiate Dictionary* may be viewed on-line <http://www.m-w.com>.

a. Most adverbs end in *ly*.

accidentally	daily	finally
carefully	definitely	steadily
cautiously	diligently	usually

b. Some adverbs may either end in *ly* or take the adjective form of the word.[13]

Please drive **slowly** (or **slow**) on this icy road.

Your order will be processed as **quickly** (or **quick**) as possible.

You may call **directly** (or **direct**) to Chicago on this line.

c. Other adverbs do not take an *ly* form. Such adverbs include the following:

again	late	not	there
almost	never	now	very
here	no	soon	well

5-26 Adverb Comparison

a. One-syllable adverbs and some two-syllable adverbs are compared by adding *er* or *est*. For comparisons between two items, use *er*; for comparisons among more than two items, use *est*.[14]

comparison of two

You live **closer** to the library than I.

My assistant left **earlier** than I.

comparison of more than two

Of all the students in the study group, you live **closest** to the library.

Who is scheduled to arrive the **earliest**—Bill, Paula, or Bob?

b. Most adverbs containing two syllables and all adverbs containing more than two syllables form the comparison by adding *more* or *most* (or *less* or *least*) to the positive form. Use *more* (or *less*) in comparing two items and *most* (or *least*) in comparing more than two items.

comparison of two

This conveyer belt travels **more slowly** than the one next to it.

Please pack these items **more carefully** than you have done in the past.

Surf soap is **less widely** used on the East Coast than in the South.

---

[13]Both forms of those adverbs that may end in *ly* or just take the adjective form are shown in the dictionary.

[14]Two-syllable adverbs that show comparison by adding *er* or *est* are considered irregular. Therefore, these forms are shown in the dictionary following the simple form.

comparison of more than two

Denver has been mentioned **most often** as the likely site for our next convention.

This conference is the **most unusually** conducted one I have ever attended.

This brand of soap is the **least widely** used of all the major brands.

5-27 Adverb Placement

a. Place adverbs as close as possible to the words they modify. The misplacement of an adverb can change the meaning of a sentence or result in an awkward-sounding sentence.

changed meaning

Only Beverly and I were invited to attend the seminar on human relations.

Beverly and I were invited to attend **only** the seminar on human relations.

awkward construction

Our costs have **nearly** risen 20 percent this year. (Awkward)

Our costs have risen **nearly** 20 percent this year. (Correct)

b. Avoid splitting an infinitive with an adverb; place the adverb after the infinitive.

We will need **to scrutinize carefully** all finalists for this position.

If you wish **to discuss** this possibility **further**, please call me.

5-28 Adverbs Vs. Adjectives

Use an adverb after a verb that shows action; use an adjective, however, after a nonaction (or linking) verb.

Verbs relating to the senses (*feel, look, smell*) may function as non-action verbs. In some cases you may test such occurrences by substituting a form of *to be* (*am, is, are, was, were*). If the sentence reads smoothly, use the adjective form for any descriptive word that modifies the verb.

action verb

You **did well** on your six-month performance evaluation.

The pedestrian **crossed** the street **cautiously**.

Most of the council members **opposed bitterly** the rezoning of this residential area.

The professional soccer team **was beaten badly** in yesterday's game.

nonaction or linking verb

If we do not brew fresh coffee every two hours, it begins to **taste bitter**. (...is bitter.)

The employees' lounge **smells terrible**. (...is terrible.)

Paul **looked angry** after he received the news. (...was angry....)

I **feel bad** about Mr. Johnson's predicament.

The entrée at the Sunday evening banquet **was delicious**.

5-29 Double Negatives

Use only one negative word or limiting adverb to express a single idea.

Do **not** release information about students to **anybody**.
(Not *nobody*)

I did **not** receive **anything** from our insurance agent. (Not *nothing*)

I **can** (not *can't* or *cannot*) **scarcely** believe that our college president would make such a statement.

We **were** (not *weren't* or *were not*) **hardly** in the office when Ms. Kawamura gave us the good news.

He **had** (not *hadn't* or *had not*) **barely** finished computing the results when the Board of Directors requested him to report his findings.

Prepositions

5-30 Prepositions as Connectors

a. Prepositions link descriptive words to other words or ideas in a sentence. The most commonly used prepositions are *of* and *for*. Occasionally used ones are *about, during, except,* and *but* (meaning *except*). Other commonly used prepositions, those listed below, can easily be identified by picturing what an airplane can do in relation to clouds: the airplane can fly _____ the clouds.

above	down	over
after	from	through
alongside	in	to
among	inside	toward
around	into	under
at	near	up
before	off	upon
behind	on	with
below	opposite	within
between	outside	without

b. Prepositions begin a phrase that ends with a noun or pronoun. This phrase is related to another word in the sentence—it describes, limits, or modifies the word in some way by clarifying *who, what, when, where, how, why,* or *to what degree.*

Our staff **of accountants** is available to assist you at any time. (*Of accountants* is related to *staff*—specifies what.)

You may park your car **behind the building**. (*Behind the building* is related to *park*—specifies where.)

5-31 Prepositional Phrases

In determining subject-verb agreement, generally ignore any prepositional phrases that separate the subject and the verb. (See Section 5–18l for subject-verb agreement principles related to prepositional phrases appearing before relative pronoun clauses [clauses beginning with *who* or *that*]).

One of your clients **is** waiting in the outer office. (Omit *of your clients* to match "One ... is.")

A large **quantity** of bathing suits **has** been ordered for the sale. (Omit *of bathing suits* to match "quantity ... has.")

Last Monday our **supply** of paper goods and kitchen utensils **was** destroyed. (Omit *of paper goods and kitchen utensils* to match "supply ... was.")

5-32 *In, Between,* or *Among?*

When a preposition has a single object, use *in.* For two separate objects, use *between;* for three or more objects, use *among.*

preposition **in**
Did our accountant discover any discrepancies **in** the auditor's report?

The judge noted several discrepancies **in** the defendant's testimony.

preposition **between**
Between you and me, I believe this stock will split before the end of the year.

There were several discrepancies **between** the two witnesses' reports.

preposition **among**
Please distribute these supplies **among** the various departments on this floor.

Among themselves the board members had consented previously to withdraw their bid to acquire this software company.

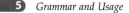

5-33 Prepositions Used With Certain Words

Certain words require particular prepositions, depending upon the meaning to be conveyed. Other words often acquire prepositions incorrectly. A list of commonly used correct combinations follows:

Agree **on** or **upon** (mutual ideas or considerations—to reach an understanding)

Agree **to** (undertake an action)

Agree **with** (a person or his or her idea)

All **of** (Use *of* when followed by a pronoun; omit *of* when followed by a noun. *All of us . . . . All the people . . . .*)

Angry **about** (a situation or condition)

Angry **at** (things)

Angry **with** (a person or a group of persons)

Both **of** (Use *of* when followed by a pronoun; omit *of* when followed by a noun. *Both of them . . . . Both the managers . . . .*)

Buy **from** (Not *off* or *off of*)

Compare **to** (Use to show a likeness.)

Compare **with** (Use to look for differences as well as similarities.)

Comply or compliance **with** (Not *to*)

Conform **to** (To act in accordance with prevailing standards.)

Conform **with** (To be similar or in agreement)

Convenient **to** (a location)

Convenient **for** (a person)

Correspond **with** (a person—by writing)

Correspond **to** (a thing)

Different **from** (Not *than*)

Discrepancy **in** (one thing)

Discrepancy **between** (two things)

Discrepancy **among** (three or more things)

From (a person) (Not *off* a person)

Help (doing something) (He could not *help* laughing at . . . .) (Not *help from*)

Identical **with** (Not *to*)

Inside (Not *inside of*)

Off (a thing) (Not *off of*)

Opposite (Not *opposite to* or *opposite of*)

Outside (Not *outside of*)

Plan **to** (Not *plan on*)

Retroactive **to** (Not *retroactive from*)

Take **off** (a thing)

Take **from** (a person)

Conjunctions

Conjunctions join words or groups of words within a sentence. While some conjunctions join equal ideas, others join contrasting ideas or introduce dependent clauses.

5-34 Coordinating Conjunctions

a. The most commonly occurring coordinating conjunctions—*and, but, or,* and *nor*—are used to join like or equal ideas within a sentence. These ideas may be words, phrases, or clauses.

words

Please place a copy of the **proposal** and the **contract** in each client's file.

You may obtain additional information from **Mr. Parr**, **Ms. Dow**, or **me**.

phrases

Please post these notices **on all bulletin boards** and **in student gathering places** throughout the campus.

Ms. Ross has agreed to **edit the manuscript** and **follow it through all the production stages**.

clauses

If you accept our offer, **we will sign a guarantee of completion by May 1** and **you will be protected against any losses until this date**.

Our advertising funds for this year have been spent, but **we are interested in considering your proposal for next year's budget.**

b. Because coordinating conjunctions join equal ideas, the ideas they join must be expressed in the same way; that is, they must have *parallel structure.* Parallel structure requires that the connected ideas have the same format. For example, if the first idea begins with a noun or pronoun, so must any others. If the first idea begins with an infinitive, then all others must begin with an infinitive. Be sure to match each idea—gerund with gerund, verb with verb, prepositional phrase with prepositional phrase, and so forth.

parallel structure with gerunds

You may obtain your free trial subscription by **calling** our toll-free number or **returning** the enclosed postcard.

We would appreciate your **paying** this bill by November 1 and **sending** us a copy of the receipt issued at the time of payment.

parallel structure with verb phrases (past participles)

The contractor has **leveled** the site and **poured** the foundation.

As you requested, we have **notified** our delinquent customers of their status, **requested** immediate payment of all overdue amounts, and **halted** any charge orders in progress.

parallel structure with clauses (subject and verb)

As soon as we receive your loan approval, **the bank will release** the money and **we will open** an escrow account.

Our local **chamber of commerce has endorsed** this project, but **chambers of commerce** in surrounding cities **are opposed** to it.

5-35 Conjunctions Used in Pairs

a. Use *either . . . or* for positive statements; use *neither . . . nor* for negative statements. The same grammatical construction should be used after each part.

positive statements, either . . . or

Either Ms. Saunders **or** Mr. Ramirez will inspect the property.

Be sure to specify a room with **either** an ocean view **or** a mountain view when you make your hotel reservations.

negative statements, neither . . . nor

XYZ Car Rental has **neither** an Explorer **nor** a Suburban available for rent next week.

Neither the patient's husband **nor** her children have been notified about the apparent success of the surgery.

b. Use the same grammatical construction after each part of the conjunctive pair *not only . . . but also*.

Our company manufactures **not only** commercial restaurant appliances **but also** household kitchen appliances. (Not: Our company *not only* manufactures commercial restaurant appliances *but also* household kitchen appliances.)

Our company **not only** manufactures and services major appliances **but also** services small appliances.

c. In comparisons use *as . . . as* for positive ideas and *so . . . as* for negative ideas.

positive ideas, **as . . . as**

Our Model 874 cellular phone has become **as** popular **as** our Model 923.

I believe that her understudy is **as** talented **as** Ms. Saito.

negative ideas, **so . . . as**

Our Model 874 cellular phone is not **so** popular **as** our Model 923.

Avocados are not **so** expensive **as** they were last year.

5-36 Subordinating Conjunctions

Words such as *if, when, as, since,* and *because* (subordinating conjunctions) may be used to introduce word groups (dependent clauses). A partial listing of subordinating conjunctions follows:

if	because	while
as	since	before
when	although	after

a. When a subordinating conjunction with its corresponding clause introduces a sentence, place a comma after the introductory clause.

If you wish any additional information, please call me at (626) 555-3782.

Before you sign the contract, you should speak with some of All-State Fencing's former clients.

b. When a subordinating conjunction with its corresponding clause follows a main clause, separate the two clauses with a comma only if the subordinating conjunction introduces an additional or nonessential (nonrestrictive) idea.

no comma separating clauses—essential (restrictive) idea

We will ship the porcelain figurines **as soon as we receive authorization from your credit card company**.

You should verify this information **before you purchase these bonds**.

comma separating clauses—additional (nonrestrictive) idea

Mr. Johnson would be pleased to supply you with any additional information, **if you need it**.

My clients have agreed to settle this matter out of court, **although I advised them against doing so**.

5-37 *As* Vs. *Like*

As is a conjunction and is used when the following construction is a clause (a word group containing a subject and a verb). *Like* is a preposition and is used when the construction results in a prepositional phrase (a phrase ending with a noun or pronoun).

5

Grammar and Usage

181

as *introducing a clause*

The shipping clerk did not package the order **as** (not *like*) **I had expected he would.**

As (not *like*) **you indicated in your E-mail message**, we cannot expect to show a profit during our first year of operation.

like *introducing a prepositional phrase*

We need to hire more qualified agents **like Terry**.

Please order another desk **like the one** you have in your office.

Interjections

5-38 Use of Interjections

Interjections impart sudden emotion or strong feeling, but they do not contribute substantially to the meaning of the sentence. When used alone, interjections are followed by an exclamation mark. When they are used within a sentence, the sentence is generally concluded with an exclamation mark. Examples of interjections used alone follow:

Absolutely not!	Never!	Well!
Ah!	No!	Whew!
Great!	Oh!	Wow!
Indeed not!	Terrific!	Yes!

interjections used alone

Whew! I'm certainly glad the work for this tax period is behind us.

Absolutely not! Only employees with security clearances are permitted in this area.

interjections in sentences

Oh, you can't expect us to have these photographs developed by tomorrow!

No, we cannot make any exceptions to this company policy!

6

Abbreviations and Symbols

c.o.d.

Abbreviations and Symbols Solution Finder

Abbreviations

6-1 Use of Abbreviations

a. Use abbreviations only when you are confident the reader understands their meaning. Confine your primary use of abbreviations to (1) business forms; (2) suitable technical documents; and (3) tables, charts, graphs, and other such visual aids.

b. Limit your use of abbreviations in running copy. If used, write out the words and place the abbreviation in parentheses the first time the words are used.

Before filing this tax return, please check with the **Internal Revenue Service (IRS)** on the legitimacy of this deduction. Several recent **IRS** rulings in this area may affect the client's ability to use these losses as a deduction.

c. Throughout your document use consistently the same form for an abbreviated word or sequence of words.

Application deadlines for admittance to **Florida State University (FSU)** are due by January 31. Housing requests for **FSU** are due by March 1. (Not: *Florida State*)

6-2 Titles

a. The abbreviations *Mr.*, *Ms.*, *Mrs.*, and *Dr.* are used for courtesy titles.

Mr. Robert Gregg   **Mrs.** Jill Binsley
Ms. Lena Sabawi   **Dr.** Jeremy Cole

b. Write out a civil, educational, military, or religious title used before and in conjunction with a person's full name or last name only. Lengthy titles (those containing more than one word) may be abbreviated, however, when they appear before a person's *full* name and brevity is required.

title written out—with full name

This semester **Professor** Donna-Mae Villanueva is teaching the advanced communications class.

title written out—with last name only

Dear **Governor** Hendricks:

The keynote convention speaker will be **Lieutenant Governor** Garabedian.

title abbreviated—with full name

You may contact **Lt. Col.** Barrie Logan for further information. (Lieutenant Colonel)

6
Abbreviations

c. **Abbreviate and capitalize personal titles (*Jr., Sr., Esq.*, etc.), professional designations (*CPA, CLU, R.N., R.P.T.*, etc.), or academic degrees (*M.D., Ph.D., Ed.D., LL.B., M.L.S.*, etc.) that follow a person's name. A comma is used before and after an abbreviation appearing within a sentence and before an abbreviation appearing at the end of a sentence. The personal titles *Jr.* and *Sr.* may appear with or without commas, depending on the individual's preference.**

Abbreviations of academic degrees and professional designations are separated by periods except for the designations *CPA* (Certified Public Accountant), *CPS* (Certified Professional Secretary), *CAP* (Certified Administrative Professional), *PLS* (Professional Legal Secretary), and *CLU* (Chartered Life Underwriter).

personal title

William J. Armstrong **Jr.** was recently elected to the Springfield Board of Education.

This suite of hotel rooms has been reserved for Charles T. Wellington, **Sr.**

Please send a copy of the report to Robert Lucio, **Esq.**, by March 1.

professional designation

Ana Tobar, **CPA**, will be in charge of the audit for Weisfeld Industries.

The surgery floor supervisor during that shift is Michael Yano, **R.N.**

academic degree

Direct all student complaints to Joy McCaslin, **Ph.D.**, our vice president of student services.

This journal article on spinal cord injuries was written by Dorothy Salazar, **M.D.**

6-3 Organizations

a. **The names of well-known business, educational, governmental, professional, military, labor, philanthropic, and other organizations or agencies may be abbreviated. No periods or spaces are used to separate the individual letters.**

business organizations

ARCO	Atlantic Richfield Company
BA	Bank of America Corporation
GE	General Electric Company
GMC	General Motors Corporation
IBM	International Business Machines Corporation
IP	International Paper Company
AA	American Airlines, Inc.

educational organizations

ERIC	Educational Resources Information Center
NYU	New York University
PCC	Pasadena City College
UCLA	University of California, Los Angeles

governmental organizations

CIA	Central Intelligence Agency
FBI	Federal Bureau of Investigation
FCC	Federal Communications Commission
FDA	Food and Drug Administration
FTC	Federal Trade Commission
HUD	Department of Housing and Urban Development
ICC	Interstate Commerce Commission
OSHA	Occupational Safety and Health Administration
SEC	Securities and Exchange Commission
SSA	Social Security Administration
UNESCO	United Nations Educational, Scientific, and Cultural Organization
USDA	U.S. Department of Agriculture
USPS	U.S. Postal Service
VA	Veterans Administration

professional organizations

ABA	American Bankers Association; American Bar Association
ABC	Association for Business Communication
AIA	American Institute of Architects
AIB	American Institute of Banking
AMA	American Medical Association
IAAP	International Association of Administrative Professionals
NBEA	National Business Education Association

other organizations

AAA	American Automobile Association
AFL-CIO	American Federation of Labor and Congress of Industrial Organizations
BBB	Better Business Bureau
NAACP	National Association for the Advancement of Colored People
NOW	National Organization for Women
YMCA	Young Men's Christian Association
YWCA	Young Women's Christian Association

b. **Television and radio station call letters are written in all capital letters without periods or spaces.**

ABC   CBS   CNN   KFI   KNXT   PBS   NBC

6

Abbreviations

c. In the names of business firms, abbreviations such as *Co.*, *Corp.*, *Inc.*, *Ltd.*, and *Mfg.* are used only if they are part of the official organizational name.

We are still awaiting the remainder of our order from Century **Mfg. Co.**

Brockton Computers, **Inc.**, submitted the lowest bid to install our network.

6-4 Dates and Time

a. Spell out days of the week and months of the year. Abbreviate them only in lists, tables, graphs, charts, illustrations, or other such visual displays where space is limited.

days and months spelled out in text

Our grand opening is scheduled for **Friday, October 9**.

By **Wednesday, January 21**, we must have our annual report ready to be mailed.

days of the week abbreviated in graphics

Sun.	Mon.	Tues. (Tue.)	Wed.	Thurs. (Thu.)	Fri.	Sat.
Su	M	Tu	W	Th	F	Sa

months of the year abbreviated in graphics

Jan.	Feb.	Mar.	Apr.	May	June (Jun.)
July (Jul.)	Aug.	Sept. (Sep.)	Oct.	Nov.	Dec.

b. The abbreviations *a.m.* (ante meridiem) and *p.m.* (post meridiem) are used for expressing clock time. They are placed in lowercase letters followed by periods. No space follows the first period.

Would you prefer to take the flight at 8:45 **a.m.** or the one at 2 **p.m.**?

All our departmental meetings are scheduled at 3:30 **p.m.**

c. United States time zones—*EST* (Eastern Standard Time), *CST* (Central Standard Time), *MST* (Mountain Standard Time), *PST* (Pacific Standard Time), *AST* (Alaska Standard Time), and *HST* (Hawaii Standard Time)—are usually abbreviated. Time zones for daylight saving time are abbreviated *EDT, CDT, MDT, PDT,* and *ADT.* Hawaii does not have daylight saving time.

Operators are available to take telephone orders from 8 a.m. until 10 p.m., **EST**.

John's flight is scheduled to arrive in Denver at 2:38 p.m., **MDT**.

d. The abbreviations *B.C.* (before Christ) and *A.D.* (anno Domini) are sometimes used in expressing dates. Both follow the year and are shown in capital letters (or small caps) with periods. In formal writing, however, *A.D.* appears before the year.

B.C.

Professor Reinhardt has substantiated that these artifacts date back to 600 **B.C.** (or B.C.)

A.D. *after the year*

Ms. Lopez's thesis deals with the rise of Christianity from 200 to 350 A.D. (or **A.D.**)

A.D. *before the year*

The Spanish legions, under the leadership of Galba, conquered Rome in **A.D.** 68 (or A.D. 68).

6-5 Standard Units of Measure

Common units of measure—distance, length, temperature, volume, and weight—are usually spelled out in business documents. Abbreviations, however, may be used on invoices, packing slips, and other business forms where space is limited. In abbreviating units of measure, place periods after one-word abbreviations and use the singular form. Omit the periods in abbreviations representing more than one word.

general business documents

All perishable goods shipped over **100 miles** should be kept below **40 degrees** Fahrenheit.

business forms, one-word abbreviations

15 **ft.** 4 **in.** (15 feet 4 inches)   7 **lb.** 6 **oz.** (7 pounds 6 ounces)

68°F (68 degrees Fahrenheit)   4 **doz.** pens (4 dozen pens)

business forms, multiple-word abbreviations

120 **wpm** (120 words per minute)   65 **mph** (65 miles per hour)

6-6 Metric Units of Measure

a. **In standard business documents metric units of measure are generally written out. However, in forms, tables, technical writing, and scientific writing, they are often abbreviated. These abbreviations are written without periods, and the singular and plural forms are the same. Common abbreviations for measurements related to distance, weight, and volume follow:**

prefixes

deka	**da**	($\times$ 10)	deci	**d**	(1/10)
hecto	**h**	($\times$ 100)	centi	**c**	(1/100)
kilo	**k**	($\times$ 1000)	milli	**m**	(1/1000)
mega	**m**	($\times$ 1 000 000)			
giga	**g**	($\times$ 1 000 000 000)			

6

Abbreviations

common units of measure

meter	**m**	centimeter	**cm**	kilometer	**km**
gram	**g**	kilogram	**kg**	milligram	**mg**
liter	**L**	milliliter	**ml**		

cubic centimeter	**cc**	square meter	**sq m**
kilobyte	**KB**	megabyte	**MB**	gigabyte	**GB**

b. The abbreviation for *liter* is a capital *L* because the lowercase letter *l* and the numeral *1* (one) in many fonts look the same. Therefore, to avoid confusion, the capital *L* is used instead.

1 **L** milk *but* 1 **ml** vaccine (abbreviation is clear)

c. Temperatures in the metric system are expressed on the Celsius scale. This term is abbreviated *C*.

37°**C** 25°**C**

d. Express abbreviations related to kilometers per hour with a diagonal.

The maximum speed limit on our city expressways is **105 km/h** (65 mph).

Slow down to **40 km/h** (25 mph) in the school crossing zone.

6–7 Business and General Terms

a. When the word *number* is not followed by a numeral, write it in full. The abbreviation *No.* is used when a numeral directly follows the word unless the word begins the sentence.

The catalog **number** of the Atlas laser diskette labels is **6-487**.

We plan to increase our stock of **No. 98702** Solar digital cameras.

Please order two **Model No. 2024D** color laser printers.

Number 138-B replacement shelves must be ordered directly from the manufacturer.

b. Most commonly abbreviated business, computer, and Internet terms are written in all capital letters with no spaces or periods separating the letters. A few business terms, when used in business correspondence, however, are written in lowercase letters separated by periods. See Section 6–11 for an additional listing of business and computer terms.

capitalized abbreviation of business terms

FIFO	(first in, first out)
LIFO	(last in, first out)
PERT	(program evaluation and review technique)
SOP	(standard operating procedures)
TQM	(total quality management)

capitalized abbreviation of computer terms

CPU   (central processing unit)
EDP   (electronic data processing)
OCR   (optical character recognition)
RAM   (random-access memory)
WYSIWYG   (what you see is what you get)

capitalized abbreviation of Internet terms

DSL   (digital subscriber line)
HTML   (hypertext markup language)
ISP   (Internet service provider)
PDF   (Portable Document Format)
WWW (World Wide Web)

lowercase letters for abbreviation in correspondence

c.o.d.   (collect on delivery)   f.o.b.   (free on board)

c. Capitalize and abbreviate the word *extension* (*Ext.*) when it appears in conjunction with telephone numbers.

For further information call 439-1884, **Ext.** 6420, any weekday between 8 a.m. and 5 p.m.

Please respond to this invitation by telephoning (800) 555-8237, **Ext.** 373.

d. Some commonly abbreviated terms are derived from Latin expressions. They are generally keyed in lowercase letters and are followed by a period at the close of each abbreviated word.

abbreviations from Latin expressions

e.g.	(for example)	viz.	(namely)
et al.	(and others)	ibid.	(in the same place)
i.e.	(that is)	loc. cit.	(in the place cited)
etc.	(and so forth)	op. cit.	(in the work cited)
cf.	(compare)	a.m.	(after midnight until noon)
pro tem.	(temporarily)	p.m.	(after noon until midnight)
id.	(the same)	B.C.	(year before Christ)
P.S.	(postscript)	A.D.	(year after Christ)
ad hoc	(for a specific purpose)	ca.	(approximately; around)
N.B.	(note well)		

6-8 Plurals

Apostrophes are not used to form the plurals of abbreviations; most plural abbreviations are formed by adding only *s* to the singular form. Some words, however, use the same abbreviation for the singular and plural forms.

6
Abbreviations

plural formed by adding s

hr., **hrs.**	IOU, **IOUs**
mgr., **mgrs.**	CPA, **CPAs**
c.o.d., **c.o.d.s**	R.N., **R.N.s**

singular and plural forms identical

deg., **deg.**   ft., **ft.**   in., **in.**

6-9 Addresses and Geographical Expressions

a. For addresses in business correspondence, street designations such as *Boulevard, Street, Avenue, Lane, Place*, and *Road* are written in full. *Boulevard*, however, may be abbreviated (*Blvd.*) if space is limited for expressing long street names.

street designation spelled out

Ms. Gita Brooks
130 Barrington **Avenue**
Iowa City, IA 52240

Paramount Real Estate Company
6840 Washington **Boulevard**
Columbus, OH 43266-0309

boulevard abbreviated with long street name

Mr. Joseph F. Campenelli
1140 San Fernando Mission **Blvd.**
San Francisco, CA 94127

b. Simple compass directions (*North, South, East, West*) that appear before a street name are spelled out. Compound directions such as *Northwest* or *Southeast*, however, are abbreviated whenever they appear either before or after the street name.

simple direction before street name

470 **East** Fountain Avenue

compound direction with street name

7500 Capitol Avenue, **N.E.**   3420 **S.W.** 43rd Street

c. The U.S. Postal Service recommends that the names of states be abbreviated on all mailings by using the official state designations. (They are displayed in capital letters with no periods or spaces.) These two-letter state designations are shown in Section 6–12 and on the page opposite the inside back cover.

However, since modern optical scanning equipment no longer requires the use of the two-letter designations, either the full state name or the two-letter state designation may be used, depending upon which form more nearly balances with the other lines of the address. If both forms provide balance, use the two-letter state designation.

two-letter state designation

Los Angeles Pierce College
6201 Winnetka Avenue
Woodland Hills, **CA** 91371

state spelled out fully

Diamond Publishing Company
11000 West Seventh Avenue
Ridgewood, **New Jersey** 07541

d. Since 1974 the U.S. Postal Service has recommended a format for addressing envelopes that uses all capital letters, abbreviations, and no internal punctuation marks. As yet, this format has not been widely accepted for individually prepared correspondence or even computer-generated form correspondence; its use has been mainly with standard bulk mailings.

e. A period is placed after each abbreviated word in geographical abbreviations. Only with the two-letter state designations recommended by the U.S. Postal Service are the periods omitted.

capital letters

U.S.A.	(United States of America)	U.K.	(United Kingdom)
G.B.	(Great Britain)	R.O.C.	(Republic of China)

capital and lowercase letters

So. Nev.	(Southern Nevada)	Ire. (Ireland)

postal service designation

MI	(Michigan)	UT (Utah)

6-10 **Abbreviation Format**

a. The capitalization of abbreviations is generally governed by the format of the original word or words. Proper nouns are always capitalized while common nouns generally appear in lowercase letters. Some common noun abbreviations, however, are capitalized.

capital letters for proper noun

Our company union is affiliated with the **AFL-CIO**.

lowercase letters for common noun

All these orders should be shipped **c.o.d.**

capital letters for some common nouns

Sales of **VCRs** this month have been greater than we expected.

Your **TV** cable company may offer high-speed Internet access.

6

Abbreviations

b. Abbreviations that appear in all capital letters are generally formatted without periods or spaces.

Exceptions are geographical expressions, most professional designations, and academic degrees, which contain periods but no spaces. Other exceptions are initials in a person's name and most abbreviations with capital and lowercase letters, which contain both periods and spaces.

general rule—no periods and no spaces
The story was first aired on **CBS** television.

For popular music from the '80s, turn your radio dial to **KNET** 160.

geographical expressions—periods with no spaces
Their travel agency in Bonn, Germany, sponsored several tours of the **U.S.A.** last summer.

Within the next month the **U.S.** Food and Drug Administration should approve this new medication.

Our new store location is 1760 Fillmore Street, **N.W.**

professional designations—periods with no spaces
Angela Ramos, **R.P.T.**, is the physical therapist who handled this case.

Will Brian Williams, **R.N.**, be the new director of our nursing program?

academic degrees—periods with no spaces
I believed Mr. Fujimoto earned an **M.S.** in computer science last year.

Sharon Lund O'Neil, **Ph.D.**, was offered the position.

initials—periods and spaces
Please deliver this report to Ms. **J. T.** Kelley.

Only Gerald **H.** Monroe applied for the position.

abbreviations with capital and lowercase letters—periods and spaces
So. Calif.   (Southern California)   **N. Mex.**   (New Mexico)

c. In abbreviations beginning with lowercase letters, a period is generally placed after each letter or group of letters representing a word. No space appears between periods and letters in compound abbreviations. Periods are not used, however, in abbreviations of metric measurements and compound abbreviations representing "measures per time."

general rule—periods

c.o.d.	(collect on delivery)	**mgr.**	(manager)
a.m.	(ante meridiem)	**qt.**	(quart)
ft.	(foot or feet)	**amt.**	(amount)

metric measurements—no periods

mm	millimeter		**ml**	milliliter
cm	centimeter		**kg**	kilogram
cc	cubic centimeter			

time measurements—no periods

rpm	revolutions per minute		**wam**	words a minute
wpm	words per minute		**mph**	miles per hour

d. If an abbreviation containing a period falls at the end of a sentence that requires a period, use only a single period. In a question or an exclamation, place a closing question or exclamation mark directly after the period appearing in the abbreviation.

period

Mr. Anzel asked to be awakened at **8 a.m.**

question mark

Did you send the order **c.o.d.?**

exclamation mark

The plane was three hours late arriving in the **U.S.A.!**

6-11 **Abbreviations of Terms Commonly Used in Business**

Abbreviation	Term
A.A.	associate in arts (degree)
acct.	account
A.D. (A.D.)	anno Domini (in the year of our Lord)
ad, advt.	advertisement
addnl.	additional
Adm.	admiral (military title)
adm., admin.	administration, administrative
ADT	Alaska Daylight Time
afft.	affidavit
agcy.	agency
agt.	agent
AI	artificial intelligence
a.k.a., AKA	also known as
a.m.	ante meridiem (before noon)
amt.	amount
ans.	answer
AP	accounts payable
approx.	approximately
APR	annual percentage rate (of interest)
Apr.	April
AR	accounts receivable
ARM	adjustable rate mortgage
A.S.	associate in science (degree)
ASAP	as soon as possible

6

Abbreviations

Abbreviation	Term
ASCII	American Standard Code for Information Interchange
assn., Assn., assoc., Assoc.	association
assoc., Assoc.	associate, associates
asst.	assistant
AST	Alaska Standard Time
ATM	automated teller machine
att.	attachment
attn.	attention
atty.	attorney
Aug.	August
AV	audiovisual
av., avg.	average
Ave.	Avenue
B.A., A.B.	bachelor of arts (degree)
bal.	balance
B.B.A.	bachelor of business administration (degree)
bbl.	barrel, barrels
B.C. (B.C.)	before Christ
BIOS	basic input-output system
bit	binary digit
bl.	bale, bales
B/L, BL	bill of lading
bldg.	building
BO	back order
bps	bits per second
Brig.	brigadier (military title)
bros., Bros.	brothers
B.S.	bachelor of science (degree)
B/S, BS	bill of sale
bu.	bushel, bushels
c	copy
C	Celsius
CAD/CAM	computer-aided drafting/computer-aided manufacturing
CAI	computer-aided instruction
cap.	capital
Capt.	captain
CAT	computer-aided transcription
cc	cubic centimeter
cc, CC	carbon copy, courtesy copy
CD	certificate of deposit, compact disc
CD-ROM	compact disk read-only memory
CDT	Central Daylight Time
CEO	chief executive officer
CFO	chief financial officer
cg	centigram
CGA	color graphics adapter

Abbreviation	Term
chg.	charge
c.i.f., CIF	cost, insurance, and freight
CLU	Chartered Life Underwriter
cm	centimeter
c/o	care of
co., Co.	company
COBOL	Common Business Oriented Language
c.o.d., COD	collect on delivery
Col.	colonel (military title)
COLA	cost-of-living adjustment
COM	computer output microfilm
comm.	commission, committee, community
cont.	continued
COO	chief operating officer
corp., Corp.	corporation
CPA	Certified Public Accountant
cpi	characters per inch
cps	characters per second
CPS	Certified Professional Secretary
CPU	central processing unit
cr.	credit
CRT	cathode-ray tube
CST	Central Standard Time
ctn.	carton
cu.	cubic
cwt.	hundredweight
D.A.	doctor of arts (degree)
D.B.A.	doctor of business administration (degree)
d.b.a., DBA	doing business as
DBMS	data base management system
D.D.	doctor of divinity (degree)
D.D.S.	doctor of dental surgery (degree)
Dec.	December
depr.	depreciation
dept.	department
disc., dis.	discount
dist.	district
distr.	distributed, distribution, distributor
div.	dividend; division
DJIA	Dow Jones Industrial Average
DOS	disk operating system
doz., dz.	dozen
DP	data processing
dpi	dots per inch
dr.	dram, drams
Dr.	doctor
Drs.	doctors
DSS	decision support system
DST	daylight saving time

Abbreviation	Term
dstn.	destination
dtd.	dated
DTP	desktop publishing
dup.	duplicate
D.V.M.	doctor of veterinary medicine (degree)
ea.	each
ed.	edition, editor
Ed.D.	doctor of education (degree)
EDP	electronic data processing
EDT	Eastern Daylight Time
e.g.	for example
EGA	enhanced graphics adapter
e-mail, E-mail	electronic mail (verb), electronic mail (noun)
enc., encl.	enclosure
EOF	end of file
e.o.m., EOM	end of month
Esq.	Esquire
EST	Eastern Standard Time
ETA	estimated time of arrival
exp.	expense
ext., Ext.	extension
F	Fahrenheit
f.a.s., FAS	free alongside ship
FAQ, FAQs	frequently asked question(s)
fax	facsimile
f.b.o., FBO	for the benefit of
Feb.	February
FIFO	first in, first out (inventory)
f.o.b., FOB	free on board
FORTRAN	FORmula TRANslator
Fri.	Friday
frt.	freight
ft.	foot, feet
FTP	file transfer protocol (Internet)
ft-tn	foot-ton, foot-tons
fwd.	forward
FY	fiscal year
FYI	for your information
g	gram
gal.	gallon, gallons
GB	gigabyte (billion bytes)
GDP	gross domestic product
gen.	general
Gen.	general (military title)
GIGO	garbage in, garbage out
GM	general manager
gov., govt.	government
gr.	gross
GUI	graphical user interface

Abbreviation	Term
hdlg.	handling
HMO	health maintenance organization
HP, hp	horsepower
HQ, hdqrs.	headquarters
HR	human relations, Human Resources (department)
hr.	hour
hrs.	hours
HST	Hawaii Standard Time
HTML	hypertext markup language
ID	identification data
i.e.	*id est* (that is)
in.	inch, inches
inc., Inc.	incorporated
incl.	includes, including
info	information
ins.	insurance
int.	interest
intl., intnl.	international
inv.	invoice
invt.	inventory
I/O	input/output
IOU	I owe you
ips	inches per second
IQ	intelligence quotient
IRA	individual retirement account
ISP	Internet service provider
Jan.	January
J.D.	doctor of jurisprudence, doctor of law (degrees)
K	thousand (in reference to computer disk or memory)
K, KB	kilobyte, kilobytes (thousand bytes)
kg	kilogram, kilograms
km	kilometer, kilometers
km/h	kilometers per hour
L	liter
l., ll.	line, lines
LAN	local area network
laser	light amplification stimulated emission radiation
lb.	pound, pounds
L/C	Letter of Credit
l.c.l., LCL	less-than-carload lot
LIFO	last in, first out (inventory)
LL.B.	bachelor of laws (degree)
lpm	lines per minute
Lt.	lieutenant
ltd., Ltd.	limited
m	meter
M.A.	master of arts (degree)

Abbreviation	Term
Maj.	major (military rank)
Mar.	March
max.	maximum
MB, M	megabyte, megabytes (million bytes)
M.B.A.	master of business administration (degree)
MC (represents *emcee*)	master of ceremonies, mistress of ceremonies
M.D.	doctor of medicine (degree)
mdse.	merchandise
MDT	Mountain Daylight Time
memo	memorandum
Messrs.	Misters
mfg., Mfg.	manufacturing
mfr.	manufacturer
mfrs.	manufacturers
mg	milligram, milligrams
mgr.	manager
mgt.	management
MHz	megahertz
mi.	mile, miles
min.	minute, minutes; minimum
MIS	management information system
misc.	miscellaneous
ml	milliliter, milliliters
mm	millimeter, millimeters
MO	mail order
MO	money order
mo.	month
mos.	months
modem	modulator/demodulator
Mon.	Monday
M.P.A.	master of public administration (degree)
mpg	miles per gallon
M.P.H.	master of public health (degree)
mph	miles per hour
Mr.	Mister
Mrs.	Mistress
M.S.	master of science (degree)
MSP	moved, seconded, and passed
MST	Mountain Standard Time
M.S.W.	master of social work (degree)
mtg.	meeting, mortgage
n/30	net in 30 days
NA	not applicable; not available
nat., natl.	national
ND	no date
No.	number
Nos.	numbers
Nov.	November
NSF	not sufficient funds

Abbreviation	Term
nt. wt.	net weight
OAG	*Official Airline Guide*
OC	overcharge
OCR	optical character recognition
Oct.	October
o.d., OD	overdraft
OK	okay
opt.	optional
org.	organization
orig.	original
O/S	out of stock
OS	operating system (computer)
OTC	over-the-counter
oz.	ounce, ounces
p.	page
PC	personal computer
pd.	paid
PDA	personal digital assistant
PDT	Pacific Daylight Time
PERT	program evaluation and review technique
p and h, P/H	postage and handling
Ph.D.	doctor of philosophy (degree)
phone	telephone
photo	photograph
PIN	personal identification number
pkg.	package
P & L, P/L	profit and loss
p.m.	post meridiem (after noon)
P.O.	post office
P.O., PO	purchase order
p.o.e., POE	port of entry
pp.	pages
ppd.	postpaid, prepaid
PR	public relations
pr., prs.	pair, pairs
pres.	president
PROM	programmable read-only memory
P.S., PS	postscript
PST	Pacific Standard Time
pt.	part; pint, pints
pt.	point
pts.	points
qr.	quire, quires
qt.	quart, quarts
qtr.	quarter, quarterly
qty.	quantity
RAM	random-access memory
R & D	research and development
recd.	received

6

Abbreviations

Abbreviation	Term
reg.	registered; regular
req.	requisition
ret.	retail
ret.	retired
retd.	returned
rev.	revised, revision
RFD	rural free delivery
rm.	ream, reams
ROM	read-only memory
rpm, RPM	revolutions per minute
R.S.V.P., RSVP	respond, if you please
rwy., ry.	railway
/S/	signed by
Sa., Sat.	Saturday
SASE	self-addressed, stamped envelope
sec.	second, seconds
sec., secy.	secretary
sect.	section
Sep., Sept.	September
Sgt.	sergeant
shpt.	shipment
shtg.	shortage
S.O., SO	shipping order
SOP	standard operating procedure
sq.	square
std.	standard
stge.	storage
stmt.	statement
Su., Sun.	Sunday
Th., Thu., Thurs.	Thursday
TQM	total quality management
treas.	treasurer
Tu., Tue., Tues.	Tuesday
TV	television
TWX	Western Union Teleprinter Exchange Service
UPC	Universal Product Code
URL	uniform resource locator (Web site address)
VAT	value-added tax
VCR	video cassette recorder
VDT	video display terminal
VGA	video graphics array
VIP	very important person
vol.	volume
V.P.	vice president
vs., v.	versus
wam	words a minute
WAN	wide area network
WATS	Wide Area Telephone Service
Wed.	Wednesday

Abbreviation	Term
whsle.	wholesale
wk.	week
wks.	weeks
w/o	without
wp	word processing
wpm	words per minute
wt.	weight
WWW	World Wide Web
WYSIWYG	What you see is what you get.
Y2K	year 2000
yd.	yard, yards
yr.	year
yrs.	years
zip, ZIP	Zone Improvement Plan

 ## Abbreviations of States and Territories

State or Territory	Two-Letter Postal Designation	Standard Abbreviation
Alabama	AL	Ala.
Alaska	AK	—
Arizona	AZ	Ariz.
Arkansas	AR	Ark.
California	CA	Calif., Cal.
Colorado	CO	Colo., Col.
Connecticut	CT	Conn.
Delaware	DE	Del.
District of Columbia	DC	D.C.
Florida	FL	Fla.
Georgia	GA	Ga.
Guam	GU	—
Hawaii	HI	—
Idaho	ID	—
Illinois	IL	Ill.
Indiana	IN	Ind.
Iowa	IA	—
Kansas	KS	Kans., Kan.
Kentucky	KY	Ky.
Louisiana	LA	La.
Maine	ME	—
Maryland	MD	Md.
Massachusetts	MA	Mass.
Michigan	MI	Mich.
Minnesota	MN	Minn.
Mississippi	MS	Miss.
Missouri	MO	Mo.
Montana	MT	Mont.
Nebraska	NE	Nebr., Neb.
Nevada	NV	Nev.

6

Abbreviations

203

State or Territory	Two-Letter Postal Designation	Standard Abbreviation
New Hampshire	NH	N.H.
New Jersey	NJ	N.J.
New Mexico	NM	N. Mex.
New York	NY	N.Y.
North Carolina	NC	N.C.
North Dakota	ND	N. Dak.
Ohio	OH	—
Oklahoma	OK	Okla.
Oregon	OR	Oreg., Ore.
Pennsylvania	PA	Pa., Penn., Penna.
Puerto Rico	PR	P.R.
Rhode Island	RI	R.I.
South Carolina	SC	S.C.
South Dakota	SD	S. Dak.
Tennessee	TN	Tenn.
Texas	TX	Tex.
Utah	UT	—
Vermont	VT	Vt.
Virgin Islands	VI	V.I.
Virginia	VA	Va.
Washington	WA	Wash.
West Virginia	WV	W. Va.
Wisconsin	WI	Wis., Wisc.
Wyoming	WY	Wyo.

6-13 **Two-Letter Postal Designations for Canadian Provinces and Territories**

Province or Territory	Designation	Province or Territory	Designation
Alberta	AB	Nova Scotia	NS
British Columbia	BC	Nunavut	NT
Labrador	LB	Ontario	ON
Manitoba	MB	Prince Edward Island	PE
New Brunswick	NB	Quebec	QC
Newfoundland	NF	Saskatchewan	SK
Northwest Territories	NT	Yukon Territory	YT

Contractions

6-14 **Contractions**

a. Contractions are similar to abbreviations in that they are shortened forms. Unlike most abbreviations, however, contractions always contain an apostrophe to indicate where letters have been omitted. The use of single-word contractions is generally limited to business forms and tables. Some common single-word contractions follow:

ack'd	(acknowledged)	rec't	(receipt)
ass't	(assistant)	add'l	(additional)
gov't	(government)	cont'd	(continued)
nat'l	(national)	'03	(2003)

b. A second kind of contraction occurs with verb forms. By using an apostrophe to indicate where letters have been omitted, two words may be combined into one. The use of verb contractions is generally limited to informal business writing. A sampling of commonly used verb contractions follows:

aren't	(are not)	weren't	(were not)
shouldn't	(should not)	I'll	(I will)
can't	(cannot)	what's	(what is)
should've	(should have)	I'm	(I am)
couldn't	(could not)	where's	(where is)
that's	(that is)	isn't	(is not)
didn't	(did not)	who's	(who is)
there's	(there is)	it's	(it is)
doesn't	(does not)	won't	(will not)
they're	(they are)	I've	(I have)
don't	(do not)	wouldn't	(would not)
wasn't	(was not)	let's	(let us)
hasn't	(has not)	you'd	(you would)
we'll	(we will)	she's	(she is)
haven't	(have not)	you're	(you are)
we're	(we are)	you've	(you have)
he's	(he is)		

Symbols

6-15 Symbols on the Standard Computer Keyboard

a. Except for the dollar sign ($) in amounts of money, the asterisk (*) in unnumbered footnotes, and the ampersand (&) in company names, avoid using symbols in running copy. Limit the use of symbols to business forms, statistical material, tables, charts, graphs, and other documents or visuals where space is limited.

dollar sign, asterisk, and ampersand in running copy

Unauthorized charges of **$247.56**, **$153.29**, and **$73.20** appeared on last month's credit card statement.

Use **ASCII*** characters to prepare your résumé for this on-line career center.

We have retained **Leavitt, Kahn & Moss** to handle this legal matter for our firm.

symbols in forms, statistical materials, and visuals

4 @ $7.95   #833   37#   46%   6'1" tall   20:1

b. Use standard keys on the computer keyboard for the following commonly used symbols:

Symbol	Description	Examples
/	abbreviated word separator	c/o, w/o
&	and (ampersand)	Johnson & Sons, Inc. AT&T
@	at, each	12 @ $59.95
	at (Internet domain)	ClarksHOW@aol.com
x	by	8 x 10 inches
"	ditto, same as (quotation marks)	10 unformatted floppy disks 20 IBM formatted " "
/	divided by (diagonal)	July Sales/Annual Sales $27,500/3
$	dollar, dollars	$2,843.62
=	equals	Price + Tax = Cost
'	foot/feet (apostrophe)	14' x 16' room, 5'6" tall
/	fraction separator (diagonal)	1/2, 2/3, 3/4
>	greater than	100 > 90
"	inch/inches (quotation marks)	8 1/2" x 11"
<	less than	90 < 100
–	minus	Price – Discount, 75 – 50
'	minute, minutes (apostrophe)	60' sessions
x	multiplied by	12 x 12 = 144
*	multiplied by (asterisk)	12 * 12 = 144
#	number	#568712, #3 pencil
%	percent	87.2%
+	plus	Principal + Interest, 8 + 4
#	pound, pounds	24# paper
:	ratio (colon)	3:1 ratio
"	second, seconds (quotation marks)	5" intervals
*	unnumbered footnote (asterisk)	. . . for diacritical marks.*
/	word separator (diagonal)	and/or

6-16 Symbols Not on the Standard Computer Keyboard

Many commonly used symbols do not appear on the standard computer keyboard. Contemporary word processing programs, though, have extended character sets and provide access to many of these symbols. With just a few keystrokes or mouse movements, you can access the following symbols:

Symbol	Description	Examples
¢	cents	85¢
©	copyright	Copyright © 2004 by South-Western Publishing
°	degree, degrees	72°
÷	divided by	144 ÷ 12 = 12
–	en dash	pages 41–47, March 11–14
—	em dash	We have three colors in this style—red, blue, and black.
½	fractions	$\frac{1}{2}$, $\frac{1}{4}$, $\frac{3}{4}$, $2\frac{1}{3}$, $25\frac{3}{8}$
≥	greater than or equal to	≥ 10
≤	less than or equal to	≤ 12
é	letter with diacritical mark	résumé, La Cañada, Fraülein
∓	minus or plus	∓4
¶	paragraph, paragraphs	¶23, ¶¶123–132
‖	parallel to	Main Street ‖ Hill Street
±	plus or minus	±$2
®	registered	Kinko's®, Pentium®
§	section, sections	§12, §§56–59
SM	service mark	The new way to office.SM
√	square root	$\sqrt{4} = 2$
Σ	sum	Σn = 286
TM	trademark	The Computer Inside.TM

7

Words Often Confused and Misused

a / an

Words Often Confused and Misused Solution Finder

All entries in this chapter appear in alphabetical order. Audible pronunciations for all these words may be obtained on-line without charge at the Merriam-Webster Web site—<http://www.m-w.com>.

A/An

A (ARTICLE; used before a word beginning with a consonant sound or a long *ū* sound)—We will need the services of ***a t***echnician to solve this network problem. ***A u***nion representative met with us yesterday.

An (ARTICLE; used before a word beginning with a vowel sound other than long *ū*)—Please make ***an a***ppointment for me to meet with Señor Lopez while I am in Puerto Rico.

A lot/Allot/Alot

A lot (ARTICLE + NOUN; combination meaning "many" or "much")—***A lot*** of our clients from Germany will be attending our user conference. We have spent ***a lot*** of time investigating your proposal.

Allot (VERB; to allocate, assign)—How much of the budget should we ***allot*** for Internet advertising next year?

Alot (misspelling of *a lot*)

A while/Awhile

A while (ARTICLE + NOUN; combination meaning "a short time")—After using speech-recognition software for ***a while***, you will wonder why you didn't rely on voice input sooner.

Awhile (ADVERB; meaning "*for* a short time")—Exercise ***awhile*** each day to maintain your good health.

Accede/Exceed

Accede (VERB; to agree or consent)—I will ***accede*** to this request for new carpeting only if the tenants sign another one-year lease.

Exceed (VERB; to surpass a limit)—Most accidents occur when drivers ***exceed*** the posted speed limit.

Accelerate/Exhilarate

Accelerate (VERB; to speed up)—We must ***accelerate*** our progress in providing speech access to the Internet if we wish to increase our sales for high-end PDAs (personal digital assistants).

Exhilarate (VERB; to make cheerful; to refresh or stimulate)—News that our office was No. 1 in sales ***exhilarated*** the entire staff. The crisp, fresh air at Blue Pines Resort ***exhilarated*** everyone who attended the retreat.

Accept/Except

Accept (VERB; to take or receive)—We do not ***accept*** two-party checks or checks written on out-of-state banks.

Except (PREPOSITION; with the exclusion of, but)—Everyone in the company ***except*** Tyler Moore has received his or her overtime bonus payment for November.

Access/Excess

Access (NOUN; admittance or approachability)—Only authorized personnel should have *access* to these student files. How many people in your company have *access* to the president?

Excess (ADJECTIVE; beyond ordinary limits; a surplus)—You may return all *excess* flooring materials for full credit within 60 days of purchase.

Ad/Add

Ad (NOUN; abbreviated form of *advertisement*)—We sold the entire lot of these municipal bonds by running an *ad* in Sunday's edition of the *Los Angeles Times*.

Add (VERB; to increase by uniting or joining)—These new computers will *add* to the productivity of our office staff.

Adapt/Adept/Adopt

Adapt (VERB; to adjust or modify)—We must readily *adapt* ourselves to new situations in this rapidly changing market.

Adept (ADJECTIVE; skilled)—All our customer service representatives must be *adept* at dealing with irate callers.

Adopt (VERB; to take and follow as one's own)—We will *adopt* Mrs. Williams' proposal to computerize our accounting system.

Add: see Ad.

Addict/Edict

Addict (NOUN; one who is habitually or obsessively dependent; devotee)—Our clinic has noted success with the rehabilitation of drug *addicts*. Many of today's teenagers are rock music *addicts*.

Edict (NOUN; order or command)—When did our manager issue this *edict*?

Addition/Edition

Addition (NOUN; the process of uniting or joining; an added part)—Increased production quotas have resulted in the *addition* of factory floor space in two of our facilities. When will the new *addition* to your home be completed?

Edition (NOUN; a particular version of printed material)—Only the tenth *edition* of this reference manual is now available from the publisher.

Adept: see Adapt.

Adherence/Adherents

Adherence (NOUN; a steady attachment or loyalty)—Strict *adherence* to all safety procedures is required of all personnel.

Adherents (NOUN; loyal supporters or followers)—The many *adherents* to the space program believe in its importance to the human race.

Adopt: see Adapt.

Adverse/Averse

Adverse (ADJECTIVE; opposing; antagonistic)—Rising interest rates have had an *adverse* effect on real estate sales and new home developments.

7

Misused Words

Averse (ADJECTIVE; unwilling; reluctant)—One of Sandy's many attributes is that she is not *averse* to working overtime to meet specific deadlines.

Advice/Advise

Advice (NOUN; a suggestion, an opinion, or a recommendation)—He could have avoided further legal problems had he followed his attorney's *advice*.

Advise (VERB; to counsel or recommend)—Did you *advise* her not to sign the contract in its present form?

Affect/Effect

Affect (VERB; to influence)—Large pay increases throughout the country will *affect* the rate of inflation. Increased costs will *affect* our pricing policies on all merchandise.

Effect (VERB; to bring about or cause to happen; to create)—Rising costs of raw materials will *effect* large price increases in our products. Our government plans to *effect* a change in the rate of inflation by tightening bank credits.

Effect (NOUN; a result or consequence)—Inflation usually has a negative *effect* on our economy. The company's new vacation policy has had no apparent *effect* on boosting employee morale.

Aggravate/Irritate

Aggravate (VERB; to make something worse or more serious; to produce inflammation in)—To bring in legal counsel at this time would only *aggravate* the situation further. By scratching the infected area, you will only *aggravate* the itching and puffiness.

Irritate (VERB; to create an annoying condition)—If you do not refund the full purchase price, you will surely *irritate* the customer.

Aid/Aide

Aid (VERB; to help or assist. NOUN; assistance)—The United States *aids* many foreign countries. Your application for financial *aid* is currently being processed.

Aide (NOUN; a person who assists another)—Please ask your *aide* to deliver these papers to Dr. Powell's office by Friday afternoon.

Aisle/Isle

Aisle (NOUN; a passageway for inside traffic)—After each showing the *aisles* of the theater are littered with empty popcorn containers and candy wrappers.

Isle (NOUN; a piece of land surrounded by water, island)—This script centers around two teenagers marooned on a tropical *isle*. The state of Hawaii has a number of beautiful tropical *isles.*

All ready/Already

All ready (ADJECTIVE; prepared)—Our college is *all ready* to offer distance learning courses in business law, marketing, and small-business management next semester.

Already (ADVERB; by or before this time)—Orders for our August sale have *already* been placed with the suppliers.

All right/Alright

All right (ADJECTIVE; satisfactory or agreeable)—Changing your vacation dates from June to July seems to be *all right* with our supervisor.

Alright (An informal spelling of *all right* that is not appropriate for business writing.)

All together/Altogether

All together (ADVERB + ADVERB; wholly as a group; counted or summed up)—We must work *all together* if the company is to survive this crisis. *All together*, 87 families signed up for the company picnic.

Altogether (ADVERB; entirely or completely; in all; on the whole)—This problem is *altogether* different from the one we faced last year. We believe he has embezzled more than $150,000 *altogether*. Although we did not reach our goal of $3 million in sales, our company's progress may *altogether* be considered successful.

All ways/Always

All ways (ADJECTIVE + NOUN; by all methods)—We must try *all ways* possible to increase Internet access for our rapidly expanding list of on-line subscribers.

Always (ADVERB; at all times, continually)—Our agency is *always* looking for qualified office personnel with experience in Word, Excel, and PowerPoint.

Allot: see A lot.

Allowed/Aloud

Allowed (VERB; permitted)—Our company is *allowed* to sell its cosmetic line only through contracted retail outlets.

Aloud (ADVERB; audibly)—The president's resignation was read *aloud* to all board members present.

Allude/Elude

Allude (VERB; to mention or refer to)—As proof of Americans' lack of concern for economy, I *allude* to the increased popularity of SUVs during recent years.

Elude (VERB; to evade or escape)—The senator has been able to *elude* severe criticisms of his program by anticipating and counteracting objections.

Allusion/Delusion/Illusion

Allusion (NOUN; an indirect reference)—Several *allusions* were made to Mr. Reed's apparent inability to submit reports in a timely fashion.

Delusion (NOUN; a false belief instilled through purposeful deception)—Investors purchased these oil stocks because they were under the *delusion* that the company's wells were active producers.

Illusion (NOUN; a perception of something that is a misinterpretation of its actual nature)—Many employees had the *illusion* that this new electronic inventory system would reduce our staff, but they were pleased to learn that it would only increase management's ability to control inventory.

Almost/Most

Almost (ADVERB; nearly)—By the end of the third quarter, this company had sold *almost* 600,000 copies of its low-end voice-recognition software through on-line sources.

Most (ADJECTIVE; the greatest in amount or number)—Patricia Lynn received the *most* votes in the election for faculty senate treasurer.

Alot: see A lot.

Aloud: see Allowed.

Already: see All ready.

Alright: see All right.

Altar/Alter

Altar (NOUN; a structure used for worship)—The wedding flowers are to be placed on the *altar* by 6 p.m.

Alter (VERB; to change)—Please *alter* your teaching schedule so that you will be available to attend the monthly meeting of department chairs.

Alternate/Alternative

Alternate (VERB ['ȯl-tər-ˌnāt], to change from one to another repeatedly; NOUN ['ȯl-tər-nət], one that substitutes for another; ADJECTIVE ['ȯl-tər-nət], separate and distinct)—Our conferences *alternate* between the northern and southern parts of the state. Jack Smith has agreed to serve as my *alternate* on the budget committee. For the next few months, motorists will be required to use an *alternate* route to the downtown area.

Alternative (NOUN; a choice between two or among several)—We were left with only two *alternatives*—either accept the lease conditions or find another location. None of the *alternatives* presented by the committee were acceptable to the Board of Directors.

Altogether: see All together.

Always: see All ways.

Among/Between

Among (PREPOSITION; ordinarily refers to more than two persons or things)—Distribute the supplies equally *among* the three departments.

Between (PREPOSITION; ordinarily refers to two persons or things; refers to more than two persons or things when they function one-on-one in a group)—The final choice for the position is *between* Ms. Harris and Mr. Thompson. There are notable differences *between* the fares quoted by American, Delta, and United to fly to Cincinnati. Use a vanilla filling *between* the layers in the wedding cake.

Amount/Number

Amount (NOUN; used with singular nouns and mass items that cannot be counted)—Only a small *amount* of the cake was eaten. The store manager has not yet determined the *amount* of money that was stolen. Because of the power failure, a significant *amount* of the frozen food had deteriorated.

Number (NOUN; used with plural nouns and items that can be counted)—Only a small *number* of spaces have been allotted for visitor parking. In 2003 the *number* of children in each classroom was reduced by three.

An: see A.

Anecdote/Antidote

Anecdote (NOUN ['a-nik-ˌdōt]; a story or a brief account of an event)—We all had to laugh at Tom's **anecdote** about the customer who insisted upon returning a product our store doesn't even sell.

Antidote (NOUN ['an-ti-ˌdōt]; a remedy that counteracts a harmful substance or circumstance)—Dr. Martin has consented to write an article about the **antidote** he has developed for common household poisons. The only **antidote** I have found for employees who are habitually late and take extended lunch breaks is to replace them.

Annual/Annul

Annual (ADJECTIVE; yearly)—The company's **annual** report will be mailed to all stockholders of record next week.

Annul (VERB; to void or abolish)—The judge recommended that we agree to **annul** the contract because its terms are not clearly stated.

Antidote: see Anecdote.

Anxious/Eager

Anxious (ADJECTIVE; worried or apprehensive)—Donna is **anxious** about taking the upcoming real estate brokers' examination.

Eager (ADJECTIVE; anticipating with enthusiasm)—Mr. Adams is **eager** to begin his new job with Girard Enterprises next week.

Any one/Anyone

Any one (ADJECTIVE + PRONOUN; any one person or thing in a group [always followed by *of*])—I would be pleased to assist **any one** of the new employees in our department.

Anyone (PRONOUN; any person at all)—If you know of **anyone** who has these qualifications, please ask that person to e-mail a résumé to our manager of human resources.

Any time/Anytime

Any time (ADJECTIVE + NOUN; an amount of time)—We did not have **any time** yesterday to review this case.

Anytime (ADVERB; whenever; at any time *whatsoever*)—You may call me **anytime** you have questions about company policies or procedures. **Anytime** we can be of service, just call our toll-free number and a service representative will assist you. Drop by our offices **anytime**. You may take your vacation **anytime** during July or August.

Any way/Anyway

Any way (ADJECTIVE + NOUN; any method)—Is there **any way** we can step up production to advance our July 1 release date?

Anyway (ADVERB; in any case)—Considering the low bids of our competitors, I don't believe we would have received the contract **anyway**.

Anyways (An informal form of *anyway* that is not appropriate for business writing.)

Appraise/Apprise

Appraise (VERB; to estimate the value or nature)—Before we can liquidate this company, we must hire an outside firm to *appraise* its assets. As I *appraise* Mr. Bell's modus operandi, he doesn't do any more work than is minimally required of him.

Apprise (VERB; to inform or notify)—Please *apprise* all employees immediately of this change in our safety policies.

As/Like

As (CONJUNCTION; used at the beginning of a clause)—I will get the patient's file to you by Friday, *as* (not *like*) I promised. Our manager always acts *as if* (not *like*) he knows more than anyone else.

Like (PREPOSITION; used when the sentence requires a preposition meaning "similar to" [followed by a noun or pronoun and any modifiers])—This adhesive compound feels *like* wet cement. I have never met anyone else *like* him. These cookies taste *like* the chocolate chip cookies my mother used to make.

Ascent/Assent

Ascent (NOUN; rising or going up)—The recent *ascent* of stock market prices has encouraged more small investors to enter the market.

Assent (VERB; to agree or consent)—All the department heads will surely *assent* to the technology plan you have outlined in this report.

Assistance/Assistants

Assistance (NOUN; help or aid)—The project could not have been completed by September 1 without your *assistance*. If you need financial *assistance*, please fill out these forms.

Assistants (NOUN; people who aid or help a superior)—The consultant's staffing report indicates that our general manager should have three *assistants*.

Assume/Presume

Assume (VERB; to take for granted as true; to take on)—I *assume* these sales figures were corrected before they were submitted to the accountant. Who will be assigned to *assume* these extra duties?

Presume (VERB; to anticipate with confidence)—After this episode we can no longer *presume* that this company will stand behind its products or fulfill the conditions of its warranties. In our justice system defendants are *presumed* innocent until proven guilty.

Assure/Ensure/Insure

Assure (VERB; to promise; to make a positive declaration)—I *assure* you that the loan will be repaid according to the terms specified in the note. Please *assure* the patient that this procedure is not painful.

Ensure (VERB; to make certain)—To *ensure* the timely completion of this project, please hire additional qualified personnel. If you cannot *ensure* that this order will reach us by October 15, we will need to place it with another vendor.

Insure (VERB; to protect against financial loss)—We *insure* all our facilities against fire, flood, and earthquake damage.

Attendance/Attendants

Attendance (NOUN; being present or attending)—At least two thirds of the committee members must be in *attendance* before the meeting may be called to order.

Attendants (NOUN; those who attend with or to others)—The two *attendants* had difficulty parking all the cars for such a large crowd.

Averse: see Adverse.

Awhile: see A while.

Bad/Badly

Bad (ADJECTIVE; an adjective or subject complement used *after* such nonaction verbs as *is*, *was*, *feel*, *look*, or *smell*)—Sales *were* **bad** today. I *feel* **bad** that your transfer request was denied. Profits for the first quarter of this year *look* **bad** in view of the additional expenses incurred by our sales staff. The air in this office *smells* **bad**.

Badly (ADVERB; used with transitive or action verbs)—We **badly** need the advice of a tax attorney before we invest any money in this project. The defeated candidate behaved **badly** before thousands of television viewers. The home team was **badly** defeated in last night's game.

Bail/Bale

Bail (NOUN; guarantee of money necessary to set a person free from jail until the trial)—**Bail** in your client's case has been set at $25,000.

Bale (NOUN; a large bundle)—One **bale** of used clothing was lost in transit. How many **bales** of hay do you order monthly to feed your horses?

Bare/Bear

Bare (ADJECTIVE; uncovered; empty; plain; or mere)—The paint had chipped and peeled so badly that the **bare** wood was showing. Our supply cabinet will soon be **bare** if we do not send a requisition to Central Supply this week. Every year our work group retreats for three days to a **bare** wooden cabin in the mountains. I had time to cover only the **bare** facts involved in this dispute.

Bear (VERB; to support, carry, or bring forth)—Unfortunately, the senior partner has had to **bear** the brunt of the financial losses. Our travel agency has hired guides who have donkeys to **bear** the luggage and provisions. As a result of the surgery, the patient was able to **bear** children.

Base/Bass

Base (NOUN; bottom part of something or foundation)—When did the **base** of this marble column crack?

Bass (ADJECTIVE; a low-pitched sound; musical instrument having a low range)—We could use his **bass** voice in our quartet. Do you play the **bass** violin?

Bazaar/Bizarre

Bazaar (NOUN; a fair for the sale of articles)—Our Lady of Lourdes Church will hold its annual **bazaar** during the Memorial Day weekend.

7

Misused Words

217

Bizarre (ADJECTIVE; strikingly out of the ordinary)—Floyd's Fashions has often been described as carrying *bizarre* clothing lines and accessories.

Bear: see Bare.

Berth/Birth

Berth (VERB; to bring into a berth. NOUN; the place where a ship lies at anchor; place to sit or sleep on a ship or vehicle)—When will the Song of Norway next *berth* in Puerto Rico? How many *berths* does your port have for ships from major cruise lines? The only sleeping accommodations not yet reserved on the train are upper *berths*.

Birth (NOUN; the emergence of a new individual from the body of its parent)—Present hospital policy permits only two family members to be present during the *birth* of a child.

Beside/Besides

Beside (PREPOSITION; by the side of)—Please place the new scanner on the table *beside* Ms. Carter's computer.

Besides (PREPOSITION; in addition to)—What other Internet service providers *besides* America Online have you contacted?

Between: see Among.

Bi-/Semi-

Bi- (prefix; two)—Our newsletter is published *bi*monthly: January, March, May, July, September, and November.

Semi- (prefix; half)—Bulletins to the staff are issued *semi*monthly, on the 1st and 15th of each month.

Biannual/Biennial

Biannual (ADJECTIVE; occurring twice a year)—The stockholders' *biannual* meetings are held in January and July.

Biennial (ADJECTIVE; occurring once every two years)—According to our society's constitution, the *biennial* election of officers should be held in November.

Bibliography/Biography

Bibliography (NOUN; a list of works consulted by an author for a production)—Be sure to include in the *bibliography* all the sources—books, magazines, newspapers, compact disks, Internet resources, etc.—you used for this report.

Biography (NOUN; history of a person's life written by someone else)—This is an exceptionally well-written *biography* of Henry Ford, the automobile magnate.

Billed/Build

Billed (VERB; charged for goods or services)—You will be *billed* $39.95 on the 15th of each month for your pest control service.

Build (VERB; to construct)—We plan to *build* a new, larger plant in Korea within the next two years.

Biography: see Bibliography.

Birth: see Berth.

Bizarre: see Bazaar.

Boarder/Border

Boarder (NOUN; one who is provided with regular meals and lodging)—Home owners in residential areas are limited in the number of **boarders** they may solicit for commercial purposes.

Border (NOUN; an outer part or edge; boundary)—Which **border** did you select for the cover page of the report? If you plan to cross the **border** into Arizona or California, do not bring any live plants with you.

Bolder/Boulder

Bolder (ADJECTIVE; more fearless or daring)—Perhaps the Board of Trustees should hire a **bolder** person to serve as president of the university.

Boulder (NOUN; a large rock)—Damage to the insured's left-front tire was apparently caused by a **boulder** in the road.

Born/Borne

Born (ADJECTIVE; brought forth by birth; originated)—This patient was **born** on February 14, 1949. One can hardly believe that the multibillion-dollar microcomputer industry was **born** in a garage fewer than three decades ago.

Borne (VERB; past participle of *bear*)—Mrs. Talbert has already **borne** six children, and she is currently expecting her seventh. Our school district has **borne** these financial burdens for more than ten years.

Bouillon/Bullion

Bouillon (NOUN ['bü(l)-,yän]; a clear soup)—For the first course of the banquet, I ordered beef **bouillon**.

Bullion (NOUN ['bul-yən]; uncoined gold or silver in bars or ingots)—Mr. Reece had hidden in his home nearly $45,000 in gold **bullion**.

Boulder: see Bolder.

Breach/Breech

Breach (NOUN; a violation of a law or agreement; a hole, gap, or break)—The judge ruled that a **breach** of contract transpired when the building was not ready for occupancy by the date agreed upon. If contract negotiations are to continue, we must narrow the **breach** between union and management negotiators.

Breech (NOUN; part of a firearm or cannon that is located behind the barrel)—They had difficulty firing the old cannon because the **breech** would not work properly.

Bring/Take

Bring (VERB; to carry toward [a place])—Please **bring** (not *take*) all your receipts when you meet with our accountant.

Take (VERB; to carry away; to carry from one place to another)—You may **take** any one of these samples. Please **take** these brochures to our Springfield office.

Build: see Billed.

Bullion: see Bouillon.

7

Misused Words

Calendar/Colander

Calendar (NOUN; a schedule of days and months for a period of time)—Please order a supply of desk *calendars* for the new year.

Colander (NOUN; a strainer)—Use a *colander* to drain the pasta thoroughly before placing it in the sauce.

Callous/Callus

Callous (ADJECTIVE; insensitive, without feeling)—Mr. Coe's *callous* remark concerning Ms. Wright's disability caused his removal from the hiring committee.

Callus (NOUN; hard, thick skin)—Pointed-toe, high-heeled shoes will cause permanent *calluses* on your toes.

Can/May

Can (VERB; to have the ability to do something)—You *can* develop a Web site without knowing hypertext markup language (HTML).

May (VERB; to express permission or possibility)—Yes, you *may* schedule your vacation for the week of July 15. *May* we have these files converted from Quark to Microsoft Word by next Friday?

Canvas/Canvass

Canvas (NOUN; a firm, closely woven cloth)—Use these *canvas* coverings to protect the new cars as they arrive on the lot.

Canvass (VERB; to survey or solicit in an area)—Do you have a volunteer who will *canvass* the residences on Jersey Street?

Capital/Capitol

Capital (NOUN; a city in which the official seat of government is located; the wealth of an individual or firm)—The *capital* of Wisconsin is Madison. Much of our company's *capital* is tied up in computers and software.

Capital (ADJECTIVE; punishable by death; foremost in importance)—Treason is a *capital* crime in most countries. The forthcoming election is *capital* in the minds of the school board members.

Capitol (NOUN; a building used by the U.S. Congress [always capitalized])—Senator Cano must be in the *Capitol* by 9 a.m. on Tuesday for the hearings. The United States *Capitol* is a major tourist attraction in Washington, D.C.

Capitol (NOUN; a building in which a state legislature convenes [capitalized only when used in full name of building])—The *capitol* was surrounded by angry pickets waving placards. Is your office located in the California State *Capitol*?

Carat/Caret/Carrot/Karat

Carat (NOUN; a unit of weight for gems)—The total diamond weight in this ring is 2.17 *carats*.

Caret (NOUN; a proofreading symbol similar to an inverted *v* that is placed at the bottom of a line to show insertions in edited copy)—Ask the editor to place a *caret* between the two words where the company name is to be inserted.

Carrot (NOUN; a vegetable)—A *carrot* can be just as delicious raw as it is cooked.

Karat (NOUN, GENERALLY USED AS ADJECTIVE; a unit of weight for gold)—All the Italian chains sold in our store are made of 18-*karat* gold.

Cease/Seize

Cease (VERB; to stop or come to an end)—Please *cease* shipment of any further orders to the Hogan Company until its current balance has been paid. When does his eligibility for financial aid *cease*?

Seize (VERB; to take possession of; to take)—Will the Internal Revenue Service *seize* all the company's assets for the payment of back taxes? You may wish to *seize* this opportunity to ask Mr. Rodriguez for a salary increase.

Ceiling/Sealing

Ceiling (NOUN; overhead inside lining of a room; upper limit)—Have you checked all the acoustical *ceilings* in this apartment complex to ensure they are free from asbestos? *Ceilings* on rent increases are controlled by the city council.

Sealing (NOUN; closing with a coating to make secure)—These glue sticks are used primarily for *sealing* envelopes.

Censor/Censure

Censor (VERB; to examine materials and delete objectionable matter. NOUN; one who censors)—Our staff will need to *censor* scenes from this movie to make it eligible for television viewing. When will the *censor* finish reviewing the script?

Censure (VERB; to criticize or condemn. NOUN; condemnation)—The city council *censured* the mayor for awarding the contract to his brother-in-law's firm. After the facts were disclosed, Senator Dillon was subjected to public *censure*.

Census/Senses

Census (NOUN; an official count of population within a specified geographical area)—The United States conducts an official *census* every ten years.

Senses (NOUN; the specialized functions of sight, hearing, smell, taste, and touch)—Our client's *senses* of hearing and touch were impaired as a result of the accident.

Cent/Scent/Sent

Cent (NOUN; a coin known as a *penny*)—At the end of the day, your tallies always balance to the last *cent*.

Scent (NOUN; a distinctive smell or odor)—The *scent* of freshly baked bread from Webby Bakery permeates our industrial complex each morning.

Sent (VERB; the past tense and past participle of *send*)—Your order was *sent* by United Parcel Service yesterday.

Cereal/Serial

Cereal (NOUN; a breakfast food made from grain)—The patient's diet calls for a daily serving of wheat *cereal*.

Serial (ADJECTIVE; arranged in a series)—In case of fire or theft, the *serial* numbers of all our equipment should be on file in your office.

Choose/Chose

Choose (VERB; to select or make a choice)—Do you know whom the general manager will *choose* to become his executive assistant?

Chose (VERB; past tense of *choose*)—The general manager *chose* Ms. Randall to be his executive assistant.

7

Misused Words

Chord/Cord

Chord (NOUN; three or more musical notes sounded at the same time)—The pianist played several **chords** before the soloist began singing "I Love You Truly." **Cord** (NOUN; a long, slender, flexible material usually consisting of several strands that are woven or twisted together; a stack of wood 4 × 4 × 8 feet cut for fuel)— Tie these two packages together with a **cord** before you deliver them. Someone had forgotten to replace in the carrying case the electrical **cord** for the laptop. Every winter we order at least one **cord** of wood for our fireplace.

Cite/Sight/Site

Cite (VERB; to quote or mention; to summon to a court appearance)— Dr. Rosenthal can **cite** many authorities who have researched the problem of pollution in major United States cities. Did the police officer **cite** you for speeding while you were in a company vehicle?

Sight (VERB; to see. NOUN; a view or spectacle)—Did you **sight** Ms. Preston among the group of reporters? The Statue of Liberty is a popular tourist **sight** in New York City.

Site (NOUN; a location)—This 20-acre land parcel is a perfect **site** for the proposed housing project.

Close/Clothes/Cloths

Close (VERB; to shut; to stop or end)—We **close** the safe at 5 p.m. every afternoon. Our accountant **closes** our books at the end of each month.

Clothes (NOUN; wearing apparel)—The previous tenant still needs to remove his **clothes** from the apartment.

Cloths (NOUN; pieces of fabric)—Use only these **cloths** to clean the new computer monitors.

Coarse/Course

Coarse (ADJECTIVE; rough texture)—This fabric is too **coarse** to be used for spring fashions.

Course (NOUN; a particular direction or route; part of a meal; a unit of learning)— We are committed to a **course** of action that we believe will increase our sales. Which menu item did you select for the main **course**? You need only three more **courses** to graduate.

Colander: see Calendar.

Collision/Collusion

Collision (NOUN; a crash)—Fortunately, no one was hurt in the **collision**.

Collusion (NOUN; an agreement to defraud)—No one suspected the seller, broker, and escrow officer of **collusion** in the sale of this unstable hillside property.

Command/Commend

Command (VERB; to order or direct. NOUN; an order)—The sergeant **commanded** his troops to return to base by 0600. This police dog has been trained to obey only its owner's **commands**.

Commend (VERB; to praise or compliment)—Please **commend** the sales staff for its fine job in promoting our product line at the Dallas convention.

Complement/Compliment

Complement (VERB; to complete or make perfect)—The paintings you selected for the reception area will ***complement*** the office decor. You may wish to select one of our fine wines to ***complement*** your meal.

Compliment (VERB; to praise or flatter)—Mr. Rose did ***compliment*** me on the fine job I had done.

Complementary/Complimentary

Complementary (ADJECTIVE; serving mutually to blend, fill out, or complete)— None of these wallcoverings are ***complementary*** to the carpeting we have selected.

Complimentary (ADJECTIVE; favorable; given free)—We appreciate receiving your ***complimentary*** letter about the exceptional service you received in our Cabazon store. To receive your ***complimentary*** copy of this recipe booklet, merely fill out and return the enclosed postcard.

Confidant/Confident

Confidant (NOUN; a trusted friend)—He has been the senator's closest ***confidant*** for many years.

Confident (ADJECTIVE; sure of oneself)—Mrs. Allen was ***confident*** she would pass the state licensing examination to work as a registered nurse.

Conscience/Conscious

Conscience (NOUN; the faculty of knowing right from wrong)—In the last analysis, his ***conscience*** prevented him from accepting the illegal funds.

Conscious (ADJECTIVE; aware or mentally awake)—Yes, we are ***conscious*** of the declining market in our industry. Most of our patients are ***conscious*** during this type of surgery.

Console/Consul

Console (NOUN; a cabinet)—The popularity of our Model 4750 home entertainment center may be attributed to its attractive ***console***.

Consul (NOUN; an official representing a foreign country)—Travel information may often be obtained from the ***consul*** of the country you wish to visit.

Continual/Continuous

Continual (ADJECTIVE; a regular or frequent occurrence)—***Continual*** complaints from customers in the Vancouver area warrant our inquiry into the activities of the Seattle office.

Continuous (ADJECTIVE; without interruption or cessation)—The ***continuous*** humming of the new air-conditioning system is disturbing everyone in the office.

Convince/Persuade

Convince (VERB; to bring a person to your point of view)—Do you think you can ***convince*** the board that our losses this year are directly related to a slowdown in the economy?

Persuade (VERB; to induce a person to do something)—An effective banner on a popular Internet site will ***persuade*** visitors to that site to purchase your products.

7

Misused Words

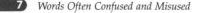

Cooperation/Corporation

Cooperation (NOUN; working together)—Only with the full ***cooperation*** of all employees will we be able to meet the contract deadline date.

Corporation (NOUN; one type of business organization)—We are looking into the possibility of forming a ***corporation***.

Cord: see Chord.

Corespondent/Correspondence/Correspondents

Corespondent (NOUN; person named as guilty of adultery with the defendant in a divorce suit)— Who was named as ***corespondent*** in this divorce case?

Correspondence (NOUN; letters or other written communications)—When did we receive the last E-mail ***correspondence*** from Mr. Flores?

Correspondents (NOUN; message or letter writers; news reporters)—Be sure to have one of our ***correspondents*** answer these customers' letters within the next three days. African ***correspondents*** have reported that several countries are still suffering severe food shortages.

Corporation: see Cooperation.

Corps/Corpse

Corps (NOUN ['kōr]; a body of persons having a common activity or occupation)— A ***corps*** of students have been soliciting funds for the stadium lights. Representatives from the Marine ***Corps*** will visit our campus next week.

Corpse (NOUN ['kòrps]; a dead body)—The identity of the ***corpse*** is still unknown.

Correspondence: see Corespondent.

Correspondent: see Corespondent.

Council/Counsel

Council (NOUN; a governing body)—We will present the request for a zoning change to the city ***council*** in the morning.

Counsel (VERB; to give advice. NOUN; advice)—Our staff ***counsels*** at least eighty students each day. In this situation your attorney gave you good ***counsel***.

Course: see Coarse.

Credible/Creditable

Credible (ADJECTIVE; believable)—The excuses offered by Ms. Ford for her many absences are hardly ***credible***.

Creditable (ADJECTIVE; good enough for praise or esteem; reliable)— Ms. Kawakami's perfect attendance record is certainly ***creditable***. Keep in mind that not all Internet resources are ***creditable***.

Deceased/Diseased

Deceased (ADJECTIVE; dead)—Two of the company's founders are already ***deceased***.

Diseased (ADJECTIVE; sick)—Be sure to spray all these ***diseased*** rose bushes with insecticide.

Decent/Descent/Dissent

Decent (ADJECTIVE; in good taste; proper)—The only *decent* solution to the problem would be to replace the customer's carpeting.

Descent (NOUN; moving downward; ancestry)—The view of the city from the sky was breathtaking as the plane began its *descent* into the Denver airport. Mr. Sirakides is of Greek *descent*.

Dissent (NOUN; differences or disagreement)—There has been considerable *dissent* among the council members concerning the resolution to expand our city's police department.

Defer/Differ

Defer (VERB; to put off or delay)—Our company has decided to *defer* moving its offices until next spring.

Differ (VERB; to vary or disagree)—Doctors' views *differ* about the best treatment for the common cold.

Deference/Difference

Deference (NOUN; yielding to someone else's wishes)—In *deference* to many shoppers' requests, our store will remain open until 9 p.m. during the summer months.

Difference (NOUN; state of being different, dissimilarity)—There is very little *difference* in product quality between these two brands.

Delusion: see Allusion.

Deprecate/Depreciate

Deprecate (VERB; to disapprove or downgrade)—The contractor's speech before the city council was solely to *deprecate* the present zoning system.

Depreciate (VERB; to lessen the value)—The tax code allows us to *depreciate* this new equipment over a five-year period.

Descent: see Decent.

Desert/Dessert

Desert (NOUN; an arid, barren land area)—Palm Springs was once a *desert* area occupied only by Agua Caliente Indians.

Dessert (NOUN; a sweet course served at the end of a meal)—Apple pie and ice cream is a traditional American *dessert*.

Device/Devise

Device (NOUN; an invention or mechanism)—The collating *device* worked perfectly during the demonstration.

Devise (VERB; to think out or plan)—Were you able to *devise* an overtime plan that would be equitable to all employees?

Dew/Do/Due

Dew (NOUN; drops of moisture)—The heavy *dew* that was forecast for this morning was instead a heavy layer of fog, which caused the airport officials to delay all flights.

Do (VERB; to perform or bring about)—What can we **do** to promote our products in foreign markets?

Due (ADJECTIVE; immediately payable)—Your payments are **due** by the 10th of each month.

Die/Dye

Die (VERB; to pass from physical life)—During the summer months water your grass twice daily so that it will not **die**.

Dye (VERB; to change a color with a coloring substance)—We can custom **dye** this carpeting to your color choice.

Differ: see Defer.

Difference: see Deference.

Disapprove/Disprove

Disapprove (VERB; to withhold approval)—Our manager will **disapprove** any reimbursement request that has not received prior approval.

Disprove (VERB; to prove false)—How can we **disprove** the witness's false testimony?

Disburse/Disperse

Disburse (VERB; to pay out; to distribute methodically)—Our accountant devised a new system to **disburse** sales commissions more rapidly. The property will be **disbursed** according to the provisions set forth in Mr. Williams' will.

Disperse (VERB; to scatter; to cause to become widely spread)—The crowd **dispersed** rapidly after the ball game. Those factories that **disperse** pollutants into the environment will continue to be subject to heavy fines. Please **disperse** this information to consumers nationwide.

Discreet/Discrete

Discreet (ADJECTIVE; showing good judgment in conduct and speech)—Ms. Doyle is **discreet** in discussing patients' cases with other hospital personnel.

Discrete (ADJECTIVE; separate)—There are several **discrete** possibilities for distributing our products in Europe and parts of Asia.

Diseased: see Deceased.

Disinterested/Uninterested

Disinterested (ADJECTIVE; impartial)—All the judges for this competition have been certified to be **disinterested** parties.

Uninterested (ADJECTIVE; indifferent)—Those employees who are **uninterested** in the success of the company are certainly not candidates for promotion.

Disprove: see Disapprove.

Dissent: see Decent.

Do: see Dew.

Done/Dun
Done (VERB; past participle of *do*)—Our company has not **done** any further research in this area.

Dun (VERB; to make persistent demands for payment. NOUN OFTEN USED AS ADJECTIVE; a variable drab color, usually a neutral brownish gray)—Ms. Green's main responsibility is to **dun** slow-paying customers. Before we move into these offices, you will need to hire a painting contractor to transform these **dun**-colored walls into a brighter atmosphere.

Due: see Dew.

Dun: see Done.

Dye: see Die.

Edict: see Addict.

Edition: see Addition.

Effect: see Affect.

E.g./I.e.
E.g. (PREPOSITION + NOUN; Latin abbreviation meaning *for example*)—Our company specializes in office furniture; **e.g.**, desks, computer stations, file cabinets, bookcases, printer tables, chairs, and reception area furniture.

I.e. (PRONOUN + VERB; Latin abbreviation meaning *that is*)—You may telephone your order anytime; **i.e.**, we have operators on duty 24 hours a day every day.

Elicit/Illicit
Elicit (VERB; to draw out or bring forth)—Did the seminar speaker attempt to **elicit** questions from the audience?

Illicit (ADJECTIVE; unlawful)—One of our agents has been cited for **illicit** business practices.

Eligible/Illegible
Eligible (ADJECTIVE; qualified to be chosen)—To be **eligible** for these employment opportunities, applicants must be at least 21 years of age.

Illegible (ADJECTIVE; unreadable)—The handwriting on this student's paper is **illegible**.

Elude: see Allude.

Emigrate/Immigrate
Emigrate (VERB; to move from a country)—The Johnsons **emigrated** from Norway in 1990.

Immigrate (VERB; to enter a country)—How many Canadians were permitted to **immigrate** to the United States last year?

Eminent/Imminent
Eminent (ADJECTIVE; prominent, distinguished)—Mr. Mendez is an **eminent** authority on labor relations.

7

Misused Words

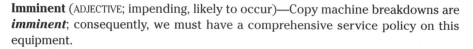

Imminent (ADJECTIVE; impending, likely to occur)—Copy machine breakdowns are *imminent*; consequently, we must have a comprehensive service policy on this equipment.

Ensure: see Assure.

Envelop/Envelope
Envelop (VERB; to wrap, surround, or conceal)—*Envelop* each tamale in a corn husk before boiling it. The chief said his fire fighters would *envelop* the fire by morning. Each day a layer of early morning fog *envelops* the city.
Envelope (NOUN; a container for a written message)—Please send me your answer in the return *envelope* provided for your convenience.

Every day/Everyday
Every day (ADJECTIVE + NOUN; each day)—I will e-mail you *every day* to give you a status report on the development of our speech-enabled PDA.
Everyday (ADJECTIVE; ordinary)—Customer complaints seem to be an *everyday* occurrence in the Litchfield office.

Every one/Everyone
Every one (ADJECTIVE + PRONOUN; each person or thing in a group [always followed by *of*])—*Every one* of us is proficient in the use of voice-recognition, word processing, spreadsheet, and presentation software.
Everyone (PRONOUN; all people in a group)—*Everyone* on the executive staff is expected to be present for the stockholders' meeting.

Example/Sample
Example (NOUN; something serving as a pattern to be imitated)—Please illustrate each of these principles with a meaningful *example*.
Sample (NOUN; a representative part or a single item from a larger whole)—When purchasing See's candy, each customer is offered a *sample*. You will need a larger *sample* population to validate the results of this study.

Exceed: see Accede.

Except: see Accept.

Excess: see Access.

Executioner/Executor
Executioner (NOUN USED AS ADJECTIVE; one who puts others [usually criminals] to death)—The *executioner*-style murders still remain unsolved.
Executor (NOUN; person appointed to carry out the provisions of a will)—Whom have you named as *executor* of your will?

Exhilarate: see Accelerate.

Expand/Expend
Expand (VERB; to enlarge)—The plan to *expand* our storage facilities was approved.

Expend (VERB; to use up or pay out)—Ms. Smith **expends** too much time dealing with insignificant matters instead of meeting major objectives. If you do not **expend** these moneys by June 30, they will revert to the general fund.

Expansive/Expensive

Expansive (ADJECTIVE; capable of expanding; extensive)—An **expansive** commercial development is planned for this 200-acre site.

Expensive (ADJECTIVE; costly)—The consultant's recommendations were too **expensive** to implement.

Expend: see Expand.

Expensive: see Expansive.

Explicit/Implicit

Explicit (ADJECTIVE; expressed clearly)—The accompanying booklet gives **explicit** instructions for assembling this computer desk.

Implicit (ADJECTIVE; implied)—Although the project manager did not state so in his progress report, I recognized an **implicit** appeal for additional engineers to assist with this complicated project.

Extant/Extent

Extant (ADJECTIVE; currently or actually existing)—Please provide me with a three-year budget for all **extant** and projected programs.

Extent (NOUN; range, scope, or magnitude)—Unfortunately, we will be unable to assess the **extent** of the damage until next week.

Facetious/Factious

Facetious (ADJECTIVE; humorous or witty, often in an inappropriate manner)—His seemingly **facetious** remark contained a kernel of truth.

Factious (ADJECTIVE; creating a faction or dissension)—A series of **factious** disputes among the three partners eventually led to the dissolution of the partnership.

Factitious/Fictitious

Factitious (ADJECTIVE; artificial)—One manufacturer created a **factitious** demand for copper alloy by spreading rumors of shortages.

Fictitious (ADJECTIVE; nonexistent; imaginary; false)—Many people believe that the reported UFO sightings are **fictitious**. This suspect has been known to operate under a number of **fictitious** names.

Fair/Fare

Fair (NOUN; an exhibition. ADJECTIVE; marked by impartiality and honesty; mediocre)—Our annual county **fair** usually begins during the first week of September. Further legislation was passed recently to enforce **fair** employment practices. He did a **fair** job.

Fare (VERB; to get along or succeed. NOUN; price charged to transport a person)—Our company did not **fare** well in its last bidding competition for state contracts. How much is the first-class airline **fare** from Chicago to New York?

7

Misused Words

Farther/Further

Farther (ADJECTIVE; a greater distance [always a measurable amount of space])—The distance from the plant to the warehouse is *farther* than I had anticipated.

Further (VERB; to help move forward. ADVERB; to a greater degree or extent. ADJECTIVE; additional)—The Arden Foundation contributed $5 million to *further* research in spinal cord injuries. Stock market prices declined even *further* after the president's announcement. Refer to my July 8 memo for *further* details.

Feasible/Possible

Feasible (ADJECTIVE; capable of being done or carried out)—Installing zip drives in all our computers is certainly *feasible*, but budget restraints prohibit our doing so.

Possible (ADJECTIVE; being within the limits of realization)—Networking all our computers should certainly be *possible* by the end of the year.

Feat/Fete

Feat (NOUN ['fēt]; an act of skill, endurance, or ingenuity)—Human beings under stress have been known to perform *feats* beyond their normal capabilities.

Fete (VERB ['fāt]; to honor or commemorate. NOUN; a large elaborate party)—A banquet is being planned to *fete* our company president upon his retirement in September. The *fete* to honor our company president will be held on August 19.

Fever/Temperature

Fever (NOUN; a rise of body temperature above the normal)—When the child was brought into the emergency room, he had a *fever* 1.4 degrees above normal.

Temperature (NOUN; degree of hotness or coldness measured on a definite scale)—Normal body *temperature* is 98.6 degrees. Be sure to record patients' *temperatures* on their charts.

Fewer/Less

Fewer (ADJECTIVE; used with items that can be counted and plural nouns)—We had *fewer* sales this month than we had last month. Reserve this checkout for customers with ten or *fewer* items. *Fewer* than half the employees elected to purchase stock options.

Less (ADJECTIVE; used with mass items that cannot be counted and singular nouns)—You will get by with *less* work if you follow my suggestions. *Less* than half the cake had been eaten by the end of the wedding reception.

Fictitious: see Factitious.

Finally/Finely

Finally (ADVERB; in the end)—The damaged CD drive was *finally* replaced.

Finely (ADVERB; elegantly or delicately; in small parts)—Visitors to the museum always admire the *finely* embroidered tapestries. Your car engine has been *finely* tuned by our expert mechanics. You may purchase these *finely* chopped nuts in 8- and 16-ounce packages.

Fiscal/Physical

Fiscal (ADJECTIVE; relating to financial matters)—The *fiscal* year for our school district begins on July 1 and ends on June 30.

Physical (ADJECTIVE; concerned with the body and its needs)—Every individual should do a minimum amount of *physical* exercise daily.

Flagrant/Fragrant

Flagrant (ADJECTIVE; glaring, scandalous)—The vice president's letting this major contract to his son-in-law's firm was a *flagrant* violation of company policy.

Fragrant (ADJECTIVE; sweet smelling)—Ann received a *fragrant* bouquet of flowers from the staff.

Flair/Flare

Flair (NOUN; a natural talent or aptitude)—Ms. Strehike has a *flair* for making people feel at ease when they enter her office.

Flare (VERB; to blaze up or spread out. NOUN; a signal light)—The gusty winds could easily cause the fire to *flare* out of control. *Flares* in the road guided motorists around the accident.

Flaunt/Flout

Flaunt (VERB; to make a gaudy or defiant display)—Although Mrs. Paige is one of the most affluent Hartford residents, she does not *flaunt* her wealth.

Flout (VERB; to mock or show contempt for; to defy)—As a new driver, the young man continued to *flout* the posted speed limit.

Flew/Flu/Flue

Flew (VERB; past tense of *fly*)—Our plane *flew* to the West Coast in record time.

Flu (NOUN; abbreviated form of *influenza*)—Nearly 15 percent of our employees were absent last week because of the *flu* epidemic.

Flue (NOUN; a duct in a chimney)—If the *flue* is closed, smoke from a burning fire cannot escape through the chimney.

Flout: see Flaunt.

Flu: see Flew.

Flue: see Flew.

Foreword/Forward

Foreword (NOUN; prefatory comments, as for a book)—Thomas S. Healy, president of the New York Public Library, wrote the *foreword* for the 1992 publication of *The New York Public Library Book of Twentieth-Century American Quotations*.

Forward (ADVERB; to or toward what is ahead)—Since its beginnings our company has moved *forward* at a rapid pace in research and development.

Formally/Formerly

Formally (ADVERB; in a formal manner)—At our next meeting you will be *formally* introduced to the other members of the committee.

Formerly (ADVERB; in the past)—Marie Martin was *formerly* the president of a large metropolitan area community college.

7

Misused Words

Former/Latter

Former (ADJECTIVE; first of two things or belonging to an earlier time)—My *former* suggestion appears to be the better one. As a *former* employee, Lois Oliver is always invited to attend the company social functions.

Latter (ADJECTIVE; second of two things or nearer to the end)—Of the two options available to us, the *latter* one seems to be more economical. Mail deliveries in your area are scheduled for the *latter* part of the day.

Forth/Fourth

Forth (ADVERB; forward)—The president requested that any objections to his relocation plan be brought *forth* by June 30.

Fourth (a numeric term; the ordinal form of *four*)—The *fourth* member of our group never arrived.

Fortunate/Fortuitous

Fortunate (ADJECTIVE; having good luck)—We were *fortunate* to obtain the services of Ladd, Ladd & Company to render the architectural drawings for our new building.

Fortuitous (ADJECTIVE; accidental; happening by chance)—Only through these *fortuitous* circumstances were we able to purchase our airline tickets at such a reduced price.

Forward: see Foreword.

Fourth: see Forth.

Fragrant: see Flagrant.

Further: see Farther.

Good/Well

Good (ADJECTIVE; meaning *of favorable quality* in describing a noun or pronoun; meaning *fit, wholesome* in describing a person's well-being)—Mr. Collins writes *good* letters. I always feel *good* after finishing my exercises at the gym.

Well (ADVERB; meaning *properly, skillfully* in describing an action; ADJECTIVE, meaning *fit, healthy* in describing a person's health)—The majority of our nursing graduates do *well* on their state board examinations. My assistant did not look *well* today.

Grate/Great

Grate (VERB; to reduce to small particles by rubbing on something rough; to cause irritation. NOUN; a frame of parallel or crossed bars blocking a passage)—In the future please use a food processor to *grate* the cheese for our pizzas. His continual talking could *grate* on anyone's nerves. Be sure to place a *grate* over this excavation when you have finished removing the dirt.

Great (ADJECTIVE; large in size; numerous; eminent or distinguished)—From the cruise ship we often sight a *great* white shark. A *great* many people have expressed an interest in purchasing our Model No. 2005 speech-enabled personal digital assistant. Many *great* performers from stage and screen will be present at our annual benefit.

Guarantee/Guaranty

Guarantee (VERB; to assure the fulfillment of a condition. NOUN; assurance of the quality or length of service of a product)—I **guarantee** that your children will enjoy immensely the adventures Disneyland has to offer. All our new cars have a three-year or 60,000-mile **guarantee**, whichever occurs first.

Guaranty (VERB; to agree to pay the debt of another in case of default. NOUN; an assurance to pay the debt of another in case of default)—The federal government will **guaranty** all loans made under this new home-buyer program. John Fletcher's car loan will be approved as soon as we receive his parents' signed **guaranty**.

Hail/Hale

Hail (VERB; to greet or summon. NOUN; rain that falls in the form of small ice balls)—On rainy afternoons you may find it difficult to **hail** a taxi in Chicago. Unfortunately, the unexpected **hail** in May has damaged our strawberry crops.

Hale (ADJECTIVE; healthy)—Let's hope you will return from this adventuresome vacation **hale** and hearty.

He/Him/Himself

He (PRONOUN; the subject of a clause or a complement pronoun)—**He** is the person I interviewed for the job. The person in our group with the best singing voice has always been **he**.

Him (PRONOUN; a direct object, an indirect object, or an object of a preposition)—The president asked **him** to head the project. Doris Waters gave **him** the information yesterday. The choice is between you and **him**.

Himself (PRONOUN; a reflexive pronoun used to emphasize or refer back to the subject)—He **himself** had to solve the problem. Rick Bogart addressed the envelope to **himself**.

Healthful/Healthy

Healthful (ADJECTIVE; beneficial to health of body or mind; promotes one's well-being or good health)—Millions of Americans consider vitamin supplements to be **healthful**. Mary tries to eat only **healthful** foods. Doctors recommend daily exercise as a **healthful** activity.

Healthy (ADJECTIVE; being well or fit; enjoying health and vigor of body, mind, or spirit)—Be sure to keep only **healthy** plants in our nursery section. Most of our clients have selected the one-year membership program to remain **healthy** and maintain their physical fitness.

Hear/Here

Hear (VERB; to perceive by the ear)—Yes, I can **hear** you clearly on my cell phone.

Here (ADVERB; in this place or at this point)—Install the telephone line **here**.

Her/Herself/She

Her (PRONOUN; a direct object, an indirect object, or an object of a preposition)—When Paulette arrived, Mr. Schultz asked **her** for the information. Barbara offered **her** a chair. The check is for **her**.

Herself (PRONOUN; a reflexive pronoun used to emphasize or refer back to the subject)—Wendy **herself** wrote and edited the audit report using voice-recognition software. Kristen often talks to **herself**.

She (PRONOUN; the subject of a clause or a complement pronoun)—***She*** locked the store and set the alarm yesterday at 6 p.m. The person who designed this spreadsheet was ***she***.

Here: see Hear.

Herself: see Her.

Hew/Hue
Hew (VERB; to cut with blows of a heavy cutting instrument)—Which famous faces have been ***hewed*** on Mount Rushmore?
Hue (NOUN; color or gradation of color; aspect)—The ***hues*** of the rainbow glistened in the sunlight. Persons from every political ***hue*** criticized the president for not informing the American public of his actions.

Him: see He.

Himself: see He.

Hoard/Horde
Hoard (VERB; to store or accumulate for future use)—Please do not ***hoard*** stationery and other supplies.
Horde (NOUN; a multitude)—A ***horde*** of people were waiting for the box office to open so they could purchase prime seats for the October 15 concert.

Hoarse/Horse
Hoarse (ADJECTIVE; low, husky sound)—Your voice is too ***hoarse*** to make these telephone calls today.
Horse (NOUN; a large animal)—For this commercial we will need at least eight ***horses***.

Hole/Whole
Hole (NOUN; an opening or open place)—Burglars had entered the jewelry store by cutting a ***hole*** through the outer wall.
Whole (ADJECTIVE; complete, entire)—Too many inexperienced managers make decisions before knowing the ***whole*** story.

Holy/Wholly
Holy (ADJECTIVE; sacred)—Visitors continually flock to Jerusalem's ***holy*** shrines.
Wholly (ADVERB; completely)—Do you agree ***wholly*** with the committee's plan to invest additional funds in the proposed shopping mall?

Horde: see Hoard.

Hue: see Hew.

Human/Humane
Human (ADJECTIVE; characteristic of people)—Please remember that all of us are guilty of possessing ***human*** frailties.
Humane (ADJECTIVE; marked by compassion, sympathy, or consideration)—The treatment of elderly people in this convalescent facility is certainly less than ***humane***.

Hypercritical/Hypocritical

Hypercritical (ADJECTIVE; excessively critical)—Many of his coworkers believe Mr. Reed to be *hypercritical* of new employees.

Hypocritical (ADJECTIVE [ˌhi-pə-'kri-ti-kəl]; falsely pretending)—Because Jodi befriended other staff members and then gossiped about their shortcomings, she was fired for her *hypocritical* behavior.

I/Me/Myself

I (PRONOUN; a subject of a clause or a complement pronoun)—*I* received information about this promotional opportunity yesterday. If you were *I*, what would you do under these circumstances?

Me (PRONOUN; a direct object, an indirect object, or an object of a preposition)—Barbara Wilson e-mailed *me* yesterday. Pat gave *me* the sales report last week. None of this mail is for *me*.

Myself (PRONOUN; a reflexive pronoun used to emphasize or refer back to the subject)—I *myself* wrote the entire script. I can blame only *myself* for losing this sale.

Ideal/Idle/Idol

Ideal (ADJECTIVE; perfect, model)—From all that I have observed, Ms. Andrews appears to be the *ideal* administrative assistant for your office. Your proposal outlines an *ideal* method for rotating our inventory.

Idle (ADJECTIVE; doing nothing)—The production line was *idle* for almost a week.

Idol (NOUN; an object for religious worship; a revered person or thing)—Was the church *idol* vandalized? Money is often the *idol* of ambitious, greedy people.

I.e.: see E.g.

Illegible: see Eligible.

Illicit: see Elicit.

Illusion: see Allusion.

Immigrate: see Emigrate.

Imminent: see Eminent.

Implicit: see Explicit.

Imply/Infer

Imply (VERB; to suggest without stating)—Did the manager *imply* that he is dissatisfied with our sales efforts?

Infer (VERB; to reach a conclusion)—From the results of this survey, we can *infer* that our advertising efforts in Miami have been aimed at the wrong population.

In behalf of/On behalf of

In behalf of (PREPOSITION + NOUN + PREPOSITION; in the interest or benefit of)—Because Ms. Shields was scheduled to be out of town, she requested Mr. Gross to present the award *in behalf of* the company.

On behalf of (PREPOSITION + NOUN + PREPOSITION; in support or defense of)—Dr. Phillips spoke *on behalf of* Ms. Jones at the hearing.

7

Misused Words

235

Incidence/Incidents

Incidence (NOUN; occurrence; rate of occurrence)—There has yet to be an *incidence* of theft within the company. The low *incidence* of traffic accidents during this holiday weekend may be attributed to our television safety campaign.

Incidents (NOUN; events or episodes)—Several *incidents* have occurred recently that require us to review our safety policies and practices.

Incite/Insight

Incite (VERB; to urge on or provoke action)—The senator's speech was an attempt to *incite* students to become more involved in public issues. Poverty, depression, and starvation *incited* riots throughout the country.

Insight (NOUN; keen understanding)—Bob's *insight* and patience resolved the issue before it developed into a major problem.

Indigenous/Indigent/Indignant

Indigenous (ADJECTIVE; native to a particular region)—I believe that this tree is *indigenous* to the Northwest.

Indigent (ADJECTIVE; poor, needy)—He entered the United States as an *indigent* refugee from war-torn Eastern Europe and is now a network supervisor.

Indignant (ADJECTIVE; insulting, angry)—Successful store managers must know how to deal with *indignant* customers.

Infer: see Imply.

Ingenious/Ingenuous

Ingenious (ADJECTIVE; marked by originality, resourcefulness, and cleverness)— Your *ingenious* plan could save our company thousands of dollars annually.

Ingenuous (ADJECTIVE; showing innocent or childlike simplicity; natural)— Mr. Warren's *ingenuous* smile and warm personality have contributed immeasurably to his successful political career.

Insight: see Incite.

Insure: see Assure.

Interstate/Intrastate

Interstate (ADJECTIVE; between states)—Since expanding our operations to Maine and Vermont, we must abide by all laws governing *interstate* commerce.

Intrastate (ADJECTIVE; within a state)—Our company, an Illinois corporation, is concerned solely with *intrastate* sales.

Irregardless/Regardless

Irregardless (an incorrect usage for *regardless* that is not acceptable for speaking or writing).

Regardless (ADVERB; despite everything)—We must vacate these premises by August 31, *regardless*!

Regardless of (PREPOSITION; without taking into account; in spite of)—*Regardless of* price, which one of these models has the best performance record? We have opened an account for Ritter's Clothing Store *regardless of* its slow-pay payment record.

Misused Words **7**

Irritate: see Aggravate.

Isle: see Aisle.

It's/Its

It's (PRONOUN + VERB; contraction of *it is*)—Although this model digital television set has become very popular, *it's* not our best-seller.

Its (PRONOUN USED AS ADJECTIVE; possessive form of *it*)—The company had *its* stockholders' meeting in Atlanta last week.

Karat: see Carat.

Later/Latter

Later (ADVERB; after the proper time)—The shipment arrived a week *later* than we had expected.

Latter (ADJECTIVE; the second thing of two things mentioned)—Your *latter* suggestion is more likely to be adopted by the hiring committee. *See also* **Former**.

Lay/Lie

Lay (VERB; to put or place; a transitive verb that needs an object to complete its meaning; *lay, laid, laid,* and *laying* are the principal parts of this verb)—Please *lay* all newly signed contracts on my desk. I *laid* the signed contracts on your desk yesterday. During the past week I have *laid* on your desk four contracts signed by Fred Miller. We are *laying* the foundation for the new building today.

Lie (VERB; to recline; an intransitive VERB that does not have an object; *lie, lay, lain,* and *lying* are the principal parts of this verb)—Where may the patient *lie* down? He *lay* in the hospital waiting room for more than three hours before a doctor examined him. These contracts have *lain* on Ms. Lee's desk since Monday. Mrs. Hartman is *lying* down.

Lead/Led

Lead (NOUN USED AS ADJECTIVE ['led]; a metallic element)—How many feet of *lead* pipe did the contractor order for this apartment house complex?

Led (VERB; past tense of *lead* ['lēd], meaning "to provide direction")—Before his retirement Mr. Andrews *led* this company from a $3 million deficit to a $6 million annual profit.

Lean/Lien

Lean (VERB; to rest against; to be inclined toward. ADJECTIVE; not fat)—Ask the children not to *lean* against these railings. Most of our employees seem to *lean* toward receiving additional medical benefits rather than salary increases. We use only first-quality *lean* ground beef in our hamburgers.

Lien (NOUN; a legal right or claim to property)—If the company refuses to pay, we will be forced to place a *lien* against its property.

Leased/Least

Leased (VERB; property rented for a specified time period)—Our company has *leased* this suite of offices for the past seven years.

Least (ADJECTIVE; smallest, slightest, lowest)—This year we showed the *least* profit since our company was established in 1982.

Led: see Lead.

Lend/Loan

Lend (VERB; to give for temporary use with the understanding that the same or equivalent will be returned)—Has the bank agreed to *lend* us additional funds to expand our warehouse facilities?

Loan (NOUN; something given for a borrower's temporary use)—Your $10,000 *loan* will be fully repaid with your August 1 payment.

Less: see Fewer.

Lessee/Lesser/Lessor

Lessee (NOUN; one to whom a lease is given)—As specified in the lease, the *lessee* must pay a monthly rent of $950 by or before the 1st of each month.

Lesser (ADJECTIVE; smaller; less important)—Although the judge ruled in favor of the defendant, he awarded a *lesser* amount than we had expected.

Lessor (NOUN; one who grants a lease)—The *lessor* for all our company cars is Allied Car Leasing Service.

Lessen/Lesson

Lessen (VERB; to make smaller)—Chris Timmins recommended that we *lessen* our efforts in the manufacturing area.

Lesson (NOUN; a unit of study; something from which one learns)—This experience was a good *lesson* for Juanita in how making assumptions can result in miscommunication.

Lesser: see Lessee.

Lessor: see Lessee.

Levee/Levy

Levee (NOUN; the bank of a river or a boat landing)—The river overflowed the *levee*.

Levy (NOUN; an order for payment)—To pay for the flood damage, the governor ordered a 1 percent *levy* on gasoline sales.

Liable/Libel/Likely

Liable (ADJECTIVE; legally responsible, obligated)—The court ruled that the company was *liable* for all damages resulting from the accident.

Libel (NOUN; a false or damaging written statement about another)—Don refused to include the statement in his article because he feared he would be sued for *libel*.

Likely (ADJECTIVE; probable. ADVERB; probably)—He is a *likely* candidate for the position. If you continue to be habitually late and absent, you are *likely* (not *liable*) to be fired.

Lie: see Lay.

Lien: see Lean.

Lightening/Lightning

Lightening (VERB [GERUND]; illuminating or brightening; lessening or alleviating)—Please select colors that will result in *lightening* the reception area. We can expect to retain Ms. Burton only by *lightening* her workload.

Lightning (NOUN; the flashing of light produced by atmospheric electricity)—During the storm flashes of *lightning* streaked across the sky.

Like: see As.

Likely: see Liable.

Loan: see Lend.

Local/Locale

Local (ADJECTIVE; limited to a particular district)—Only residents of the *local* area were eligible for financial assistance.

Locale (NOUN [lō'kal]; a particular location)—This parcel of land is an ideal *locale* for a shopping center.

Loose/Lose

Loose (ADJECTIVE; not fastened, not tight or shut up)—A *loose* connection was the probable cause of the power failure on the fifth floor of the Fisher Building.

Lose (VERB; to fail to keep; to mislay)—We do not want to *lose* any of our accounts in the Philippines. If you *lose* your keys, please call Mr. Drew in Plant Facilities.

Magnate/Magnet

Magnate (NOUN; a powerful or influential person)—As the first *magnate* of the automobile industry, Henry Ford changed the lifestyle of people throughout the world.

Magnet (NOUN or ADJECTIVE; something that has the ability to attract)—Picking up the spilled paper clips with a *magnet* was an easy task. This *magnet* school has many talented musicians.

Main/Mane

Main (ADJECTIVE; principal or most important part)—Our *main* selling feature is still customer service.

Mane (NOUN; the heavy hair on the neck of a horse or lion)—The horse's *mane* had become entangled in the wire fence.

Manner/Manor

Manner (NOUN; method; a customary or particular way)—Unless this Internet service provider changes its *manner* of doing business, it will lose many more customers. Chancellor Phelps' congenial *manner* has endeared him to both faculty and students alike.

Manor (NOUN; a main house or mansion)—Although the décor of the *manor* dates back to the early twentieth century, its interior is still well maintained and elegant.

Marital/Marshal/Martial

Marital (ADJECTIVE; pertaining to marriage)—Use "*marital* bliss" as the primary appeal in your advertising copy for this client.

Marshal (NOUN; a military or law enforcement rank; the head of a ceremony)—If you wish to have a *marshal* serve these papers, you must pay an additional $40 fee. Jack Williams was asked to act as honorary *marshal* of the parade.

Martial (ADJECTIVE; warlike, military)—Several bands played *martial* music at the Veterans Day commemoration.

May: see Can.

May be/Maybe

May be (VERB; a verb phrase [a helping verb and a main verb] derived from the infinitive *to be*)—This *may be* the last year we will lease these facilities.

Maybe (ADVERB; perhaps)—*Maybe* you could ask the sales representatives to e-mail this information to you as they call upon their various accounts.

Me: see I.

Medal/Meddle

Medal (NOUN; a metal disk; an award in the form of a metal disk)—This morning I found a gold religious *medal* lying on the sidewalk outside the church. The fire-fighter received a *medal* for his heroic efforts.

Meddle (VERB; to interfere)—Please ask your assistant not to *meddle* in the dispute between Sandra and her supervisor.

Miner/Minor

Miner (NOUN; a person who works in a mine)—The discovery of gold in Brazil in the 1980s attracted nearly 40,000 *miners*, initiating a gold rush that still exists today.

Minor (NOUN; a person under legal age. ADJECTIVE; a lesser thing)—Please post a sign that reads "No *minors* allowed." Your forgetting to fax the proposal yesterday proved to be of *minor* consequence.

Mode/Mood

Mode (NOUN; style or preferred method)—What *mode* of transportation will you use to reach the airport?

Mood (NOUN; feeling or disposition)—Before you ask Mr. Smith for a salary increase, be sure he is in a good *mood*.

Moral/Morale

Moral (ADJECTIVE; pertaining to right and wrong, ethical)—Too many *moral* issues were apparent in this investment strategy for our company to become involved.

Morale (NOUN; a mental condition)—Announcement of an across-the-board 7 percent pay increase instantly boosted employee *morale*.

Morning/Mourning

Morning (NOUN; the time from sunrise to noon)—Would you be able to schedule an appointment for me to see Dr. Rose on Friday *morning*?

Mourning (NOUN; showing signs of grief)—Please allow the family to observe this period of *mourning* without any interruptions concerning business matters.

Most: see Almost.

Mourning: see Morning.

Myself: see I.

Naval/Navel

Naval (ADJECTIVE; relating to a navy)—Last week Mr. Marsh's son accepted an assignment with *naval* intelligence.

Navel (NOUN; a depression in the middle of the abdomen)—According to Dr. Chin, the incision will leave a small scar directly below the *navel*.

Number: see Amount.

On behalf of: see In behalf of.

Ordinance/Ordnance

Ordinance (NOUN; a local regulation)—Most cities have an *ordinance* banning excessive noise after 10 p.m.

Ordnance (NOUN USED AS ADJECTIVE; military weapons)—We should know by the end of the month whether we will receive the army *ordnance* contract.

Overdo/Overdue

Overdo (VERB; to do in excess, exaggerate)—Exercise is healthful if one does not *overdo* it.

Overdue (ADJECTIVE; late)—Your payment is 15 days *overdue*.

Pair/Pare/Pear

Pair (NOUN; two of a kind; made of two corresponding parts)—The *pair* of shoes the customer attempted to return showed signs of considerable wear.

Pare (VERB; to reduce in size or trim; to peel)—All department heads have been instructed to *pare* their budgets by at least 10 percent. Be sure to *pare* the carrots before grating them.

Pear (NOUN; a fruit)—Our market carries three brands of canned *pears*.

Partition/Petition

Partition (NOUN; something that divides)—Office efficiency increased substantially after each workstation was separated by a *partition*.

Petition (NOUN; a formal written request)—Have you signed the *petition* to create curb cutouts at all major intersections in the downtown business district?

Passed/Past

Passed (VERB; past tense or past participle of *pass*, meaning "to go by" or "circulate")—Once you have *passed* the intersection, look for our store on the right side of the street. Lisa *passed* out copies of the job announcement to all eligible employees in the company.

Past (NOUN or ADJECTIVE; time gone by or ended)—Our weak profit picture is all in the *past*. From *past* experience we have learned not to extend credit to this company.

7
Misused Words

241

Patience/Patients

Patience (NOUN; calm perseverance)—Jamie's *patience* in working with disabled children is certainly to be admired. Accessing the Internet with an older, slower modem requires considerable *patience*.

Patients (NOUN; people undergoing medical treatment)—Is George Allison one of Dr. Hedge's *patients*?

Peace/Piece

Peace (NOUN; truce; tranquillity)—As long as hostilities persist, there can be no *peace* among these nations. Since Ms. Seraydarian began the project, she has not had a moment's *peace*.

Piece (NOUN; a part of a defined quantity)—Each of the three beneficiaries inherited a *piece* of the prime property.

Peak/Peek

Peak (ADJECTIVE or NOUN; highest point; top)—Our *peak* sales period is from September through November. KLAC's transmitter is located at the *peak* of Mount Baldy.

Peek (VERB; to glance)—Some of the buyers have already had a *peek* at the new fall fashions by major designers.

Peal/Peel

Peal (VERB; to give out a loud sound or succession of sounds)—The bells *pealed* from the church tower.

Peel (VERB; to remove by stripping. NOUN; skin or rind)—Ask the customer to *peel* off the mailing label and affix it to the enclosed postcard. Do any of these recipes require the use of lemon *peel*?

Pear: see Pair.

Peek: see Peak.

Peel: see Peal.

Peer/Pier

Peer (VERB; to gaze. NOUN; one belonging to the same social group)—Do customers often *peer* into the bakery shop window before entering the store? Most teenagers imitate the behavior of their *peers*.

Pier (NOUN; a structure extending into navigable waters)—The new *pier* will have shops and restaurants as well as spaces for sidewalk vendors.

Persecute/Prosecute

Persecute (VERB; to harass persistently)—If your new supervisor continues to *persecute* you, contact your union representative at Ext. 3543.

Prosecute (VERB; to conduct legal proceedings against someone)—The district attorney may not have enough evidence to *prosecute* the case.

Personal/Personnel

Personal (ADJECTIVE; private; individual)—Be careful about disclosing *personal* information over the Internet. Each employee has a *personal* parking space.

Personnel (NOUN; employees. ADJECTIVE; relating to employment)—All ***personnel*** have been asked to work overtime until the inventory is completed. Your annual performance evaluation will be placed in your ***personnel*** file.

Perspective/Prospective

Perspective (NOUN; a mental picture or outlook)—I believe his ***perspective*** is distorted by greed.

Prospective (ADJECTIVE; likely to be or become, expected)—Have you been able to locate a ***prospective*** buyer for the property on Lake Street? What are the ***prospective*** benefits to be derived from the reorganization of our marketing channels?

Persuade: see Convince.

Peruse/Pursue

Peruse (VERB; to read hastily or casually)—Each morning at breakfast I ***peruse*** the newspaper for any items of interest to our industry.

Pursue (VERB; to follow in order to overtake; to proceed with a course of action)—As he used his cell phone to notify the police, the onlooker continued to ***pursue*** the hijacker. May I suggest you ***pursue*** this sales lead further.

Petition: see Partition.

Physical: see Fiscal.

Piece: see Peace.

Pier: see Peer.

Plaintiff/Plaintive

Plaintiff (NOUN; one who initiates a lawsuit to obtain a remedy for injury to his or her rights)—The attorney for the ***plaintiff*** in this case has petitioned the court for an extension.

Plaintive (ADJECTIVE; expressive of suffering or woe)—In a ***plaintive*** voice the witness described how the gunmen carried out the robbery.

Pole/Poll

Pole (NOUN; a long, slender object that is usually cylindrical)—The teachers will need a ***pole*** to open the top row of windows in these classrooms.

Poll (NOUN; counting of opinions or votes cast; place where votes are cast [usually *polls*])—Our latest ***poll*** shows that consumers prefer Revel original toothpaste over Revel mint toothpaste. Be sure to urge all registered voters to go to the ***polls*** next Tuesday.

Populace/Populous

Populace (NOUN; the masses; population of a place)—The winning candidate must have the support of the ***populace***. During the flood the ***populace*** of Evansville was evacuated.

Populous (ADJECTIVE; densely populated)—Our fast-food chain has established restaurants only in ***populous*** areas.

Pore/Pour

Pore (VERB; to read studiously or attentively. NOUN; a small opening in a membrane)—How long did the auditors *pore* over these books before discovering discrepancies in the entries? Hot water will open the *pores* of your skin, and cold water will close them.

Pour (VERB; to dispense from a container; to move with a continuous flow)—Please ask the servers to *pour* the water before the guests are seated. Even before the game ended, spectators began to *pour* out of the stadium.

Possible: see Feasible.

Practicable/Practical

Practicable (ADJECTIVE; describes an idea or plan that in theory seems to be feasible or usable; capable of being put into practice)—The plan to build cars fueled exclusively by electricity seems to be *practicable*, but there is presently no mass market for such a vehicle.

Practical (ADJECTIVE; describes an idea or plan that is feasible or usable because it has been successfully tried or proved by past experience; fit for actual practice)—Because gasoline prices in Europe are high, most Europeans find small, economy cars to be the *practical* solution to controlling transportation costs.

Pray/Prey

Pray (VERB; to make a request in a humble manner; to address a god)—I *pray* that these bureaucrats will give consideration to my suggestion. Children may not be required to *pray* in public schools.

Prey (VERB; to have an injurious or destructive effect. NOUN; victim)—Ms. Rice should not let this experience constantly *prey* on her thoughts. Do not become *prey* to the get-rich-quick schemes of swindlers.

Precede/Proceed

Precede (VERB [pri-'sēd]; to go before)—Mrs. Andrews' presentation will directly *precede* the convention's first general session.

Proceed (VERB [prō-'sēd]; to go forward or continue)—Please *proceed* with your analysis of the utility company's financial statements.

Precedence/Precedents

Precedence (NOUN ['pre-cə-dən(t)s]; priority)—Please give *precedence* to training our middle management personnel in the use of voice-recognition software.

Precedents (NOUN ['pre-cə-dənts]; things done or said that can be used as an example)—There are no legal *precedents* in our state for this particular case.

Presence/Presents

Presence (NOUN; condition of being present; stately or distinguished bearing of a person)—Please ensure the *presence* of all supervisors and managers at this leadership seminar. Everyone was impressed by the confidence and *presence* with which the new president addressed the faculty.

Presents (NOUN; gifts or things given)—Company employees donated a record number of *presents* to needy children this year.

Presume: see Assume.

Prey: see Pray.

Principal/Principle

Principal (NOUN; a capital sum; head of a school)—Each month your loan statement shows the amount of **principal** and the amount of interest paid the previous month. As **principal** of Lindberg High School, Mrs. Brereton was proud that so many seniors attended college upon graduation.

Principal (ADJECTIVE; highest in importance)—The **principal** reason for offering employees tuition reimbursement is to encourage them to upgrade their skills.

Principle (NOUN; an accepted rule of action; a basic truth or belief)—This applicant's knowledge of accounting **principles** is questionable. Our country was founded on the **principle** that all persons are created equal.

Proceed: see Precede.

Propose/Purpose

Propose (VERB; to suggest)—I **propose** that we borrow sufficient funds to purchase all the new equipment at once.

Purpose (NOUN; a desired result)—The **purpose** of this meeting is to discuss procedures for increasing our sales through e-commerce.

Prosecute: see Persecute.

Prospective: see Perspective.

Purpose: see Propose.

Pursue: see Peruse.

Quiet/Quite

Quiet (ADJECTIVE; peaceful; free from noise)—Our client wishes to purchase a three-bedroom home in a **quiet** residential neighborhood. The **quiet** operation of this laser color printer is one of its main sales features.

Quite (ADVERB; completely or actually)—Our salespeople seem to be **quite** satisfied with the new commission plan.

Raise/Raze/Rise

Raise (VERB; to lift something up, increase in amount, gather together, or bring into existence; a transitive verb that needs an object to complete its meaning; *raise, raised, raised,* and *raising* are the principal parts of this verb)—Please do not **raise** your voice. The company **raised** our sales quota 10 percent last month. We have **raised** $350 for Mrs. Morgan's retirement gift. A number of our stockholders are **raising** questions about the proposed merger.

Raze (VERB; to tear down to the ground)—When does the company plan to **raze** this old warehouse and build a new one in its place?

Rise (VERB; to go up or to increase in value; an intransitive verb that does not have an object; *rise, rose, risen,* and *rising* are the principal parts of this verb)—Our sales should **rise** beyond the $1 million mark this quarter. The rocket **rose** 30,000 feet before it exploded. Our sales have **risen** for the third month in a row. Production has been **rising** steadily since the new equipment was installed.

Real/Really

Real (ADJECTIVE; actual, true; genuine)—By providing us with competent temporary employees during this tax season, your staffing agency has been of ***real*** assistance. The diamonds in this necklace do not look ***real***.

Really (ADVERB; very, certainly)—Susan was ***really*** disappointed that Robert did not accept the position.

Reality/Realty

Reality (NOUN; that which is real, that which exists)—The public must face the ***reality*** that videocassettes will be obsolete as DVDs become the movie medium.

Realty (NOUN or ADJECTIVE; real estate)—The last ***realty*** company that tried to sell my property could not find a qualified buyer.

Receipt/Recipe

Receipt (NOUN; a written acknowledgment of receiving goods or money)—No refunds can be made without a ***receipt***.

Recipe (NOUN; a set of instructions)—Mama Lucia's has always kept secret the ***recipe*** for its delicious spaghetti sauce.

Regardless: See Irregardless.

Residence/Residents

Residence (NOUN; place where one lives)—This house has been Mrs. Scott's ***residence*** for the past 30 years.

Residents (NOUN; people who live in a place)—One of the retirement home ***residents*** reported that the heater in her room emits only cold air. The ***residents*** of Nashville have elected a new mayor.

Respectably/Respectfully/Respectively

Respectably (ADJECTIVE; in a correct or decent manner)—The vagrant was dressed ***respectably*** for his court appearance.

Respectfully (ADVERB; a manner denoting high regard; word used in the complimentary close of a letter to show high regard for the addressee)—Please remember to treat all our customers ***respectfully***. Letter closing: ***Respectfully*** yours.

Respectively (ADVERB; each in turn or in order)—Janice Jackson, John Zelinsky, and Al Turnbull were first-, second-, and third-prize winners, ***respectively***.

Ring/Wring

Ring (VERB; to give out a resounding sound)—Do not allow your cell phone or beeper to ***ring*** during class sessions; please set these devices to "silent."

Wring (VERB; to squeeze or twist)—The care instructions for these garments caution consumers to "Hand wash only. Do not ***wring*** dry; blot dry with towel."

Rise: see Raise.

Role/Roll

Role (NOUN; proper function of a person or thing; a part or character assumed)—Mr. Hayworth is quite successful in his ***role*** as mediator for grievances within the company. What ***role*** will you play in this theater production?

Roll (VERB; to move by turning or rotating. NOUN; something wound around a core;

a list of names)—Ask the plumber to *roll* back the bathroom carpeting before attempting any plumbing repairs. Please order 3 dozen *rolls* of transparent packaging tape from Hillsdale Stationers. How many students are on your *roll*?

Rote/Wrote

Rote (NOUN; mechanical or repetitious procedure)—All fourth-grade children are expected to learn the multiplication tables *one* through *ten* by *rote*.

Wrote (VERB; past tense of *write*)—We *wrote* to all our clients last week informing them of our merger with American Financial Corporation.

Rout/Route

Rout (NOUN ['raut—sounds like *out*]; a disorderly assembly or disastrous defeat)—The game turned into a *rout* after the opposing team scored 28 points during the first quarter.

Route (NOUN ['rüt]; a course taken in traveling from one point to another)—Our delivery *routes* were changed based upon the consultant's recommendations.

Sample: see Example.

Scene/Seen

Scene (NOUN; place of an occurrence; an exhibition of anger)—The police arrived at the *scene* of the robbery shortly after the security guard telephoned them. How would you handle a hostile customer who was creating a *scene*?

Seen (VERB; past participle of *to see*)—I have not *seen* our sales manager for three days.

Scent: see Cent.

Sealing: see Ceiling.

Seize: see Cease.

Semi-: see Bi-.

Senses: see Census.

Sent: see Cent.

Serial: see Cereal.

Set/Sit

Set (VERB; to place; to position; to arrange; a transitive verb that generally needs an object to complete its meaning; *set, set, set,* and *setting* are the principal parts of this verb)—Please *set* the package on my desk. He *set* the clocks ahead one hour for daylight saving time. I have *set* the times for all your medical appointments this week. We are *setting* higher quotas for our sales personnel this year.

Sit (VERB; to be seated or occupy a seat; an intransitive verb that does not have an object; *sit, sat, sat,* and *sitting* are the principal parts of this verb)—*Sit* here, Ms. Brown. I *sat* for more than an hour awaiting his return. He has *sat* in that chair all day watching television. If Mr. Weaver calls, tell him I am *sitting* in on a meeting of the department heads.

7

Misused Words

Sew/So/Sow

Sew (VERB; to fasten by stitches with thread)—Please have someone in the Alterations Department ***sew*** a button on this coat.

So (ADVERB; to that degree. CONJUNCTION; in a way indicated; in order that; therefore)—We are ***so*** interested in entering the Brazilian market that we have set up an office in Rio. ***So*** that we may update our files, please complete the enclosed form and mail it to us in the return envelope. Our company is moving its offices to Columbus, Ohio; ***so*** now we are in the process of recruiting new personnel in this city.

Sow (VERB; to scatter seed)—This machine can ***sow*** more seed in a day than any 15 farmhands.

Shall/Will

Shall (HELPING VERB; denotes future time in the first person in formal writing)—I ***shall*** give your request the utmost consideration. We ***shall*** initiate legal proceedings on November 1.

Will (HELPING VERB; used with all three persons in business style)—I (or We) ***will*** call you tomorrow. You ***will*** receive your refund when you return the merchandise. He (or She or They) ***will*** finish the project according to schedule unless he (or she or they) encounter(s) bad weather conditions.

She: see Her.

Shear/Sheer

Shear (VERB; to cut, strip, or remove)—The mechanic had to ***shear*** off the bolts before he could remove the wheel.

Sheer (ADJECTIVE; transparently thin; utter; steep)—None of these ***sheer*** fabrics are suitable for the kind of draperies we have in mind. Attending this seminar was a ***sheer*** waste of time. A number of mountain climbers have successfully scaled these ***sheer*** cliffs.

Shone/Shown

Shone (VERB; past tense and past participle of *shine*)—If flashing red lights had been ***shone*** through the dense fog, this serious accident might have been avoided.

Shown (VERB; past participle of *show*)—The PowerPoint slide presentation describing our new products has been ***shown*** to all our salespeople and is available for their use in sales presentations.

Should/Would

Should (HELPING VERB; denotes future time in the first person in formal writing)—We ***should*** appreciate your returning the signed contracts by Friday, March 23.

Would (HELPING VERB; used with all three persons in business style)—I (or We) ***would*** appreciate receiving a copy of that report. She (or He or They) said that she (or he or they) ***would*** be willing to work overtime if the report isn't finished by 5 p.m. Did you say that you ***would*** be interested in having a demonstration of our new Model 1100 fax machine?

Shown: see Shone.

Sight: see Cite.

Sit: see Set.

Site: see Cite.

So: see Sew.

Soar/Sore

Soar (VERB; to fly aloft or about; to rise or increase dramatically)—These miniature aircraft are built to **soar** through the sky without motor or battery power. News of the merger will cause the price of our stock to **soar**.

Sore (ADJECTIVE; painfully sensitive)—If you overdo an exercise program, your muscles will become **sore**. Last year's financial losses have become a **sore** point for our company president.

Sole/Soul

Sole (NOUN; the undersurface of a foot. ADJECTIVE; being the only one)—When you walk, distribute your weight evenly between the **sole** and the heel of your foot. John is the **sole** heir to his father's fortune.

Soul (NOUN; the immaterial essence of an individual; living example of moral principle)—Most contemporary religions believe that the **soul** of an individual continues on after his or her physical death. Mr. Perry is the **soul** of honesty and integrity.

Some/Somewhat

Some (ADJECTIVE; an indefinite amount)—Before we move into our new offices, we will need to have a contractor make **some** structural alterations.

Somewhat (ADVERB; to some degree)—Our sales force feels that your sales projections for next year are **somewhat** optimistic.

Some time/Sometime/Sometimes

Some time (ADJECTIVE + NOUN; a period of time)—Our staff will need **some time** to review your proposal before we can make a decision.

Sometime (ADVERB; an indefinite time, anytime)—Your order should be delivered **sometime** early next week.

Sometimes (ADVERB; occasionally)—**Sometimes** our firm needs to hire personnel from temporary agencies.

Somewhat: see Some.

Sore: see Soar.

Soul: see Sole.

Sow: see Sew.

Staid/Stayed

Staid (ADJECTIVE; sedate, composed)—A **staid** individual, like Bill, is needed for this position.

7

Misused Words

Stayed (VERB; past tense and past participle of *stay*)—She **stayed** long after regular hours to finish the report.

Stationary/Stationery

Stationary (ADJECTIVE; not movable)—Only two of the interior walls in this suite are **stationary**.

Stationery (NOUN OR ADJECTIVE; writing material)—Prepare this letter on Mr. Parks' personal **stationery**. Our order for additional **stationery** supplies is scheduled to arrive next week.

Statue/Stature/Statute

Statue (NOUN; a carved or molded image of someone or something)—Meet me in front of the **statue** of Lincoln at 2 p.m.

Stature (NOUN; the height of an object or a body; status gained by attainment)—The **stature** alone of the pyramids is overwhelming. Dr. Sunayama is a person of great **stature** within the community.

Statute (NOUN; law enacted by a legislature)—**Statutes** in this state prohibit gambling in any form.

Stayed: see Staid.

Straight/Strait

Straight (ADJECTIVE; free of bends, curves, or angles. ADVERB; in a direct manner)—Use a ruler with a **straight** edge to draw these lines. Ms. Torti always seems able to go **straight** to the source of a problem.

Strait (NOUN; a narrow space or passage connecting two bodies of water)—The ship and its cargo were damaged while going through the **strait**.

Suit/Suite

Suit (NOUN ['süt]; an action filed in court; a set of garments)—A & Z Computer Corporation has already filed **suit** against Compco for patent infringements. Be sure to wear a dark-colored business **suit** for the interview.

Suite (NOUN ['swēt]; a group of things forming a unit; a set)—Were you able to reserve a **suite** for the week of April 3 at the Hyatt Regency? (Here *suite* refers to a group of rooms.) How many pieces are featured in this bedroom **suite**? (In this example *suite* refers to pieces of furniture in a set.)

Sure/Surely

Sure (ADJECTIVE; an adjective or subject complement meaning "certain" or "positive")—Nancy was **sure** she had made the right decision to accept the position.

Surely (ADVERB; certainly or undoubtedly)—Our employees will **surely** be pleased with the new benefits in their contract.

Take: see Bring.

Tare/Tear/Tier

Tare (NOUN ['tar—sounds like *care*]; a deduction from the gross weight of goods and their container made to allow for the weight of the container)—The **tare** on this shipment is 210 pounds.

Tear (NOUN ['tir]; a saline fluid that flows from the eye, usually signifying distress or extreme joy)—A *tear* flowed down the child's face as she viewed her brother in the hospital bed.

Tear (VERB ['tar]; to pull apart or rip. NOUN ['tar]; a rip)—When you open the envelope, be careful not to *tear* its contents. The customer returned the sweater because it had a *tear* in the sleeve.

Tier (NOUN ['tir]; rows, levels, or ranks placed one above the other)—Our company's season tickets are on the first *tier* of the stadium.

Temperature: see Fever.

Than/Then

Than (CONJUNCTION; used to show comparison)—Ms. Espinoza has more experience *than* I in writing contract proposals.

Then (ADVERB; at that time)—Once all the data has been gathered, you may *then* begin organizing the report.

That/Which

That (PRONOUN; refers to animals or things; introduces a restrictive or essential subordinate clause)—All dogs *that* are found wandering in the streets will be impounded. We have in stock, Ms. Wells, all the items *that* you ordered.

Which (PRONOUN; refers to animals or things; introduces a nonrestrictive or nonessential subordinate clause)—The security staff recommended that we acquire a watchdog, *which* would be kept inside the plant at night. Our new credit system, *which* will be installed next week, will cost more than $50,000.

Their/There/They're

Their (PRONOUN USED AS ADJECTIVE; the possessive form of *they*)—As a result of *their* recommendation, we installed an Apex Security System in our main warehouse.

There (ADVERB; at that place or at that point)—Please be *there* promptly at ten o'clock in the morning.

They're (PRONOUN + VERB; contraction of *they are*)—Although the union representatives rejected our first offer, *they're* willing to consider our second proposal.

Theirs/There's

Theirs (PRONOUN; possessive form of *they*)—This copy of the contract is *theirs*.

There's (PRONOUN + VERB; contraction of *there is* or *there has*)—*There's* still much to be done before we can open our new store. *There's* been too much time and money spent in attempting to obtain a zoning change for this property.

Them/They

Them (PRONOUN; a direct object, an indirect object, or an object of a preposition)—I asked *them* to wait outside. I sent *them* a bill last week. I waited for *them* all morning.

They (PRONOUN; subject of a clause or a complement pronoun)—*They* are meeting with the Board of Directors this afternoon. The two persons who cochaired the committee were *they*.

Then: see Than.

There: see Their.

There's: see Theirs.

They: see Them.

They're: see Their.

Threw/Through/Thru

Threw (VERB; past tense of *throw*)—As I reviewed all the documents in the files, I ***threw*** away those documents that were no longer needed.

Through (PREPOSITION; in one end and out the other; movement within a large expanse; during the period of; as a consequence of)—While you are in Atlanta, will your schedule permit a tour ***through*** the plant? The pigeons flew gracefully ***through*** the air. You may order this software at a 15 percent discount from June 15 ***through*** June 30. We have retained this account ***through*** your diligent efforts.

Thru (A variation of *through* that is not acceptable for business writing.)

Tier: see Tare.

To/Too/Two

To (PREPOSITION; function word to indicate direction toward. THE SIGN OF AN INFINI-TIVE; for example, *to go*)—Please return these materials ***to*** me when you have finished reviewing them. She wanted ***to*** see for herself the condition of the plant cafeteria.

Too (ADVERB; also; to an excessive extent)—I was there ***too***. Because the office was ***too*** noisy, I had difficulty hearing you on the telephone.

Two (NOUN; the number between *one* and *three*)—There was just too much work for the ***two*** of us to finish by five o'clock.

Tortuous/Torturous

Tortuous (ADJECTIVE; winding, twisting)—The ***tortuous*** road leading to Hana Bay has been the scene of many automobile accidents.

Torturous (ADJECTIVE; causing pain)—Filling out all these forms is a ***torturous*** task.

Toward/Towards

Toward (PREPOSITION; in the direction of)—Set up these workstations so that all the screens on the computer monitors face ***toward*** the west wall.

Towards (Secondary form of *toward*; use *toward* instead of *towards* in business writing.)

Uninterested: see Disinterested.

Us/We

Us (PRONOUN; a direct object, an indirect object, or an object of a preposition)—The vice president took ***us*** on a tour of the plant. The manager gave ***us*** a copy of the annual report. The reception was planned for ***us***.

We (PRONOUN; the subject of a clause or a complement pronoun)—*We* must decide upon a definite course of action by 3 p.m. The singers selected to perform for this special broadcast were *we*.

Vain/Van/Vane/Vein

Vain (ADJECTIVE; unduly proud or conceited)—Tom would be more popular with his fellow workers if he were not so *vain*.

Van (NOUN; a covered truck)—Our hospital *van* is used primarily for transporting patients.

Vane (NOUN; a thin object used to show wind direction)—The weather *vane* indicated that the wind was coming from a westward direction.

Vein (NOUN; a tubular vessel that carries blood to the heart; mode or style)—The laboratory technician was able to locate easily a *vein* in the elderly patient's arm to draw sufficient blood for the tests ordered by the doctor. Although Mr. Bates had been warned about his unfriendly attitude toward other employees, he continued to behave in that *vein*.

Vary/Very

Vary (VERB; to change)—The new advertising manager said that for the time being he would not request us to *vary* any procedures.

Very (ADVERB; extremely)—These figures are *very* difficult to verify from the information available.

Vein: see Vain.

Vice/Vise

Vice (NOUN; immoral habit; personal fault)—Drug abuse by America's populace is a *vice* that must be curtailed. Cigar smoking is his only *vice*.

Vise (NOUN; a clamp. ADJECTIVE; strong hold or squeeze)—Please order a *vise* for our new carpenter. He shook my hand with a *vise*-like grip.

Waive/Wave

Waive (VERB; to relinquish; to refrain from enforcing)—Do you *waive* your right to a jury trial? You must petition the dean of academic affairs to *waive* this requirement.

Wave (VERB; to swing something back and forth or up and down)—The angry customer was determined to *wave* his bill in everyone's face.

Waiver/Waver

Waiver (NOUN; the relinquishment of a claim)—Please sign the enclosed *waiver* to release our company from any further responsibility for your injury.

Waver (VERB; to shake or fluctuate)—I believe Mr. Doyle is beginning to *waver* concerning our request to update our accounting software.

Wave: see Waive.

Waver: see Waiver.

We: see Us.

Weather/Whether

Weather (VERB; to bear up against. NOUN; the state of the atmosphere)—We are pleased that you were able to *weather* the high rate of employee turnover during the summer months. Tomorrow's *weather* forecast predicts scattered showers and a high temperature of 50 degrees.

Whether (CONJUNCTION; an introduction of alternatives)—We will not know until next week *whether* our company or Artistry in Motion will be awarded the contract.

Well: see Good.

Whether: see Weather.

Which: see That.

Who/Whom

Who (PRONOUN; the subject of a subordinate clause or a complement pronoun)—I was the person *who* invited you to attend. I cannot tell you *who* the caller might have been.

Whom (PRONOUN; a direct object or an object of a preposition)—*Whom* have you hired as your assistant? Here is the address of the person with *whom* we met for legal assistance. (See Section 5-7j for a further explanation of how to use *who* and *whom*.)

Whole: see Hole.

Wholly: see Holy.

Whom: see Who.

Who's/Whose

Who's (PRONOUN + VERB; a contraction of *who is*)—Please let me know *who's* taking over for you during August.

Whose (PRONOUN USED AS ADJECTIVE; possessive form of *who*)—Mr. Long is the vice president *whose* position was eliminated.

Will: see Shall.

Would: see Should.

Wring: see Ring.

Wrote: see Rote.

Your/You're

Your (PRONOUN USED AS ADJECTIVE; possessive form of *you*)—*Your* assistant informed me that you had invited the mayor to the reception.

You're (PRONOUN + VERB; contraction of *you are*)—If *you're* interested in contacting the authors of *HOW 10*, please e-mail us at ClarksHOW@aol.com.

8

Proofreading and Editing

Proofreading and Editing Solution Finder

Spelling

Proofreading and editing have taken on new roles as spelling checkers and grammar checkers have become integral parts of word processing programs. In many ways the burden of proofreading and editing has been lightened, but only to add different approaches and tasks.

The process of producing documents with correct spellings has been automated to a great extent. However, standard dictionaries and other resources still play a major role in proofreading and/or editing documents for spelling errors.

The increasing popularity of speech-recognition software has added yet another dimension to the proofreading and editing process. Although all dictated words are spelled correctly, the words dictated may not always match the words printed on the screen. Words that sound alike but are spelled differently (to, too, two) require correction—as do words that are misunderstood entirely.

8-1 Use of the Dictionary to Locate Correct Spellings

a. Use a recognized up-to-date collegiate, desk, or unabridged dictionary to locate any spellings of words you do not know or about which you are unsure. The dictionary used for all spellings in this manual is the 2002 printing of *Merriam-Webster's Collegiate Dictionary*, 10th edition, published by Merriam-Webster, Incorporated.[1]

b. When the dictionary offers two spellings for a word in the same entry, use the first spelling.

judgment   not: judgement   **canceled**   not: cancelled

c. When verifying the spelling of words, match the word with its correct counterpart in the dictionary. For example, if the word is used as a noun in the sentence, then compare it with the noun spelling of this word in the dictionary. As an illustration of differences in spellings, note that *under way* used as an adverb is two words but *underway* as an adjective is one. Similar situations occur with many other words.

mark up (verb)	markup (noun)
break down (verb)	breakdown (noun)
set up (verb)	setup (noun)
double-space (verb)	double space (noun)

---

[1]Merriam-Webster maintains a free-access dictionary and thesaurus Internet Web site at <http://www.m-w.com>.

d. The spellings of irregular plural nouns and irregular verb forms appear in the dictionary directly after the main word in the entry. Therefore, when in doubt about the formation of these words, consult your dictionary for their spellings. (See Sections 5-4 and 5-12 for additional information and examples related to irregular plural nouns and verb forms.)

irregular plural nouns

company	companies		tomato	tomatoes
half	halves		child	children
analysis	analyses		alumnus	alumni

irregular verb forms

bring	brought	brought
sing	sang	sung
run	ran	run
lie	lay	lain
see	saw	seen

e. The spellings of irregular adjective and adverb comparisons appear in the dictionary directly after the main word in the entry. Check your dictionary to verify these spellings. (See Sections 5-21 and 5-26 for rules and additional examples on adjective and adverb comparisons.)

irregular adjective comparisons

costly	costlier	costliest
good	better	best

irregular adverb comparisons

early	earlier	earliest
far	farther	farthest

f. To locate easily the spellings of unfamiliar words in the dictionary, acquaint yourself with the various letter combinations that represent sounds in the written English language. Both consonants and vowels may have different letter combinations that represent the same sound. The chart below presents just a few of the sounds and combinations with which you should become familiar.

Sound	Letter Combinations to Represent the Sound
ā	*a*lienate, *ai*de, g*au*ge, st*ea*k, f*ei*gn, w*eigh*t
ak	*ac*tual, *acc*olade, *ac*knowledgment, *acq*uiesce, *aq*ueduct
ar	*aer*osol, *air*borne, *ar*eas, *arr*ogant
as	*as*piration, *asc*ending, *ass*ertive
aw	f*a*ther, *au*dacity, t*augh*t, *aw*esome, *o*stracize, *ough*t
ē	*e*dict, *ea*sement, d*ee*m, rec*ei*pt, p*eo*ple, f*ia*sco, p*ie*ce
er	simil*ar*, *er*adicate, *ear*nings, *err*oneous, f*ir*mly, w*or*risome, t*ou*rnament, *ur*banization

Sound	Letter Combinations to Represent the Sound
f	*f*elony, e*ff*icient, *ph*onetic, rou*gh*age
g	*g*rimace, *gh*astly, *gu*ardian
h	*h*azardous, *wh*olly
ī	a*i*sle, h*eigh*t, *i*dentify, t*ie*d, th*igh*, h*y*draulic
j	ju*dg*ment, *g*ermane, exa*gg*eration, *j*eopardize
k	*c*oincide, a*cc*ountant, *ch*emistry, *k*ilometer, *q*uandary
m	*m*iraculous, pa*lm*istry
n	*gn*aw, *kn*otty, *mn*emonic, *n*arrative, *pn*eumonia
ō	b*eau*, *o*dor, fl*oa*t, d*oe*skin, p*ou*ltry, d*ough*nut, sn*ow*
oi, oy	sp*oi*l, ann*oy*ance
oo	n*eu*tral, fl*ew*, ad*ieu*, t*o*mb, l*oo*se, l*ou*ver, thr*ough*, n*u*trition, tr*ue*, s*ui*t
ow	ann*ou*nce, fl*ow*er
r	*r*etrieve, *rh*ythm, *wr*est
s	*c*ertainty, *s*alable, *ps*ychologist, *sc*intillate
sh	ma*ch*inery, espe*ci*ally, *s*urely, con*sc*ience, *sch*nauzer, nau*se*ous, *sh*rewd, preci*si*on, substan*ti*al
t	*pt*omaine, *t*ranslate
ū	b*eau*tiful, f*eu*d, sk*ew*ed, *u*niform, f*ue*l, *yu*letide
w	*ch*oir, *q*uarterly, *w*asteful, *wh*imsical

8-2   Use of Word Processing Spelling Checkers

a. Use the spelling check feature of your word processing program to check the spelling of any document you have created. All words in the dictionaries of your word processor will be used to correct the words you have keyboarded. Any word not in the dictionary of your word processor will be flagged and must be verified through a standard dictionary, a reputable on-line reference site,[2] or other sources. Spellings of names of individuals and many other proper nouns fall into this category.

Frequently used technical terms or proper nouns not appearing in the main dictionary of a word processor may be added to a supplemental dictionary. By clicking the *Add* option during a spelling check, the word is added to your supplemental dictionary. Right-clicking on the word and then selecting the *Add* option from the drop-down menu also adds the word to your supplemental dictionary. Be careful, though, not to add misspellings to your dictionary.

b. Most word processors provide a "spell-as-you-go" feature. A wavy red line under a word signals the keyboarder that he or she has entered a word that is misspelled according to the dictionaries of

---

[2]The Merriam-Webster free on-line dictionary may be accessed at <http://www.m-w.com>.

the word processor. For standard words the person keyboarding may right click on the word to obtain a list of choices to correct the spelling of the underlined word.

Word processors also provide a "correct-as-you-go" feature. A limited number of misspellings along with their correct spellings are stored in a listing. When the keyboarder enters the misspelling exactly as shown in the list, it is corrected automatically, e.g., *adn* to *and*. Misspellings and corrections may be added to the list. This feature is useful if a keyboarder often misspells a certain word or wishes to have letters, words, numbers, or symbols formatted in a particular way, e.g., *pc* for *Pierce College*.

8-3 Use of On-Line Resources

a. For up-to-date spellings of emerging terminology or words with spellings that appear to be in transition, such as Internet terms, consult a reputable on-line dictionary reference. Merriam-Webster provides a Web site at which you may obtain the latest dictionary and thesaurus entries free of charge. The Web site address is www.m-w.com.

b. At the Merriam-Webster Web site, you may also e-mail questions to the editors requesting assistance with the appropriate spellings for words and expressions that appear to be in transition.

Proofreading

Proofreading is the process of checking a document against an original to ensure that it conforms with the original in all respects. Proofreaders are responsible for checking a prepared document to correct only spelling errors, typographical errors, and any additions or omissions that do not conform to the document with which it is being compared. The proofreader does not make changes in wording or content.

8-4 Proofreading On-Screen Documents

a. Use the spelling check feature of your word processing program before beginning the proofreading process. Follow these guidelines to check spelling in the document:

(1) Enable the "check spelling as you type" feature of your word processing program. Any words not in the dictionaries of your word processor will appear with a wavy red underline.

(2) Correct a word with a wavy red underline by right clicking on it. Select the correct spelling from the drop-down list that appears. If the word is not listed, check your original copy or an up-to-date dictionary for the correct spelling.

(3) Correct proper nouns and technical vocabulary by checking their spellings with the original copy. Spellings of technical words not in the dictionary of the word processor should be verified with the dictionary or another appropriate source such as a medical dictionary, legal dictionary, dictionary of business terms, or dictionary of computer terms.

b. **Check for consistency of style throughout the document before actually beginning to read the text.**

(1) Assess the appropriateness of margins (top, bottom, left, and right).

(2) Check the line spacing between paragraphs, before and after main or text headings, within letter closing lines, etc.

(3) Inspect to ensure that the document contains no widow or orphan lines (single lines of a paragraph at the top or bottom of a page). To avoid such occurrences within a multiple-page document, activate the widow-orphan line protection feature of your word processing program. At the same time check to ensure that the last word on the page does not break and carry over to the following page.

widow line—last line of a paragraph at top of page or column

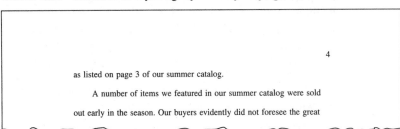

orphan line—first line of a paragraph left at bottom of page or column

(4) Inspect to ensure that no isolated text headings appear at the end of a page. At least two lines of text from the paragraph following the heading must accompany it on the same page. Use the keep-lines-together feature of your word processing program to force any isolated headings to the next page.

(5) Evaluate the general appearance of the document through the page preview feature of your word processing program. Check headers, footers, and page numbering carefully.

c. **Read the text for accuracy. Check it carefully against the original copy. Place the original copy on a copy stand next to your screen. Read a group of words in the original copy; then compare those words with the corresponding ones on the screen. Continue this process until you have proofread the entire document. Use the following criteria to evaluate the keyboarded document:**

   (1) Are any letters transposed or omitted? Are all words spelled correctly? The spelling check feature of your word processing program will have located most spelling errors, but it will not have detected such errors as using *form* for *from*, *an* for *and*, or *effect* for *affect*.

   (2) Have any letters, words, sentences, or paragraphs been omitted? Pay close attention to ensure that no *s*'s have been dropped from plural nouns or *ed*'s from the past tense or the past participle of verb forms. Ensure that no words, sentences, or paragraphs have been skipped.

   (3) Have any words, phrases, or sentences been repeated? Repeated words are flagged by your word processing spell checker, but repeated phrases or sentences are not detected electronically.

   (4) Are all names and unfamiliar words spelled correctly? When proofreading names and unfamiliar words or terminology, check each spelling meticulously—letter by letter.

   (5) Have all figures been typed correctly? Are all calculations correct? Double-check all figures carefully with the original source. For long numbers verify the number of digits and then compare the digits in groups of three. If the numbers are in a column with a total, use a calculator to check the total in the original document and then check the same total in the document being proofread.

d. **Print the document only when you are satisfied that it has been proofread properly and all aspects are correct.**

8-5 Proofreading Printed Copy

a. **Check for consistency of style throughout the document before actually beginning to read the text.**

   (1) Assess the appropriateness of margins (top, bottom, left, and right).

   (2) Check the line spacing between paragraphs, before and after main or text headings, within letter closing lines, etc.

   (3) Inspect to ensure that the document contains no widow or orphan lines (single lines of a paragraph at the top or bottom of a page). See Section 8–4b for illustrations of widow and orphan lines. At the same time ensure that the last word on the page does not break and carry over to the following page.

   (4) Inspect to ensure that no isolated text headings appear at the end of a page. At least two lines of text from the paragraph following the text heading must appear on the same page.

   (5) Evaluate the general appearance of the document. Check headers, footers, and page numbering carefully.

b. Using the original copy as a model, proofread the printed document for accuracy. Read the document carefully, and ask yourself the following questions to correct any keyboarding errors:

(1) Are any letters transposed or omitted? Are all words spelled correctly? The spelling check feature of the word processing program will have located most spelling errors, but it will not have detected such errors as using *you* for *your*, *to* for *too*, or *lose* for *loose*.

(2) Have any letters, words, sentences, or paragraphs been omitted? Pay close attention to ensure that no *s*'s have been dropped from plural nouns or *ed*'s from the past tense or the past participle of verb forms. Ensure that no words, sentences, or paragraphs have been skipped.

(3) Have any words, phrases, or sentences been repeated?

(4) Are all names and unfamiliar words spelled correctly? When proofreading names and unfamiliar words or terminology, check each spelling meticulously—letter by letter.[3]

(5) Have all figures been typed correctly? Are all calculations correct? Double-check all figures carefully with the original source. For long numbers verify the number of digits and then compare the digits in groups of three. If the numbers are in a column with a total, the easiest method of proofreading is to use a calculator to check the total in the original document and then check the same total in the document being proofread.

c. When proofreading hard copy, make your corrections with a colored pen or pencil. Use the pen-and-forefinger technique to maintain attention and keep your eyes focused on the line being proofread.

To use this technique, hold the pen in the hand with which you will be making corrections and place the copy to be proofread on that side. Place the original on the opposite side, and use the forefinger of that hand to follow along as you compare the two copies.

d. When proofreading hard copy, use the standardized proofreaders' marks shown in Section 8-6 and also on the inside back cover of this manual to show your corrections.

8-6 Standardized Proofreaders' Marks to Show Corrections

a. Standardized proofreaders' marks are used to show corrections in handwritten, typewritten, computer-generated, or printed copy. These symbols are used so that anyone who reads the document will interpret the corrections in the same way. Use the following marks and symbols to make changes in words or word groups:

---

[3]The printed version of *Merriam-Webster's Collegiate Dictionary,* 10th edition, contains sections on abbreviations and symbols for chemical elements, foreign words and phrases, biographical names, and geographical names.

Proofreading

263

Instruction	Mark or Symbol	Example	Marginal Note
Boldface word(s).	∼∼∼	received by <u>November 1</u>	bf
Capitalize letter.	≡	to the Retailers <u>a</u>ssociation	cap
Capitalize letters.	≣	from <u>Unesco</u>	caps
Change word(s).	——	~~In view of the fact that~~ you have *Because*	
Close up space.	⌒	You can, never the less, receive	
Delete letter.	/	occas*s*ion	
Delete stroke or letter.	⌿	policy and send us an fax	
Delete word(s).	——⌿	a ~~postal~~ money order for $50	
Hyphenate word(s).	=	up=to=date records	
Insert a space.	#	In#addition, you will be	
Insert apostrophe.	∨	its a good deal	
Insert colon.	⊙	follows pen, ink, and paper.	
Insert comma.	⋏	On Tuesday, May 23 we	
Insert em dash.	⊢M	comments––all are welcome!	
Insert en dash.	⊢N	January 14–16	
Insert here (caret).	∧	Insert at place. *this*	
Insert parentheses.	( )	end of this month(April 30)	
Insert period.	⊙	by 10 am tomorrow	
Insert question mark.	⑦	Do you agree(?)	
Insert quotation marks.	∨ ∨	article, Access on the Web, that	
Insert semicolon.	⌃;	now therefore, you	
Insert word(s).	∧	your latest form *income tax*	
Italicize word(s).	——	<u>The Wall Street Journal</u>	ital
Join to word.	⌒	in our computer laboratory *micro*	
Lowercase letter.	/	of the Association	lc
Lowercase letters.	/	the UNITED STATES OF AMERICA	lc

Instruction	Mark or Symbol	Example	Marginal Note
Restore word(s).	. . . . . .	our ~~furniture~~ warehouse in Toledo	stet
Roman type.	——	book titles in *italic* type	rom
Small capital letters.	═══	our red tag sale on	sm caps
Spell out word or number.	◯	③stores on Fifth Ave.	sp
Transpose letters.	∽	all thier profits.	tr
Transpose words.	⊔⌐	to legibly print your name	tr
Underscore word(s).	——	We cannot overemphasize	u'score

b. **Use the following symbols to move words or word groups:**

Instruction	Mark or Symbol	Example	Marginal Note
Align horizontally.	══	In the past two years	
Align vertically.	‖	(1) New courses (2) New curriculum	
Center.	] [	]PROOFREADERS' MARKS[	
Combine paragraphs.	no ¶	no ¶You may also wish to	
Double-space copy.		As a result of this investigation, we have decided to reduce expenses.	ds
Indent 0.5 inch.	.5"	.5"During the last month	
Insert line space.	>	COMPUTER SALES SUMMARY February 2001	+1 l#
Move as shown.	◯	for the next year	
Move to next line.	⌐	give the contract to Mr.	
Move to the left.	⊏	You may wish to	
Move to the right.	⊐	You may wish to	
New paragraph.	¶	¶Many customers do not	
Single-space copy.		As a result of this investigation, we have decided to reduce expenses.	ss

Editing

The proofreading process involves the comparison of a document with an original to assess the correctness of the prepared copy. Editing is a more challenging process because editors do not have "correct" copies upon which they may rely to determine whether the copy they are reading has been prepared properly. Editors themselves are responsible for determining the accuracy and appropriateness of all language and format applications.

8-7 Preparing to Edit

a. If possible, use the document word processing file to spell check the document electronically. If you are the document originator or preparer, use the spell-as-you-go feature of your word processor to flag potential spelling errors. These potential spelling errors are shown with a wavy red underline. You may correct common errors from a drop-down menu by right clicking on the underlined word and then selecting the correct word from the list that appears.

b. If possible, use the document word processing file and the grammar checker of your word processor to flag any potential grammar errors. Follow these guidelines in using an electronic grammar checker:

   (1) Keep in mind that you will need to make judgments when using a grammar checker. Not all flagged items are errors, and often the suggested corrections are incorrect.

   (2) Use a reliable reference to verify any grammatical constructions about which you are unsure. Although electronic grammar checkers can be helpful to the expert grammarian, they can be a hindrance to the novice because of their high incidence of error.

   (3) Use the correct-grammar-as-you-go feature if you are the document originator or preparer. A wavy blue or green line under a word or sequence of words signifies a potential grammar error. Right clicking on the potential error produces a drop-down menu that provides an opportunity to correct the error or investigate further the reason the grammar checker has flagged the error.

c. Edit documents from printed copy. If you are the document originator or the person who has prepared the document, print it for editing.

d. Assemble all the materials you will need to edit a document:

   (1) An up-to-date (printed within the past three years) collegiate, desk, or unabridged dictionary, e.g., *Merriam-Webster's Collegiate Dictionary*, 10th edition[4]

---

[4]Merriam-Webster provides free on-line Internet access to entries in this dictionary at its Web site: <http://www.m-w.com>.

(2) An up-to-date (published within the past three years) reference manual, e.g., *HOW 10: A Handbook for Office Professionals,* 10th edition

(3) An up-to-date (published within the past five years) thesaurus, e.g., *Roget's II: The New Thesaurus*[5]

(4) Reference sources from which the document was created; e.g., rough drafts, authorization letters, file copies, and meeting notes

(5) Any other published references that may relate to the document; e.g., mailing lists, telephone directories, zip code directories, maps, encyclopedias, books, magazines, and newspapers

(6) Addresses (URLs) of any Internet references or resources that may be needed

8-8 Editing the Document

a. Work from printed copy to edit a document. Because the editor does not just "check" a document against another source, you will probably need to read the material several times. As an editor you must evaluate the overall effectiveness of a document in terms of its attaining the goal for which it was written. Therefore, you will wish to read the material critically with several criteria in mind:

(1) Are there any omissions in ideas or content? All important ideas should be included in the document as well as any information to substantiate the ideas. Check to make sure the document is complete in every respect.

(2) Is the document well organized so that the reader can easily follow the ideas as they are presented? Coherent writing results in clarity and allows the reader to understand easily the purpose and contents of the document. The editor needs to make sure that ideas are placed in logical order and that each sentence flows smoothly and lucidly from the previous sentence.

(3) Is the document correct in every way—content, format, grammar, spelling, punctuation, capitalization, and number expression? Be sure to check the accuracy of all the data. In addition, make sure that all the conventions of correct language usage have been observed and that the document has been formatted appropriately.

(4) Is the content easily understood? Examine the document to ensure that the ideas are presented vividly and with ample illustrations so that the reader can picture concretely what the writer had in mind.

(5) Have all the ideas been expressed in as few words as possible? Look at each sentence to make sure that it does not contain extra wording. Evaluate sentences and paragraphs to see whether they contribute to achieving the overall purpose of the document. Any excess words, sentences, or paragraphs should be deleted.

---

[5]Merriam-Webster provides free on-line Internet access to its thesaurus at its Web site: <http://www.m-w.com>.

(6) Are all abbreviations, number expressions, and other format consid-erations handled in the same way? Check for inconsistencies in these areas and in the contents of the document.

(7) Are the tone and language appropriate for accomplishing the pur-pose of the document? Check to make sure that letters are written in a friendly and courteous manner. Reports, in contrast, should have a more formal tone. Match the formality of tone and language with the purpose of the document.

b. Use proofreaders' marks and symbols to indicate changes made during the editing process. These marks and symbols are explained and illustrated in Section 8-6 and on the inside back cover of this manual.

c. Consider double-spacing rough drafts of documents that are to be edited. Double spacing not only makes the document easier to read but also makes changes easier to interpret.

8-9 Editing Documents Created With Speech-Recognition Software

a. Speech-recognition programs enable document originators to voice type text into word processing programs, E-mail templates, and calendaring programs as well as permit users to voice input in spreadsheet, database, and presentation programs. Users may also navigate the Internet with voice commands.

With continuous voice dictation a document originator no longer needs the keyboard to enter text; words appear on the computer screen as they are spoken. Speech-recognition software not only permits continuous voice dictation for text entry but also enables the document originator to issue voice commands to edit, navigate, and format documents.

Major developers of speech-recognition software include ScanSoft (Dragon NaturallySpeaking), IBM, and Microsoft. Prices range from moderate to high, with the more expensive versions containing additional features and enhancements. System suggestions for optimum performance of speech-recognition software—and pro-gram features and available enhancements—are listed here:

(1) Minimum system components include a Pentium III 500 MHz proces-sor (or equivalent); at least 256 MB of RAM; Windows 98, Millennium, 2000, XP, or NT; 300 MB of free hard disk space; a sound card sup-porting 16-bit recording; a high-quality noise-canceling micro-phone/headset; speakers; a CD-ROM drive to install the program; and Microsoft Internet Explorer 5.0 (or higher) to navigate the Internet. Naturally, the faster the processor and the greater the amount of ran-dom access memory, the better the software will perform.

(2) Low-end speech-recognition programs provide a CD-ROM that con-tains the software needed to use the program, a headset-microphone

recommended for use with the software, and a booklet of instructions. These programs are capable of producing text from continuous speech and implementing voice program commands in most Microsoft Windows-based programs and on the Internet.

Words are spelled correctly based on the large dictionary of the software. In addition, most low-end programs permit users to expand the vocabulary of the program. Developers boast of dictation speeds up to 160 words a minute and from 95 percent to 99 percent accuracy in transferring the spoken word to text.

(3) Medium-priced speech-recognition programs include all the features of the low-end programs. They may provide a higher quality microphone and have larger built-in dictionaries. Often, too, they permit direct dictation into a larger selection of programs.

Additionally, medium-priced speech-recognition programs provide audio playback for the text dictated, read documents and E-mail messages aloud in a human-sounding voice, and transcribe sound files from handheld recorders—permitting a remote voice-to-text system.

Documents may be dictated anywhere, anytime on a pocket-size digital voice recorder. Upon plugging in the mobile recorder to your desktop computer and transferring the voice files to your speech-recognition program, the software will transcribe your documents into any one of a wide selection of text-based programs—where you can review, edit, and format them.

(4) High-end speech-recognition programs add new dimensions to this software. In addition to allowing specialized and/or multiple vocabularies, high-end speech-recognition programs may have a variety of advanced features such as saving dictation for outside correction, creating macros, providing custom templates, permitting direct dictation in additional application programs, or supporting scripting.

b. All speech-recognition programs require a training time for each user. Training times vary, depending upon the software package and the voice of the user—anywhere from 15 minutes to an hour. As each user continues to dictate into the program and follows the recommended procedures for correcting transcription errors, the transcription accuracy of the program improves. Most software developers claim from 95 percent to 99 percent transcription accuracy for their programs.

c. Speech-recognition software plays a major role in originating documents in medical, legal, business, and government offices. Although documents created with speech-recognition software do not contain spelling errors or "typos," they still require editing.

d. Documents created with speech-recognition software are subject to most of the same criteria as documents created using a keyboard. However, because the software occasionally substitutes other words for those dictated, exchanges singular and plural

Proofreading

forms, and misinterprets past and past participle forms, special attention must be given to correcting these kinds of errors. The following guidelines can assist you in editing documents created with speech-recognition software:

(1) Read the text carefully for meaning. Because speech-recognition software is generally perceived to attain between 95 and 99 percent accuracy, undetected word-recognition errors may result in nonsense-sounding sentences.

(2) Pay close attention to word endings. Speech-recognition software may add or omit the *s* at the end of nouns and verb forms. Similarly, the software may add or omit the *ed* at the end of a verb form. Only by reading the text slowly and carefully for meaning can such errors be detected.

(3) Check carefully for errors in number recognition and format. These kinds of errors can easily occur and go unnoticed. Use the same strategies recommended for proofreading numbers in Section 8-5b.

(4) Double-check the spelling of proper nouns. Although speech-recognition software "learns" the spelling of unusual proper nouns and differentiates among the various spellings of other proper nouns, it may occasionally substitute an incorrect spelling.

(5) Do not rely on the Read Back feature of your speech-recognition software to assist you with the proofreading or editing process. The Read Back feature merely reads back the words exactly as they appear on the screen—errors and all. The copy is not read as it was dictated.

(6) Use any available voice files to assist you with the proofreading or editing process. If the document was created on a mobile digital voice recorder, replay the voice recording of the document as you edit it. This recording will assist you in recognizing words misinterpreted by the speech-recognition software.

9

Using the Internet

http://

Using the Internet

Using the Internet Solution Finder

Accessing the World Wide Web

Connecting to the Internet

Evaluating Web Sites   9-4

Using the Internet

The Internet, an extensive system of connected computers, comprises a vast number of networks that are made up of more than 147 million host computers.[1] This on-line global network, which is accessible worldwide, has more than 390 million users[2] and has promoted information exchange between almost every segment of our society.

From major universities and giant corporations to the single user at a home computer, all may access the wealth of information that the Internet provides. In the United States alone, more than 79 million active users *regularly* connect to the Internet at home[3] and more than 42 million active users *regularly* connect to the Internet at work.[4] Nielsen//NetRatings also projected on these same Web pages that the United States "Current Internet Universe Estimate" (active users and occasional users) for home and work is 167 million and 50.6 million users, respectively.

Business people need to gather information for general operations, decision making, and document preparation. Major sources were previously limited to printed reference materials. With advances in technology, however, other forms of information exchange—on-line resources—provide access to the information needed by today's fast-paced business environment.

E-commercing, the sale of goods and services through Web sites, has had a major impact on the purchasing patterns of both consumers and businesses. Fledgling enterprises and long-established business organizations have flocked to the Internet to capture a part of this burgeoning consumer marketplace. Sales through e-commercing are growing rapidly.

9-1 Using the Internet

a. Although many people use the Internet to plan a vacation, join a newsgroup, or pursue personal interests, such personal applications are separate from accessing information that relates directly to business operations. Major business interests today rely on accessing the Internet's World Wide Web and its exploding abundance of vital resources.

The World Wide Web provides the following kinds of information often needed for research, planning, and implementation:

---

[1]"Internet Domain Survey, January 2002," *Internet Software Consortium*, <http://www.isc.org/ds/WWW-200201/index.html> (8 August 2002).

[2]"Hot off the Net, June 2002 Global Internet Index Average Usage," *Nielsen//NetRatings*, <http://www.nielsen-netratings.com/hot_off_the_net.jsp> (13 October 2002).

[3]"Average Web Usage, Week end of September 29, 2002, U.S. (Home)," *Nielsen//NetRatings*, <http://pm.netratings.com/nnpm/owa/NRpublicreports.usageweekly> (13 October 2002).

[4]"Average Web Usage, Week end of September 29, 2002, U.S. (Work)," *Nielsen//NetRatings*, <http://pm.netratings.com/nnpm/owa/NRPublicReports.Usages> (13 October 2002).

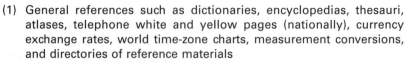

(1) General references such as dictionaries, encyclopedias, thesauri, atlases, telephone white and yellow pages (nationally), currency exchange rates, world time-zone charts, measurement conversions, and directories of reference materials

(2) Stock and bond market quotations, company profiles, and a multitude of other business and financial resources

(3) Travel information and resources—airline schedules and reservations, hotel reservations, rental cars, restaurants, attractions and events, mapped driving routes, train schedules, and bus schedules

(4) Current news and weather—locally, nationally, and internationally

(5) Articles published in major newspapers and magazines worldwide

(6) Services, rates, and tracking for domestic and international mail service providers such as the United States Postal Service, United Parcel Service, FedEx, and other private carriers

(7) Products and services provided by companies throughout the world

(8) Career services and company profiles

(9) Government information and services.

b. **Individuals, businesses, and major corporations are increasingly using the Internet to market products and services. By creating Web sites and advertising their addresses (uniform resource locators— URLs), they are soliciting sales through e-commercing, the trading of goods and services through the Internet.**

9-2 Connecting to the Internet

The Internet is a collection of millions of computers linked together on a vast network, which permits all its component computers to communicate with one another.

An individual or home computer is usually linked to the Internet through an Internet service provider (ISP). A computer in a business or university connects directly to a local area network (LAN) inside the organization. The LAN is then usually connected to an ISP using a high-speed phone line (a T line).

Local ISPs connect to larger ISPs, which maintain fiber-optic "backbones" for a nation or a region, as shown by the diagram on page 275.[5] Backbones around the world are connected through fiber-optic lines, undersea cables, and satellite links. In this way, every computer on the Internet is connected to every other.

a. **For individuals or small businesses, computer connections to the Internet may be achieved in a number of ways. The most common access requires a computer, a modem, a telephone line, communications software, an on-line service provider, and a browser.**

---

[5]Marshall Brain, "The Internet," *HowStuffWorks,* n.d., <http://www.howstuffworks.com/web-server1.htm> (8 August 2002).

Individual Computer Connectivity to Internet Backbones

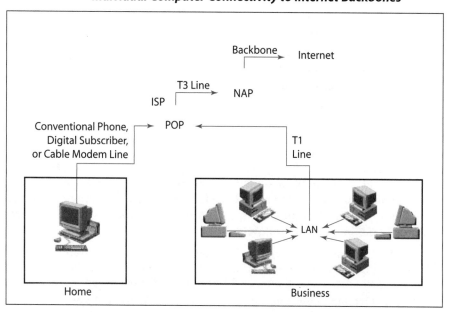

Modern computers provide as standard features a built-in modem with preloaded communications software. Users need only to plug in to a regular telephone jack, and they are ready to be connected to an on-line service.

Telephone line connections to on-line services may be achieved in one of the following ways:

(1) *Through an Internet service provider with a local telephone number.* Internet service providers (ISPs) supply E-mail capabilities and access to the Internet. Some providers furnish software for accessing (browsing) the Internet's World Wide Web (WWW); others require members to obtain their own browsers. Two popular Web browsers are Netscape and Microsoft Internet Explorer.

To locate an Internet service provider in your local area, consult your Yellow Pages under "Internet Access" or "Internet Services." Internet service providers may also be located through an Internet connection at www.thelist.com.

(2) *Through a commercial on-line service provider such as America Online, AT&T WorldNet, MSN, CompuServe, or Prodigy.* In addition to providing E-mail capabilities, Internet access, and a World Wide Web browser, commercial on-line services often provide features such as these:

News and weather

Stock reports and other financial news

Sports scores, headlines, and news

Magazine and newspaper articles

Reference (dictionaries and encyclopedias) and educational sources

Computing support

Professional forums

Travel information

Entertainment options

Shopping opportunities

Home and leisure activities

Web page postings

Chat rooms

b. **Advances in technology have brought faster Internet access to individual and small-business computer users. One such advance, digital subscriber lines (DSL), refers to digital technologies for fast two-way data connections over ordinary telephone lines. Features of DSL include the following:**

(1) *Increased access speed.* You may access audio, video, and enhanced graphics over the Internet with download speeds that are up to 50 times faster than a 28.8 KBPS (kilobytes per second) modem.

(2) *Instantaneous Internet access.* With DSL technology there is no waiting-to-receive mode because there is no need to dial in—the connection is always on.

(3) *E-mail capability.* DSL services provide from one to two E-mail accounts, depending upon the level of service selected, with the opportunity to purchase additional ones.

(4) *Flat monthly fee.* Digital subscriber lines are available at a flat monthly fee for unlimited Internet connection time. Providers offer several subscription levels.

DSL connections are currently available in major United States cities and are continually being made available in other cities through AT&T, local telephone companies, and Internet service providers. For DSL availability in your location, requirements, and cost, visit the following Web sites:

(1) AT&T's DSL Web site at www.ipservices.att.com/ipaccess/dsl/

(2) Web site of your local telephone company

(3) *The List* Web site at www.thelist.com to locate Internet service providers that offer DSL connections

c. **Advances in high-speed Internet access have resulted in the development of cable modems. Cable modems work with signals from television cables, which use fiber optics for distant connections and coaxial cable locally to the individual computer or office network. Cable modems are capable of much higher speeds than conventional modems. The cables have the capacity (contain enough bandwidth) to carry television signals as well as multiple Internet connections. Some features of cable modem connections follow:**

(1) *Increased access speed.* You may access audio, video, and enhanced graphics over the Internet with an average speed of 1 megabyte per second (approximately 20 times faster than a 56 KBPS modem).[6]

(2) *Instantaneous Internet access.* The connection to the cable service is always active; users have split-second access to the Internet and its resources.

(3) *Connectivity as an Internet service provider or a commercial on-line service provider.* With cable modem access, subscribers may continue to use their commercial services such as America Online, CompuServe, and others. These commercial services provide other features besides Internet access. Some cable television companies, however, are also acting as commercial providers by providing on-line content services.

(4) *E-mail capability.* Providers of cable modem on-line access allow customers to send and receive E-mail. Subscribers may have between one and five accounts, depending upon the cable company and level of service selected.

(5) *Independent from television viewing.* Although local cable television companies provide cable modem Internet access from computers, the on-line access does not interfere with television viewing. Cable modems use a group of cable frequencies that are not used for television signals at this time.

(6) *Flat monthly fee.* Cable modem services are available at a flat monthly fee for unlimited Internet connection time.

Cable modem on-line computer connections are available through the local cable television company that services your area. Such connections generally require a cable modem, an Ethernet card, and a cable line. For availability in your location, requirements, and cost, visit the Web site of your local cable television company.

Another technology provides Internet access through your television and its remote control without the use of a computer. Visit www.msntv.com for further information on this access mode.

d. Wireless Fidelity (Wi-Fi) is an emerging network technology that permits homes and small businesses to connect multiple computers to the Internet through a single DSL or cable modem connection. Features of this wireless network follow:

(1) *Increased access speed.* You may access audio, video, and enhanced graphics over the Internet with a speed up to 11 megabytes per second (nearly 200 times faster than a dial-up modem).[7]

(2) *Internet access for multiple computers.* The wireless network permits more than one computer to access the Internet through a single DSL or cable connection.

---

[6]"About Cable Internet Access," *Cable Modem,* n.d., <http://www.cable-modem-internet-access.com/about/> (8 August 2002).

[7]"All Net, All the Time," *BusinessWeek,* April 29, 2002, 100.

(3) *Mobility.* With a wireless PC card adapter for your laptop, you can use other wireless networks in airports, hotels, coffee shops, businesses, etc., to access the Internet and your E-mail account. Public wireless networks are expected to number more than 15,000 by 2003.[8]

(4) *No extra monthly fee.* Home and small-business users encounter no extra monthly fee for the additional connections.

(5) *Monthly fee for use of remote sites.* Those laptop users wishing to access wireless networks (Wi-Fi hot spots) as they travel to various parts of the United States should subscribe to a service that has a network of thousands of Wi-Fi hot spots. These services charge a monthly fee.

Components needed for a home or small-business wireless network include (1) a broadband wireless router, (2) a wireless USB adapter for each desktop computer that is going to be wireless, (3) a wireless PC card adapter for any laptop that is going to be wireless, and (4) a DSL or cable modem connection to the Internet. The following diagram illustrates the components and their relationship to a wireless network.[9]

Components of a Wireless Network

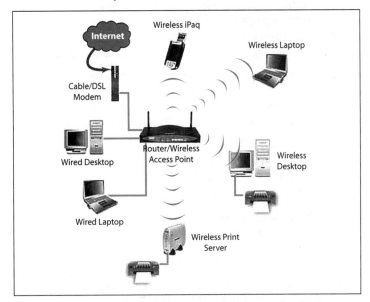

e. **Large corporations, universities, colleges, and government agencies obtain Internet access through Internet providers (IPs). These organizations lease special high-bandwidth telephone lines (T lines) that can support a large number of users simultaneously, such as those in a local area network (LAN) for a whole company.**

---

[8]Ibid.

[9]"Welcome to WiFiDirect!" *WiFiDirect* , n.d., <http://www.wifidirect.com/> (8 August 2002).

(1) T-1 Line: A high-bandwidth telephone line that provides an Internet connection and transmits data at 1.5 megabytes per second.

(2) T-3 Line: A high-bandwidth telephone line that provides an Internet connection and transmits data at 45 megabytes per second.[10]

Large corporations, universities, colleges, and government agencies furnish Internet access free of charge to their employees and students. On-site computers are available for easy access. In many cases users at remote sites (home computers) may dial in to the host computer at the university, college, or agency site and gain Internet access from there.

9-3   Accessing the World Wide Web

a. **The World Wide Web provides an interactive, graphical presentation of information that connects similar data at different locations. On-line documents known as *Web pages* contain hypertext, highlighted words that link you to other areas containing related information. With just a mouse click, hypertext enables you to do the following:**

(1) Migrate easily to documents, graphics, or other Web pages

(2) Connect to other kinds of Internet resources such as newsgroups

(3) Download text, graphics, photos, sounds, music, and movies to a computer

b. **Using the World Wide Web requires a Web browser in addition to the standard communications software that comes preloaded on today's computers. Commercial on-line service providers supply their subscribers with a browser; many local Internet service providers make Web browsers available to their members at no cost or for a nominal fee. Two popular browsers, Netscape and Microsoft Internet Explorer, are available for free download.**

c. **Locating information through your Web browser may be accomplished in several ways:**

(1) *Through an Internet address.* Any Internet site may be reached through its address (uniform resource locator [URL]). Each Web page has a specific address, and by typing the correct address in the appropriate box shown on your Web browser screen, you will be transported to that page. (See Chapter 15 for business-related sites.)

All World Wide Web addresses begin with *http://* (Hypertext Transfer Protocol); the succeeding letters, numbers, and symbols must be entered exactly as shown to access the site. In most cases you need not key *http://*. By keying the remaining letters in the address box, you can access the site. For example, *http://www.usps.com* may be accessed by keying *www.usps.com* instead of the full address.

---

[10]Walt Howe, "Glossary of Internet Terms, Letter T," *Walt's Internet Glossary,* 21 March 2002, <http://www.walthowe.com/glossary/t.html> (8 August 2002).

Internet addresses in running copy may often appear with commas that relate to the sentence punctuation or periods that conclude a sentence. Remember that a URL has no spaces or commas. It does not end with a period or any other punctuation mark—except perhaps a slash (/).

Internet addresses are shown in angle brackets (< >) in footnotes and bibliographical references. In accessing referenced sites, enter only the information *within* the angle brackets.

(2) *Through a search site.* Web browsers have at least one search site available, or search sites may be accessed through their own addresses. Search sites permit you to locate information by entering keywords.

If you were trying to find job listings on the Internet using a search site, you might enter *employment jobs resumes career postings.* This search string will give you the information you need; it relies on a series of keywords to capture the various employment-related information that is available. From the list produced by this search, you can connect directly to any of the sites listed.

(3) *Through a link in a Web site.* Hypertext permits Web sites to link to other Web sites. By clicking on an icon, underlined text, or highlighted text, you can be transported from one information source to another. Related information is frequently linked through hypertext, so often you can locate needed information through a link.

d. **Search sites provide access to locating information on the Internet. Specific search sites may be accessed by entering their addresses (URLs) in the address box of your browser. These resources use various means for classifying sites, and they produce results based upon search strings entered in a search box. From the same search string, different search sites commonly produce different results. That is why persons researching a topic often rely on two or three search sites to gather information. Popular and reliable search sites, along with their Internet addresses, include the following:**

(1) AltaVista   www.altavista.com

(2) Dogpile   www.dogpile.com

(3) Excite   www.excite.com

(4) Google   www.google.com

(5) HotBot   hotbot.lycos.com

(6) Infoseek   infoseek.go.com

(7) LookSmart   www.looksmart.com

(8) Lycos   www.lycos.com

(9) Metacrawler   www.metacrawler.com

(10) MSN   www.msn.com

(11) Netscape   www.netscape.com

(12) WebCrawler   www.webcrawler.com

(13) Yahoo!   www.yahoo.com

e. Search strings composed of isolated keywords often produce thousands of results, many of which are unrelated to the search question. Any document containing any of the keywords is included in the results. Consequently, to refine search results, many people use Boolean operators in their search strings.

Not every search site recognizes Boolean operators, but they improve results with the major search sites: AltaVista, Excite, HotBot, Google, Infoseek, and Lycos.[11] The search results may be reduced or expanded by using Boolean operators.

You just need to apply a few concepts to use Boolean operators effectively: *AND* (+) and *OR,* the value *NOT* (–), the limiter *NEAR,* and grouping operators (parentheses and quotation marks). Key Boolean operators in all capital letters.

(1) *Basic Boolean operators* AND *and* OR. The operator *AND* retrieves items containing all terms connected by *AND.* The search string *stocks AND bonds* retrieves only items containing both words—*stocks* and *bonds.* Some search sites permit the use of a plus sign to replace the *AND* operator. In this case the plus sign is keyed directly before the linked word without an intervening space. Thus *stocks AND bonds* would appear as *stocks +bonds.* Several items may be linked with the *AND* operator, and each linked word refines the search further.

The operator *OR* retrieves items containing either term. The search string *stocks OR bonds* retrieves all items containing either *stocks* or *bonds.* *OR* is useful for synonyms (e.g., *cars* OR *automobiles*) and when different terms (e.g., *colleges* OR *universities*) will retrieve what you want. While the operator *AND* will refine your search, the operator *OR* will produce more search results.

(2) *Basic Boolean operator* NOT. *NOT* excludes terms that would otherwise clutter retrieval. Any items that contain the word or phrase following the *NOT* operator are excluded from the search results. Therefore, *jaguar NOT car* will search for sites with *jaguar* but will eliminate any item that also includes the word *car.*

Be careful in using the *NOT* operator; you may exclude items that contain important information and have only an incidental reference to the word you are excluding. The reference *DSL NOT modem* would exclude any items with the word *modem,* even if it was used only to compare DSL transmission speeds with modem speeds. Use this operator only with a search that is returning too many results or with a word or phrase that is often associated with your topic but unrelated to it.

For the *NOT* operator, some search sites use the minus sign. The minus sign is placed directly before the word or phrase to be

---

[11]For a chart illustrating which Boolean operators are available in the various search sites, consult M. A. Tate, "Selected Web Search Engines: Search Characteristics," *Wolfgram Memorial Library, Widener University,* 15 July 2002, <http://www2.widener.edu/Wolfgram-Memorial-Library/pyramid/setblsch.htm> (23 August 2002).

excluded without an intervening space. To exclude *tigers* from your search on information about cats, you would key *cats NOT tigers* (or *cats –tigers*) in your search string.

(3) *Advanced operator NEAR. NEAR* is an *AND* search in which the terms must appear within a specified word count of one another to be included in the results. Generally, most search sites that support the *NEAR* operator have a set value of ten words as a maximum distance. Consequently, the search string *2005 NEAR calendar NEAR holidays* would have a better chance of locating a calendar of holidays for the year 2005 than would the search string *2005 AND calendar AND holidays. NEAR* increases the chance that the terms are actually related to each other in the item.

A few search sites allow you to specify the maximum number of words that may be between terms in a site for it to be included in the results. Use the following syntax for this refinement: term NEAR# term (e.g., *Greek NEAR15 restaurant*). Other search sites permit the tilde (~) to substitute for the word *NEAR*. The tilde is keyed directly before the following word or phrase without an intervening space: *2005 ~calendar ~holidays.*

(4) *Grouping operators.* Grouping operators determine the order in which Boolean operators are applied or signify words that should be treated as a single unit.

Place parentheses around the words and Boolean operators that are to be evaluated together. Just as in mathematical equations, the parentheses signify that the items within parentheses are to be treated as a unit. The parentheses say, "Do this first." For example, if you entered *brokerages AND Internet OR Web* and then entered *brokerages AND (Internet OR Web)*, you would get quite different results. The first string would give you all items containing both the words *brokerages* and *Internet* and all items containing the word *Web.* The second string would give you all items containing *brokerages* and *Internet* and all items containing *brokerages* and *Web.*

Use quotation marks (double quotes) around words that should be considered as a single unit. Examples are *"Internet service provider"* and *"Mona Lisa"* and *"money market"* and *"municipal bonds."* Only those items containing the exact words shown in quotation marks will be retrieved.

(5) *Wild cards.* The asterisk may be used in AltaVista and several other search sites as a wild card to represent any combination of letters. Its most common use is with truncated words like *educat** to retrieve all forms of the word (*educate, educates, educated, educating, education,* etc.).

(6) *Case-sensitive searches.* Most search sites are not case sensitive with lowercase letters; that is, if you enter the word *web*, the search will return items with *web* and *Web.* If, however, you capitalize the word in the search string, you are likely to receive only items in which the word is capitalized.

9-4 Evaluating Web Resources

The World Wide Web maintains a valuable collection of information. As it has grown, however, the Web has accumulated outdated, inaccurate, and biased sites. Resourceful Internet users should evaluate objectively the information contained in the sites they visit.

In 1998 Jim Kapoun suggested five criteria for evaluating Web pages.[12] Since then other authors have patterned their criteria after his.[13] Still others have incorporated Kapoun's criteria but have expanded their perspective to include additional standards.[14] The following criteria to evaluate Web sites are based on those devised by Jim Kapoun and the other authors cited here:

(1) *Purpose of use.* If the site is for research, business, or educational use, stricter standards should be applied than if the site is for entertainment or personal interests.

- Assess the purpose of the Web page or site.
- Consider whether the Web page fits in with your purpose.

(2) *Creditability of Web documents.* Review the document to determine the creditability of the authors and the host.

- Determine who authored the document and whether that person is separate from the Webmaster.
- Check to see whether the author has any credentials listed on the Web page. If so, do they meet your standards for the purpose of your visit? If no credentials are listed, are they available from another source?
- Determine whether the author has provided an E-mail address or other contact information.
- Evaluate the domain of the document in terms of whether it is hosted by an educational institution (*.edu*), a government agency (*.gov*), a nonprofit organization (*.org*), an Internet service provider (*.net*), a military organization (*.mil*), or a commercial organization (*.com*). Critique the organizational information available or the absence of information about the organization sponsoring the site.

(3) *Accuracy of information in Web documents.* Assess the purpose of the Web document and the reason it was produced as you evaluate its accuracy.

- Determine whether the purpose of the site is clear and the content reflects its purpose. Is the site meant to entertain, persuade, educate, or sell?

---

[12]Jim Kapoun, "Teaching Undergrads Web Evaluation: A Guide for Library Instruction," *C&RL News,* July/August, 522–523, as cited in Paul McMillin, *Five Criteria for Evaluating Web Pages,* Cornell University Library, 18 September 1998, <http://www.library.cornell.edu/okuref/webcrit.html> (8 August 2002).

[13]"Five Criteria for Evaluating Web Resources," *Library Research Guide,* Daemen College, n.d., <http://www.daemen.edu/library/criteriawebsites.html> (8 August 2002).

[14]"Evaluating Web Resources: Checklist to Evaluate a Web Page," *Search the Web,* Learning Resource Centre Library, Algonquin College, 18 February 2002, <http://www.algonquinc.on.ca/lrc/search/evalchecklist.html> (8 August 2002).

- Determine whether the subject matter is covered adequately.
- Assess the quality of the content and whether it compares favorably with other sources in the field.
- Determine whether the facts are similar to those reported in related print materials or other on-line sources. Are the facts well researched and documented?
- Determine whether the page contains original work, not simply links to external sources. Do those links in the site lead to quality sources that complement the theme of the document?
- Check whether appropriate copyright information is available.
- Assess whether the spelling, grammar, and punctuation are correct.

(4) *Objectivity of Web documents.* Determine whether the author provides opinions instead of facts — or is the site a mask for advertising?

- Assess the intended audience. Why was this page written and for whom?
- View the page as you would any television infomercial to determine whether the site is free of bias.
- Assess the document to determine what opinions (if any) are expressed by the author.
- Determine whether the information is primary or secondary in origin.
- Identify whether the site exhibits objective writing by presenting controversial issues from more than one viewpoint.
- Count the number of embedded advertisements in the site as well as pop-up advertisements that occur upon accessing and viewing pages in the site.

(5) *Currency of Web documents.* Determine whether the information contained in the Web page is up-to-date.

- Determine when the Web page was first produced by locating any information related to a creation date at the bottom of the page. Note specifically when the page was last updated.
- Determine whether the information on the page is outdated.
- Assess the currency of any links contained on the page.
- Determine whether there are any dead links on the page. If so, how many?

(6) *Design and usability of the page or site.* Determine how easily the page may be accessed and how easily the information can be located.

- Determine whether the page has a proper title and other information that permits it to be cited properly.
- Determine whether the site organization is logical and easy to maneuver. Does it provide a search feature?
- Evaluate the format of pages in terms of text, graphics, and background. Is there a balance of text and images? Does the background enhance readability or detract from it?
- Learn whether access to the page is free or charges apply.
- Evaluate the reading level of the page in terms of its intended audience.
- Determine what add-ins are required, if any, to view the page.

10

Electronic Messaging

Electronic Messaging Solution Finder

E-Mail Messaging

Facsimile (Fax) Transmittals

Networks

Networks

Computer communication is a key factor in information exchange. Computers that are linked together can communicate with each other and are part of a network. Electronic messages are transmitted through networks.

10-1 Local Area Networks

a. Local area networks generally use telephone wires, coaxial cable, or fiber optics to link computers that are geographically close; that is, computers within a building, several adjacent buildings, or the same geographical area.

b. Local area networks may also be connected by Wireless Fidelity (Wi-Fi).

  (1) Wireless Fidelity is integrated with a wired network to expand the number of client stations without any additional wiring. It may also be integrated with a single wired workstation to create a wireless network.

  (2) Connectivity is achieved through the purchase of wireless technology hardware: a wireless broadband router/access point and appropriate network cards for all the computers in the network. The wired network or wired workstation must have at least DSL or cable-modem connectivity to provide Internet access to the wireless clients in the network.

c. Data can be transmitted within seconds from one location to another. The receiving station may store or print the information for further use.

10-2 Wide Area Networks

Local networks can be linked to larger networks that enable individuals and companies to send and receive information throughout the United States and worldwide. These wide area networks or global networks use combinations of telephone lines, underground cables, fiber optics, and satellites to transmit information within minutes.

Facsimile (Fax) Transmissions

10-3 Fax-to-Fax Messaging

a. Facsimile transmission of computer-generated, typewritten, and handwritten documents; charts, graphs, and diagrams; photographs; and other kinds of hard copy has become an everyday occurrence. It is one of the most popular methods of electronic document transmission used by modern businesses today.

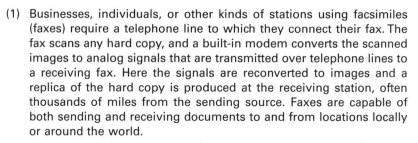

(1) Businesses, individuals, or other kinds of stations using facsimiles (faxes) require a telephone line to which they connect their fax. The fax scans any hard copy, and a built-in modem converts the scanned images to analog signals that are transmitted over telephone lines to a receiving fax. Here the signals are reconverted to images and a replica of the hard copy is produced at the receiving station, often thousands of miles from the sending source. Faxes are capable of both sending and receiving documents to and from locations locally or around the world.

(2) Costs include the purchase of a facsimile, paper to reproduce the transmitted replicas, installation and monthly service charges for a telephone line, and regular local and long-distance telephone rates for on-line transmission. Simple documents are sent and received in a matter of minutes.

(3) Fax transmissions require a cover sheet. Standard cover sheets may be purchased from office supply stores, or individualized cover sheets may be created from word processing templates. Individualized cover sheets may also be created on a word processor without the aid of a template.

Fax cover sheets generally contain the following information or provisions:

- Name of the addressee
- Company name, if any
- Destination fax number
- Destination city (also include state or country if lesser-known city)
- Name, complete address, fax number, telephone number, and E-mail address of originator
- Date (and time, optional)
- Subject line
- Space for any message
- Number of pages transmitted, including the cover page (also provide statement that the page count includes the cover page)
- Request to telephone if transmission is unsuccessful

An example of a fax cover sheet is shown on page 289.

b. **Use of fax transmission is not restricted to those individuals and businesses that have stations on-site. This high-speed, low-cost method of document transmission is also available to the general public at copy centers, private postal centers, stationery stores, and various other businesses in major cities throughout the United States.**

10-4 Computer Fax Messaging

Most computers purchased in today's market are equipped with built-in fax software, a modem, and a fax-management system. These features enable fax transmissions to occur between computers and between computers and faxes.

fax cover sheet

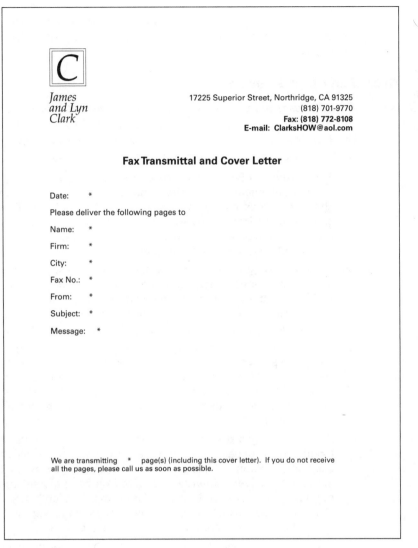

James
and Lyn
Clark

17225 Superior Street, Northridge, CA 91325
(818) 701-9770
Fax: (818) 772-8108
E-mail: ClarksHOW@aol.com

Fax Transmittal and Cover Letter

Date: *

Please deliver the following pages to

Name: *

Firm: *

City: *

Fax No.: *

From: *

Subject: *

Message: *

We are transmitting   *   page(s) (including this cover letter). If you do not receive
all the pages, please call us as soon as possible.

E-Mail Messages

E-mail (electronic mail) is a system by which people communicate
through computers and networks. Members of a system have an
electronic "mailbox" in their computers and an "address" to which
communiqués are directed. Messages sent to the mailbox by other
E-mail participants are stored until recipients open their "mailboxes." After reading the messages, recipients may print them,
store them on the computer, or delete them.

The rate of information exchange through E-mail messages conveyed on the Internet is rising faster than any other method of message transmission. Advances in accessing the Internet have brought E-mail messaging to the "fingertips" of anyone who has a computer.

10-5 Purpose and Function

E-mail messages are not substitutes for business letters or memorandums. They are used to convey short messages, request information, respond to inquiries, acknowledge receipt of merchandise or mail, or act as cover documents for attached files.

(1) The purpose of E-mail is to convey *short* messages quickly and easily without encountering the expense of long-distance telephone charges or mail carrier express charges. Not only are E-mail messages economical and easily created but also they are convenient— they may be received in a matter of minutes (more often even seconds) and read at the recipient's discretion.

(2) The E-mail originator composes a message and "sends" it on its way. Intraorganizational messages are directed to the recipient's computer mailbox via the organization's network. Messages directed outside an organizational network must be transmitted through the Internet.

(3) An E-mail message sent through the Internet leaves the originator's computer and first arrives at the host computer of the originator's on-line access source. Here the message is routed from computer to computer until it reaches the host of the recipient's on-line access source. Once at this destination, the message is in residence until the recipient opens his or her mailbox and retrieves the message from the host computer.

(4) E-mail messages do not replace letters or memorandums that are lengthy, need paper copies, require confidentiality, or discuss significant information or issues. Messages of this nature that are for immediate delivery should be prepared on company letterhead or a memorandum form and sent by fax to the recipient's fax. Also, the U.S. Postal Service and private mail carriers offer overnight delivery to most cities in the continental United States.

(5) Keep in mind that electronic mail is not protected or private. Because network security is fallible, you must assume that anyone with a computer has the potential to read your message. Be careful not to include any information in E-mail messages that you would not want disclosed publicly or that would cause you embarrassment. Also, remember that with a click of the mouse, you can inadvertently send your message to the wrong person.

10-6 **E-Mail Features**

Internet service providers,[1] E-mail applications software,[2] and Internet-based E-mail providers[3] provide users with a comprehensive E-mail system. Although these systems differ in appearance, they basically offer the same features.

a. *An E-mail address book.* In the E-mail address book, you may store E-mail addresses of those persons to whom you write on a regular basis. Stored addresses may be inserted directly into an E-mail message, thereby reducing the chance for error.

(1) Address books provide template forms for recording the name and E-mail address of individuals. Some E-mail address books permit users to include additional information such as company affiliation, address, telephone number, and fax number.

(2) Address books allow users to enter multiple E-mail addresses in a group file. Group files permit you to send the same message simultaneously to all members in the group.

b. *A message-composition template.* This template permits you to create and send E-mail messages. It contains a set of boxes into which you can enter information and a series of buttons that permit you to activate E-mail options. An illustration of a message-composition template is shown on page 292.

E-mail composition templates generally contain the following guides and options:

(1) *The guide word* To:. Clicking on an individual's or a group's address in the address book will enter the recipient's E-mail address after the guide word *To:.* You may also type in the recipient's address. Do so carefully because one wrong character or space will prevent your message from being delivered—at least to its intended destination.

(2) *The guide abbreviation* cc:. If you want others to receive courtesy copies of your message, enter their E-mail addresses after the abbreviation *cc:*—either from your address book or by typing them in.

(3) *The guide abbreviation* bcc:. Most forms provide for sending blind courtesy copies. Copies are sent to the E-mail addresses listed, but all other recipients do not see that the message was also sent to the addresses designated to receive blind courtesy copies. Some forms do not have a separate notation for blind courtesy copies. Instead, users code (e.g., place in parentheses) E-mail addresses after the guide abbreviation *cc:* to indicate that they are to be treated as blind courtesy copies.

---

[1]Examples of Internet service providers are America Online (AOL) and EarthLink.

[2]Examples of E-mail applications software are Microsoft Outlook and Lotus Notes. Applications software is used primarily by organizations for both internal and Internet E-mail.

[3]Examples of Internet E-mail providers are MSN Hotmail and Yahoo!

Microsoft Outlook 2002 message-composition template

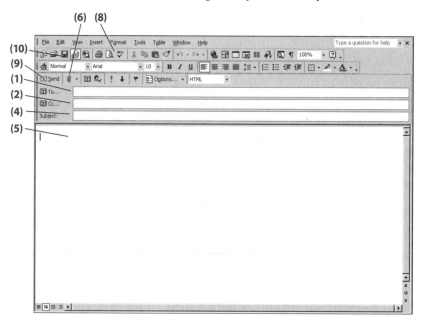

The blind copy feature is useful when a message is sent to a large group of individuals. It prevents showing a long list of E-mail addresses before the actual message appears. This feature also respects the privacy of others' E-mail addresses by not displaying them with the message.

(4) *The guide word* Subject:. Type a brief and descriptive phrase that summarizes the topic of your E-mail message after the guide word *Subject:*. Use initial capital letters for each principal or main word[4] in the subject line.

(5) *The message-composition window.* Type your message in the message-composition window. If possible, limit your message to a screenful or two of data. For transmitting lengthy messages and other pertinent data, use attachments.

(6) *The* Attachments *button and window.* You may attach files to be downloaded by the recipient. Keep in mind, though, that the recipient must have the application program in which the file was created to open the file. Use the attachments button and then the attachments window to select (browse) the path and file name of any document or image you wish to send with your E-mail message or to designate a Web site you wish to attach to your message.

(7) *A* Draft *or* Send Later *button.* The *Draft* or *Send Later* option permits you to interrupt composing an E-mail message and store it for editing at another time. This feature is useful if you need to collect additional data or verify information before sending the message.

---

[4]See Section 3-6 for an explanation of *principal* or *main* words.

(8) *A spelling checker.* Most E-mail systems provide a spelling checker by which you can electronically correct any spelling errors. Some also contain a thesaurus that may be accessed to locate synonyms for words used in your E-mail messages. A few programs provide dictionaries that permit you to look up word meanings as you are composing your message.

(9) *The* Send *button.* The *Send* button routes the message and any attachments to your recipients.

(10) *The save feature.* E-mail systems provide an option for you to store a copy of your outgoing messages.

c. *An in box.* **The in box receives your incoming E-mail messages. From there you are able to open and read the messages sent to you. Your incoming E-mail message is formatted into a template provided by your E-mail system. Information in the template shows who sent the message, who received courtesy copies (not blind courtesy copies), the subject line, the message, and whether any attachments are included. Two timesaving features appear on templates for incoming messages:**

(1) *The* Reply *and the* Reply All *buttons.* The *Reply* and the *Reply All* features simplify your providing responses to incoming messages. By clicking the *Reply* button within an incoming E-mail message, you will obtain a fresh composition template. The address of the sender is inserted automatically in the address box, and the subject preceded by *Re:* appears in the subject line. All that is needed before you click *Send* is your reply in the message-composition window. By using the *Reply All* feature, you send your response to the E-mail message originator as well as to all those who received courtesy copies of the original message.

(2) *The* Forward *button.* By using the *Forward* feature, you may direct a message in your in box to another person. This feature may be used when another person should see the message contents or when someone else should take responsibility for answering the message because it has been directed to the wrong person.

d. *An out box.* **Some E-mail systems permit you to compose messages off-line and save them in an out box until you go on-line. Messages remain in the out box until you connect to your Internet access provider and send them. Such practices reduce Internet traffic (and in some cases access costs) and are a courtesy to the Internet community.**

e. *An E-mail filing cabinet.* **E-mail systems provide procedures for deleting, saving, and organizing both incoming and outgoing messages.**

(1) Messages in the in box may be deleted before or after they have been read. Recognizable "spam" (junk mail) may be deleted even before it is opened.

(2) Folders may be created to save and organize incoming and outgoing messages. Messages may later be deleted when they are no longer considered important enough to keep.

f. *A print feature.* **You may print incoming and outgoing messages through the** *File-Print* **menu in your E-mail system.**

g. *Other features.* **Depending upon your software, your E-mail system may have one or more of these features:**

(1) Notify senders that you are unavailable to answer their E-mail messages until a certain date because you are "out of the office"

(2) Create signature files

(3) Mark messages as "unread" (to be read later)

(4) Use various fonts and font attributes

(5) Use E-mail stationery

(6) Paste pictures within messages

(7) Send messages as greeting cards

(8) File messages automatically

(9) Schedule messages to be sent at a later time

(10) Filter "junk mail" (unwanted, unsolicited E-mail messages)

(11) Inform the sender when a message is received

(12) Inform the sender when a message is opened and read

10-7 E-Mail Systems

a. Large organizations—commercial enterprises, educational institutions, government entities, and other such organizations—provide E-mail capabilities for their employees or their employees and students.

(1) E-mail messages within organizations are commonly sent through a computer network established to serve the organization. Stations are connected by either coaxial cable (within a building) or by other wire (between buildings or sites). Messages are transmitted from station to station by cable or other wire. E-mail messages sent outside an organizational network are transmitted through the Internet, a worldwide global network.

(2) Each member of the organization is given a mailbox that may be accessed through a unique user name and password. The E-mail message originator composes a message and "sends" it on its way. Intraorganizational messages are directed to the recipient's computer mailbox via the organization's network. Messages directed outside an organizational network must be transmitted from the organization's network to an Internet backbone computer, where it is routed through the Internet.

(3) Access to the E-mail mailbox is generally obtained from a computer located within the organization. Increasingly, however, organizations

are furnishing employees with telephone numbers that provide dial-up access to their organizational E-mail mailboxes from home computers or other computers outside the organization.

(4) Most large organizations use E-mail applications software (such as Microsoft Outlook or Lotus Notes) for their E-mail systems. See the message composition template on page 292.

b. Internet service providers (ISPs) provide E-mail services to their clients as part of their subscription fee for Internet access.

(1) Individual users or small businesses may obtain access to E-mail messaging through their Internet service provider (ISP). Those services that furnish Internet access also provide subscribers from one to a multiple number of E-mail accounts.

(2) Users of subscription electronic mail must have a modem, DSL, or cable connection and a subscription to an Internet service provider (ISP).

(3) Internet service providers supply the connection to the Internet. Commonly known Internet service providers are America Online, EarthLink, CompuServe, and MSN. Thousands of others are scattered in cities throughout the United States and may be easily located through a city's *Yellow Pages* under "Internet access" or on-line at www.thelist.com. Internet service providers usually furnish the communications software needed for E-mail and other Internet access. See Section 9-2 for additional information.

(4) Internet service providers supply each subscriber with a screen name (a user I.D.) that is unique for that subscriber. The screen name followed by the at sign (@) and the Internet name of the Internet service provider comprise the subscriber's E-mail address. Examples of E-mail addresses are *ClarksHOW@aol.com, lrdr@telis.org,* and *jslevin@pacificnet.net.* An explanation of extensions following the Internet name of the E-mail provider follows:

Identifier	Definition
com	commercial organization
edu	educational site
gov	government organization
mil	military
net	organization administering a network
org	miscellaneous organization

(5) Messages are sent from one E-mail address to another through the Internet. An originator's message is sent to the computer of his or her Internet service provider, where it is directed along the Internet to the computer of the recipient's access point. Here it is stored until the recipient logs on to his or her on-line provider's computer and retrieves the message.

(6) Subscribers generally have access to their E-mail only when they are logged on to their particular Internet service provider. Some Internet service providers, however, maintain Internet Web sites where

subscribers may access their E-mail accounts from computers other than their own to read and write mail.

(7) Internet service providers furnish an on-screen form to compose and send messages. The E-mail message template illustrated below is from AmericaOnline.

America Online message-composition template

c. **A number of Internet sites provide free Internet E-mail accounts to anyone on-line who requests one.**

(1) Internet E-mail accounts are unique. Not only are they usually free to anyone worldwide who has any Internet connection but also they may be accessed *anywhere* at *anytime* from *any* computer that is connected to the Internet. Individuals, then, may communicate with friends, relatives, business associates, colleagues, classmates, and all other persons worldwide—from any connected computer.

(2) Many major sites provide free Internet E-mail accounts. Among the most popular are MSN Hotmail at www.hotmail.com, Netscape Webmail at webmail.netscape.com, Yahoo! Mail at mail.yahoo.com, and Lycos MailCity at www.mailcity.com. Messages are stored on a computer owned by the host (for those sites mentioned—Microsoft, Netscape, Yahoo! and Lycos), not on the computer of an Internet service provider, the message originator, or the message recipient. Consequently, messages may be retrieved, stored, reread, and deleted from any computer as long as it is connected to the Internet.

(3) Messages from an Internet E-mail account may be sent to the mailbox of any E-mail address, regardless of the source of its Internet access. Conversely, messages from any E-mail address with access to the Internet may be sent to the mailbox of any Internet E-mail account.

(4) Internet E-mail accounts offer features and templates similar to those offered by Internet service providers. The template shown below illustrates the message-composition template used for Hotmail messages.

(5) Internet E-mail messaging has advanced from sending simple messages to adding font attributes to text, attaching documents, and including graphic images. Internet E-mail accounts permit the transfer of word processing, spreadsheet, and database documents. Attachments, however, have varying size limitations according to the Internet mail service.

Documents prepared in Microsoft Word, WordPerfect, PowerPoint, and Excel arrive in the recipient's mailbox ready to be downloaded in the format they were sent. Such attachments can easily be read once they are downloaded (from anywhere) and brought up in the program in which they were created. Files may be stored on disk and/or printed for reference.

(6) Most Internet E-mail sites can filter unwanted E-mail and block junk E-mail. These sites permit each user to store from 2000 KB–5000 KB of messages and attachments for each log-in name. For a minimal annual fee, however, users may increase the storage capacity of their account.

MSN Hotmail message-composition template

10–8 **Message Preparation**

a. Just as business letters and memorandums are forms of one-way communication, so are E-mail messages. Since an E-mail message will not be accompanied by facial expressions or voice inflections, it will be taken at face value. No opportunities exist for the receiver to ask questions, clarify statements, or obtain feedback. Therefore, writers of E-mail messages must plan and write their messages as carefully as they would any other form of written communication.

b. Begin your E-mail message with a friendly greeting. Examples of such greetings follow:

Hi, Bob,	Thank you, Paula,
Hello, Anna	Dear John Morrow,
Greetings, Don,	Dear Sandra,

c. Use the following guidelines to construct your messages. Review them to ensure that they are

(1) *Courteous.* Make your message "smile" by using words such as *please, thank you, appreciate,* and *gladly.* Select positive words to convey your ideas; avoid negative words, innuendos, and accusations. Above all, keep your tone friendly.

(2) *Complete.* Ensure that all the necessary information has been included to achieve the purpose of your E-mail message. Make sure you have not left out any important data.

(3) *Coherent.* Check that all the ideas have been placed in logical order so that one idea flows naturally from the previous one. Make sure that the reader can easily follow your train of thought and that you finish discussing one idea before moving on to the next.

(4) *Clear.* Construct your sentences so that they are worded clearly. Make sure that "who does what" and "what is what" leaves no question in the reader's mind. Avoid long, complicated sentences. Place modifiers as close as possible to the words they modify, and do not use ambiguous pronouns.

(5) *Concrete.* Write in terms of specifics, and use concrete nouns instead of generalities. Dates and times should be expressed explicitly. Likewise, assignments and expectations need to be described in precise terms that are understood similarly by both the writer and the reader.

(6) *Concise.* Use as few words as possible to construct your message, but make sure you have included all the necessary information. Avoid including extra words and extraneous ideas. Remember to keep your E-mail messages as short as possible.

(7) *Correct.* Use the spelling checker of your E-mail software. If your software does not have a spelling checker, keep a dictionary handy as you compose your messages. Proofread your messages carefully for typographical errors, repeated words, omitted words, words used

incorrectly, spelling errors, and grammatical errors. E-mail messages represent you as much as any other kind of written communication.

d. Conclude your E-mail message with a "signature," even if it is only your first name. Some people prefer also to sign off with a cordial farewell remark such as *Best wishes*, especially in informal messages to people whom they know.

Signature lines vary in content. Some people may use only their name. Others will include their name, title, organization, and telephone number. Whatever you choose to use, place the information in no more than five lines.

10-9 E-Mail Emoticons (Smileys)

Because E-mail messages are one-way communications, the "Internet community" has developed a series of symbols to express emotion — *emoticons,* often called "smileys." Some writers of E-mail messages use emoticons to express emotion in their messages. Emoticons should be used only in personal E-mail messages or in E-mail messages to business associates with whom you have a close working relationship. Commonly used emoticons are these:

(1) :-) This basic smiley is used to show approval or indicate that a statement is made jokingly.

(2) ;-) The wink smiley is flirtatious; it means that what I have just said is a joke.

(3) :-(The frowning smiley is used to show disappointment with a situation.

(4) :-I The indifferent smiley is used to show that the outcome of a situation makes no difference to the writer.

Many more E-mail emoticons are popular in the Internet community. One site that illustrates and explains E-mail emoticons is *The Unofficial Smiley Dictionary*, paul.merton.ox.ac.uk/ascii/smileys.html.

10-10 E-Mail Netiquette

Netiquette (net etiquette) is a set of behaviors that should be adhered to when using the Internet. Excluding conduct prohibited by federal laws, the Internet community itself has devised etiquette standards for Internet use. Those applying to E-mail follow:

(1) Construct your E-mail messages off-line, where possible, so you do not unnecessarily tie up the network.

(2) Use E-mail to accomplish a specific purpose. Do not tie up the network with E-mail messages that are needless or unnecessary. At the same time, send courtesy copies only to people who will benefit from or who need the information contained in your E-mail message.

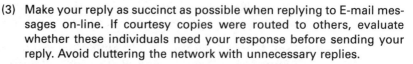

(3) Make your reply as succinct as possible when replying to E-mail messages on-line. If courtesy copies were routed to others, evaluate whether these individuals need your response before sending your reply. Avoid cluttering the network with unnecessary replies.

(4) Be courteous in your E-mail messages. Sending rude messages is known as "flaming" and is frowned upon by the Internet community.

(5) Avoid using a series of all capital letters in the body of your message. Besides hindering readability, all capital letters are considered the E-mail equivalent of shouting and may be construed as rude.

(6) Use the following substitutions if your E-mail software does not support font attributes (boldface, italics, underlining):

- Enclose a word or phrase in asterisks to indicate a mild emphasis. Asterisks used in this way may be equated with using boldface type.
- Place an underline before and after the title of a published work to represent italics or a continuous underline, thus distinguishing it as a title.

asterisks for boldface type

The deadline for submitting the grant application is *May 15.*

Megatone Utilities checks for *all* boot-sector viruses as well as for file viruses.

single underlines for italics or a continuous underline

On page 23 of the July 28 issue of _BusinessWeek_, you will find an analysis of profits in the telecommunications industry for the past three years.

Please send me three copies of _Learning the Internet for Personal and Business Applications_.

(7) Keep your E-mail messages short, generally no more than one or two screenfuls of data. If you send a long message, tell the recipient at the beginning so he or she has the option to download it for later reading.

(8) Do not send chain letters over the Internet.

E-Messaging 10

11

Address Format and Forms of Address

Address Format and Forms of Address Solution Finder

Addressing

11

General Address Format

11-1 **General Address Format**

a. Use combinations of the following to address general business correspondence: full name of person with appropriate courtesy title, professional title, company name, street address, city, state, and zip code (5 digits or 9 digits, depending upon the availability of the 9-digit code).

Coordinate the person's name, title, and company name so that line endings in the inside address are as nearly even as possible. Use the two-letter postal state designation or spell out the state name to achieve further a balanced appearance. (See Section 6-9c.)

Use the same format for both the inside address of the letter and the envelope used to mail it.

addressed to individual

Ms. Marie LaGrasta-Sundy
8730 Beach Boulevard, Apt. 2
San Clemente, CA 92672-2036

Dear Ms. LaGrasta-Sundy:

Mr. Joseph A. Caruana
2231 Washington Avenue
Des Moines, Iowa 50310

Dear Mr. Caruana:

addressed to individual within company

Mr. Shawn T. Stein, Manager
Policy Issue Department
General Insurance Company of America
600 Prospect Avenue, Suite 600
Hartford, Connecticut 06105-2920

Dear Mr. Stein:

Ms. Jill R. Binsley
Vice President of Operations
Bank of America
5420 Bayshore Boulevard
Tampa, Florida 33611-4122

Dear Ms. Binsley:

addressed to company

F. M. Tarbell Company
2740 S.W. Troy Street
Portland, OR 97219-2553

Ladies and Gentlemen:

Cinamerica
Post Office Box 20077
Encino, CA 91416-0077

Ladies and Gentlemen:

b. An address may have a maximum of six lines and a minimum of two lines.

maximum six-line address

Ms. Brenda Ingram-Cotton
Chief Operations Manager
Quality Control Department
Neware Aluminum Accessories
3600 Chelwood Park Blvd., N.E.
Albuquerque, NM 87111-5416

minimum two-line address

Phillips Foods, Inc.
Morristown, NJ 07960-3305

Names and Titles

11-2 **Courtesy Titles**

a. Abbreviate the courtesy titles *Mr.* and *Mrs.* when they are used with the names of individuals. The courtesy title *Ms.* ends with a period, although it is not an abbreviation. Always spell out the courtesy title *Miss*; do not conclude it with a period.

In the salutations of business letters, use the courtesy title with the last name only.

courtesy title with full name

Mr. Marvin Weston	**Ms.** Frances Shannon
Mrs. Charlene Pollyea	**Miss** Natalia Granados

courtesy title in salutation

Dear **Mr.** Weston:	Dear **Ms.** Shannon:
Dear **Mrs.** Pollyea:	Dear **Miss** Granados:

b. When the name of an individual does not signify whether the person is a man or a woman, omit the courtesy title. Use the same format for the salutation in a business letter.

name does not signify gender

Chris V. Stauber	Cary Antonovich	T. R. Najjar
Casey R. Elliott	Lynn Sebastian	B. Kelly Clemens
Cory Williams	Jaime Bennett	Duong Nguyen

salutation for name that does not signify gender

Dear T. R. Najjar:	Dear Chris V. Stauber:
Dear Cory Williams:	Dear B. Kelly Clemens:

c. When addressing a woman, use the courtesy title *Ms.* unless *Mrs.* or *Miss* is specified by the addressee. Use the courtesy title *Miss* for young girls under the age of thirteen.

woman does not indicate a title preference

Ms. Laura Rankin	**Ms.** Robin Togo

girl under age thirteen

Miss Kristen Fielding	**Miss** Claudia Martinez

d. The courtesy title *Master* is used for addressing young boys, usually below the age of thirteen.

Master William J. Clark   **Master** Charles Bentley

e. The abbreviated courtesy title *Esq.* (*Esquire*) is sometimes used after the surname of a lawyer. In such cases no courtesy title precedes the name.

David R. Grossman, **Esq.**   Lorraine H. Clark, **Esq.**

f. Female correspondents who have a courtesy title preference other than *Ms.* should indicate this preference in the signature lines of their correspondence by enclosing the title in parentheses before their names. Correspondents who have names that do not signify gender may also indicate a courtesy title preference by enclosing it in parentheses before their names in a signature line.

female with courtesy title preference other than Ms.

(Mrs.) Susan K. Willett   (Dr.) Barbara Wilson

male or female whose name does not indicate gender

(Ms.) K. C. Roberts   (Ms.) Lonnie Abrams

(Mrs.) Chris Dobrian   (Mrs.) Lee Haberman

(Mr.) Dana Lopez   (Mr.) Leslie Mitchell

11-3 Professional Titles

a. Except for *Dr.* and long professional titles consisting of more than one or two words, write out and capitalize all professional titles when they precede the names of individuals. *Professor, Dean, The Reverend, Governor, Senator, Colonel, Lieutenant*, and *The Honorable* are examples of titles that are capitalized and written in full.

Doctor abbreviated

Dr. Alan Strozer   **Dr.** Shannon T. Goar

professional title written out

Professor Marie Flatley   **The Honorable** Brian K. Stanfield

long professional title abbreviated

Lt. Col. Ret. Leonard C. Williams (Lieutenant Colonel Retired)

b. In addressing business correspondence or completing signature lines, capitalize and write out professional titles that follow an individual's name.

single-line address format

Mr. Kevin McDonald, **Dean**   Ms. Patrice A. Halby, **Vice President**

11

Addressing

two-line address format

Ms. Melanie L. Fielding
Plant Superintendent

Mr. Adam T. Livingston Jr.
Assistant Vice President

single-line signature format

(Dr.) Jennifer Loucks, **Chair**

(Mrs.) Joyce Moore, **President**

William A. Murillo, **Manager**

Rebecca L. Dentino, **Supervisor**

two-line signature format

John S. Minasian
Chairman of the Board

(Mrs.) Brenda Browning
Collections Manager

(Ms.) Orolyn L. Ruenz-Clark
Vice President of Operations

Bradley C. Johnson
Customer Service Representative

c. Capitalize professional titles *not* appearing in address format or signature lines only when they precede and are used directly with an individual's name in place of a courtesy title. Do not capitalize titles following an individual's name.

title preceding name

President Lloyd W. Bartholome will deliver the main address.

One of the senators from Michigan, **Senator** Scot Ober, will be the luncheon speaker.

title following name

Lloyd W. Bartholome, **president** of A & P Enterprises, will deliver the main address.

The Honorable Scot Ober, **senator** from Michigan, has agreed to deliver the main address.

d. Only one courtesy or professional title with the same meaning should appear with a single name. Use *Dr.* or *M.D.*, but not both titles, with the same name.

titles with the same meaning

Dr. Jason V. Glaser   *or*   Jason V. Glaser, **M.D.**

Dr. Cheng Wong   *or*   Cheng Wong, **D.D.S.**

titles with different meanings

Dr. Susan Cornner, **Professor**

e. Do not capitalize professional titles that substitute for individuals' names.

The **general** has canceled his weekly staff meeting.

Did the **governor** appear for the press conference?

11-4 Company Names

Spell out company names in full unless the company itself uses abbreviations in its official name.[1] *Inc.* and *Ltd.* usually appear in abbreviated form, but some companies write these words in full.

company name written in full

Pacific Mutual Life Insurance Company   Schultz and Sons

Merriam-Webster, Incorporated   Neilson Corporation

company name containing abbreviation

Consolidated Factors, **Ltd.**   McKnight, Larson **&** Crosby

International Computer **Corp.**   Lyons Investment Group **Inc.**

Places

11-5 Buildings and Units

Capitalize the names of buildings and the names of any units within the building. Place the unit, suite, or apartment location after the building name, but separate the two with a comma.

If an address contains a unit location without a building name, place it after the street address. Separate the street address and the unit location with a comma. Use numerals for all unit numbers.

building name with unit location

Plaza Medical Center, **Suites 450–460**   Tishman Building, **Suite 600**

California State Capitol, **Office 243F**   Bayview Apartments., **Unit 7**

unit location without building name

220 Main Street, **Suite 100**   18564 Clark Street, **Apt. 4**

5670 Fair Oaks Avenue, **Unit 12**   5426 S.W. 43rd Street, **#205**

11-6 Street Addresses

a. Use numerals to express house or building numbers. Only the house or building number *one* is written in word form.

house or building number one

One Lakeview Terrace   **One** Riverwalk Place

house or building number in numerals

8 Burbank Lane   **420** Fourth Avenue, Apt. 112

17225 Plumber Street   **10239-3** White Oak Avenue

---

[1]The official name of a company may be determined from its printed letterhead or from any of its contracts.

b. Spell out simple compass directions (*North, South, East,* and *West*) that appear in a street address. Compound compass points (*Northeast, Northwest, Southeast,* and *Southwest*) in an address are abbreviated. Any compound compass directions following the street address are preceded by a comma.

simple compass point in street address

3214 **West** 47th Street   2160 Century Park **East**

1090 **North** Grand Boulevard   640 Manchester Street **South**

compound compass point within street address

3028 **N.E.** 19th Street   127 **S.W.** Madison Street

compass point following street address

1603 F Street, **N.W.**   3750 Broxten Avenue, **S.E.**, Apt. 18

c. All street-number names *ten* and below are written in words using ordinal numbers—*first, second, third,* etc. Street-number names above *ten,* however, are written in numerals. Use ordinal numbers (*11th, 12th, 13th,* etc.) when expressing these street names.

street-number name ten or below

1482 **Sixth** Avenue   742 East **First** Street

street-number name above ten

890 South **21st** Street   3624 West **59th** Place

2036 **42nd** Street   9680 **123rd** Street

d. Spell out street designations such as *Boulevard, Avenue, Street, Place, Drive,* and *Lane.* Only the street designation *Boulevard* may be abbreviated (*Blvd.*) with exceptionally long street names.

street designation spelled out

18394 Lankershim **Boulevard**

street designation abbreviated

9263 North Coldwater Canyon **Blvd.**

e. Spell out where possible mailing designations such as *Rural Route* or *Post Office Box* that are used in the place of street addresses. Abbreviate the mailing designation only with long addresses.

postal designation spelled out

Post Office Box 450   **Rural Route** 2, Box 1620

postal designation abbreviated

P.O. Box 1629, Terminal Annex

f. Apartment, suite, and unit numbers are expressed in numerals and are generally included on the same line as the building name. In addresses without building names, these numbers appear on the same line with the street address. The term *Apartment* may be abbreviated when it appears on the same line as the street address.

With long street addresses, apartment numbers may be placed on the following line. The term *Apartment* in these cases is spelled out.

apartment, suite, or unit number with building
Redlands Medical Plaza, **Suite 540**

unit or apartment number with street address
6176 Arroyo Road, **Unit 2**

4150 West 21st Street, **Apt. 6**

no specific designation with street address
16932 Wilshire Boulevard, **C-110**

apartment number on line following street address
8564 Kensington Street, S.W.
Apartment 230

11-7 City, State, and Zip Code

a. Spell out in full the names of cities.

Saint Louis   New York   Fort Worth   Los Angeles

b. Use the two-letter post office designation for state names or spell out in full the state name. Select either style based upon (1) the degree of formality of the correspondence or (2) the one that provides better balance for setting up the entire address. Should both be equally suitable, use the two-letter postal designation. Use the same form for both the inside address and the envelope used to mail the correspondence.

A list of two-letter state and territory designations for the United States may be found in Section 6-12 and on the page opposite the inside back cover.

state two-letter zip code designation

Ms. Jessica Morton	Mr. Richard A. Chui
108 Academy Avenue	9540 Barr Drive, Apt. 204
Weymouth, MA 02188-4204	Indianapolis, IN 46229-1214

state name written in full

Mr. William R. Stephenson	Mrs. Shirley Schnair-Goldman
257 American Legion Highway	1124 Jefferson Boulevard
Revere, Massachusetts 02151	Flint, Michigan 48507-4201

c. Zip codes are keyed a single space after the state.

Atlanta, GA 30331-8732   *or*   Atlanta, Georgia 30331

Address Format for Foreign Correspondence

11-8 Address Format for Foreign Correspondence

a. Addresses for foreign correspondence contain combinations of the following: (1) full name of addressee with appropriate courtesy title, (2) professional title of addressee, (3) company name, (4) street address, (5) city and any city numbering codes or section name, (6) state or region, if applicable, and (7) destination country.

b. Sequencing of the address components varies among countries. Some countries place the name of the addressee first but place the city information before the street address. Some place the house number after the street name or the postal code before the city name. Others follow the familiar street address, city, state, and postal code format used in the United States. Where possible, follow the conventions of the destination country. For mail posted from the United States, however, always place the name of the destination country in all capital letters as the last line of the mailing address.

Mr. Atsushi Ishiki	Alexandria
1-6-302 Wutsukusigaoka	Stanly
1 Chome—C1Z Midoriku	237 Zaky Badway Mohamed St.
Yokohama	Mrs. Iman Gaber El-Desoky
JAPAN	EGYPT

c. If possible, use courtesy titles that reflect the language of the country. *Herrn, Frau,* and *Fraülein* (German); *Señor, Señora,* and *Señorita* (Spanish); and *Monsieur, Madame,* and *Mademoiselle* (French) are just a few examples of foreign courtesy titles that represent the English *Mr., Mrs.,* and *Miss*.

In most foreign countries a comparable term for *Miss* is used for young women. Adult women are addressed with the courtesy title comparable to the English *Mrs.,* regardless of their marital status.

Use English courtesy titles in those cases where the comparable title is unknown or impractical to reproduce on English-based keyboards. However, use the extended character sets of your word processor to form the characters that are supported by the software.

Le Lien	Srta. Kristina Chagas Tavares
c/o Mr. Lucien Aubert	Rua 706, n°=152/178
14, rue Roger-Radisson	Balneario Camboriú, SC
69322 Lyon	CEP 88330
FRANCE	BRAZIL

d. When addressing foreign correspondence, use the English version of a country name (*GERMANY*, not *DEUTSCHLAND*) to ensure the correspondence is routed to the correct country from the United States. For city names, however, use the foreign spelling to hasten delivery within the country (*Köln*, not *Cologne*; *Wien*, not *Vienna*; *Venezia*, not *Venice*). If possible, use all the appropriate letters and diacritical marks in spelling names, streets, cities, and other parts of the address. Consult the geographical reference section of your dictionary for assistance in selecting the correct name and its spelling.[2]

Herrn Paul-Erich Rünz
Diplomat-Kaufman
Gemarkenstraße 290
5000 Köln 80—Dellbrück
GERMANY

On-Line Address Formats

The Internet,[3] which is accessible to users worldwide, has promoted information exchange between virtually any segment of our society. From individuals in major universities and giant corporations to the single user at a home computer, all may access the wealth of information Internet access provides and all may communicate with each other through E-mail.

11-9 Internet Addresses

Internet popularity has soared since the introduction of the World Wide Web (WWW) and its first browser, Netscape Navigator, in 1992. Companies, government offices, educational institutions, organizations, and individuals have established Web sites—computer "pages" on which they provide information, sell products or services, and/or recruit employees. Each page has an address so it can be reached easily by merely typing in the address. An Internet address is known as a *uniform resource locator—URL*, pronounced "you are el." A description of URL parts follows:

(1) A typical Internet address (URL) might appear as **http://www.odci. gov/cia/publications/factbook/index.html** in a listing.

(2) The first part, **http://**, indicates the type of protocol needed to retrieve the information at the site. In this case **http** represents *hypertext transfer protocol*. World Wide Web sites are accessed by Web browsers using this protocol.

---

[2]The spellings shown here are based on those contained in *Merriam-Webster's Collegiate Dictionary*, 10th ed. (Springfield, Mass.: Merriam-Webster, Incorporated, 2002). Note that in this dictionary the foreign spelling is shown after the English spelling in the primary reference and also listed separately in a secondary reference.

[3]See Chapter 9 for additional information on accessing and using the Internet. See Chapter 15 for useful Internet site addresses.

(3) The **www** following the protocol type symbolizes World Wide Web. The name of the host computer, **odci** (Office of the Director of Central Intelligence), is followed by its identifier, **gov**, which distinguishes the Web site as a government entity. Note the common URL identifier extensions in the following table:

Identifier	Definition
com	commercial organization
edu	educational site
gov	government organization
mil	military
net	organization administering a network
org	miscellaneous organization

(4) The link **cia** from the host computer moves to the Web site of The Central Intelligence Agency where **publications**, **factbook**, and **index.html** are accessed.

(5) Keying in **http://www.odci.gov/cia/publications/factbook/index. html**,[4] therefore, will take you directly to the contents for *The World Factbook 2001* or an updated version. The **html** extension after **index** represents "hypertext markup language." Clicking on any item in the contents will access the text in the current world fact book.

11–10 E-Mail Addresses

Just as everyone has an address for mail delivery by the U.S. Postal Service and private mail carriers, anyone who wishes to send and receive mail through the Internet must have an Internet E-mail (electronic mail) address.

(1) An E-mail address is divided into two basic parts: the user name and the user domain. The user name is the combination of letters and/or numbers assigned to a specific user upon signing up with an on-line service or other E-mail provider. The user domain identifies the location of the computer that receives the user's mail—the on-line service or other E-mail provider.

(2) The user name and the user domain are separated by @ (an "at" sign). Examples of E-mail addresses follow:

E-Mail Address	Explanation
ClarksHOW@aol.com[5]	The user name is *ClarksHOW* (James and Lyn Clark); the on-line service provider is America Online, an on-line service provider that is classified as a commercial organization.
jdoe@plantronics.com	The user name is *jdoe* (John Doe); the E-mail provider is Plantronics, a commercial organization.

[4]Normally you may omit typing *http://* when entering a Web site address in the address box of your browser.

[5]See Section 11-9 for an explanation of extensions *com, edu, gov, mil, net,* and *org.*

E-Mail Address	Explanation
allison.jones@sdsu.edu	The user name is *allison.jones* (Allison Jones); the E-mail provider is San Diego State University, an educational site.
bsmith@csupomona.edu	The user name is *bsmith* (B. Smith); the E-mail provider is California State Polytechnic University, Pomona—an educational site.
JLConnor87@earthlink.net	The user name is *JLConnor87* (Jason L. Connor); the on-line service provider is EarthLink, an access provider that is classified as an organization administering a network.
lyndiamilton@aplus.net	The user name is *lyndiamilton* (Lyndia Milton); the on-line service provider is Aplus.Net, an access provider that is classified as an organization administering a network.
az678@lafn.org	The user name is *az678* (Mary Smith); the E-mail/Internet service provider is Los Angeles Free Net, a miscellaneous organization.

Forms of Address

11-11 Personal and General Professional Titles

The following table lists the proper forms of address, salutation, and complimentary close for correspondence addressed to a general individual, two or more general individuals, certain professionals, and a company:

Addressee	Address on Letter and Envelope	Salutation and Complimentary Close
Man	Mr. (full name) (local address)	Dear Mr. (last name): Sincerely,
Married woman	Mrs. (husband's first name, last name) (local address)	Dear Mrs. (last name): Sincerely,
	Mrs. or Ms. (wife's first name, last name)[6] (local address)	Dear Mrs. or Ms. (last name): Sincerely,
Single woman	Ms. (full name) (local address)	Dear Ms. (last name): Sincerely,
Woman, marital status unknown	Ms. (full name) (local address)	Dear Ms. (last name): Sincerely,

---

[6]This form is also used for a woman who is separated or divorced from her husband.

313

Addressee	Address on Letter and Envelope	Salutation and Complimentary Close
Widow	Mrs. (husband's first name, last name) (local address)	Dear Mrs. (last name): Sincerely,
	Mrs. or Ms. (wife's first name, last name) (local address)	Dear Mrs. or Ms. (last name): Sincerely,
Two or more men	Mr. (full name) Mr. (full name) (local address)	Dear Mr. (last name) and Mr. (last name): *or* Dear Messrs. (last name) and (last name): *or* Gentlemen: Sincerely,
Two or more women	Mrs. (full name) Mrs. (full name) (local address)	Dear Mrs. (last name) and Mrs. (last name): *or* Dear Mesdames (last name) and (last name): *or* Mesdames: Sincerely,
	Mrs. (full name) Ms. (full name) (local address)	Dear Mrs. (last name) and Ms. (last name): Sincerely,
	Ms. (full name) Ms. (full name) (local address)	Dear Ms. (last name) and Ms. (last name): *or* Dear Mses. (last name) and (last name): Sincerely,
One woman and One man	Ms. (full name) Mr. (full name) (local address)	Dear Ms. (last name) and Mr. (last name): Sincerely,
Married couple	Mr. and Mrs. (husband's full name) (local address)	Dear Mr. and Mrs. (last name): Sincerely,
Married couple with different last names	(title) (full name of husband) (title) (full name of wife) (local address)	Dear (title) (husband's last name) and (title) (wife's last name): Sincerely,
Professional married couple with same title and same last name	(title in plural form) (husband's first name) and (wife's first name) (last name) (local address)	Dear (title in plural form) (last name): Sincerely,
Professional married couple with different titles and same last name	(title) (full name of husband) (title) (full name of wife) (local address)	Dear (title) and (title) (last name): Sincerely,

Addressee	Address on Letter and Envelope	Salutation and Complimentary Close
President of a college or university (Doctor)	Dr. (full name), President (name of institution) (local address)	Dear Dr. (last name): Sincerely,
Dean of a school or college	Dean (full name) School of (name) (name of institution) (local address)	Dear Dean (last name): Sincerely,
	Dr. or (Mr./Mrs./Ms.) (full name) Dean of (title) (name of institution) (local address)	Dear Dr. or (Mr./Mrs./Ms.) (last name): Sincerely,
Professor	Professor (full name) (name of department) (name of institution) (local address)	Dear Professor (last name): Sincerely,
	Dr. (full name), Professor (name of department) (name of institution) (local address)	Dear Dr. (last name): Sincerely,
	Dr. or (Mr./Mrs./Ms.) (full name) Assistant (or Associate) Professor (name of department) (name of institution) (local address)	Dear Dr. or (Mr./Mrs./Ms.) (last name): Sincerely,
Physician	(full name), M.D. (local address) *or* Dr. (full name) (local address)	Dear Dr. (last name): Sincerely,
Lawyer	(Mr./Mrs./Ms.) (full name) Attorney-at-Law (local address) *or* (full name), Esq. (local address)	Dear (Mr./Mrs./Ms.) (last name): Sincerely,
Service personnel	(full rank, full name, and abbreviation of service designation) (*Retired* is added to rank if applicable.) (unit assignment) (local address)	Dear (rank) (last name): Sincerely,
	Example: Lieutenant Colonel, United States Air Force Lieutenant Colonel Cory Adams, USAF Headquarters Squadron, 22nd Bomb Group March Air Force Base Riverside, California 92506	Dear Colonel Adams: Sincerely,

Addressee	Address on Letter and Envelope	Salutation and Complimentary Close
Service personnel *(continued)*	Example: Brigadier General Retired, United States Marine Corps Brig. Gen. Ret. Casey Rhodes, USMC (local address)	Dear General Rhodes: Sincerely,
Company or corporation, men	(full name of organization) (local address)	Gentlemen: Sincerely,
Company or corporation, men and women	(full name of organization) (local address)	Ladies and Gentlemen: Sincerely,
Company or corporation, women	(full name of organization) (local address)	Ladies: Sincerely,

11-12 Government Officials

The following table shows the proper forms of address, salutation, and complimentary close for specific government officials:

Addressee	Address on Letter	Salutation and Complimentary Close
President of the United States	(Mr./Mrs./Ms.) (full name), President The White House 1600 Pennsylvania Avenue, N.W. Washington, DC 20500	Dear (Mr./Madam) President: Respectfully,
Former president[7]	Honorable (full name) Former President of the United States (local address)	Dear (Mr./Mrs./Ms.) (last name): Sincerely,
President-elect	Honorable (full name) President-Elect of the United States (local address)	Dear (Mr./Mrs./Ms.) (last name): Sincerely,
Wife of the president	Mrs. (full name) The White House Washington, DC 20500	Dear Mrs. (last name): Sincerely,
Assistant to the president	Honorable (full name) Assistant to the President The White House Washington, DC 20500	Dear (Mr./Mrs./Ms.) (last name): Sincerely,
Vice president of the United States	The Vice President United States Senate Washington, DC 20510 *or* The Honorable (full name) Vice President of the United States United States Senate Washington, DC 20510	Dear (Mr./Madam) Vice President: Sincerely,
Chief Justice of the United States	The Chief Justice of the United States The Supreme Court of the United States Washington, DC 20543	Dear (Mr./Madam) Chief Justice: Sincerely,

---

[7]This form of address may be adapted to address other former high-ranking government officials.

Addressee	Address on Letter	Salutation and Complimentary Close
Associate Justice	Honorable (full name) Associate Justice of the United States The Supreme Court of the United States Washington, DC 20543	Dear (Mr./Madam) Justice: Sincerely,
United States senator	Honorable (full name) United States Senate Washington, DC 20510 or Honorable (full name) United States Senator (local address)	Dear Senator (last name): Sincerely,
United States senator-elect	(Mr./Mrs./Ms.) (full name) Senator-Elect, United States Senate (local address)	Dear (Mr./Mrs./Ms.) (last name): Sincerely,
United States representative	Honorable (full name) House of Representatives Washington, DC 20515 or Honorable (full name), Member United States House of Representatives (local address)	Dear (Mr./Mrs./Ms.) (last name): Sincerely,
Cabinet Member	Honorable (full name) Secretary of (name of department) Washington, DC 00000	Dear (Mr./Madam) Secretary: Sincerely,
	Honorable (full name) Postmaster General Washington, DC 20260	Dear (Mr./Madam) Postmaster General: Sincerely,
	Honorable (full name) Attorney General Washington, DC 20503	Dear (Mr./Madam) Attorney General: Sincerely,
Deputy secretary, assistant secretary, or undersecretary	Honorable (full name) Deputy Secretary of (name of department) Washington, DC 00000	Dear (Mr./Mrs./Ms.) (last name): Sincerely,
	Honorable (full name) Assistant Secretary of (name of department) Washington, DC 00000	
	Honorable (full name) Undersecretary of (name of department) Washington, DC 00000	
Head of independent office or agency	Honorable (full name) Comptroller General of the United States General Accounting Office Washington, DC 20548	Dear (Mr./Mrs./Ms.) (last name): Sincerely,
	Honorable (full name) Chairman, (name of commission) Washington, DC 00000	Dear (Mr./Madam) Chairman: Sincerely,

11
Addressing

Addressee	Address on Letter and Envelope	Salutation and Complimentary Close
Head of independent office or agency *(cont.)*	Honorable (full name) Director, Bureau of the Budget Washington, DC 20503	Dear (Mr./Mrs./Ms.) (last name): Sincerely,
American ambassador	Honorable (full name) American Ambassador (address and city) (country)	Sir: or Madam: (formal) Very truly yours, *or* Dear (Mr./Madam Ambassador: (informal) Sincerely,
American consul general or American consul	(Mr./Mrs./Ms.) (full name) American Consul General (or American Consul) (address and city) (country)	Dear (Mr./Mrs./Ms.) (last name): Sincerely,
Foreign ambassador in the United States	His Excellency (full name) Ambassador of (country) (local address)	Excellency: (formal) Very truly yours, *or* Dear (Mr./Madam Ambassador: (informal) Sincerely,
Governor of state	Honorable (full name) Governor of (name of state) (address) (city), (state) 00000	Dear Governor (last name): Sincerely,
Lieutenant governor	Honorable (full name) Lieutenant Governor of (name of state) (address) (city), (state) 00000	Dear (Mr./Mrs./Ms.) (last name): Sincerely,
State senator	Honorable (full name) (name of state) State Senate (address) (city), (state) 00000	Dear Senator (last name): Sincerely,
State representative, assemblyperson, or delegate	Honorable (full name) (name of state) House of Representatives (or State Assembly or House of Delegates) (address) (city), (state) 00000	Dear (Mr./Mrs./Ms.) (last name): Sincerely,
Mayor	Honorable (full name) Mayor of (name of city) (address) (city), (state) 00000	Dear Mayor (last name): Sincerely,
President of a board of commissioners	Honorable (full name), President Board of Commissioners of (name of city) (address) (city), (state) 00000	Dear (Mr./Mrs./Ms.) (last name): Sincerely,
Judge	Honorable (full name) (name of court) (local address)	Dear Judge (last name): Sincerely,

11-13 Religious Dignitaries

The following table shows the proper forms of address, salutation, and complimentary close for specific religious dignitaries:

Addressee	Address on Letter and Envelope	Salutation and Complimentary Close
Catholic clergy		
Cardinal	His Eminence (given name) Cardinal (last name)	Your Eminence: (formal)
		or
	Archbishop of (diocese) (local address)	Dear Cardinal (last name): (informal) Sincerely,
Archbishop	The Most Reverend (full name) Archbishop of (diocese) (local address)	Your Excellency: (formal) or Dear Archbishop (last name): (informal) Sincerely,
Bishop	The Most Reverend (full name) Bishop of (city) (local address)	Your Excellency: (formal) or Dear Bishop (last name): (informal) Sincerely,
Monsignor	The Right Reverend Monsignor (full name) (local address)	Right Reverend Monsignor: (formal) or Dear Monsignor (last name): (informal) Sincerely,
	or	
	The Very Reverend Monsignor (full name) (local address)	Very Reverend Monsignor: (formal) or Dear Monsignor (last name): (informal) Sincerely,
Priest	The Reverend (full name), (add initials of order, if any) (local address)	Reverend Sir: (formal) Dear Father (last name): (informal) Sincerely,
Mother superior	Mother (full name), (initials of order, if used) Superior, (name of convent) (local address)	Dear Mother (full name): Sincerely,
Nun	Sister (full name), (initials of order, if used) (name of convent) (local address)	Dear Sister (full name): Sincerely,
Monk	Brother (full name), (initials of order, if used) (local address)	Dear Brother (full name): Sincerely,
Jewish clergy	Rabbi (full name) (local address)	Dear Rabbi (last name): Sincerely,

Addressee	Address on Letter and Envelope	Salutation and Complimentary Close
Protestant clergy		
Bishop	The Right Reverend (full name) Bishop of (name) (local address) *or*	Right Reverend Sir: (formal) *or* Dear Bishop (last name): (informal) Sincerely,
	The Reverend (full name) Bishop of (name) (local address)	Reverend Sir: (formal) *or* Dear Bishop (last name): (informal) Sincerely,
Dean	The Very Reverend (full name) Dean of (name of church) (local address)	Very Reverend Sir: (formal) *or* Dear Dean (last name): (informal) Sincerely,
Minister	The Reverend (full name) (title, if any) (name of church) (local address)	Dear Reverend (last name): *or* Dear (Dr./Mr./Mrs./Ms.) (last name): Sincerely,
Chaplain	Chaplain (full name) (full rank, service designation) (post office address of organization and station) (local address)	Dear Chaplain (last name): Sincerely,
Lay clergy	Deacon (full name) (name of church) (local address)	Dear Deacon (last name): Sincerely,
	(Brother/Sister) (full name) (name of church) (local address)	Dear (Brother/Sister)(last name): Sincerely,

11-14 Undetermined Individual or Group

Although addressing correspondence to an undefined or undetermined individual or group should generally be avoided, circumstances sometimes provide no other alternative. In these cases the letter contains no inside address. The phrase *To Whom It May Concern:* replaces the standard salutation, and the complimentary close is either *Sincerely yours,* or *Yours very truly,*.

12

Business Letters and Memorandums

Business Letters and Memorandums Solution Finder

Letter Styles

12-1 Full Block

Business letters may be formatted in several styles.[1] The full block letter style is the most streamlined style because all parts and all lines begin at the left margin.

full block letter

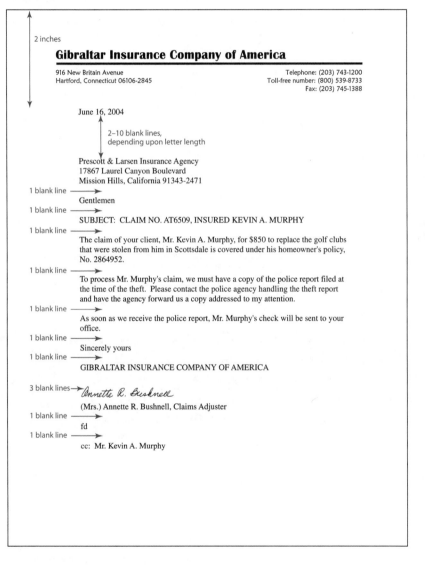

---

[1]All letters appearing in this chapter have been designed by the authors for illustrative purposes. They are not reproductions of actual letters.

12-2 **Modified Block**

a. The modified block letter style with blocked paragraphs is the most popular letter style used in business. All lines except the return address (if used), the date, and the closing lines begin at the left margin.

modified block letter with blocked paragraphs

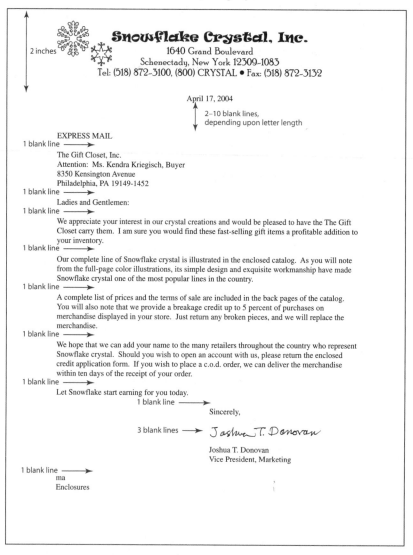

b. The modified block letter style with indented paragraphs is also used frequently. All lines except the first line of each paragraph, the return address (if used), the date, and the closing lines begin at the left margin.

modified block letter with indented paragraphs

2 inches

2122 Celes Street
Woodland Hills, CA 91364
April 10, 2004

2–10 blank lines,
depending upon letter length

Nabisco, Inc.
Special Products Division
East Hanover, NJ 07936

1 blank line ——————→

Gentlemen:

1 blank line ——————→

I have been buying Milk-Bone biscuits for about ten years and have been pleased with my dog's oral health.

1 blank line ——————→

Recently I noticed that you placed on the market two new Milk-Bone flavors: beef and cheese. However, these flavors come in the large size only. Since I have a medium-size dog, he won't eat the larger biscuits. If you were to produce these new flavors in small and medium sizes also, dogs of all sizes could enjoy these new Milk-Bone dog biscuits.

1 blank line ——————→

Please let me know if you plan to make these new flavors in three sizes. In the meantime, my dog Ozzie will continue to enjoy munching on your original Milk-Bone dog biscuits.

1 blank line ——————→ Sincerely,

3 blank lines ——————→ *Angela Dellaria*

Angela Dellaria

12
Business Letters

12-3 Social Business

The social business letter style is used for social business correspondence. In this informal format the inside address is placed after the closing lines. The salutation may be followed by a comma instead of a colon, and the typed signature line is optional. Paragraphs are either indented or blocked.

No subject or attention lines are used in the social business letter style. Reference initials, enclosure notations, and copy notations are usually omitted on the original, but these parts may be included below the inside address on the file copy or on the copies for distribution. Leave a double space after the inside address, and single-space on all copies except the original any needed notations.

social business letter

2 inches

United Bank of Iowa
Park Fair Shopping Center • Des Moines, Iowa 50313-2167 • Tel: (515) 273-9600 • Fax: (515) 273-9590

January 23, 2004

4–10 blank lines,
depending upon letter length

Dear Tyler,

1 blank line ⟶

    Congratulations on your appointment as president of Parkfair Mutual Bank and executive vice president of the parent holding company, Parkfair Financial Corporation.

1 blank line ⟶

    You are certainly deserving of this promotion because you have contributed immeasurably to the rapid growth and development of Parkfair and its parent holding company. I know, too, that under your leadership both organizations will continue to move forward in the banking industry.

1 blank line ⟶

Sincerely,

3 blank lines ⟶

Morgan S. Stanley

2 blank lines ⟶

Mr. Tyler T. Hezzelwood, President
Parkfair Mutual Bank
5800 West Camelback Road
Phoenix, Arizona 85033-4613

12–4 Simplified

In the simplified style all parts of the letter begin at the left margin. A subject line keyed in all capital letters replaces the salutation. Two blank lines are left before and after the subject line. No complimentary close is used in the simplified letter style. Instead, the signature line is keyed on the fifth line (leave four blank lines) below the last line of the message. Use all capital letters and a single line for the signature line.

simplified letter

2 inches

Worldwide Insurance Company

400 Berkeley Street • Boston, MA 02117 • Tel. (617) 555-3765 • Fax (617) 555-3785

June 7, 2004

2–10 blank lines, depending upon letter length

Mr. Wooil Lee
A-1 Insurance Agency
470 West Fairmont Street
Grand Rapids, MI 49502-1036

2 blank lines

POLICY NO. S119294, INSURED DUNCAN R. HANNAH

2 blank lines

We have completed our investigation of the accident claim submitted by your agency on behalf of Duncan R. Hannah.

1 blank line

According to our claims adjuster, Mr. Hannah was injured while in the employ of the Millstone Manufacturing Company. His injuries were incurred in an industrial accident on April 27 and are therefore considered job related. Consequently, the expenses of this accident are covered by Workers' Compensation insurance. Only those expenses beyond the amount allowed by Workers' Compensation are covered by our company.

1 blank line

Please submit a complete listing of Mr. Hannah's expenses in regard to this accident. As soon as we receive verification from the Workers' Compensation Board on the amount allowable in Mr. Hannah's case, we will process the proper claim forms.

1 blank line

If you have any questions or need any additional information, please let us know.

4 blank lines

B. Andrew Feragamo

B. ANDREW FERAGAMO, CLU, VICE PRESIDENT

1 blank line

mrd

12

Business Letters

Letter Format and Placement of Major Parts

12-5 Margins and Vertical Placement With Word Processing Software

a. Use a 2-inch top margin for the first page of a business letter printed on letterhead stationery. Any second and succeeding pages of a business letter have 1-inch top margins. Use left justification.

Choose the side margins according to the number of words in the letter and the size of the font used to prepare it. Set the margins *after* keying the letter and using the word count feature of your word processing program.

The following tables may be used as guidelines for preparing standard and long letters. The first table applies to 12-point fonts; the second table applies to 11-point and 10-point fonts.

12-point fonts[2]

Margin Settings for Business Letters
Printed in 12-Point Fonts

Letter Length	Number of Words	Margin Settings		Line Length
		Left	Right	
Standard	Up to 200	1.5"	1.5"	5.5 inches
Long	200+	1"	1"	6.5 inches

11-point and 10-point fonts [3]

Margin Settings for Business Letters
Printed in 11-Point and 10-Point Fonts

Letter Length	Number of Words	Margin Settings		Line Length
		Left	Right	
Standard	Up to 200	1.75"	1.75"	5 inches
Long	200+	1.25"	1.25"	6 inches

b. Leave 2 or 3 blank lines between the date and inside address in letters with two or more pages. Balance single-page letters vertically by regulating the number of lines between the date and the inside address. Use the following procedures on your word processing program to achieve this balance *after* the margins have been set:

(1) Count the number of blank lines between the date and the inside address. (Example: 3 blank lines)

(2) Directly after the *last* line of the letter (usually reference initials or an enclosure notation), press the *Enter* key until the page break is reached. Count the number of blank lines from the last line of the letter until the page break. (Example: 6 blank lines)

(3) Total the two line counts. (Example: 6 + 3 = 9) Divide this total by two. (Example: 9 ÷ 2 = 4.5) Disregard any fractional part. (Example: 4 blank lines)

(4) Insert or delete blank lines, if necessary, to ensure that the number of blank lines between the *date and the inside address* EQUALS the

---

[2] This table may also be used for fonts measuring 10 characters per inch. Other names used to describe this font size are *10 cpi, 10 pitch,* and *pica.*

[3] This table may also be used for fonts measuring 12 characters per inch. Other names used to describe this font size are *12 cpi, 12 pitch,* and *elite.*

result obtained in Step (3) above. Do not, however, leave fewer than two or more than ten blank lines between the date and the inside address. (Example: Insert 1 additional blank line between the date and the inside address.)

(5) Delete any extra blank lines at the bottom of the page.

examples for balancing a letter vertically on the page

Blank Lines Between Date and Inside Address	Blank Lines Between Letter End and Page Break	Sum of Blank Lines	Blank Lines ÷ 2 (Remainder Dropped)	Revised Number of Blank Lines Needed Between Date and Inside Address	Number of Blank Lines to be Inserted or Deleted
4	2	4+2=6	6÷2=3	3	−1
3	7	3+7=10	10÷2=5	5	+2
4	1	4+1=5	5÷2=2.5=2	2	−2
3	8	3+8=11	11÷2=5.5=5	5	+2
4	−1	4−1=3	3÷2=1.5=1	At least 2	−2

12-6 Return Address

a. No return address is needed for business letters prepared on paper containing a complete company letterhead. Similarly, business letters prepared on word processing programs with a letter template do not require a return address.

printed company letterhead

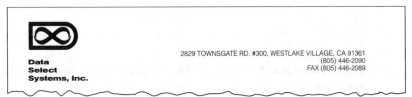

letterhead produced from a word processing template

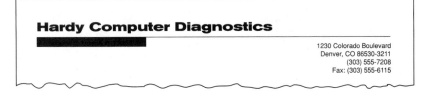

b. When plain bond paper or letterhead paper without a mailing address is used, a return address must be included.

On plain bond paper begin the return address so that the date is 2 inches from the top edge of the paper. Although the date appears directly below the last line of the return address, it is not considered part of the return address.

On letterhead paper without a mailing address, begin the return address a double space below the last line in the letterhead or end it so the date is 2 inches below the top edge of the paper. Select the option that places the return address in the lower position.

c. *Modified block or social business letter styles.* In the modified block or social business styles, each line of the return address may be centered. Lines in the return address may also (1) begin at the center of the page, (2) begin 0.5 inch to the left of the page center, or (3) align at the right margin. The return address in a modified block letter style is illustrated in Section 12-2b, page 325.

Full block or simplified letter styles. In the full block and simplified letter styles, all lines begin at the left margin.

return address in modified block or social business letter style without letterhead

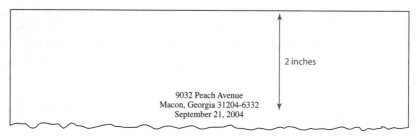

```
                              9032 Peach Avenue
                           Macon, Georgia 31204-6332
                              September 21, 2004
```
2 inches

return address in full block or simplified letter style without letterhead

```
   Holbrook Linen Supply
   1700 Farrell Boulevard
   Boise, Idaho 83706-3793
   March 21, 2004
```
2 inches

letterhead with return address ending 2 inches from top edge of paper—modified block or social business letter

Techline Computer Supplies
A Subsidiary of Compton Corporation

1403 South Queen Street
Honolulu, HI 96819-5912
June 17, 2004

2 inches

letterhead with return address begun a double space below letterhead—full block or simplified letter

Committee for the Preservation of State Historical Sites
A Nonprofit Organization

Endorsed by

_____   _____   _____   _____
_____   _____   _____   _____

1 blank line ——►
8940 East State Street
Minneapolis, MN 55431-3642
November 14, 2004

12
Business Letters

12-7 Date

a. On letterhead paper with a mailing address, place the date a double space below the last line in the letterhead or allocate a 2-inch margin from the top edge of the paper. Select the procedure that places the date in the lower position.

Modified block and social business letter styles. In modified block and social business letters, the date may be (1) centered, (2) begun at the center of the page, or (3) aligned with the right margin.

Full block and simplified letter styles. In full block or simplified letters, place the date at the left margin.

date 2 inches below top edge of paper—modified block or social business letter

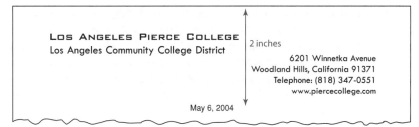

LOS ANGELES PIERCE COLLEGE
Los Angeles Community College District

2 inches

6201 Winnetka Avenue
Woodland Hills, California 91371
Telephone: (818) 347-0551
www.piercecollege.com

May 6, 2004

date placed a double space below letterhead—full block letter

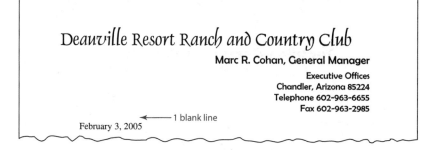

b. In letters requiring return addresses, place the date on the line directly below the last line of the return address. A date used with the return address in a complete letter is illustrated in Section 12-2b, page 325.

date with return address

12-8 **Addressee and Delivery Notations**

a. Addressee notations such as *Personal* and *Confidential* are entered in all capital letters a double space above the inside address.

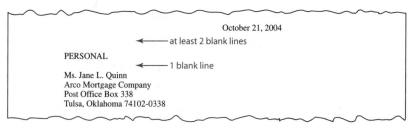

b. Delivery notations such as *Certified Mail, Express Mail, Federal Express, Air Mail, Registered Mail, Fax Transmittal,* and *Messenger Delivery* are entered in all capital letters either (1) a double space above the inside address or (2) a single or double space below the reference initials or enclosure notation, whichever appears last. A delivery notation is illustrated in a complete letter in Section 12-2a, page 324.

delivery notations a double space above inside address

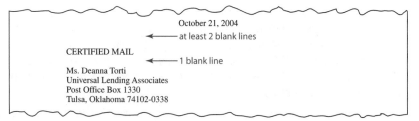

October 21, 2004

◄—— at least 2 blank lines

CERTIFIED MAIL ◄—— 1 blank line

Ms. Deanna Torti
Universal Lending Associates
Post Office Box 1330
Tulsa, Oklahoma 74102-0338

October 21, 2004

◄—— at least 2 blank lines

FAX TRANSMITTAL ◄—— 1 blank line

Ms. Deanna Torti
Universal Lending Associates
Post Office Box 1330
Tulsa, Oklahoma 74102-0338

delivery notation after reference initials or enclosure notation

mls
Enclosure
EXPRESS MAIL
copy to Dylan Busse

c. If an addressee and a delivery notation appear in the same letter, place the addressee notation on the third line above the inside address and the delivery notation on the line directly below. Use all capital letters for both notations. Leave *at least* two blank lines between the date and the addressee notation.

addressee and delivery notations in same letter

January 22, 2005

◄—— at least 2 blank lines

CONFIDENTIAL
EXPRESS MAIL ◄—— 1 blank line

Mr. Vincent D. Perotti
Vice President, Marketing
Investment Online, Inc.
4000 Washington Boulevard
Chicago, IL 60612-6427

12-9 Inside Address

a. The inside address follows the date and any addressee or delivery notations. It contains some or all of the following: courtesy title, full name, professional title, department name, company name, street or mailing address, city, state, and zip code. Single-space and begin at the left margin those parts necessary to direct the letter to the addressee.

Place the courtesy title and full name on the first line. The professional title and department name have no specific line designations; they should be positioned to balance with the remaining parts of the inside address. The street or mailing address appears on a separate line. Arrange the city, state, and zip code together on another separate line.

arrangement of an inside address

Ms. Morgan A. Stanley
Manager, Policy Issue Department
Atlantic-General Insurance Company
400 West Jefferson Boulevard, Suite 100
Charlotte, North Carolina 28212-7610

Mr. Byron Hart, Manager
Department of Human Resources
Citizens Federal Bank
5282 East Ninth Street
Charlotte, NC 28212-4310

b. Abbreviate only the courtesy titles *Mr.*, *Mrs.*, and *Dr.* The courtesy title *Ms.* is not an abbreviation; its only form is *Ms.*

Spell out all street designations such as *Street*, *Avenue*, and *Boulevard*. *Boulevard* may be abbreviated, however, with exceptionally long street names. Spell out the state name or use the two-letter post office designation, whichever form achieves balance with the remaining lines. A listing of two-letter state and territory designations for the United States may be found in Section 6-12 and on the page opposite the inside back cover.

An inside address may contain from a minimum of two lines to a maximum of six lines.

two-line inside address

Cedar Creek Inn
Cedar Rapids, IA 52406

six-line inside address

Mr. M. J. Fujimoto
Airline Training Specialist
Division of Personnel Instruction
TransAmerica-Continental Airlines
12700 East Funston Street
Wichita, Kansas 67207-3402

c. *Modified block, full block, and simplified letter styles.* In the modified block, full block, and simplified letter styles, the inside address usually follows the date. The number of blank lines between the date and the inside address is determined by the length of the letter.

Refer to Section 12-5 for detailed instructions on setting margins and determining the number of blank lines to leave between the date and the inside address.

inside address in modified block letter

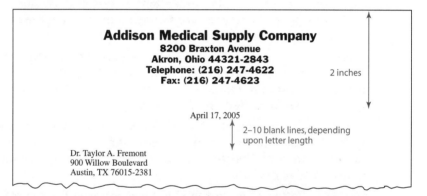

d. *The social business letter style.* In the social business letter, the inside address is placed after the closing lines. If the typed signature line is omitted, leave five or six blank lines after the complimentary close before beginning the inside address. If a typed signature line is included, leave two blank lines after the typed signature before beginning the inside address.

social business letter without typed signature

social business letter with typed signature

Sincerely,

John | 3 blank lines

John R. Billings

↕ 2 blank lines

Dr. Willard R. Moss, Professor
University of Tennessee
847 Union Street
Memphis, Tennessee 38103

12-10 Attention Line

a. The attention line is used for directing correspondence to an individual or department within a company while still officially addressing the letter to the organization. It is also useful for directing correspondence to a person whose name is unknown.

b. The modern trend is to place the attention line in the inside address on the line directly below the company name and use the same format for the envelope address.[4]

Modified block and full block letter styles. As an alternative to including the attention line in the inside address, it may be placed at the left margin a double space below the last line of the inside address in the modified and full block styles.

Use (1) a combination of initial capital letters and lowercase letters or (2) all capital letters. Using a colon after the word *Attention* is optional. An attention line is illustrated in a complete letter in Section 12-2a, page 324.

Simplified letter style. In the simplified letter style, the attention line is included in the inside address and placed directly below the organization's name. The word *Attention* may or may not be followed by a colon.

Social business letter style. The attention line is not used in the social business style.

attention line included in inside address

Valley Manufacturing Company
Attention: General Manager
18600 Sierra Bonita Boulevard
San Bernardino, CA 91763-5201

---

[4]Correspondence using an attention line is addressed to the company, not an individual. Therefore, the name of the company should appear before the attention line. The U.S. Postal Service recommendation to place the attention line before the company name does not follow this protocol.

attention line at left margin below inside address

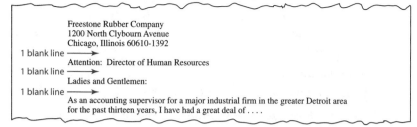

Freestone Rubber Company
1200 North Clybourn Avenue
Chicago, Illinois 60610-1392
1 blank line ⟶
Attention: Director of Human Resources
1 blank line ⟶
Ladies and Gentlemen:
1 blank line ⟶
As an accounting supervisor for a major industrial firm in the greater Detroit area
for the past thirteen years, I have had a great deal of . . . .

12-11 Salutation

a. The content of the salutation depends upon to whom the letter is addressed in the inside address and the degree of familiarity between the addressee and the writer. See Section 12-11b–f.[5]

Modified block and full block letter styles. Begin the salutation at the left margin, and place it a double space below the last line of the inside address or the attention line, if used. Conclude the salutation with a colon for the mixed punctuation format; use no ending punctuation mark for the open punctuation format.

Simplified letter style. Omit the salutation in this letter style.

Social business letter style. In the social business style, position the salutation at the left margin after the date. Use the mixed punctuation format; place a colon or a comma after the salutation.

salutation in a modified block or full block letter

Mr. Charles B. Wayama
Empire Check Printing
200 Renaissance Center
Detroit, MI 40610-1392
1 blank line ⟶
Dear Mr. Wayama:
1 blank line ⟶
For the past eight years, our bank has been using your company to print checks
for our checking account customers. During this time we have been . . . .

salutation in a social business letter

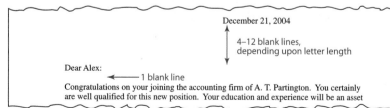

December 21, 2004

4–12 blank lines,
depending upon letter length

Dear Alex: ⟵ 1 blank line
Congratulations on your joining the accounting firm of A. T. Partington. You certainly
are well qualified for this new position. Your education and experience will be an asset

---

[5]See Sections 11-11 through 11-14 for additional information on the proper use of formal titles, salutations, and complimentary closes.

b. In letters addressed to individuals, use one of the following salutations, depending upon the degree of formality desired. Use a colon (or a comma in the social business letter) after the salutation if mixed punctuation is used; use no punctuation mark if open punctuation is used.

informal salutation

Dear Carson: Dear Drew:

standard business letter salutation to a single addressee

Dear Mr. Forrester: Dear Miss Sanders:

Dear Ms. Lopez: Dear Mrs. Chin:

standard business letter salutation to two or more men

Dear Mr. Donovan and Mr. Stephenson:
> *or*

Dear Mr. Donovan, Mr. Stephenson, and Mr. Stern:
> *or*

Dear Messrs. Donovan, Stephenson, and Stern:
> *or*

Gentlemen:

standard business letter salutation to two or more women—courtesy title **Ms.**

Dear Ms. Franklin and Ms. Kellogg:
> *or*

Dear Ms. Franklin, Ms. Horike, and Ms. Kellogg:
> *or*

Dear Mses. Franklin, Horike, and Kellogg:
> *or*

Ladies:

standard business letter salutation to two or more young girls— courtesy title **Miss**

Dear Miss Bradshaw and Miss Lambert:
> *or*

Dear Miss Bradshaw, Miss Lambert, and Miss Hoover:
> *or*

Dear Misses Bradshaw, Lambert, and Hoover:
> *or*

Ladies:

standard business letter salutation to two or more women—courtesy title **Mrs.**

Dear Mrs. Marsee and Mrs. O'Donnell:
> *or*

Dear Mrs. Bedrosian, Mrs. Marsee, and Mrs. O'Donnell:
> *or*

338

Dear Mesdames Bedrosian, Marsee, and O'Donnell:
>> *or*

Mesdames: *or*   Ladies:

standard business letter salutation to two or more persons with different courtesy titles

Dear Ms. Sterling and Mr. Michel:

Dear Mrs. Andrino, Ms. Hopi, Mr. Lopez, and Ms. Mullens-King:

Ladies: (women only)

Gentlemen: (men only)

Ladies and Gentlemen:

Dear Colleagues: (or other appropriate general reference designation)

standard salutations to persons with professional titles

Dear Dr. Marcus:

Dear Professor Bredow:

Dear Colonel Andrews:

formal salutations for certain government officials and religious dignitaries

Sir:

Excellency:

Reverend Sir:

Your Eminence:

c. If the gender of an addressee is unknown, use the full name of the person without a courtesy title. Use the courtesy title *Ms.* for a woman unless another title is specified by the addressee.

full name without courtesy title

Orolyn Ruenz (Dear Orolyn Ruenz:)

Chris Ravetch (Dear Chris Ravetch:)

B. C. Weyenberg (Dear B. C. Weyenberg:)

courtesy title for a woman

Ms. Diana Reember (Dear Ms. Reember:)

Ms. Min Nguyen (Dear Ms. Nguyen:)

d. In correspondence addressed to companies, associations, or other groups, use one of the following salutations:

salutations for groups composed of men and women

Ladies and Gentlemen: Gentlemen and Ladies:

salutation for groups composed entirely of men

Gentlemen:

salutations for groups composed entirely of women

Mesdames: Ladies:

e. Letters addressed to a firm but directed to the attention of an individual within the company receive the salutation used to open a
letter to a group: *Gentlemen*, *Ladies and Gentlemen*, *Gentlemen
and Ladies*, *Mesdames*, or *Ladies*.

Arroyo Textile Manufacturing Company
Attention Accounts Receivable Manager
2850 Central Avenue, N.W.
Albuquerque, New Mexico 87105-1742
                     ← 1 blank line
Ladies and Gentlemen:
                     ← 1 blank line
On September 10 we purchased from your company twelve 50-yard bolts of Royal
Luster velvet upholstery fabric (Invoice No. GY-14953). Payment for . . . .

f. Letters to an undetermined individual or group of individuals
should generally be avoided. When used, such letters contain no
inside address and use *To Whom It May Concern:* as the salutation.

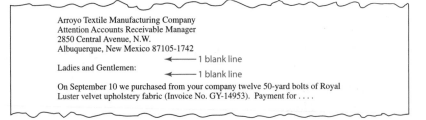

April 7, 2005

4–12 blank lines,
depending upon letter length

To Whom It May Concern:
               ← 1 blank line
I am pleased to recommend . . . .

12-12 Subject Line

a. The subject line briefly describes the contents of the letter.

Modified block and full block letter styles. For modified and full
block letters, begin the subject line at the left margin a double
space below the salutation. Double-space after the subject line.

Use (1) initial capital letters for the main words[6] or (2) all capital
letters. The word *Subject* followed by a colon usually introduces the
line. The subject line is illustrated in a full block letter in Section
12-1, page 323.

---

[6]*Main* words are (1) the first and last words and (2) all words except the articles *a, an,
the;* the conjunctions *and, but, or, nor;* the word *to* used with an infinitive; and prepositions
containing two or three letters (*of, for, on,* etc.).

If an attention line appears in the same letter a double space below the inside address, use the same format for both the attention and the subject lines.

subject line at left margin

Dear Mr. Sullivan:
←——— 1 blank line
Subject: Anticipated Cost Reductions
←——— 1 blank line
Within the next few weeks, we expect to see significant price reductions in the cost of several raw materials we use for the production of our woven synthetic . . . .

Dear Mr. Sullivan:
←——— 1 blank line
ANTICIPATED COST REDUCTIONS
←——— 1 blank line
Within the next few weeks, we expect to see significant price reductions in the cost of several raw materials we use for the production of . . . .

two-line subject with book title

Dear Ms. Kriegisch:
←——— 1 blank line
Subject: Alternate Distribution Channels for the Seventh Edition of Our Statistics Textbook, *Statistical Analysis*
←——— 1 blank line
The seventh edition of one of our best-selling textbooks, *Statistical Analysis*, has generated considerable interest among many members of the international . . . .

attention and subject lines in the same letter

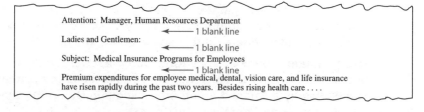

Attention: Manager, Human Resources Department
←——— 1 blank line
Ladies and Gentlemen:
←——— 1 blank line
Subject: Medical Insurance Programs for Employees
←——— 1 blank line
Premium expenditures for employee medical, dental, vision care, and life insurance have risen rapidly during the past two years. Besides rising health care . . . .

Simplified letter style. The subject line replaces the salutation in the simplified style. Begin the subject line at the left margin a triple space below the inside address. Type it in all capital letters without the term *Subject:*. Triple-space between the subject line and the first line of the body of the letter.

Social business letter style. A subject line is not used in the social business letter style.

b. Insurance companies, financial institutions, attorneys, and government offices often use the abbreviation *Re:* or *In re:* (meaning "in the matter of") in place of the word *Subject:* at the beginning of the subject line.

Re: Policy 489-6342, Insured Michael T. Block

IN RE: TOLBERT VS. FEINBERG

c. When initiating or replying to correspondence that has a special policy number, order number, account number, or other such reference, include this information in a subject line or in a specific reference below and aligned with the date.

If guide words are not printed on the letterhead, supply labels such as *When replying, refer to:, File No.:, In reply to:, Re:, Your reference:, Refer to:*, etc. These notations are typed in initial capital and lowercase letters; they are placed a double space below the date.

standard subject line

> Dear Mr. Urun:
> ◄——— 1 blank line
> Subject: Invoice No. 4398 Dated May 23
> ◄——— 1 blank line
> Four of the seven computer workstations billed on your May 23 invoice, No. 4398, have not yet been installed and are scheduled for installation . . . .

notation below and aligned with date—modified block letter

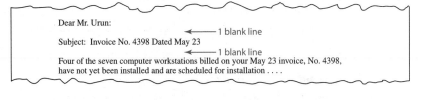

> June 8, 2004
> 1 blank line ——►
> In re: Policy 893621P

d. Some companies prefer to place the subject line above the salutation. In such cases begin the subject line a double space below the inside address. If an attention line follows the inside address, then begin the subject line a double space below the attention line.

Use (1) initial capital letters with lowercase letters or (2) all capital letters. The caption *Subject, Re,* or *In re* precedes the content and is followed by a colon. If an attention line appears in the same letter, use the same format for both lines.

Double-space after the subject line to begin the salutation.

subject line above salutation

> Ms. Midori S. Washida, Manager
> Great Midwestern Bank
> 4430 Greenbriar Street
> Iowa City, IA 52247-0321
> ◄——— 1 blank line
> Subject: Account 183-573245, John R. Hagle
> ◄——— 1 blank line
> Dear Ms. Washida:

subject and attention lines above salutation

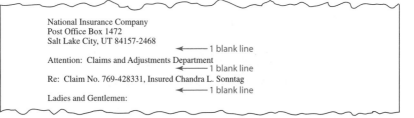

National Insurance Company
Post Office Box 1472
Salt Lake City, UT 84157-2468
← 1 blank line
Attention: Claims and Adjustments Department
← 1 blank line
Re: Claim No. 769-428331, Insured Chandra L. Sonntag
← 1 blank line
Ladies and Gentlemen:

12-13 Body of the Letter

a. The body of the letter contains the message. It begins a double space below the salutation or the subject line, if used. Single-space paragraphs within the body of the letter and double-space between each paragraph.

Modified block and social business letter styles. The first line of paragraphs in the modified block or social business letter styles may be either blocked or indented 0.5 inch.

Full block and simplified letter styles. Always block the first line of paragraphs in the full block and simplified letter styles.

body of letter with blocked paragraphs

Dear Mr. Feinberg:
← 1 blank line
Your Zippo portable sound system arrived yesterday, along with your explanation of the needed repairs.
← 1 blank line
As you suggested, the station tuning mechanism has been replaced under the terms of the warranty. In examining your system, however, our service representative noticed that the speaker had been damaged from an apparent jarring or dropping. The installation cost (parts and labor) for a new speaker would be $54.98.

body of letter with indented paragraphs

Dear Mrs. Russell:
← 1 blank line
We learned a great deal from your interesting presentation on the dynamics of color that you gave to Dr. Sullivan's business management class last Saturday. Thank you for sharing your valuable ideas with us.
← 1 blank line
The class especially appreciated the material you gave us on the Wilson color wheel. Everyone agreed that this information will certainly be helpful in making color selections for the employee work environment and ensuring comfortable working conditions.

b. Quoted materials, listings, tables, and graphics are often included within the body of a letter. All these visual enhancements are placed within the left and right margins. See Section 1-25 for instructions on formatting long quotations, Section 13-9 for

12

Business Letters

preparing horizontal and vertical listings, and Section 13-11 for preparing tables and charts.

listing within the body of a letter

To proceed with the escrow on the property you purchased at 6176 Arroyo Road in Palm Springs, please send us the following items by September 20:

———— 1 blank line

0.5"
• A loan application (form enclosed) completely filled out and notarized by a bank official
0.5"

———— 1 blank line

• Verification of employment to include a letter from your employer stating your length of employment and current earnings

———— 1 blank line

• Copies of your last six months' paycheck stubs

———— 1 blank line

• Copies of your federal income tax returns for the previous two years

———— 1 blank line

As soon as we receive these items, we will be able to contact prospective lenders to obtain a loan. Interest rates among lenders vary, but we will attempt to . . . .

quoted material within the body of a letter

recommendations have been based on an economic forecast published in one of our leading trade magazines. This forecast appeared in an article on pages 101–103 of the September issue of *Bankers' Financial World*:

———— 1 blank line

0.5"
Although interest rates for the next quarter will remain at the same low rate, building of new homes and commercial buildings will continue to decline. The large number of bank foreclosures on real property during the last year has driven values down so low that builders are ceasing to develop new projects.
0.5"

———— 1 blank line

The article, "Foreclosures and Their Rippling Effect on the Banking Industry," was written by Joseph L. Langham, a prominent economist and professor at Stanford University. Dr. Langham is noted for his success in predicting trends and . . . .

table within the body of a letter

We certainly appreciate your interest in purchasing a catalog that illustrates our fine Foster porcelain figurines. The following catalogs are presently available for purchase:

———— 1–2 blank lines

2004/05 Foster Catalog Set		
Current Retail Pricing		
Catalog or Supplement	Price for Members	Price for Nonmembers
Foster Core Catalog	$16.25	$32.50
Foster Limited Edition Catalog	8.75	17.50
Gres Supplement	2.50	5.00
Elite Catalog	10.00	20.00
Limited Edition Gres Catalog	7.50	15.00
Gres Catalog	5.00	10.00
Complete Catalog Set With Price List	$50.00	$100.00

———— 1–2 blank lines

Both the *Foster Core Catalog* and the *Foster Limited Edition Catalog* contain color photographs of the figurines currently available. All other catalogs contain black-and-white photographs. As a member of the Foster Collectors' Society, you are eligible for the members' price. Shipping and handling . . . .

12-14 Complimentary Close

a. The complimentary close begins the closing lines of a letter. The complimentary close selected to conclude a business letter must conform to the formality of the salutation. Sample salutations as well as suitable complimentary closes are listed here.

formal correspondence

Salutation	Complimentary Close
Dear Mr. President	Respectfully Very truly yours Sincerely yours
Excellency	Respectfully Very truly yours Sincerely yours
Dear Senator Monroe	Respectfully Very truly yours Sincerely yours

general business correspondence

Salutation	Complimentary Close
Dear Mr. Soloman	Sincerely yours Sincerely
Dear Ms. Rodriguez	Sincerely yours Sincerely
Dear Dr. Hsueh	Sincerely yours Sincerely
Ladies and Gentlemen	Sincerely yours Sincerely

informal business correspondence

Salutation	Complimentary Close
Dear Bill	Sincerely yours Sincerely Cordially yours Cordially
Dear Karen	Sincerely yours Sincerely Cordially yours Cordially

b. Place the complimentary close a double space below the last line of the message. Capitalize only the first word. Conclude the complimentary close with a comma for the mixed punctuation format; use no ending punctuation mark for the open punctuation format.

Modified block and social business letter styles. For the modified block and social business letter styles, begin the closing lines at the center of the page.

Full block letter style. Begin the closing lines at the left margin when using the full block letter style.

Simplified letter style. The complimentary close is omitted in the simplified letter style.

complimentary close begun at page center

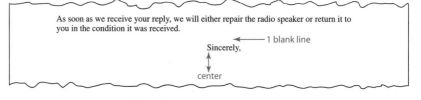

As soon as we receive your reply, we will either repair the radio speaker or return it to you in the condition it was received.

◄──── 1 blank line

Sincerely,

↑
center

complimentary close begun at left margin

May I please have an opportunity to review my qualifications with you? Just call me at 349-8211, and I will be pleased to come to your office for an interview.

◄──── 1 blank line

Sincerely yours,

12-15   Signature Block

a. The signature block identifies the writer of the letter by name. In most cases the writer's professional title is also included.

Modified and full block letter styles. Some business firms include the name of the company in the closing lines. In such cases the name of the company is placed in all capital letters a double space below and aligned with the complimentary close.

Company signature lines are used only in the modified block and full block letter styles. Use of the company name in the closing lines is illustrated in a full block letter in Section 12-1, page 323.

modified block letter

Don't delay; act now to receive a copy of *Your Banking Future*—while the supply lasts. Just sign the enclosed postcard and drop it in the mail today.

◄──── 1 blank line

Sincerely yours,

◄──── 1 blank line

BRADSTREET TRAINING INSTITUTE

◄──── 3 blank lines

Morgan Riley, Director

full block letter

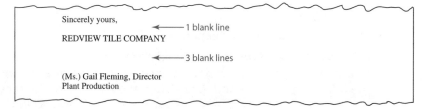

Place the writer's signature line or lines on the fourth line below the previous line, which will be either the complimentary close or the company name. Align the first letter of the individual's name with the first letter of the complimentary close and/or the company name.

modified block letter

full block letter

Place combinations of names, titles, and organizational sectors so that the contents of the signature lines appear balanced. The name and title may appear on the same line or on separate lines, depending upon the length of each item. Use commas to separate categories within the same line, but do not use commas to conclude any of the signature lines.

single-line signature line

John Wright, President   Sandra R. Bennett, M.D.

two-line signature line

Deborah T. Washington   Joshua S. Ross, Supervisor
Manager, Credit Department   Data Processing Department

Robert F. Tavelman
Accounts and Sales Representative

three-line signature

Danielle Cooper, Ed.D.
Curriculum Specialist, English
Division of Secondary Education

Simplified letter style. In the simplified letter style, the entire signature line is typed in all capital letters on a single line. It begins at the left margin on the fifth line below the last line of the message.

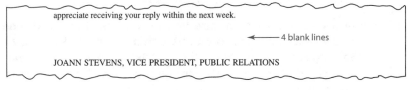

> appreciate receiving your reply within the next week.
>
> ◄───── 4 blank lines
>
> JOANN STEVENS, VICE PRESIDENT, PUBLIC RELATIONS

Social business letter style. In the social business letter style, the printed signature line may be omitted. If it is included, only the individual's name, not title, is written.

typed signature line omitted

> Sincerely,
>
> ◄───── 5–6 blank lines
>
> Dr. Marie Hannah
> 2362 Bogie Road
> Palm Springs, CA 92284

typed signature line included

> Cordially yours,
>
> ◄───── 3 blank lines
>
> Phyllis Ramon
>
> ◄───── 2 blank lines
>
> Mr. Winston L. Bell
> 638 Ladley Avenue
> Evanston, IL 60204-3246

b. Signature lines containing the names of men are generally not preceded by the courtesy title *Mr.* Only with initials, international names, and gender-equal names should a man use *Mr.* if the addressee does not know him. *Mr.* may be written with or without parentheses.

If a man has the title *Dr.,* either (1) place the abbreviation of the degree after the name of the individual or (2) place the title *Dr.*—with or without parentheses—before the name of the individual.

signature lines containing name of man to be addressed as **Mr.**

Gordon R. Bezowski	(Mr.) Huy Cao Nguyen
Regional Manager	Assistant Vice President
Mr. R. L. Rothstein	(Mr.) Leslie Neible
Realtor Associate	Customer Service Representative

signature lines containing name of man to be addressed as **Dr.**

Cory V. Thompson, Ph.D.	Vahi Urun, D.D.S.
Professor of Business	
(Dr.) Lawrence C. Simi	Dr. Lawrence C. Simi
Dean, Academic Affairs	Dean, Academic Affairs

c. Signature lines containing the names of women should be preceded by a courtesy title if the writer prefers to be addressed as *Mrs.* instead of the standard *Ms.* in any return correspondence. Courtesy titles (*Ms.* or *Mrs.*) should also be used before female names that are not readily distinguishable as male or female, names containing only initials, and international names. The title is usually placed in parentheses, but it may appear without them.

If a woman has the title *Dr.,* either (1) place the abbreviation of the degree after the name of the individual or (2) place the title *Dr.*—with or without parentheses—before the name of the individual.

signature lines containing name of woman

Sally Abramowitz, Manager	Alice H. Duffy, Coordinator
Production Department	Training and Development

signature lines distinguishing courtesy title of woman

(Mrs.) Miho Tabata	*or*	Mrs. Miho Tabata
Administrative Assistant		Administrative Assistant
(Mrs.) Kelly Krusee	*or*	Mrs. Kelly Krusee
Sales Associate		Sales Associate
(Ms.) M. R. Stevens	*or*	Ms. M. R. Stevens
General Manager		General Manager
(Ms.) Tran Huynh	*or*	Ms. Tran Huynh
Vice President		Vice President

signature lines containing name of woman addressed as **Dr.**

Ermonia C. Gevorkian, D.B.A.	Cynthia R. Randall, M.D.
Associate Professor	
(Dr.) Alexis Noonan, Chair	Dr. Alexis Noonan, Chair
Mathematics Department	Mathematics Department

d. Correspondence that is signed by a person other than the one whose name appears in the signature line usually shows the initials of the person signing the letter.

Sincerely yours,

Wallace C. Murietta (lc)

Wallace C. Murietta
Chairman of the Board

e. **When more than one signature is required in a business letter, arrange the signature lines in order of rank. If ranking is unimportant, arrange the signature lines in alphabetical order.**

Modified block letter style. **In the modified block letter, align multiple signatures vertically beginning at the horizontal center of the page. Leave three blank lines between each signature block.**

Full block letter style. **In a full block letter, arrange multiple signatures (1) side by side or (2) aligned vertically at the left margin with three blank lines separating each typed signature block.**

multiple signature lines in modified block letter

Sincerely yours,

◄——— 3 blank lines

Barbara D. Lewis, Vice President
Financial and Estate Planning

◄——— 3 blank lines

David L. Satilow, Manager
Trust Department

side-by-side signature lines in full block letter

Sincerely,

◄—— 3 blank lines

| John P. Gerberding | (Ms.) Leslie R. Leigh | Mark F. Sarafian |
| Vice President | Director of Marketing | Sales Manager, Central |

vertically aligned signature lines in full block letter

Sincerely,

◄——— 3 blank lines

John P. Gerberding
Vice President

◄——— 3 blank lines

(Ms.) Leslie R. Leigh
Director of Marketing

◄——— 3 blank lines

Mark F. Sarafian
Sales Manager, Central

12-16 Reference Initials

a. Reference initials are used to show who keyed and formatted the letter. In all letter styles except the social business style, the preparer's initials are placed in lowercase letters at the left margin a double space below the last line in the signature block.

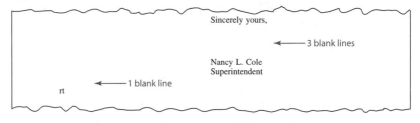

```
                                    Sincerely yours,

                                                    ◄──── 3 blank lines

                                    Nancy L. Cole
                                    Superintendent
                    ◄──── 1 blank line
        rt
```

b. The initials of both the writer and the preparer *may* be included in the reference notation, although the writer's initials are generally omitted. When the person whose name appears in the signature lines is the one who wrote the letter, his or her initials appear in capital letters before the preparer's initials. The initials are separated by a colon or a diagonal line.

```
                                    Sincerely yours,
                                                    ◄──── 1 blank line
                                    JAMESTOWN PLUMBING SUPPLY

                                                    ◄──── 3 blank lines

                                    Owen F. Toburg, Manager
                        ◄──── 1 blank line
        OFT:md
```

c. When correspondence is written by a person other than the one whose name appears in the signature lines, the writer's name or capitalized initials precede the initials of the preparer. Separate the name or initials of the writer from the preparer's initials by a colon or a diagonal line.

```
                                    Sincerely yours,

                                                    ◄──── 3 blank lines

                                    Stephen T. Pendleton
                                    Chief Executive Officer
                        ◄──── 1 blank line
        KWashburn/rt
```

12

Business Letters

12-17 Enclosure or Attachment Notations

a. If any enclosures are included with the letter, an enclosure notation is placed on the second line (or next line to conserve space) below the reference initials. Begin the enclosure notation at the left margin. If more than one enclosure is included, be sure to list them or include the number with the enclosure notation. Following are some examples:

one enclosure

Enclosure   Enc.   Check enclosed   Enclosure: Wilson Contract

more than one enclosure

Enclosures: Check for $375   2 Enc.   Enc. 2
               Copy of Invoice A18743

Enclosures 2   Enclosures (2)   2 Enclosures

b. When an enclosure is attached to the letter, the word *Attachment* or its abbreviation may be used in place of the enclosure notation. If more than one item is attached, be sure to include a listing or the number with the attachment notation.

one attachment

Attachment   Attachment: Meeting Minutes   Att.

more than one attachment

Attachments: Application for admission   Attachments 2
               Student information form

2 Attachments   Att. 2

12-18 Copy Notations

a. When copies of correspondence are directed to individuals other than the addressee, note the distribution at the bottom of the letter. The copy notation is placed on the second line (or next line to conserve space) following the enclosure notation, if used. Otherwise, it appears a single or double space below the reference initials. However, if a delivery notation follows the reference initials or enclosure notation, the copy notation is placed below it.

copy notation following reference initials

copy notation with additional notations

b. Copies of correspondence are prepared with a photocopier or a printer. The traditional *cc* notation, which formerly represented *carbon copy*, now represents *courtesy copy*. This notation is appropriate for copies produced by any method. Some writers use only *c* for *copy*.

Copy notations may include a combination of the courtesy title, name, position, department, company, and complete address of an individual. Following are some examples of appropriate copy notations:

cc: Mr. Kelly T. Mayo
    2432 Grand Avenue
    Oklahoma City, OK 73103

c: Kirby P. Thompson, President, Investments Online

cc Alicia Morley, Escrow Officer

c Vahi Urun

Some companies prefer to note copies made on a photocopier in the following ways:

copy: Ms. Janene Sassine	c: Marketing Department Staff
copies: José Acevedo Dawn Mellert	C: Mrs. Phuong Nguyen

copy to Mr. Bill Hughes, Plant Manager, Marlborough Paper Company

c. If copies are directed to more than one individual, list the individuals according to rank. If the individuals are equal in rank or ranking is unimportant, alphabetize the list. The list may be prepared either vertically or horizontally.

ranked list

cc: R. F. Gillham, President
    T. L. McMillan, Vice President
    F. S. Lopez, General Manager

alphabetized list

cc Marcus L. Brendero, Anne S. Langville, David M. Silverman

d. If sending a copy of the letter to other individuals is unnecessary or inappropriate for an addressee to know, use a blind copy notation. The blind copy notation appears only on copies of the letter, not on the original.

The blind copy notation may be placed (1) one inch from the top edge of the page at the left margin or (2) where the regular copy notation normally appears. Examples of blind copy notations follow:

bcc: David P. Dougherty   bcc Ms. Marty Hayes

12-19 Postscripts

A postscript may be used to emphasize an idea or add an idea that was unintentionally omitted from the body of the letter. The postscript is placed in last position; it may be keyed or handwritten with or without the abbreviation *P.S.* or *PS.*

Treat the postscript as any other paragraph in the letter. If the first line is blocked, then block the first line and all succeeding lines. If the first line is indented, then indent the first line and begin the remaining lines at the left margin.

with abbreviation P.S. *or* PS

```
rt
                 ◄────── 1 blank line
Enclosure
                 ◄────── 1 blank line
P.S.  Don't miss this opportunity to order your subscription of Living World Today.
Remember that this offer ends October 31.

                          at least 1 inch
```

```
cr
Enc. 2
          ◄────── 1 blank line
     PS Don't miss this opportunity to order your subscription of Living World
Today.  Remember that this offer ends October 31.

                          at least 1 inch
```

without abbreviation P.S. *or* PS

```
JNT:rg
Enclosure
            ◄────── 1 blank line
Don't miss this unique opportunity to order Living World Today.  Remember that
this offer ends October 31.

                      at least 1 inch
```

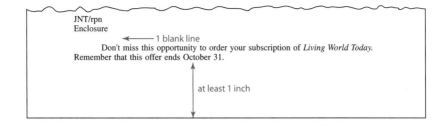

JNT/rpn
Enclosure
◄────── 1 blank line
Don't miss this opportunity to order your subscription of *Living World Today.*
Remember that this offer ends October 31.

at least 1 inch

12-20 Computer File Notations

Some companies prefer to place within the document the path and file name of letters produced on word processors. Since these notations are file references, they should appear only on file copies— not on copies sent to the addressee or other recipients. Place computer file notations a single space below the last keyed line of the letter on the file copy only.

Marie La Grasta, Manager
Western Regional Sales

jr

cc: Robert Levy
c:\dayton\corres\ackerman.doc

12-21 Second-Page Headings

a. **Prepare headings for second and succeeding pages on plain paper. Allow a 1-inch top margin, and use the same side margins that appear on the first page. These continuation-page headings include the name of the addressee, the page number, and the date. Either a horizontal or a vertical format may be used.**

b. **Before resuming the message, space down three lines from the last line of the heading. Two blank lines should separate the heading and the continuation of the message.**

horizontal format

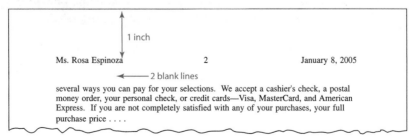

1 inch

Ms. Rosa Espinoza   2   January 8, 2005
◄────── 2 blank lines
several ways you can pay for your selections. We accept a cashier's check, a postal money order, your personal check, or credit cards—Visa, MasterCard, and American Express. If you are not completely satisfied with any of your purchases, your full purchase price . . . .

vertical format

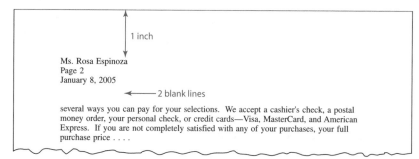

c. If a page does not end at the conclusion of a paragraph, include *at least* the first two lines of any new paragraph begun at the bottom of the page. Do not divide the last word on the page. Likewise, carry forward to the next page *at least* the last two lines from a paragraph begun on the previous page. Use the widow/orphan line protection feature of your word processing program to prevent single lines of a paragraph from being isolated at the top or the bottom of a page.

Leave at least 1 inch, but no more than 1.5 inches, at the bottom of each page—except, of course, for the last one.

d. The closing lines of a business letter should not be isolated on a continuation page. At least two lines of the message must precede the complimentary close or signature lines (when no complimentary close is used).

Punctuation Style

12-22 Mixed Punctuation

The most popular punctuation style for business letters is mixed punctuation. In this format a colon follows the salutation and a comma appears after the complimentary close. No other closing punctuation marks are used except those concluding an abbreviation or ones appearing within the body of the letter.

business letter with mixed punctuation

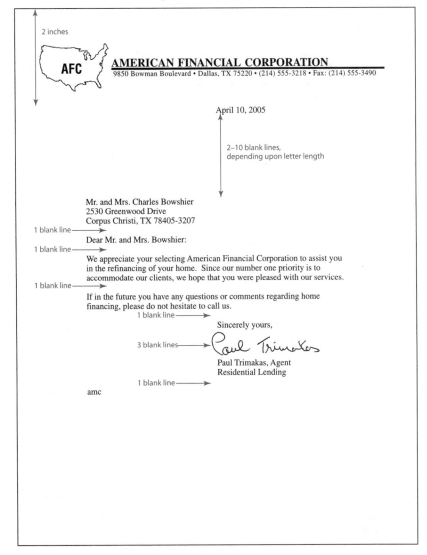

12-23 **Open Punctuation**

Writers of business letters sometimes use open punctuation. No closing punctuation marks except those concluding an abbreviation appear after the letter parts. The only other ending punctuation marks are ones used within the body of the letter.

business letter with open punctuation

Security Midwest Bank

1230 South Capitol Boulevard
Boise, Idaho 83706-1980

(208) 555-7649
Fax: (208) 555-8739

---

2 inches

August 10, 2004

2–10 blank lines,
depending upon letter length

Mrs. Carol Werner
243 Skycliffe Avenue
Boise, Idaho 83704-2037

1 blank line ────▶
Dear Mrs. Werner

1 blank line ────▶

The upcoming merger between Security Midwest Bank and the Bank of Idaho is an important event within the financial industry. However, in certain markets it is clear that the resulting merger may limit banking competition to a greater extent than federal or state governments allow. Consequently, Security Midwest Bank has agreed to sell its Hidden Valley Office to Union Bank to ensure a competitive environment in this market.

1 blank line ────▶

Before the actual sale can take place, Union Bank will need approval from several federal regulatory agencies. Until then, business will be carried on as usual at the Hidden Valley Office. You will be notified well in advance should there be any changes to your personal or business accounts.

1 blank line ────▶

The decision to divest your branch to Union Bank was not entered into lightly. Union Bank has been in Idaho for over 110 years and is now the fifth largest bank in the state with over 120 offices. We are confident that it will continue to meet your financial needs with the quality of products and service you have come to expect. You will receive a letter from Union Bank within the next few weeks.

1 blank line ────▶

You have our assurance that the transfer of your relationship will be handled with utmost care to make this change as convenient as possible.

1 blank line ────▶

Thank you for being a Security Midwest Bank customer.

1 blank line ────▶

Sincerely yours

Liam E. McAllister ◀──── 3 blank lines

Liam E. McAllister, Vice Chairman

1 blank line ────▶
amc

Addressing Envelopes

12-24 Automated Envelope Addressing

Use the envelope feature of your word processing program to prepare envelopes for your correspondence and other mailings. Adapt the default settings to correspond to your needs by following these guidelines:

(1) Select the envelope size from the menu of types provided by your software. If the correct envelope size is not available, create and select it. Be sure that your printer will support the envelope size selected.

(2) Adjust the left and top margin settings of your return address placement to accommodate any lines to be added to a printed return address or to accommodate a keyed return address. See Section 12-25b.

(3) Adjust the left and top margin settings of your mailing address placement to accommodate the envelope size selected. See Section 12-26 for the margin settings to be used for No. 10 (legal-size), No. 6¾ (letter-size), No. 7 (monarch), and No. 5⅜ (baronial) envelopes.

(4) Use the option to insert a bar code, if desired.

envelope printed with envelope feature of a word processing program

Continental Insurance Company
460 North Ashley Drive
Tampa, Florida 33601-1469

CONFIDENTIAL   CERTIFIED MAIL

Mr. Thomas R. Paige, Manager
Allied Insurance Agency
6200 Beachwood Boulevard
Tampa, Florida 33609-2147

|ılılıılıılıılıılıılıılıılıılıılıılıılıl|

12-25 Return Address

a. The return address is usually printed in the upper left corner of the envelope. In large companies the writer's or sender's initials or name and location are placed above the company name and return address. This practice facilitates routing the letter to the sender in case of nondelivery by the post office.

Jeffrey Edwards, Trust Department
United Bank of Iowa
1640 Medina Road
Des Moines, Iowa 50313-2167

b. On an envelope without a printed return address, place the return address in the upper left corner. Single-space the lines and include (1) the name of the individual; (2) the title of the individual, if applicable; (3) the company name, if applicable; (4) the mailing address; and (5) the city, state, and zip code. Begin the return address 0.3 inch from the top and 0.4 inch from the left edge of the envelope.

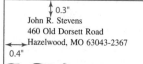

```
         ↕ 0.3"
    John R. Stevens
    460 Old Dorsett Road
  →Hazelwood, MO 63043-2367
  0.4"
```

12-26 Mailing Address

a. Single-space the mailing address, using at least two lines. The last line of the address should contain the city, state, and zip code. If the envelope is used to mail correspondence, key the address exactly as it appears in the inside address.

b. On legal-size envelopes, No. 10 envelopes (9.5 by 4.13 inches), allow a 2-inch top margin. Begin the address 4.25 inches from the left edge of the envelope.

No. 10 envelope

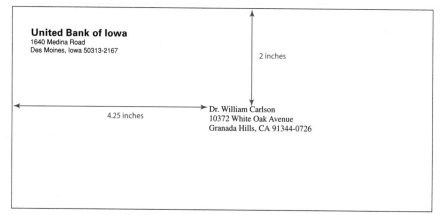

United Bank of Iowa
1640 Medina Road
Des Moines, Iowa 50313-2167

2 inches

4.25 inches

Dr. William Carlson
10372 White Oak Avenue
Granada Hills, CA 91344-0726

c. On letter-size envelopes, No. 6¾ envelopes (6.5 by 3.63 inches), allow a 1.75-inch top margin. Begin the mailing address 2.5 inches from the left edge of the envelope.

No. 6¾ envelope

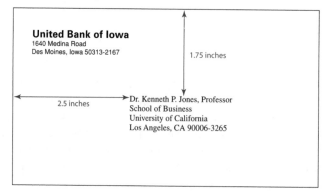

United Bank of Iowa
1640 Medina Road
Des Moines, Iowa 50313-2167

1.75 inches

2.5 inches

Dr. Kenneth P. Jones, Professor
School of Business
University of California
Los Angeles, CA 90006-3265

Business Letters

12

d. No. 7 (7.5 by 3.88 inches) and No. 5⅜ (5.94 by 4.63 inches) envelopes are used less frequently than the standard No. 10 and No. 6¾ envelopes. On No. 7 envelopes allow a 1.75-inch top margin; on No. 5⅜ envelopes allow a 2-inch top margin. Begin typing the mailing address 0.5 to 1 inch left of the envelope center, depending upon the length of the address lines.

No. 7 envelope

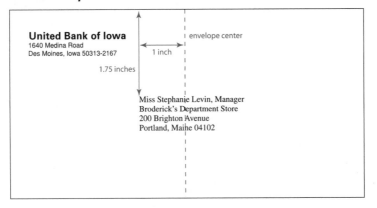

No. 5⅜ envelope

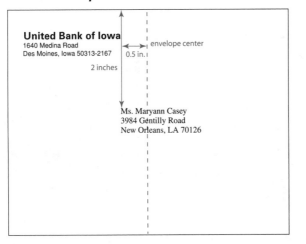

e. Letter-size manila envelopes (9 by 12 inches or 10 by 12 inches) may have the address keyed directly on the envelope or have a label with the address affixed to the envelope. In either case, position the envelope so that the flap and opening are on the right side. Place the first line of the mailing address 4.5 inches (for 9- by 12-inch envelopes) or 5 inches (for 10- by 12-inch envelopes) from the top edge and 4.5 to 5 inches from the left edge, depending upon the length of the address lines.

letter-size manila envelope

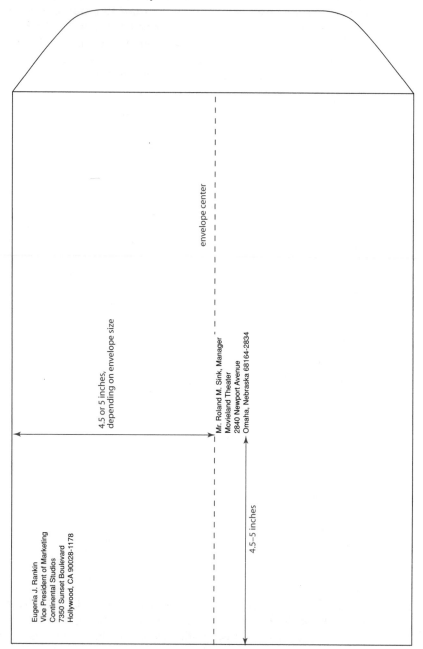

4.5 or 5 inches,
depending on envelope size

envelope center

Eugenia J. Rankin
Vice President of Marketing
Continental Studios
7350 Sunset Boulevard
Hollywood, CA 90028-1178

Mr. Roland M. Sink, Manager
Movieland Theater
2840 Newport Avenue
Omaha, Nebraska 68164-2834

4.5–5 inches

12-27   Addressee Notations

If an attention line appears in the inside address of a letter, include it within the envelope address. If an attention line is placed below the inside address in the letter, treat it the same as you would any other addressee notation.

Place an attention line or an addressee notation such as *Personal*, *Confidential*, *Please Forward*, or *Hold for Arrival* a double space below the last line of the return address or 1.5 inches from the top edge of the envelope, whichever position is lower. Begin keying 0.5 inch from the left edge of the envelope, and use all capital letters.

attention line included with address

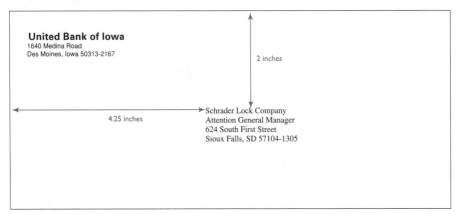

addressee notation below return address

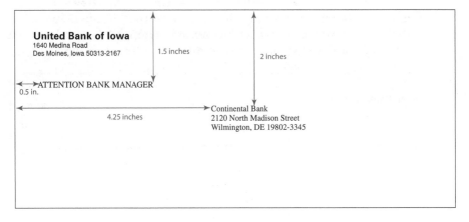

12-28   Delivery Notations

a.   Place delivery notations such as *Air Mail* (for foreign destinations), *Certified Mail,* or *Registered Mail* in all capital letters below the stamp, 1.5 inches from the top edge of the envelope. End the notation 0.5 inch from the right edge of the envelope.

Envelope delivery notations are less significant than they were previously, except for *Air Mail*, which is used exclusively for international mailings. *Express Mail* and other fast-delivery options provided by private courier services have their own supplier-provided envelopes. *Registered Mail* must be presented at the post office for mailing, where it is marked and routed appropriately. *Certified Mail*, too, is usually taken to the post office and marked accordingly.

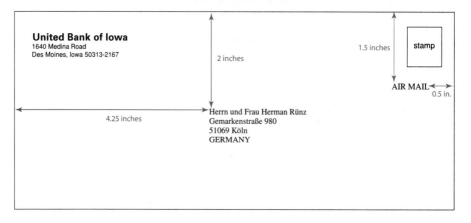

b. If an addressee notation and a delivery notation are on the same envelope, key both in all capital letters. The addressee notation appears a double space below the last line of the return address or 1.5 inches from the top edge of the envelope, whichever position is lower. Begin this notation 0.5 inch from the left envelope edge. Delivery notations are placed below the stamp, 1.5 inches from the top edge of the envelope. They end 0.5 inch from the right edge.

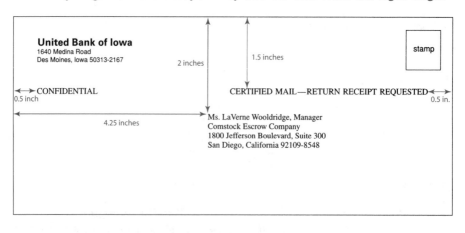

12-29 **Computer-Generated Address Labels**

Word processing programs as well as database programs can easily generate mailing labels from a database merge file or a database file. Addresses are compiled and formatted for printing on pre-defined label forms prepared commercially by companies such as Avery or 3M. The following example was prepared on a word processor using an Avery 5162 address label form for a laser printer.

Mr. George R. Simms, Vice President Great Western Bank 19300 Devonshire Street Chatsworth, CA 93471-1046	Ms. Elizabeth Candiotti, President Woodland Hills Chamber of Commerce 20220 Ventura Boulevard, Suite 130 Woodland Hills, CA 91365-3281
Ms. Veronica Richmond, Director Human Resources Department Harman International 6200 Balboa Boulevard Northridge, CA 91324-1954	Dr. Sandra L. Washington, President California State University, Northridge 18600 Nordhoff Street Northridge, CA 91327
Mr. Charles E. Buchanan, Manager Coldwell Banker Realty 8750 Arroyo Parkway Camarillo, CA 92374-3209	Mr. Anthony Murillo, Vice President International Operations Amgen Corporation 30375 Victory Boulevard Thousand Oaks, CA 94509-1001

12-30 **Zip + 4**

a. To process mail faster and more economically, the U.S. Postal Service has assigned four additional digits to the zip codes of mailing addresses that do not have their own separate zip codes. This series of four digits is separated from the zip code with a hyphen.

Tampa, FL 33626-6213   Boise, Idaho 83702-4819

Jackson, MS 39203-1073   Reno, Nevada 89503-2103

b. The use of zip + 4 is recommended by the U.S. Postal Service. Bulk mailers may obtain reduced rates for the use of zip + 4.

c. Zip + 4 codes may be located through various media available for purchase from the U.S. Postal Service[7] and from various private software companies. Zip + 4 codes for specific addresses may be retrieved free of charge at the U.S. Postal Service Web site at www.usps.com/zip4/.

---

[7]For information about zip + 4 products, telephone the National Customer Support Center, U.S. Postal Service, (800) 238-3150.

Folding and Inserting Correspondence

12–31 **No. 10 and No. 7 Envelopes**

a. Fold up one third of the page.

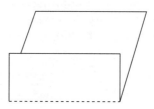

b. Fold down the upper third of the page so that the top edge is approximately ⅓ inch above the first fold.

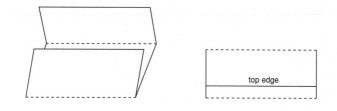

c. Insert the page so that the top edge is near the top edge of the envelope.

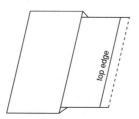

12–32 **No. 6¾ Envelopes**

a. Fold up one half of the page so that the bottom edge is approximately ⅓ inch below the top edge.

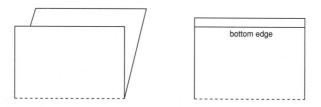

b. From the right side fold over one third of the page.

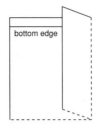

c. Fold over the second third of the page so that the left edge is approximately ⅓ inch from the right fold.

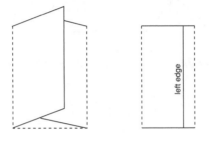

d. Insert the page so that the left edge is near the top edge of the envelope.

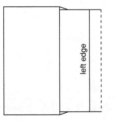

12-33 Window Envelopes

a. Fold up one third of the letter.

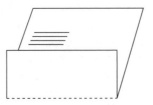

b. Turn the folded letter face down.

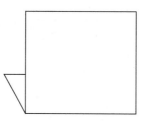

c. Fold down the upper third of the letter so that the top edge meets the first fold.

d. Insert the letter so that the address appears in the window of the envelope.

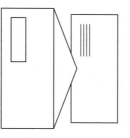

Memorandums

12-34 Usage

While letters generally involve the transmission of written messages sent outside an organization, memorandums are used for internal written communication. Once the major form of internal written communication, memorandums have declined in use since the advent of E-mail messaging.

12-35 Preparation

a. Procedures for preparing memorandums vary widely from office to office, but a few general guidelines exist. Most organizations have printed memorandum forms or custom word processing templates. These forms or templates contain guide words for directing the message to an addressee, specifying the name of the writer, providing the date written, and identifying the subject content.

Although the arrangement and design may vary, these basic elements are found in most printed memorandum forms.

printed memorandum forms or custom templates

Northridge Manufacturing Company
Interoffice Memorandum

To:

From:

Date:

Subject:

Mattel Toys Memo   MAT-3497-8

TO: DATE:

FROM: REFERENCE:

SUBJECT:

GENERAL MOTORS ACCEPTANCE CORPORATION
INTRAORGANIZATION LETTERS ONLY

TO: ADDRESS:

FROM: ADDRESS:

SUBJECT: DATE:

b. Memorandums may be prepared on preprinted memorandum forms using word processing software. For standard 8$\frac{1}{2}$- by 11-inch printed memorandum forms, create a form document to assist you with completing the preliminary lines: *Date:, To:, From:, Subject:,* etc. Each time you are required to use this printed form, you can use the form document to assist you with the proper placement of information after each guide word.

(1) Use 1-inch top and bottom margins and 1.25-inch left and right margins.

(2) Use a ruler to measure the horizontal and vertical position of the first letter to be keyed after each guide word in the memorandum form.

(3) Move your cursor to the horizontal and vertical position (as shown in the status line of your program) of the first letter to be keyed after the first guide word; key an asterisk (*). Follow the same procedure for each guide word in the printed form. If any preliminary parts will be completed with standard information, key in this standard information instead of an asterisk.

(4) Triple-space after the asterisk marking the beginning of the last guide word, usually the one that introduces the subject line.

(5) Save the form document as a separate file.

When a memorandum needs to be prepared, open the form document and save it with a new name. Use the search feature of your program to locate the asterisks and substitute the variable information needed for the current memorandum.

c. **Companies that do not have standardized forms for preparing memorandums use company letterhead, custom templates with plain paper, word processing templates with plain paper, or plain paper. In these cases apply the following procedures:**

(1) A memorandum is usually prepared on 8½- by 11-inch paper. For short memorandums, however, a half sheet (8½ by 5½ inches) may be used, although this size is usually avoided because of handling and filing difficulties.

(2) On 8½- by 11-inch paper, begin the preliminary lines 2 inches from the top edge of the paper. For memorandums prepared on half sheets, begin the preliminary lines 1 inch from the top edge of the paper.

(3) Use 1.25-inch left and right margins for memorandums prepared on 8½- by 11-inch paper and 1-inch margins for memorandums prepared on half sheets.

(4) Key in bold with initial capital letters the guide words **Date:**, **To:**, **From:**, and **Subject:** at the left margin. Double-space the guide words. Align the information following the guide words after the colon in the **Subject:** guide word.

(5) Any other guide words the company may wish to use should be placed on the same lines as the **Date:**, **To:**, or **From:** headings and begin after the information for those guide words.

(6) Triple-space after **Subject:**, and begin keying the body of the memorandum at the left margin. Single-space the message, but double-space between paragraphs.

(7) If you regularly prepare memorandums on plain paper or letterhead stationery, create a form document or macro for the preliminary lines of the memorandum.

d. Reference initials are used to show who keyed and formatted the memorandum. The preparer's initials are placed in lowercase letters at the left margin a double space below the last line of text.

When a memorandum is written by a person other than the one whose name appears after the *From:* guide word, the writer's name or capitalized initials precede the initials of the preparer. Separate the name or initials of the writer from the preparer's initials by a colon or a diagonal line.

e. If any enclosures or attachments are included with the memorandum, an enclosure or attachment notation is placed on the second line (or next line to conserve space) below the reference initials. Begin the notation at the left margin. If more than one enclosure or attachment is included, be sure to list the items or include the number with the notation. Following are examples of enclosure and attachment notations:

Enclosure	Enc. Directory	Enclosure:	Mason Contract
Enclosures: Receipt from agent		2 Enc.	Enc.
Copy of application			
Enclosures 2	Enclosures (2)	2 Enclosures	
Attachment	Attachment: Survey results		Att.
Attachments: Application for admission		Attachments 2	
Student information form			
2 Attachments		Att. 2	

f. When copies of memorandums are directed to individuals other than the addressee, note the distribution at the bottom of the memorandum. The copy notation is placed on the second line (or next line to conserve space) following the enclosure notation, if used. Otherwise, it appears a single or double space below the reference initials. For copy notations in memorandums, use the same formats and procedures as shown for business letters in Section 12-18.

cc: Matthew L. Parker, Agent
5600 North Western Avenue
Oklahoma City, OK 73103

c: Donna Huberman   cc Cory Pallini, Supervisor

c Vahi Urun, Vice President, Operations

copy: Ms. Jenell Warren   c: Sales Department Staff

copies: Bill Acevedo   C: Mrs. Phuong Nguyen
Kristen Mellert

copy to Mr. Joseph Basil, Manager, Capital Paper Company

12 Business Letters

cc: R. F. Gillham, President
    T. L. McMillan, Vice President
    F. S. Brotherton, General Manager

cc Marcus L. Brendero, Anne S. Langville, David M. Silverman

memorandum prepared on company letterhead

---

2 inches

SPRINGFIELD DEPARTMENT OF WATER AND POWER

To: Brenda Ingram-Cotton, Public Relations
1 blank line →

From: James D. Bell, Manager, Construction Projects
1 blank line →

Date: May 19, 2004
1 blank line →

Subject: RINALDI-NORTHRIDGE 230-KV TRANSMISSION LINE SEGMENT
2 blank lines →

Beginning August 1, 2004, our department will begin constructing a 6.7-mile, 230-kilovolt transmission line segment. This line will be placed between four existing transmission lines that link the DWP's Rinaldi Receiving Station in Granada Hills with Receiving Station J in Northridge.
1 blank line →   1.25 inches (left) / 1.25 inches (right)

The transmission lines will serve the electrical needs of the western portion of the San Fernando Valley and part of the west Los Angeles area. The project will include the construction of approximately 45 lattice steel, double-circuit towers and the installation of conductors.
1 blank line →

Before we begin this project, we will need to inform residents affected by this construction of its inception. Notices should be sent by your department to those persons residing south of Rinaldi, east of Wilbur, north of Nordhoff, and west of Zelzah.
1 blank line →

A fact sheet explaining a transmission line and its location should be sent to residents in July. This fact sheet should also explain the need for the transmission line segment as well as the source of the power for this segment. Other details that might be included should cover the visual impacts to the surrounding areas, the environmental review process performed, potential health effects of electric and magnetic fields, and the construction schedule.
1 blank line →

The attached report regarding the project provides information that you may wish to use for your fact sheet. If you have any questions about the information contained in the report, I will be happy to answer them.
1 blank line →

amc
1 blank line →

Attachment
1 blank line →

cc: Marion R. Klein, Vice President, Planning

---

memorandum prepared using a word processing template

interoffice
MEMORANDUM

to: All Employees
from: Donna Anderson
subject: GROUP HEALTH NSURANCE
date: November 9, 2004

2 blank lines ——►

1.25 inches

As you know, Stanley Hutchinson, your employee representative, proposed to the Board of Directors last January that we consider adopting an employee group health insurance plan. He pointed out the many medical expenses incurred by our employees throughout the year and the benefits a group health insurance policy would have in helping meet some of the medical expenses resulting from sickness and injuries.

1.25 inches

1 blank line ——►

After careful study of several group health insurance policies, the board concluded that the group policy proposed by the Edgewater Insurance Company would give the most comprehensive medical coverage for its cost. As a result, the board voted unanimously to adopt this policy at no cost to the employees, effective June 1.

1 blank line ——►

Attached is a brochure that explains in detail the health-care services covered by the Edgewater policy. If you have any questions, please call Don Curry at Ext. 7351. He will be glad to assist you.

1 blank line ——►

rm

1 blank line ——►

Attachment

12
Business Letters

memorandum prepared on blank paper

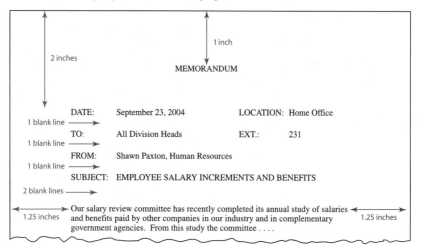

1 inch

2 inches

MEMORANDUM

DATE: September 23, 2004   LOCATION: Home Office

1 blank line ——►

TO: All Division Heads   EXT.: 231

1 blank line ——►

FROM: Shawn Paxton, Human Resources

1 blank line ——►

SUBJECT: EMPLOYEE SALARY INCREMENTS AND BENEFITS

2 blank lines ——►

1.25 inches

Our salary review committee has recently completed its annual study of salaries and benefits paid by other companies in our industry and in complementary government agencies. From this study the committee . . . .

1.25 inches

g. When a memorandum contains more than one page, the heading for the second and succeeding pages should have a 1-inch top margin. Show the name of the person or group to whom the memorandum is addressed, the page number, and the date. This information may be arranged vertically at the left margin or be placed on a single line with the name beginning at the left margin, the page number centered, and the date aligned with the right margin. Triple-space after the heading before continuing the body of the memorandum.

vertical second-page heading

horizontal second-page heading

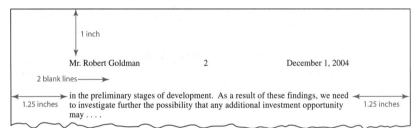

13

Reports and Other Business Documents

Ibid.

Reports and Other Business Documents Solution Finder

General Formats for Reports and Manuscripts

13-1 **Purpose, Content, and General Style**

Reports are used in business mainly to convey information, analyze data, or support proposals. Those reports written for public distribution, such as reports to stockholders, are printed and usually appear in booklet form. Other reports, those for internal use or limited distribution, are generated internally using word processing software. Regardless of their final form—printed, desktop published, or keyed and printed from word processing software—the report formats recommended here should be used for the preparation and editing process. Except for printed and desktop published reports, these formats also represent the final product.

All reports and manuscripts contain a title page and the body of the report. Other parts may be added, depending upon the length, complexity, and formality of the document. The parts of a report or manuscript may include the following:

Title page
Letter of transmittal
Summary (or Executive summary)
Table of contents
List of tables (and/or List of illustrations)
Contents of the report (main body)
Endnotes (if applicable)
Bibliography
Appendix (or Appendixes)

a. Reports and manuscripts may be prepared with *either* 1.25-inch left and right margins *or* 1-inch left and right margins, depending upon the preference of the originator. If the report or manuscript is to be bound on the left, allow an additional 0.25 inch for the left margin.

b. The first page of major parts (title page, table of contents, bibliography, etc.) and the opening page of sections or chapters require a 2-inch top margin, 2.25 inches for top-bound documents.

section opener with 2-inch top margin

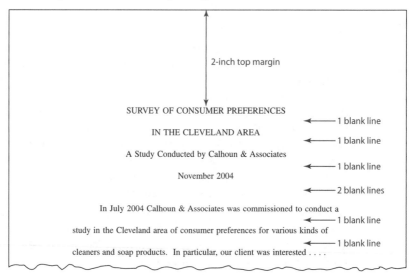

2-inch top margin

SURVEY OF CONSUMER PREFERENCES
◄——— 1 blank line

IN THE CLEVELAND AREA
◄——— 1 blank line

A Study Conducted by Calhoun & Associates
◄——— 1 blank line

November 2004
◄——— 2 blank lines

In July 2004 Calhoun & Associates was commissioned to conduct a
◄——— 1 blank line

study in the Cleveland area of consumer preferences for various kinds of
◄——— 1 blank line

cleaners and soap products. In particular, our client was interested . . . .

The opening pages of major sections are included in the page count, but the page number is usually not printed on the page.

section opener without page number

in our industry have been experiencing a steady market decline in this area for

the past three years, even though economic conditions are seemingly in a state

1- to 2-inch bottom margin

If a page number is to be included on the section opener, select one of the following formats:

(1) **Page number 1 inch from bottom edge of page.** Center the page number on a line 1 inch from the bottom edge of the paper. Leave at least one blank line separating the page number from the last line of text.

in our industry have been experiencing a steady market decline in this area for

the past three years, even though economic conditions are seemingly in a state

◄——— at least 1 blank line

1

1-inch bottom margin

(2) **Page number 0.5 inch from bottom edge of page.** Center the page number on a line 0.5 inch from the bottom edge of the paper. Leave at least two blank lines separating the page number from the last line of text.

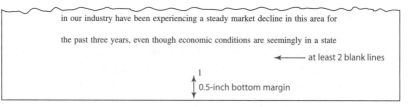

c. **Number preliminary pages (those preceding the contents of the report) consecutively in lowercase Roman numerals (*i, ii, iii, iv, v,* etc.). Count the title page as page *i* even though no number is shown on that page; number the letter of transmittal *ii,* if used.**

Create a footer or use the page-numbering feature of your word processing program to number any preliminary pages. Suppress the footer or page numbering on the title page. Use one of the following two formats:

(1) **Page number 1 inch from bottom edge of page.** Center the page number on a line 1 inch from the bottom edge of the paper. Leave at least one blank line separating the page number from the last line of text.

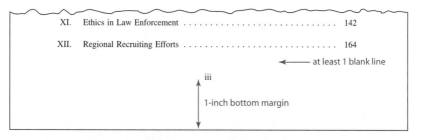

(2) **Page number 0.5 inch from bottom edge of page.** Center the page number on a line 0.5 inch from the bottom edge of the paper. Leave at least two blank lines separating the page number from the last line of text.

VI.   Income Projections from United States Regions 92

Eastern Region Projections 94

Western Region Projections 103

←——— at least 2 blank lines

iii

0.5-inch bottom margin

Discontinue the footer or this mode of pagination at the conclusion of the preliminary parts.

d. **Use a 1-inch top margin (1.25 inches for top-bound documents) for all pages except those with main headings. The page number begins the page.**

Create a header or use the page-numbering feature of your program to number pages. Select one of the following page-numbering formats; use consistent formats for numbering the preliminary pages and the remaining pages of the report or manuscript.

(1) **Page number 1 inch from top edge of page.** Place the page number in Arabic numerals 1 inch below the top edge of the paper. Align the page number with the right margin, and leave one or two blank lines before beginning the text.

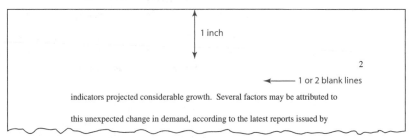

(2) **Page number 0.5 inch from top edge of page.** Place the page number in Arabic numerals 0.5 inch below the top edge of the paper and 0.5 inch from the right edge of the paper. Leave two blank lines before beginning the text.

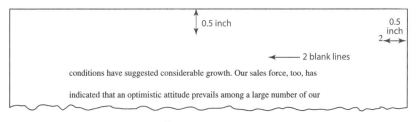

e. **In the body of the report, indent the first line of paragraphs 0.5 inch. Indent long quotations and vertical listings 0.5 inch from both the left and right margins.**

Use a tab to indent each paragraph and the "left-right indent" feature of your word processing program to indent long quotations and vertical listings.

0.5 inch

←—→Besides providing local advertising, screening prospective tenants, and

collecting rents for your rental property, we provide you with an annual

statement for your income tax records. In addition, we have available at cost

to each of our clients the following services:

    • Appliance, electrical, or plumbing repairs by a reputable,
      licensed service center

0.5 inch   0.5 inch

←—→• Daily, weekly, or monthly cleaning service to include linen ←—→
      change, kitchen and bathroom maintenance, dusting and
      vacuuming, and window cleaning

    • Painting and general maintenance or repairs

0.5 inch

←—→As you can see, we are a full-service rental agency. We have been

serving the Coachella Valley for over . . . .

f. **A single line that belongs to a paragraph may not be isolated at the top or bottom of a different page. In addition, an isolated text heading may not be the last line on a page. Conclude the report or manuscript text between 1 and 2 inches from the bottom edge of the page, ensuring that *at least* two lines of a paragraph appear at the bottom of a page. A minimum of two lines (one full line and at least one word on a second line) must appear at the top of a page for any paragraphs carried over from a previous page.**

Use the widow/orphan protection feature of your word processing program to prevent single lines of a paragraph from appearing on a separate page. For any text headings appearing as the last line on the page, use the line and page-break control feature to keep lines together and force the heading to the next page.

concluding lines of page

We have been advertising this product line for the past six months in the

Dallas area. Television, radio, and newspaper campaigns have focused on all

continuation of paragraph on next page

6

hair-care products in our Lustre Plus line. Billboard advertising has been confined

to featuring only our shampoo and conditioner.

Preliminary results from this advertising campaign show between a 25 and

30 percent increase in sales for . . . .

g. **In your word processing program, create macros, create styles, or use system shortcuts to change line spacing instantly (single spacing, double spacing, triple spacing). Use these macros, styles, and/or shortcuts to produce the following results in formatting the report or manuscript:[1]**

(1) Double-space and center main headings (all capital letters) and any secondary headings (uppercase and lowercase letters); triple space before beginning the first line of text. Always triple-space after a main heading if no secondary heading is used.

(2) Double-space the textual material in the body of the report; indent the first line of each paragraph 0.5 inch.

(3) Triple-space before and double-space after first- and second-degree text headings. Third-degree headings are considered part of the paragraph they introduce and are spaced like regular text.

(4) Single-space and indent 0.5 inch from the left and right margins any long quotations; omit the quotation marks. Long quotations are those consisting of more than three lines *or* more than two sentences. Double-space before and after the long quotation.[2]

(5) Vertical listings consisting of single-line items may be single or double spaced. For listings with items containing more than one line, single-space the items and leave one blank line between items. Double-space before and after the vertical listing.

(6) Tables and illustrations should be centered between the left and right margins. Either double- or triple-space before and after any tables and illustrations that interrupt the text narrative. Be consistent in your choice of spacing before and after all visual displays within the text material.

h. **Use the spelling check feature of your word processing program to correct any spelling or typographical errors.**

---

[1]See the following sections in this chapter for specific instructions and examples for the preparation of report and manuscript parts, main headings, secondary headings, text headings, vertical listings, report or manuscript text (body), tables, and illustrations.

[2]See Chapter 1, Punctuation, Section 1-48, for an additional example of a long quotation formatted for inclusion in a manuscript or report.

i. If you must frequently prepare manuscripts or reports, use the styles feature of your word processing program to format your reports.

report page with text headings and a table

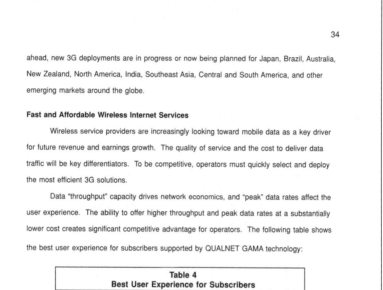

34

ahead, new 3G deployments are in progress or now being planned for Japan, Brazil, Australia, New Zealand, North America, India, Southeast Asia, Central and South America, and other emerging markets around the globe.

Fast and Affordable Wireless Internet Services

Wireless service providers are increasingly looking toward mobile data as a key driver for future revenue and earnings growth. The quality of service and the cost to deliver data traffic will be key differentiators. To be competitive, operators must quickly select and deploy the most efficient 3G solutions.

Data "throughput" capacity drives network economics, and "peak" data rates affect the user experience. The ability to offer higher throughput and peak data rates at a substantially lower cost creates significant competitive advantage for operators. The following table shows the best user experience for subscribers supported by QUALNET GAMA technology:

Table 4 Best User Experience for Subscribers		
Air Interface	Effective Peak Data Rate	Download Time
GSM IS-95A GAMA	9.6 kbps 14.4 kbps	41 minutes 28 minutes
GPRS IS-95B GAMA	57.6 kbps 64.0 kbps	7 minutes 6 minutes
GAMA2000 1X WGAMA GAMA2000 1xEV-DO	307 kbps 2,000 kbps 2,400 kbps	78 seconds 12 seconds 10 seconds

Easy Migration Path

From entry-level "voice-only" networks to rich, high-end voice/data solutions, QUALNET supports wireless service providers around the globe by providing flexible technology choices. Engineers in the QUALNET Technology Group include easy migration into the designs of the

13

Reports

Parts of a Report or Manuscript

13-2 Title Page

a. The title page generally contains the following information, but its contents are not restricted to these items:

(1) The name or title of the report or manuscript

(2) The name and title of the person and/or the name of the group or organization for whom it was written

(3) The name and title of the person and/or the name of the group who wrote it

(4) The date it was submitted

b. Use the following guidelines to prepare a title page. To prepare the title page easily, access the center-page feature of your word processing program.

(1) Allow 2-inch top and bottom margins.

(2) Center all lines horizontally.

(3) Type the title of the report or manuscript in all capital letters. Single-space any titles containing more than one line.

(4) Space equally between the top and bottom margins all other parts following the title.

(5) Count the title page in the pagination, but do not number the page.

An illustration of a title page appears on page 385.

13-3 Letter of Transmittal

a. The letter of transmittal, if used, introduces the reader to the report or manuscript. Although the content of the transmittal letter will depend upon the complexity and scope of the report or manuscript, it should basically tell the reader the following:

(1) What the topic is

(2) Why the report was written

(3) How the report was compiled (method of research)

(4) Who worked on it or helped with its development

(5) What major findings or conclusions resulted (if a synopsis or summary page is not included)

b. The letter of transmittal should be friendly and concise, usually concluding with the writer expressing appreciation for the opportunity to produce the report or manuscript. Use the following guidelines to prepare the transmittal letter:

(1) Use any acceptable business letter style.

(2) Place the letter of transmittal after the title page.

(3) Number the page with a lowercase Roman numeral centered at the bottom of the page. Place the page number 1 inch or 0.5 inch from the bottom edge of the page, depending upon the page-numbering format selected for the document. See Section 13-1c for further information on the page-numbering formats.

An illustration of a letter of transmittal appears on page 386.

title page

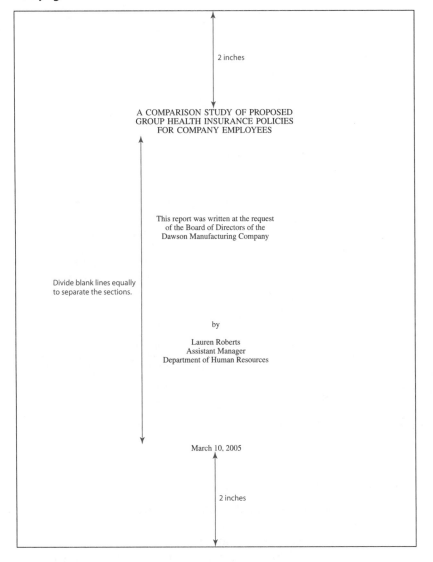

letter of transmittal

Dawson Manufacturing Company

170 East Parkland Avenue　　　　　　　　**(214) 363-5757**
Dallas, Texas 75214　　　　　　　　　　**Fax: (214) 363-5783**

March 10, 2005

Mr. Clifford Powell, President
Dawson Manufacturing Company
170 East Parkland Avenue
Dallas, Texas 75214

Dear Mr. Powell:

As requested by our Board of Directors, I have prepared a report comparing the employee group health insurance policies that were submitted by eight companies.

The policies were compared in the following ways:

1. Company cost per employee
2. Cost to employees
3. Kinds of illnesses and/or injuries covered
4. Hospital, out-patient, and home-visit coverage
5. Total annual health benefits allowed
6. Miscellaneous coverages such as medicines, X rays, physical therapy, private nursing, etc.
7. Family members covered
8. Annual deductible and copayment

As shown by the summary table on page 19, the Edgewater policy is superior in all categories except one–company cost per employee. I recommend we select the Edgewater proposal. The additional $28.16 annual cost per employee is relatively small considering the substantial benefits over any one of the other less expensive policies.

Thank you for the opportunity to conduct this study. I appreciate the help and cooperation I received from the employees' representative and from the representatives of the insurance companies.

If you have any questions or if I can be of further assistance, please let me know.

Sincerely,

Lauren Roberts

Lauren Roberts, Assistant Manager
Department of Human Resources

mw

ii

↑
0.5 in.
↓

13-4 Summary of the Report

Long reports—especially those not including a letter of transmittal or those including a letter of transmittal without a synopsis—usually require a summary, sometimes referred to as an *executive summary*. Use the following guidelines to prepare the summary:

(1) Allow a 2-inch top margin. Center the main heading *SUMMARY* or *EXECUTIVE SUMMARY* in all capital letters on the line directly following the top margin. Triple-space after the main heading.

(2) Double-space the text of the summary; indent the first line of each paragraph 0.5 inch. Begin by stating the purpose of the report. Briefly describe the procedures used in preparing the report, and end with a concise presentation of the conclusions and recommendations.

(3) Number the summary page or pages with lowercase Roman numerals centered at the bottom of the page. Place the page number 1 inch or 0.5 inch from the bottom edge of the page, depending upon the page-numbering format used for the document. See Section 13-1c.

13-5 Table of Contents

The content and format of a table of contents vary with the length and complexity of the report or manuscript, but the following guidelines may be used for its preparation:

(1) Allow a 2-inch top margin. Center the main heading *TABLE OF CONTENTS* or *CONTENTS* in all capital letters on the next line.

(2) Place the word *Page* a triple space below the *TABLE OF CONTENTS* heading; align it with the right margin.

(3) Use all capital letters and double-space the listing for the preliminary sections of the report (e.g., *LETTER OF TRANSMITTAL, SUMMARY,* or *LIST OF TABLES*). Begin a double space below *Page* and at the left margin. Although it is counted and paginated with a lowercase Roman numeral, the table of contents is not included in this listing.

(4) Begin the major division heading of the report (e.g., *Chapter, Section, Unit,* or *Topic*) at the left margin. The major division heading may either appear on the same line as *Page* or be placed a double space below the preliminary parts.

(5) Number major sections of the report, if desired, by using uppercase Roman numerals. Align the longest numeral with the left margin, and indent the shorter numerals so the periods following the numerals are aligned. Use a decimal tab in your word processing program to achieve this alignment.

(6) Use all capital letters for listing major sections of the report. Those sections of lesser degree should be indented, placed in capital and lowercase letters, single spaced, and arranged in the same sequence as they appear in the report.

(7) Use leaders (a line of alternating periods and spaces) to assist the reader in locating the page number of a particular section, and align vertically the leaders for each section or subsection of the report. Although all major headings must have corresponding page numbers, the assignment of page numbers to subheadings appearing in the table of contents is optional. To obtain leaders in your word processing program, set a right decimal tab with dot leaders adjacent to the right margin.

(8) Number the page or pages containing the table of contents with lowercase Roman numerals centered at the bottom of the page. Place the page number 1 inch or 0.5 inch from the bottom edge of the page, depending upon the page-numbering format selected for the

document. See Section 13-1c for further information on the page-numbering formats.

table of contents

2-inch top margin

TABLE OF CONTENTS

←—— 2 blank lines

Page

←—— 1 blank line

iii

0.5 inch

13-6 List of Tables or List of Illustrations

a. When a report or manuscript contains several tables, include as a helpful reference to the reader a list of tables after the table of contents. Guidelines for formatting the list of tables follow:

(1) Center the heading *LIST OF TABLES* in all capital letters 2 inches from the top edge of the page.

(2) Triple-space after the *LIST OF TABLES* heading. Place the word *Table* at the left margin, and align the last letter of the word *Page* with the right margin.

(3) Indent 0.25 inch from the left margin. Key the number of each table followed by spacing of 0.25 inch and the table title. Capitalize the principal or main words in the title,[3] and single-space the lines in each title. Double-space between titles.

(4) Use leaders (a line of alternating periods and spaces) to assist the reader in locating the page number of a particular table. To obtain leaders in your word processing program, set a right decimal tab with dot leaders adjacent to the right margin.

(5) Number pages in the list of tables with lowercase Roman numerals centered at the bottom of the page. Place the page number 1 inch or 0.5 inch from the bottom edge of the page, depending upon the page-numbering format selected for the document. See Section 13-1c for further information on the page-numbering formats.

list of tables

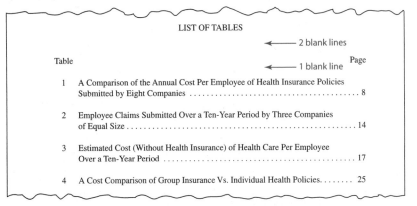

b. A list of illustrations may be used for a report or manuscript that contains figures or a combination of tables and figures. For one that contains only figures, use the same format described in the previous section for a list of tables. Change the title to *LIST OF ILLUSTRATIONS* and the word *Table* to *Figure*. Use the following guidelines to format a list of illustrations that contains both tables and figures:

(1) Center the heading *LIST OF ILLUSTRATIONS* in all capital letters 2 inches from the top edge of the page.

(2) Triple-space after the *LIST OF ILLUSTRATIONS* heading, and center the subheading *A. Tables* in capital and lowercase letters. Double-space after the subheading. Place *Table* at the left margin, and align the last letter of the word *Page* with the right margin. Double-space before beginning the listing.

---

[3]See Section 3-6 for an explanation of *principal* or *main* words.

(3) Indent 0.25 inch from the left margin. Key the number of each table followed by spacing of 0.25 inch and the table title. Capitalize the main words[4] and single-space each title. Double-space between titles. Use leaders (a line of alternating periods and spaces) to assist the reader in locating the page number. To obtain leaders in your word processing program, set a right decimal tab with dot leaders adjacent to the right margin. Triple-space after the last title.

(4) Center the subheading *B. Figures* in capital and lowercase letters. Double-space after the subheading; place *Figure* at the left margin and align the last letter of the word *Page* with the right margin. Double-space before beginning the listing.

(5) Indent 0.25 inch from the left margin. Key the number of each figure followed by 0.25-inch spacing and the figure title. Capitalize the principal or main words, and single-space each title. Double-space between titles. Use leaders to assist the reader in locating the page number.

(6) Number the list of illustrations with lowercase Roman numerals centered at the bottom of the page. Place the page number 1 inch or 0.5 inch from the bottom edge of the page, depending upon the page-numbering format selected for the document. See Section 13-1c for further information on the page-numbering formats.

list of illustrations

LIST OF ILLUSTRATIONS

⟵ 2 blank lines

A. Tables

⟵ 1 blank line

Table   Page

⟵ 1 blank line

1   A Comparison of the Annual Cost Per Employee of Health Insurance Policies Submitted by Eight Companies 8

⟵ 1 blank line

2   Employee Claims Submitted Over a Ten-Year Period by Three Companies of Equal Size... 14

⟵ 1 blank line

3   Estimated Cost (Without Health Insurance) of Health Care Per Employee Over a Ten-Year Period 17

⟵ 1 blank line

4   A Cost Comparison of Group Insurance Vs. Individual Health Policies 25

⟵ 2 blank lines

B. Figures

⟵ 1 blank line

Figure   Page

⟵ 1 blank line

1   Per Capita Dollar Increase in Medical Care for Working-Age Population, 1994–2003 5

⟵ 1 blank line

2   Per Capita Dollar Increase of Group Medical Insurance Coverage for Working-Age Population, 1994–2003 6

⟵ 1 blank line

3   Comparison of Assets of Eight Major Health Insurance Carriers (in Millions of Dollars) 28

---

[4]See Section 3-6 for an explanation of *principal* or *main* words.

13-7 Preparing the Body of the Report or Manuscript

a. Allow a 2-inch top margin on pages that begin the body of the report or manuscript or major sections of the body. Center the heading in all capital letters; double-space multiple-line main headings. Triple-space after the main heading if it is not followed by a secondary heading.

b. Secondary headings are often used to explain or elaborate on a main heading. These headings begin a double space below the main heading and appear in capital and lowercase letters. All lines are centered, and multiple lines are double spaced. Triple-space after the secondary heading.

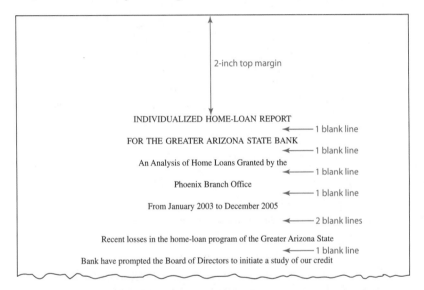

c. Double-space the body of the report or manuscript. Indent the first line of each paragraph 0.5 inch to offset it clearly from the previous one.

Use the widow/orphan feature of your word processing program to adjust page endings so that single lines from a paragraph are not at the top or bottom of a page. (These single lines are often called *widow and orphan lines*.) If page and paragraph endings do not coincide, be sure to place at least two lines of a new paragraph at the end of a page and carry over at least two lines from the previous paragraph to a new page (one complete line and a minimum of one word on a second line). Example pages from the body of a report appear on pages 392 and 393.

d. Use the following guidelines to number the pages of the report or manuscript:

(1) For pages with main headings, either omit the page number or center it at the bottom of the page. Place the page number either 1 inch or 0.5 inch from the bottom edge of the page, depending upon the page-numbering system selected. See Section 13-1b for further explanation and illustrations.

(2) For pages without main headings, place the page number either 1 inch or 0.5 inch from the top edge of the page, depending upon the page-numbering system selected. See Section 13-1d for further explanation and illustrations.

body of report

2-inch top margin

SECTION I ←——— 1 blank line

INTRODUCTION ←——— 2 blank lines

The following report provides a comparison of the employees' health and major medical insurance programs submitted by eight major insurance companies.

←——— 2 blank lines

Purpose of the Report ←——— 1 blank line

Last January Norman Rittgers, one of the employee representatives of our company, requested that company-sponsored health insurance be considered by the Board of Directors as a supplement to our wage and salary schedule. As a result, the board directed the Department of Human Resources to (1) contact insurance companies to determine what health insurance coverages were available and (2) compare the coverages to determine which policy would most cost effectively meet our employees' health insurance needs.

←——— 2 blank lines

Scope of the Report ←——— 1 blank line

The scope of this investigation was limited to an analysis of the written proposals and copies of policies submitted by the participating insurance companies. Of the 28 insurance companies contacted, the majority provided only verbal explanations as to what the estimated coverage and cost of a group health and major medical insurance program would be for our employees. Only eight of these companies submitted written documents for our consideration. Proposals and policies from these companies were evaluated according to the following criteria:

at least 1 inch

body of report (continued)

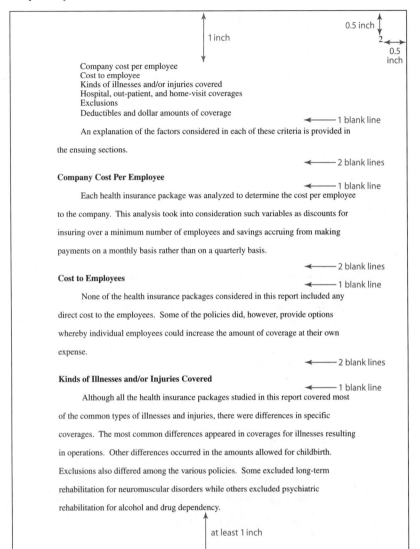

13-8 **Text Headings**

a. Text headings of different degrees signal content in a report or manuscript and contribute to its readability. A common classification of text headings includes first-, second-, and third-degree headings. Text headings are usually boldfaced, but they may have a larger font size with or without bolding. Guidelines for formatting each text heading follow and are repeated in the context of its corresponding illustration.

393

(1) **First-degree text headings**. Center a first-degree text heading, and capitalize the first letter of each main word. The heading may be bold-faced and/or keyed in a larger font size than the report or manuscript text. Triple-space before a first-degree text heading, and double-space after it.

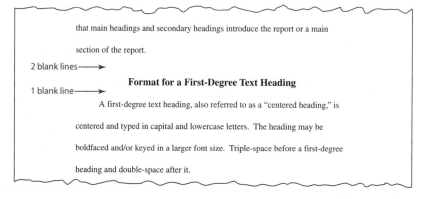

that main headings and secondary headings introduce the report or a main

section of the report.

2 blank lines ──▶

Format for a First-Degree Text Heading

1 blank line ──▶

A first-degree text heading, also referred to as a "centered heading," is

centered and typed in capital and lowercase letters. The heading may be

boldfaced and/or keyed in a larger font size. Triple-space before a first-degree

heading and double-space after it.

(2) **Second-degree text headings**. Begin the second-degree text heading at the left margin. Capitalize the first letter of each main word. Boldface the heading, or use a larger font size with or without bold-ing. If enlarged, the font size must be smaller than the one used for first-degree text headings and larger than the one used for the report or manuscript text. Triple-space before a second-degree text heading, and double-space after it.

use a larger font. Triple-space before a first-degree heading and double-

space after it.

2 blank lines ──▶

Format for a Second-Degree Text Heading

1 blank line ──▶

A second-degree heading is often called a "margin heading" or a "side

heading" because it begins at the left margin. Use capital and lowercase

letters. Boldface the heading, or use a larger font size with or without bolding.

If changed, the font size must be smaller than that used for first-degree text

headings and larger than that used for the report or manuscript text. Triple-

space before a second-degree heading, and double-space after it.

(3) **Third-degree text headings**. The third-degree text heading begins a paragraph, so it is indented from the left margin the same amount of space as the first line of any other paragraph—usually 0.5 inch. Capitalize only the first word and any proper nouns. Boldface the heading and conclude it with a period. Use the same font size as the report or manuscript text. Double-space before a third-degree text

heading, and begin keying the paragraph text one or two spaces after the period that concludes the heading.

used for the report or manuscript text. Triple-space before a second-degree text

heading and double-space after it.

1 blank line ⟶

Format for a third-degree text heading. Because the third-degree

heading is part of the paragraph that follows, it is also referred to as a "paragraph

heading." Only the first word and proper nouns in the heading are capitalized.

The third-degree heading is boldfaced (in the same typeface and size as

the report or manuscript text) and followed by a period. Double-space before

a third-degree heading, and begin keying the paragraph on the same line

directly after the heading.

b. Text headings indicate divisions of a topic or subtopic; therefore, if a first-, second-, or third-degree heading is used, it must be followed by at least one or more matching headings. For example, if you use one first-degree heading in the report or manuscript, you must use at least one other first-degree heading in the same document.

c. All text headings should be separated by at least two lines of text, regardless of their place in the heading hierarchy. In other words, a lesser-degree text heading may not follow another heading without any intervening text.

d. Text headings must be used in ascending order of degree from first degree to third degree, *but* the first-degree heading may be omitted if only one or two levels of headings are required in a report. The following table illustrates what heading levels may be used based upon the number of levels or divisions required:

Number of Text Headings Required	Levels of Text Headings to Be Used
3	First-degree heading, Second-degree heading, and Third-degree heading
2	First-degree heading and Second-degree heading *or* Second-degree heading and Third-degree heading
1	First-degree heading *or* Second-degree heading

13-9 Listings

a. Both vertical and horizontal listings are often used in letters, memorandums, reports, and manuscripts. Whether to use a horizontal listing or a vertical listing depends upon (1) the number of items in the listing, (2) the number of words contained in each item, and (3) the degree of emphasis intended.

Vertical listings are more emphatic than horizontal listings. They may be numbered, unnumbered, or bulleted. Lengthy and complex listings are more readily understood in the vertical format.

Horizontal listings are less emphatic. They are generally used with short listings that are few in number. Each item in a horizontal listing is preceded by an Arabic numeral or a lowercase letter enclosed in parentheses.

b. *Numbered vertical listings* are numbered in consecutive order with Arabic numerals. In all business documents, use the following guidelines for listing numbered items vertically:

(1) Introduce a vertical listing with a complete sentence.

(2) Indent the listing 0.5 inch from both the left and right margins. In business letters and memorandums, vertical listings *may* align with the left and right margins of the main text.

(3) Number each item; use the features of your word processing program to align the text approximately two spaces after the period in the number. (Any second and succeeding lines should begin directly under the first word, not the number, of the item.) Single-space items that are more than one line.

(4) Use parallel construction; that is, use all complete sentences, all the same kind of phrases, or all single words that begin with the same part of speech and have the same form. Place a period after each item *only* in listings that contain complete sentences.

(5) Capitalize the first word in each listed item.

(6) Double-space before the first item, between items, and after the last item in the listing.

numbered vertical listing—complete sentences

```
0.5 inch
   ←→ When explaining our investment programs to new clients, be sure to

use the following procedures:
0.5 inch                                          ←——— 1 blank line
   ←→ 1.  Introduce yourself to the clients, and be sure you solicit the 0.5 inch
          correct pronunciation of their names.              ←→
                                                  ←——— 1 blank line
       2.  Begin sessions by using the clients' surnames with a
           courtesy title.
                                                  ←——— 1 blank line
       3.  Enter into a discussion that discloses their leisure activities
           and interests.
                                                  ←——— 1 blank line
       4.  Move into a discussion about their future and plans for . . . .
```

c. *Unnumbered vertical listings* are similar in most respects to numbered vertical listings. Use the following guidelines for listing unnumbered items vertically:

(1) Introduce a vertical listing with a complete sentence.

(2) Indent the listing 0.5 inch from both the left and right margins.

(3) Use parallel construction; that is, use all complete sentences, all the same kind of phrases, or all single words that begin with the same part of speech and have the same form. Place a period after each item *only* in listings containing complete sentences.

(4) Capitalize the first word in each listed item.

(5) Double-space before the first item, between items, and after the last item in the listing. Single-space items that are more than one line.

unnumbered vertical listing—words or phrases

```
0.5 inch
   ←→ This position requires that the employee be qualified to perform the

   following duties:                                    ←——— 1 blank line

       Greet and develop rapport with clients
                                                        ←——— 1 blank line
       Answer questions regarding the investment opportunities
       available through our company
   0.5 inch                                             ←——— 1 blank line
   ←→ Evaluate clients' investment portfolios and other holdings ←→  0.5 inch
                                                        ←——— 1 blank line
       Obtain current information and forecasts on . . . .
                                                        ←——— 1 blank line
```

```
0.5 inch
   ←→ In our new complex all workstations will be equipped with the following

   computers and peripherals or their equivalents:
   0.5 inch                                             ←——— 1 blank line
   ←→ HP Pavilion desktop computer,  Model 9290
                                                        ←——— 1 blank line
       HP Windows keyboard
                                                        ←——— 1 blank line
       HP multimedia monitor
                                                        ←——— 1 blank line
       HP LaserJet 6 printer
                                                        ←——— 1 blank line
```

13
Reports

unnumbered vertical listing—complete sentences

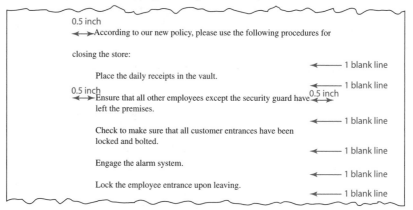

Unnumbered vertical listings consisting of words or phrases that are keyed on single lines *may* be single spaced, although a double space still appears before and after the listing. Such a listing is shown below.

unnumbered vertical listing—words or phrases single spaced

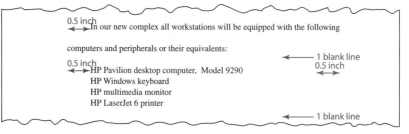

d. *Bulleted listings* are similar to numbered listings. Typographic symbols (small solid circles, hollow circles, solid squares, hollow squares, check marks, etc.) replace the numbers. These symbols may be accessed through various options in word processing programs. In all business letters, memorandums, reports, and manuscripts, use the following guidelines for listing bulleted items vertically:

(1) Introduce a vertical listing with a complete sentence.

(2) Indent the listing 0.5 inch from both the left and right margins. In business letters and memorandums, vertical listings *may* assume the left and right margins of the main text.

(3) Insert the typographical symbol; use the features of your word processing program to align the text after the typographical symbol. (Any second and succeeding lines should begin directly under the first word, not the symbol, of the item.) Single-space items that are more than one line.

(4) Use parallel construction; that is, use all complete sentences, all the same kind of phrases, or all single words that begin with the same part of speech and have the same form. Place a period after each item *only* in listings containing complete sentences.

(5) Capitalize the first word in each listed item.

(6) Double-space before the first item, between items, and after the last item in the listing.

bulleted vertical listing—words or phrases

bulleted vertical listing—complete sentences

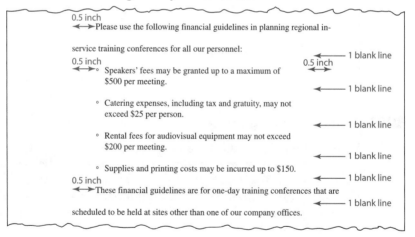

e. **Horizontal listings may be part of a sentence, or they may be introduced by a complete thought followed by a colon. Whenever a horizontal listing contains three or more items, the items are separated by commas or semicolons. Use commas to separate words or phrases; use semicolons to separate complete thoughts or items that contain internal commas. Use the following guidelines for listing items horizontally:**

(1) Use a colon to introduce the list *only when it is preceded by a complete thought.*

(2) Capitalize the first word of each item *only if it is a proper noun.*

(3) Identify the listed items by enclosing either lowercase letters or numbers in parentheses before each item. Do not conclude a line with only a letter or number enclosed in parentheses; at least one word of the item must appear after the letter or numeral. Use the nonbreaking space feature of your word processing program to wrap an isolated number or letter to the next line.

horizontal listing—items separated by commas

as requested. Each team will consist of (a) an administrator, (b) a scientist,

(c) two engineers, (d) an administrative assistant, and (e) a secretary. The

team will function under the supervision of our project coordinator, who will

horizontal listing—items separated by semicolons

on Tuesday, June 10. While I am in New York, would you please take care of

the following items: (1) complete the negotiations with AAA Computer System

Services for an additional one-year contract; (2) respond to and follow through

on the inquiry from Medco Financial Services regarding our medical software

line; and (3) contact dental offices to review, test, and evaluate our newly

developed line of software. If you are unable to complete any of these items,

13-10 Methods of Citing Sources

When either direct quotations or other information needs to be cited in a report or manuscript, any one of a number of methods may be used. The most common ones include footnotes, bibliographical notes, endnotes, the MLA (Modern Language Association) style of notation, and the APA (American Psychological Association) style of notation.

The MLA style of notation is generally used in literary writings while the APA style of notation is predominantly used by writers in the social sciences. Business writers, on the other hand, usually employ a conventional footnote or endnote style because they can more easily associate the cited information with its source and authenticate its contents. Therefore, the following styles shown for footnotes and endnotes are recommended for use in business reports.[5]

a. Use the *footnote* feature of your word processing program to ensure that notations and corresponding documentation appear consistently on the same page. Guidelines for preparing footnotes for off-line sources are listed below:

(1) Indicate the presence of a footnote by typing a superior (slightly raised) figure after the material to be documented. Place the footnote itself at the bottom of the page on which the reference notation appears. By accessing the footnote feature of a word processing program, these procedures may be performed automatically.

(2) Set off the footnotes from the rest of the page with a 1.5- or 2-inch line at the left margin, at least a single space after the last line of text on the page. Double-space after this line. Single-space all footnotes. By accessing the footnote feature of a word processing program, these formats will be performed automatically.

(3) Indent 0.5 inch, and number each footnote consecutively with a superior (slightly raised) figure at the beginning of the footnote. By accessing the footnote feature of a word processing program, these procedures will be performed automatically.

(4) Begin the footnote by keying the name of the author, if any, in a first-name, last-name sequence.

(5) Provide the complete title of the cited reference. Place the titles of magazine articles, sections of books, newspaper columns, and other such section or segment titles in quotation marks. Italicize the titles of books, pamphlets, magazines, newspapers, and other complete works with subdivisions.

(6) Include next, where applicable, the publishing information. Enclose in parentheses the geographical location of the publisher followed by a colon, the name of the publisher, and the date of publication. Eliminate the state name from the geographical location when the city is commonly known; otherwise, use the standard state abbreviation with the city name.

(7) Follow the complete title of magazines and newspapers with the date of publication.

(8) Conclude footnotes with the page location of the cited material.

(9) Separate the parts of a footnote with commas.

---

[5]The formats suggested here for footnotes and endnotes for published and unpublished works (except for noted deviations) are based on the traditional format alternatives contained in the following sources:

The Chicago Manual of Style, 14th ed. (Chicago and London: The University of Chicago Press, 1993), 487–635.

Kate L. Turabian, *A Manual for Writers of Term Papers, Theses, and Dissertations,* 6th ed., revised by John Grossman and Alice Bennett (Chicago and London: The University of Chicago Press, 1996), 116–164.

The AMA Style Guide for Business Writing (New York: American Management Association, 1996), 44, 81–84.

book, one author

[1]Charlene L. Parsons, *Introduction to Microcomputing: Basic Concepts*, 4th ed. (Mason, Ohio: South-Western Publishing, 2003), 117–132.

book, two authors

[2]R. Thomas Petrowski and Diane C. Robbins, *Principles of Small Business Management*, 5th ed. (New York: John Wiley & Sons, Inc., 2000), 237.

book, more than two authors

[3]Patricia Whitman, David Kane, James E. Wellington, and Ida Mason, *Fundamentals of Finance and Banking* (New York: McGraw-Hill, Inc., 2003), 208–214.

book, editor(s) only

[4]John M. Sakasian and Carol L. Jones, eds., *Readings in Organizational Communication* (Belmont, Calif.: Wadsworth Publishing Company, 2003), 307–309.

CD-ROM

[5]"Securities and Exchange Commission," *Microsoft Bookshelf '02*, CD-ROM (Microsoft Corporation, 2002).

company memorandum

[6]Angela Garcia, "Medical Insurance Programs Available to Employees" (Boston: Interstop Corporation memorandum, 23 August 2003).

company report—published

[7]Shel Holtz, "A Partnership in Japan," *Insights* (Irvine, Calif.: Allergan, Inc., published report, February 2004), 2.

company report—unpublished (internal)

[8]Terry Thomsen, "An Analysis of Current Manufacturing Facilities" (Detroit: General Motors, Chevrolet Division, unpublished report, May 2004), 32–37.

correspondence

9George Bush (as vice president of the United States), response letter to author, 17 October 1986.

encyclopedia article—signed

10Robert D. Patton, "Management," *The 2002 World Book Encyclopedia* (Chicago: World Book, Inc., 2002), 13:97.

encyclopedia article—unsigned

11"Adams, John," *2002 Encyclopaedia Britannica Print Set* (Chicago: Encyclopaedia Britannica, Inc., 2002), 1:83–84.

film, videocassette, digital video disk (DVD), or audiocassette

12*Barriers to Effective Global Communication*, videocassette (Chicago: Visual Education Corporation, 2000).

government publication

13*Statistical Abstract of the United States*, U.S. Bureau of the Census (Washington, D.C.: U.S. Government Printing Office, 2000), 256.

interview

14Jeremy Moore (CEO, Great Western Federal Bank), interview by author, Woodland Hills, Calif., 14 October 2003.

magazine article with author

15A. T. Stadthaus, "Security Issues Plaguing Wireless Fidelity," *BusinessWeek*, 28 July 2003, 32–33, 57.

magazine article without author

16"The Declining Dollar in Our International Economy," *Changing Times*, December 2000, 40–42.

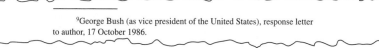

newspaper article with author

[17]Andrew R. Donovan, "Technology Insights," *Los Angeles Times*, 21 March 2003, San Fernando Valley edition, sec. D, p. 6, cols. 3–4.

paperback book

[18]John T. Mathews, *Successful E-Commercing in a Global Economy* (Upper Saddle River, N.J.: Prentice Hall Inc., 2003), 105.

professional journal article (with volume number)

[19]Thomas D. Clark, Sherrie E. Human, Heidi Amshoff, and Mike Sigg, "Getting Up to Speed on the Information Highway: Integrating Web-Based Resources Into Business Communication Pedagogy," *Business Communication Quarterly,* 64:1 (March 2001): 43–44.

radio or television broadcast

[20]"Work Camps Around the World," *60 Minutes* (Los Angeles: Repeat KCBS telecast, 26 July 2004).

secondary source citation

[21]Robert Willis and Margaret Elwood, *Succeeding in the International Marketplace* (New York: Penguin Books, 2001), 84, as cited in Michael Crosby, *Nonverbal Communication in a Cross-Cultural Economy* (New York: Random House, Inc., 2003), 109.

table, source in

[22]Leonard J. Cogan and Carey D. Paransky, table "U.S. Merchandise Trade Dollars by Country, 2001," *International Trading Benefits* (New York: Random House, Inc., 2002), 127.

unpublished book or booklet

[23]John Wooden, "John Wooden Basketball Fundamentals Camp, Player's Notebook" (Unpublished and undated booklet), 9.

unpublished book or booklet without author, section

[24]"A History of Bruin Basketball," The UCLA Alumni Association, Occasional Paper #9 (Unpublished booklet, 1975), 2.

Once a reference has been cited, a shortened form *may be* used when the same reference is shown again. These shortened forms— *Ibid., loc. cit.,* and *op. cit.*—are explained and illustrated in the following paragraphs.

Ibid. is used when the reference cited is identical to the one in the preceding footnote. If the reference source is the same but the page numbers differ, use *Ibid.* with appended page numbers.

Ibid.—identical reference

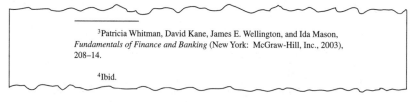

³Patricia Whitman, David Kane, James E. Wellington, and Ida Mason, *Fundamentals of Finance and Banking* (New York: McGraw-Hill, Inc., 2003), 208–14.

⁴Ibid.

Ibid.— same reference but different page number(s)

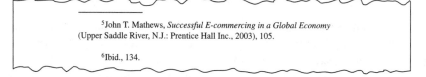

⁵John T. Mathews, *Successful E-commercing in a Global Economy* (Upper Saddle River, N.J.: Prentice Hall Inc., 2003), 105.

⁶Ibid., 134.

The notation *loc. cit.* means "in the place cited." It is used when the reference and the same page numbers have been previously cited but intervening citations have occurred. Begin the citation with the last name of the author. For two authors separate the last names with *and*; for more than two authors, just add *et al.* after the last name of the first author. Conclude the citation with *loc. cit.*⁶

loc. cit.

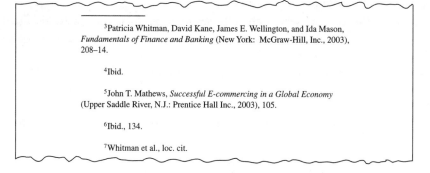

³Patricia Whitman, David Kane, James E. Wellington, and Ida Mason, *Fundamentals of Finance and Banking* (New York: McGraw-Hill, Inc., 2003), 208–14.

⁴Ibid.

⁵John T. Mathews, *Successful E-commercing in a Global Economy* (Upper Saddle River, N.J.: Prentice Hall Inc., 2003), 105.

⁶Ibid., 134.

⁷Whitman et al., loc. cit.

---

⁶*The Chicago Manual of Style* recommends the use of the short-title form in place of the term *loc. cit.* (pp. 582–583).

The notation *op. cit.* (meaning "in the work cited") also refers to a previously cited reference, but different page numbers are being referenced and intervening references have occurred.[7] Begin the citation with the last name of the author. For two authors separate the last names with *and*; for more than two authors, merely add *et al.* after the last name of the first author. Conclude the citation with *op. cit.* and the new page number(s).

op. cit.

[5]John T. Mathews, *Successful E-Commercing in a Global Economy* (Upper Saddle River, N.J.: Prentice Hall Inc., 2003), 105.

[6]Ibid., 134.

[7]R. Thomas Petrowski and Diane C. Robbins, *Principles of Small Business Management,* 5th ed. (New York: John Wiley & Sons, Inc., 2000), 237.

[8]Mathews, op. cit., 147.

Formats for citing on-line Internet sources (World Wide Web [WWW] sites, E-mail messages, Web discussion forum postings, listserv messages, newsgroup messages, real-time communication, linkage data, telnet sites, FTP [file transfer protocol] sites, and gopher sites) have emerged only within the past several years. Use the following guidelines for citing World Wide Web sites:[8]

(1) Use the footnote feature of your word processing program to achieve the formats used for other types of sources.

(2) Begin with the author's full name, if known. Continue with the full title of the document in quotation marks, the title of the complete work (if applicable) in italics, the name of a sponsoring body or government organization (if applicable), and the date of publication or last revision (if available; otherwise, use *n.d*). Separate each item with a comma.

(3) Enclose within angle brackets (< >) the complete address (URL).

(4) Enclose in parentheses the date (day, month, year) the site was visited.

(5) Conclude the citation with a period.

---

[7]*The Chicago Manual of Style* recommends the use of the short-title form in place of the term *op. cit.* (pp. 582–583).

[8]The formats suggested here are adaptations based on *The Chicago Manual of Style* as contained in the following sources:

Andrew Harnack and Eugene Kleppinger, "Using Chicago Style to Cite and Document Sources," *Online! A Reference Guide to Using Internet Sources* (New York: Bedford/St. Martin's, 2001), 158–164.

Andrew Harnack and Eugene Kleppinger, "Using Chicago Style to Cite and Document Sources," *Citation Styles … online!,* 2001, <http://www.bedfordstmartins.com/online/citex.html> (18 September 2002).

personal Web site

¹Jill R. Binsley, *Jill R. Binsley, Assistant Professor, Computer Applications and Office Technologies, Los Angeles Pierce College, Woodland Hills, California,* n.d., <http://www.piercecollege.com/usr/binslejr/> (26 June 2002).

general Web site

²Peter Vogt, "A Winning Strategy: Tactics for an Effective Job Search," "Finding Your First Job," *Monster Career Center,* n.d., <http://content.monster.com/firstjob/strategy/> (26 June 2002).

on-line book

³Andrew Harnack and Eugene Kleppinger, *Online! A Reference Guide to Using Internet Sources,* 2001, <http://www.bedfordstmartins.com/online/> (26 June 2002).

on-line article in a magazine

⁴Frederik Balfour, Mark L. Clifford, Moon Ihlwan, and Michael Shari, "How the Crisis Changed Asia and How It Didn't," *BusinessWeek Online,* 1 July 2002, <http://www.businessweek.com/magazine/content/02_26/b3789002.htm> (26 June 2002).

on-line government publication

⁵"United States Postal Service Transformation Plan," *United States Postal Service,* n.d., <http://www.usps.com/strategicdirection/transform.htm/> (26 June 2002).

⁶Graham R. Mitchell, Kelly H. Carnes, Esq., and Cheryl Mendonsa, *America's New Deficit: The Shortage of Information Technology Workers,* Office of Technology Policy, Department of Commerce, n.d., <http://www.ta.doc.gov/reports/itsw/itsw.pdf> (26 June 2002).

Use the following guidelines for citing E-mail messages:

(1) Use the footnote feature of your word processing program to achieve the formats used for other types of sources.

(2) Begin with the author's full name followed by the subject line placed in quotation marks.

(3) Supply next the date the message was sent (day, month, year).

(4) Designate the type of message (*personal E-mail, distribution list, office communication*).

(5) Enclose in parentheses the date (day, month, year) of access.

(6) Separate items with a comma except the date of access.

(7) Conclude the citation with a period.

⁷Brenda Ingram-Cotton, "CBEA 2003 Breakout Session Speakers," 27 May 2003, distribution list (28 May 2003).

b. *Bibliographical notes,* **references to the bibliography, may be used as alternatives to formal footnotes. The reference to the bibliography is shown in parentheses at the end of the cited material by referring first to the number of the reference in the bibliography followed by a colon and the page number(s) of the source. The complete source appears in the bibliography following the body of the paper (see Section 13-12).**

bibliographical note

. . . Income has risen 16 percent during the last fiscal period. To offset this

increased income, however, expenses have risen 21 percent over the same

period. (6:10–11)

c. **Another alternative to footnotes or bibliographical notes is *endnotes*. Indicate the presence of an endnote by typing a superior (slightly raised) figure after the reference material to be documented. Endnotes are placed on a separate page at the end of the body of the report or at the end of each chapter in a long report. Use the endnotes feature of your word processing program and the following guidelines to prepare endnotes:**

(1) Allow a 2-inch top margin. Center the heading *NOTES* or *ENDNOTES* in all capital letters.

(2) Triple-space after the heading. Single-space each note, but double-space between notes.

(3) Number the notes consecutively using Arabic numerals followed by a 0.3-inch left indent.

(4) Use the same content and sequence for endnotes as shown for footnotes in Section 13-10a. Use a footer to number the page at the bottom, or omit (but count) the page number—select whichever style was used for the beginning pages of other major sections in the body of the report.

(5) Use a 0.5- or 1-inch top margin for any second and succeeding pages, depending upon the page-numbering format selected. Be sure to follow the same format used for the body of the report.

endnotes page

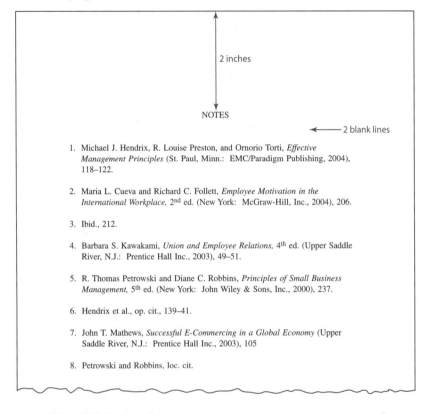

2 inches

NOTES

2 blank lines

1. Michael J. Hendrix, R. Louise Preston, and Ornorio Torti, *Effective Management Principles* (St. Paul, Minn.: EMC/Paradigm Publishing, 2004), 118–122.

2. Maria L. Cueva and Richard C. Follett, *Employee Motivation in the International Workplace,* 2nd ed. (New York: McGraw-Hill, Inc., 2004), 206.

3. Ibid., 212.

4. Barbara S. Kawakami, *Union and Employee Relations,* 4th ed. (Upper Saddle River, N.J.: Prentice Hall Inc., 2003), 49–51.

5. R. Thomas Petrowski and Diane C. Robbins, *Principles of Small Business Management,* 5th ed. (New York: John Wiley & Sons, Inc., 2000), 237.

6. Hendrix et al., op. cit., 139–41.

7. John T. Mathews, *Successful E-Commercing in a Global Economy* (Upper Saddle River, N.J.: Prentice Hall Inc., 2003), 105

8. Petrowski and Robbins, loc. cit.

13

Reports

d. The *MLA (Modern Language Association) referencing style,*[9] used predominantly in the humanities, is another method for citing sources. In this style a short description of the source and the pertinent page number(s) appear in parentheses after the information cited. The main purpose of the parenthetical reference is to point the reader to a specific work in the Works Cited, the MLA version of a bibliography.

---

[9]For a complete discussion of the preparation of reports and manuscripts according to the MLA style, consult Joseph Gibaldi, *MLA Handbook for Writers of Research Papers,* 5th ed. (New York: The Modern Language Association of America, 1999).

For a concise interpretation of citing on-line sources according to the MLA style, consult Andrew Harnack and Eugene Kleppinger, "Using MLA Style to Cite and Document Sources," *Online! A Reference Guide to Using Internet Sources* (New York: Bedford/St. Martin's, 2001), 116–121. OR Andrew Harnack and Eugene Kleppinger, "Using MLA Style to Cite and Document Sources," *Citation Styles . . . online!,* 2001, <http://www.bedfordstmartins.com/online/citex.html> (2 September 2002).

Use the following guidelines to cite sources according to the MLA referencing style:

(1) Begin with the last name of the author or authors. If the work has more than three authors, use only the first author's last name followed by *et al.* with no intervening punctuation, e.g., Greenburg et al.

(2) Begin the citation with the title of the work or a shortened version of the title, e.g., *Employment Trends in Manufacturing* or *Employment Trends*, if a work has no author listed.

(3) Follow the author or title reference with the relevant page number(s), but do not use any intervening punctuation.

(4) Place the citation in parentheses directly after the referenced material. Examples of such references would be (Greenburg et al. 113) and (*Employment Trends in Manufacturing* 65–67).

(5) Include only the page number(s) in the citation if the author(s) or source is named in the context of the text.

(6) Provide a full description of all cited sources in the Works Cited.[10]

MLA referencing style

According to several recent surveys, investment in desktop and laptop computers continues to be a major investment item for United States corporations. Advances in technology have forced corporations to update continually with hopes of obtaining a competitive edge. (McAllister and Doyle 32). Between now and the year 2007, corporations will spend between $20 billion and $25 billion on individual workstations and their peripherals (*U.S. News and International Report* 114).

MLA page reference only

According to McAllister and Doyle (32), investment in desktop and laptop computers continues to be a major investment item for United States corporations. Advances in technology have forced corporations to update continually with hopes of obtaining a competitive edge. Between now and the year 2007, as reported in *U.S. News and International Report*, corporations will spend between $20 billion and $25 billion on individual workstations and their peripherals (114).

---

[10]Refer to Section 13-12c of this manual for information on preparing the Works Cited, the MLA version of a bibliography.

e. Another method for citing sources is the *APA (American Psychological Association) style*,[11] which is used predominantly by writers in the sciences.

To cite a specific part of a source or a direct quotation in this style, place in parentheses the last name of the author(s), the year of publication, and the pertinent page number(s) after the information to be cited. To cite a complete source, place in parentheses the last name of the author(s) and the year of publication.

The main purpose of the parenthetical reference is to point the reader to a specific work in the reference list—the APA version of a bibliography. Use the following guidelines to cite sources according to the APA referencing style:

(1) Begin the citation with the last name of the author. If a source has two authors, cite both authors' last names each time the source is referenced. For sources with three to five authors, cite each author's last name in the first reference; additional references require only the first author's last name followed by *et al.*

(2) Join the names in a multiple-author citation with an ampersand (&) instead of the word *and* when they appear in parentheses or in the reference list, e.g., (Hendrix, Preston & Torti, 2003).

(3) Begin the citation with the first two or three words of the entry in the reference list—usually the title of the work—if a work has no author listed. Use quotation marks around titles of articles or chapters; italicize the names of books or magazines. Capitalize the main words, e.g., (*Employment Trends*, 2003).

(4) Follow the author or title reference with the date of publication. For direct quotations or specific material, include any relevant page number(s) preceded by *p.* or *pp.* Additional examples of such references are (Hendrix et al., 2003) and ("Marketing Aspects," 2004, pp. 87–88).

(5) Include only the date of publication (and any applicable page numbers for direct quotations or specific material) in the citation if the author(s) or source is named in the context of the text. Omit the parenthetical reference for an entire work if both the source and date appear in the text.

13

Reports

---

[11]For a complete discussion of the preparation of reports and manuscripts according to the APA style, consult *Publication Manual of the American Psychological Association,* 5th ed. (Washington, D.C.: American Psychological Association, 2001).

For a concise interpretation of citing on-line sources according to the APA style, consult Andrew Harnack and Eugene Kleppinger, "Using APA Style to Cite and Document Sources," *Online! A Reference Guide to Using Internet Sources* (New York: Bedford/St. Martin's, 2001), 136–140. OR Andrew Harnack and Eugene Kleppinger, "Using APA Style to Cite and Document Sources," *Citation Styles . . . online!,* 2001, <http://www.bedfordstmartins.com/online/citex.html> (18 September 2002).

(6) Provide a full description of cited sources in the reference list, the APA version of a bibliography.[12] However, personal letters, telephone calls, and other material that cannot be retrieved are not listed in the reference list. These sources are cited only in the text, e.g., "B. Baity (personal communication, November 5, 2003) confirmed that . . . ."

APA referencing style

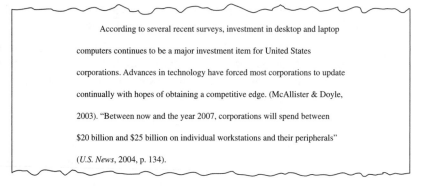

According to several recent surveys, investment in desktop and laptop computers continues to be a major investment item for United States corporations. Advances in technology have forced most corporations to update continually with hopes of obtaining a competitive edge. (McAllister & Doyle, 2003). "Between now and the year 2007, corporations will spend between $20 billion and $25 billion on individual workstations and their peripherals" (*U.S. News*, 2004, p. 134).

APA year and page reference only

According to McAllister and Doyle (2003), investment in desktop and laptop computers continues to be a major investment item for United States corporations. Advances in technology have forced most corporations to update continually with hopes of obtaining a competitive edge. "Between now and the year 2007," as reported in *U.S. News and International Report*, "corporations will spend between $20 billion and $25 billion on individual workstations and their peripherals" (2004, p. 114).

f. **Business writers may use a reference style that suits their purpose. In citing sources, though, use a style that meets the following criteria:**

(1) The citation can be easily located from its point of reference within the report.

(2) The citation contains sufficient information so that the reader can readily locate the source and authenticate the information cited.

(3) All citations, regardless of media, are complete and expressed in a similar and consistent format.

---

[12]Refer to Section 13-12d of this manual for information on how to prepare a reference list, the APA version of a bibliography.

13-11 Illustrations

Visuals in the form of tables, pie charts, column charts, bar charts, and line charts may be used to illustrate data in a report or manuscript. Where possible, a table or chart should appear on the same page as the narrative describing it. If there is insufficient space on the same page for the table or chart and its explanation, then the illustration should be placed on the following page. A statement such as "As shown in Table 3 on page 9, ..." must be used in the narrative to direct the reader to the illustration. The type of illustration used will vary according to the kind of data presented; guidelines for preparing each type of illustration follow:

a. *Tables* arrange data in an orderly fashion by employing a system of headings and columns to present information. Either open tables or ruled tables may be used in business documents.

Although the length, style, and number of table columns will vary according to the type of data presented, use the following general procedures to set up tables:

(1) Use the Tables feature of your word processing program to create tables. For open tables eliminate the lines and condense the row height. For ruled tables select the line enhancements or one of the preformatted table formats provided by your word processing program.

(2) Leave two blank lines before and after a table if it does not appear on a separate page. (Some authorities prefer three blank lines before and after the table; be consistent in the use of whichever of the two formats you choose.)

(3) Number each table consecutively with Arabic numerals if more than one table appears in the report. Center *Table* and its corresponding number over the proposed position of the table. (If only one table appears in a report, begin the table with its title.)

(4) Double-space, and then center under the table number the title of the table; use all capital letters. If a subtitle is needed, center and use capital and lowercase letters. Place the subtitle a double space below the main title. Triple-space after the last line of either the main title or the subtitle in an open table.

(5) Center the entire table between the left and right margins of the report or manuscript. Allow a sufficient amount of space for each column, keeping in mind that the column heading is part of the column.

(6) Use capital and lowercase letters for column headings. Boldface and center each column heading.

(7) Center both horizontally and vertically a table appearing on a separate page.

13

Reports

an open table

1 blank line——►

Table 1

**A COMPARISON OF THE MONTHLY COST PER EMPLOYEE
OF HEALTH INSURANCE POLICIES
SUBMITTED BY EIGHT COMPANIES**

1 blank line——►

March 3, 2005

2 blank lines——►

Company	Plan A[1]	Plan B[2]	Plan C[3]
Chicago General	$375.00	$492.50	$545.00
Concord	325.00	450.00	520.00
D & D Life	385.50	485.50	585.50
Edgewater	312.50	443.50	511.50
Lincoln	415.00	500.00	635.00
Morgan	309.34	440.25	524.15
New Jersey	350.00	475.00	530.00
Western	405.60	585.00	620.30

[1]$500,000 maximum coverage
[2]$1,000,000 maximum coverage
[3]$1,500,000 maximum coverage

enhanced ruled table

1 blank line——►
1 blank line——►

Table 1

**A COMPARISON OF THE MONTHLY COST PER EMPLOYEE
OF HEALTH INSURANCE POLICIES
SUBMITTED BY EIGHT COMPANIES**

1 blank line——►
1 blank line——►

March 3, 2005

Company	Plan A[1]	Plan B[2]	Plan C[3]
Chicago General	$375.00	$492.50	$545.00
Concord	325.00	450.00	520.00
D & D Life	385.50	485.50	585.50
Edgewater	312.50	443.50	511.50
Lincoln	415.00	500.00	635.00
Morgan	309.34	440.25	524.15
New Jersey	350.00	475.00	530.00
Western	405.60	585.00	620.30

**[1]$500,000 maximum coverage
[2]$1,000,000 maximum coverage
[3]$1,500,000 maximum coverage**

b. *Pie charts* are used to illustrate the parts of a whole when that whole represents 100 percent of something. To achieve maximum clarity in this type of visual, do not exceed seven or eight segments in the illustration.

simple pie chart with exploded segment

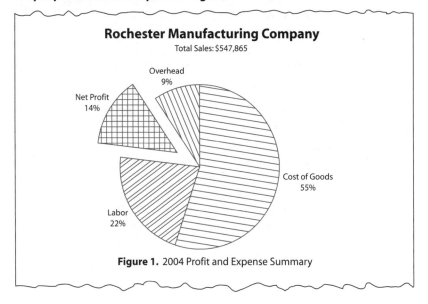

Rochester Manufacturing Company
Total Sales: $547,865

Overhead 9%
Net Profit 14%
Cost of Goods 55%
Labor 22%

Figure 1. 2004 Profit and Expense Summary

3-D pie chart

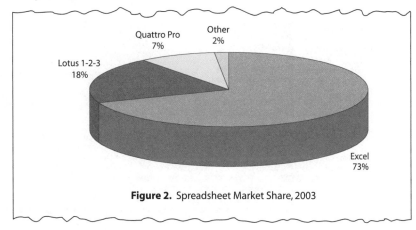

Quattro Pro 7%
Other 2%
Lotus 1-2-3 18%
Excel 73%

Figure 2. Spreadsheet Market Share, 2003

If possible, use the graphics feature of your spreadsheet program to create and import charts into your word processing program. Follow these guidelines to create pie charts:

(1) Begin the illustration two blank lines (some authorities prefer three) below the last line of text.

(2) Slice the pie in appropriate wedges, showing the largest wedge first. Start at the 12 o'clock position of the circle and move clockwise. The remaining wedges may or may not be in descending order of size, but the size of each wedge should be proportional to the percentage of the whole it represents.

(3) Identify what each wedge represents and its corresponding percentage. If the wedges are too small, use a legend to identify what each wedge represents.

(4) Center numbers and titles of pie charts in capital and lowercase letters a triple space below the bottom of the chart. Some software, however, may not permit this format. In those cases where the program requires a different format, use the format dictated by the program. Leave two blank lines (or three, depending upon the number of lines left before the chart) before resuming the narrative.

c. **Bar charts** and **column charts** are used to compare quantities within a class or over a time period. Bar charts are oriented horizontally, and column charts are oriented vertically. These charts require both a vertical axis and a horizontal axis. One axis represents the quantity, and the other represents the varying items in the class or the time period over which the quantities are measured.

horizontal 3-D bar chart comparing a single variable

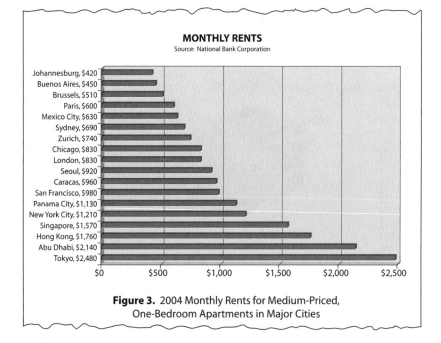

Figure 3. 2004 Monthly Rents for Medium-Priced, One-Bedroom Apartments in Major Cities

column chart comparing multiple variables

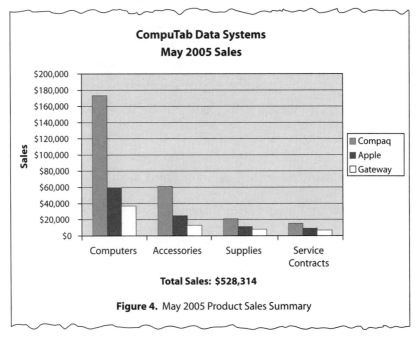

Figure 4. May 2005 Product Sales Summary

3-D stacked column chart

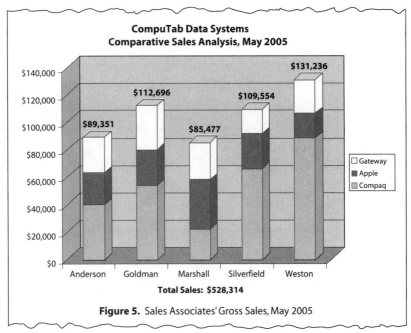

Figure 5. Sales Associates' Gross Sales, May 2005

Use your spreadsheet program and the following guidelines for constructing bar or column charts:

(1) Leave two (some authorities prefer three) blank lines before and after a column or bar chart when it interrupts the narrative.

(2) Use the horizontal axis in bar charts to represent the different quantities for each variable or time period; use the vertical axis to represent the variables or time periods.

(3) Use the vertical axis in column charts to represent the different quantities for each variable or time period; use the horizontal axis to represent the variables or time periods.

(4) Label clearly both the horizontal and vertical axes.

(5) Ensure that all bars are of uniform width. If the bars are not touching, they should be placed equidistantly in the chart.

(6) Center the figure numbers and titles of bar and column charts in capital and lowercase letters a triple space below the bottom of the chart. Some software, however, may not permit this format. In those cases where the program requires a different format, use the format dictated by the program.

d. *Line charts* are used to illustrate movement or trends over a time period. They may also be used to compare two or more sets of data over a time period.

line chart plotting multiple variables

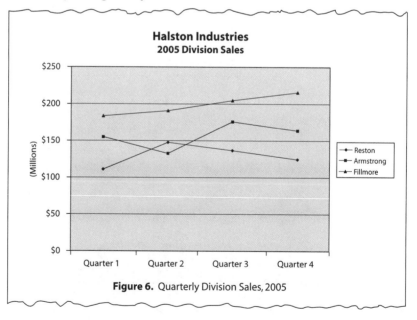

Figure 6. Quarterly Division Sales, 2005

Use your spreadsheet program and the following guidelines to construct line charts that plot both single and multiple variables:

(1) Leave two (some authorities recommend three) blank lines before and after a line chart that interrupts text.

(2) Place a straight vertical line at the left of the line chart to portray the quantity scale. The bottom of the scale represents the lowest quantity, and the top of the scale represents the largest quantity.

(3) Place at a right angle to the bottom of the vertical line a horizontal line that extends to the right side of the line chart. This horizontal line represents the time periods encompassed by the chart.

(4) Mark each quantity and time period equidistantly on its scale.

(5) Plot quantities above their respective time periods. Connect the cross points with a line, mark the cross points with a symbol, or use both symbols and connecting lines. When two or more factors are plotted on the same graph, use a different color, symbol, or line style for each set of data.

(6) Center the figure numbers and titles of line charts a triple space below the last line contained in the chart. Capitalize all main words in the title. Some software, however, may not permit this format. In those cases use the format dictated by the program.

13-12 Bibliography

a. The bibliography[13] follows immediately after the body of the report or manuscript and contains all sources cited in the text. Any source material that is not cited but that has contributed directly to the development of a report or manuscript should also be included.

b. List the items in the bibliography alphabetically by authors' last names or the first entry of the reference. Use the following guidelines to prepare a bibliography:

(1) Center the heading *BIBLIOGRAPHY* in all capital letters 2 inches from the top edge of the page.

(2) Triple-space between the heading and the first reference.

(3) Single-space each reference and double-space between references. If a reference requires more than one line, use the hanging indent feature of your word processing program to indent the second and succeeding lines 0.5 inch.

---

[13]The formats suggested here for bibliographical references (except for noted deviations) are based on the traditional format alternatives contained in the following sources:

The Chicago Manual of Style, 14th ed. (Chicago and London: The University of Chicago Press, 1993), 487–635.

Kate L. Turabian, *A Manual for Writers of Term Papers, Theses, and Dissertations,* 6th ed., revised by John Grossman and Alice Bennett (Chicago and London: The University of Chicago Press, 1996), 165–230.

The AMA Style Guide for Business Writing (New York: American Management Association, 1996), 41–44, 221.

Andrew Harnack and Eugene Kleppinger, *Online! A Reference Guide to Using Internet Sources* (New York: Bedford/St. Martin's, 2001), 164–165. AND Andrew Harnack and Eugene Kleppinger, "Using Chicago Style to Cite and Document Sources," *Citation Styles . . . online!,* 2001, <http://www.bedfordstmartins.com/online/citex.html> (2 September 2002).

(4) Type a 0.5-inch underline followed by a period in place of an author's name if he or she has more than one reference listed. Begin this procedure with the second reference for that author.

(5) Alphabetize the reference by title when the author is unknown.

(6) End the citations for magazines, journals, or other such source articles with page references.

(7) Enclose within angle brackets (< >) the complete uniform resource locator (URL) for Internet sites.

unsigned encyclopedia article

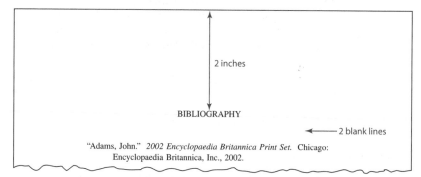

2 inches

BIBLIOGRAPHY

←——— 2 blank lines

"Adams, John." *2002 Encyclopaedia Britannica Print Set.* Chicago: Encyclopaedia Britannica, Inc., 2002.

film, videocassette, digital video disk (DVD), or audiocassette

Barriers to Effective Global Communication. Videocassette. Chicago: Visual Education Corporation, 2000.

business correspondence

Bush, George (as vice president of the United States). Response letter to author, 17 October 1986.

professional journal with volume and issue number

Clark, Thomas D., Sherrie E. Human, Heidi Amshoff, and Mike Sigg. "Getting Up to Speed on the Information Highway: Integrating Web-Based Resources Into Business Communication Pedagogy." *Business Communication Quarterly*, 64:1 (March 2001), 43–44.

source in table

Cogan, Leonard J., and Carey D. Paransky. Table. "U.S. Merchandise Trade Dollars by Country, 2001." *International Trading Benefits.* New York: Random House, Inc., 2002, 127.

newspaper column with author

Donovan, Andrew R. "Technology Insights." *Los Angeles Times*, 21 March 2003.

magazine article without author

"The Declining Dollar in Our International Economy." *Changing Times*.
December 2000, 40–42.

magazine article with author

Drew, Richard. "Multinational Corporations in the International Marketplace."
BusinessWeek, 17 August 2004, 19–20.

company memorandum

Garcia, Angela. "Medical Insurance Programs Available to Employees."
Boston: Interstop Corporation memorandum, 23 August 2003.

section in unpublished book or booklet without author

"A History of Bruin Basketball." The UCLA Alumni Association, Occasional
Paper #9. Unpublished booklet, 1975, 2.

published company report

Holtz, Shel. "A Partnership in Japan." *Insights.* Irvine, Calif.: Allergan, Inc.,
published report, February 2004, 2.

signed encyclopedia article

Karlen, Delmar. "Criminal Justice: 1. Criminal Justice in England and the
U.S." *The Encyclopedia Americana.* International ed. Vol. 8.
Danbury, Conn.: Grolier Incorporated, 1999.

paperback book

Larson, Harold G., and Charlene L. Morimoto. *Principles of Small Business
Management.* 6th ed. Chicago: The University of Chicago Press, 2004.

interview

Moore, Jeremy (CEO, Great Western Federal Bank). Interview by author,
Woodland Hills, Calif., 14 October 2003.

book, one author

Morrison, Alice T. *Microcomputers: Introductory Concepts and Applications.*
2nd ed. Mason, Ohio: South-Western Publishing, 2005.

13

Reports

book, same author

_____. *Microcomputers: Business and Accounting Spreadsheet Applications.*
Mason, Ohio: South-Western Publishing, 2004.

book, two authors

Patterson, L. David, and Kathy Lim. *Principles of Real Estate.* 4th ed.
New York: John Wiley & Sons, Inc., 2004.

book, three or more authors

Rodriguez, Rose P., Charles T. Bove, and Saad Najjar. *Fundamentals of
Accounting.* 3rd ed. St. Paul, Minn.: EMC/Paradigm Publishing, 2003.

book, editor(s) only

Sakasian, John M., and Carol L. Jones, eds. *Readings in Organizational
Communication.* Belmont, Calif.: Wadsworth Publishing Company, 2003.

CD-ROM

"Securities and Exchange Commission." *Microsoft Bookshelf '02.* CD-ROM.
Microsoft Corporation, 2002.

government publication

Statistical Abstract of the United States. U.S. Bureau of the Census.
Washington, D.C.: U.S. Government Printing Office, 2000.

internal unpublished company report

Thomsen, Terry. "An Analysis of Current Manufacturing Facilities." Detroit:
General Motors, Chevrolet Division, unpublished report, May 2004.

Internet, World Wide Web (WWW)

Walker, Janice R., and Todd Taylor. "Basic CGOS (The Columbia Guide to
Online Style) Style." *Columbia University Press.* 15 May 2002.
<http://www.columbia. edu/cu/cup/cgos/idx_basic.html> (29 June 2002).

secondary source citation

Willis, Robert, and Margaret Elwood. *Succeeding in the International Marketplace.*
New York: Penguin Books, 2001. As cited in Michael Crosby, *Nonverbal
Communication in a Cross-Cultural Economy.* New York: Random House,
Inc., 2003.

unpublished book or booklet

> Wooden, John. "John Wooden Basketball Fundamentals Camp, Player's Notebook." Unpublished and undated booklet.

radio or television broadcast

> "Work Camps Around the World." *60 Minutes*. Los Angeles: Repeat KCBS telecast, 26 July 2004.

c. **Reports prepared according to the MLA (Modern Language Association) style title the bibliography *Works Cited*.[14] References are listed alphabetically as in any other bibliography. Guidelines for formatting the Works Cited follow:**

(1) Place the title *Works Cited* 1 inch from the top edge of the page; number the page in the upper right corner, 0.5 inch from the top edge and aligned with the right margin.

(2) Double-space after the heading, and double-space within and between the entries. Begin each entry at the left margin, but use the hanging indent feature of your word processor to indent any subsequent lines 0.5 inch from the left margin.

Works Cited—MLA bibliographical style

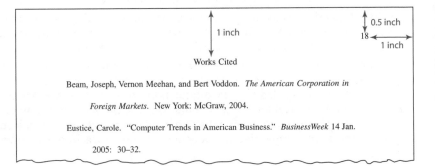

13

Reports

> Works Cited
>
> Beam, Joseph, Vernon Meehan, and Bert Voddon. *The American Corporation in Foreign Markets*. New York: McGraw, 2004.
>
> Eustice, Carole. "Computer Trends in American Business." *BusinessWeek* 14 Jan. 2005: 30–32.

---

[14]For a complete discussion of arrangements and formats for the Works Cited according to the MLA style, consult Joseph Gibaldi, *MLA Handbook for Writers of Research Papers*, 5th ed. (New York: The Modern Language Association of America, 1999), 114–202.

For a concise interpretation of citing on-line sources according to the MLA style, consult Andrew Harnack and Eugene Kleppinger, "Using MLA Style to Cite and Document Sources," *Online! A Reference Guide to Using Internet Sources* (New York: Bedford/St. Martin's, 2001), 121–131. OR Andrew Harnack and Eugene Kleppinger, "Using MLA Style to Cite and Document Sources," *Citation Styles . . . online!*, 2002, <http://www.bedfordstmartins.com/online/citex.html> (2 September 2002).

d. **Reports prepared according to the APA (American Psychological Association) style refer to the bibliography as a *reference list*.**[15] **References are listed alphabetically as in any other bibliography. Guidelines for formatting the reference list follow:**

(1) Begin the reference list on a new page, and place the title *References* 1 inch from the top edge of the page. (Use 1-inch bottom, left, and right margins.)

(2) Number all pages in the upper right corner. Align numbers with the right margin between the top edge of the page and the first line of text. Place a shortened version of the report or manuscript title on the same line, separating the title and page number by approximately 0.5 inch.

(3) Double-space after the title, and double-space within and between the entries.

(4) Begin the reference at the left margin. Use the hanging indent feature of your word processing program to indent the second and succeeding lines the same amount of space used for paragraphs within the body of the report or manuscript (usually 0.5 inch).

(5) Provide authors' last names and first initials in inverted order for book entries. Use an ampersand (&) instead of the word *and* to link multiple names. Follow the authors' names with the date of publication enclosed in parentheses.

(6) Capitalize only the first word and any proper nouns in the title or subtitle of a work. Italicize the name of the work.

(7) Provide next the facts of publication, listing the city first. Give the two-letter U.S. Postal Service state designation for little-known cities. The location is followed by a colon and the name of the publisher.

(8) List the names of magazine article authors in the same format used for authors of books. Follow with the publication date enclosed in parentheses. Do not place quotation marks around magazine article titles, and capitalize only the first word or proper nouns. Capitalize all main words and italicize the names of periodicals; include the volume or issue number (if any). Conclude the reference with page numbers.

---

[15] For a complete discussion of arrangements and formats for the reference list according to the APA style, consult *Publication Manual of the American Psychological Association,* 5th ed. (Washington, D.C.: American Psychological Association, 2001), 215–281, 313–314.

For a concise interpretation of citing on-line sources according to the APA style, consult Andrew Harnack and Eugene Kleppinger, "Using APA Style to Cite and Document Sources," *Online! A Reference Guide to Using Internet Sources* (New York: Bedford/St. Martin's, 2001), 140–148. OR Andrew Harnack and Eugene Kleppinger, "Using APA Style to Cite and Document Sources," *Citation Styles . . . online!,* 2001, <http://www.bedfordstmartins.com/online/citex.html> (2 September 2002).

reference list—APA bibliographical style

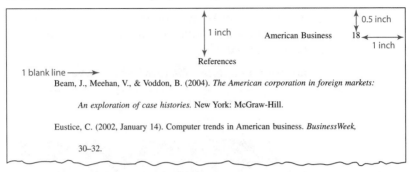

13-13 Appendix

a. The appendix follows the bibliography and contains supportive material. This material may include such items as letters, copies of questionnaires, maps, contracts, lists, tables, and other documents not shown elsewhere.

b. The appendix may be preceded by a page entitled *APPENDIX* or *APPENDIXES* (keyed in all capital letters and centered both horizontally and vertically). If the report or manuscript contains one appendix, the name of the appendix may be centered a double space below the *APPENDIX* heading. If the report or manuscript contains more than one appendix, the introductory page may show a list of appendixes included. In this case (1) both the title and the listing are centered vertically or (2) the title is placed 2 inches from the top edge of the page with the listing beginning a triple space thereafter. The appendixes should be numbered with their corresponding alphabetic letters.

introductory appendix page

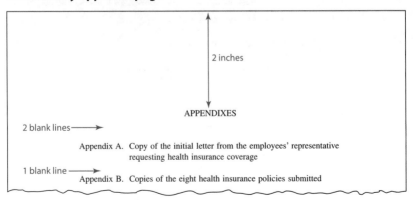

13–14 Word Processing Templates

Word processing programs—Microsoft Word and WordPerfect, specifically—provide templates to simplify the process of preparing and formatting reports.[16]

professional report template—Microsoft Word 2002

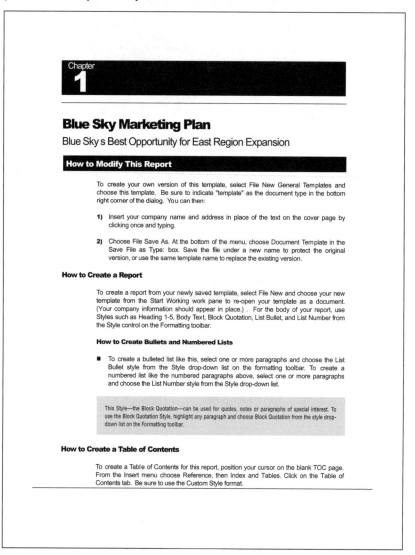

Chapter

1

Blue Sky Marketing Plan

Blue Sky's Best Opportunity for East Region Expansion

How to Modify This Report

To create your own version of this template, select File New General Templates and choose this template. Be sure to indicate "template" as the document type in the bottom right corner of the dialog. You can then:

1) Insert your company name and address in place of the text on the cover page by clicking once and typing.

2) Choose File Save As. At the bottom of the menu, choose Document Template in the Save File as Type: box. Save the file under a new name to protect the original version, or use the same template name to replace the existing version.

How to Create a Report

To create a report from your newly saved template, select File New and choose your new template from the Start Working work pane to re-open your template as a document. (Your company information should appear in place.) . For the body of your report, use Styles such as Heading 1-5, Body Text, Block Quotation, List Bullet, and List Number from the Style control on the Formatting toolbar.

How to Create Bullets and Numbered Lists

■ To create a bulleted list like this, select one or more paragraphs and choose the List Bullet style from the Style drop-down list on the formatting toolbar. To create a numbered list like the numbered paragraphs above, select one or more paragraphs and choose the List Number style from the Style drop-down list.

> This Style—the Block Quotation—can be used for quotes, notes or paragraphs of special interest. To use the Block Quotation Style, highlight any paragraph and choose Block Quotation from the style drop-down list on the Formatting toolbar.

How to Create a Table of Contents

To create a Table of Contents for this report, position your cursor on the blank TOC page. From the Insert menu choose Reference, then Index and Tables. Click on the Table of Contents tab. Be sure to use the Custom Style format.

---

[16]Microsoft at its Web site <http://office.microsoft.com/> (17 August 2002) provides access to free downloads for additional Microsoft Word business-form templates.

professional report template—Microsoft Word 2002 (**continued**)

More Template Tips

There are three ways to view the various style names of template text:

1) In Normal view, choose Tools Options. Click the View tab. In the Style Area Width box, dial up a number such as 1 and click OK. Observe the style name next to each paragraph; or

2) In Print Layout view, click on any paragraph. View the style name on the Formatting toolbar; or

3) From the Format menu choose Theme, then Style Gallery. In the Preview section click on Example or Style Samples.

How to Create a Table

Choose Insert from the Table menu. Be sure to choose the Professional AutoFormat if you are using a Professional style template.

To modify an existing table, such as the table below, position your cursor in any cell. To modify the table, access the Table menu to select the desired action and/or result.

Competitor Ranking	Current Share	Share in 3 Yrs.
Largest competitor	50%	30%
Second largest competitor	25%	20%
Third largest competitor	15%	12%

Table: Projected growth of competitors over 3 years.

How to Edit Table Text

You can edit and format table text like regular text. Simply select text and type to replace, and use the Format menu to change the font and/or paragraph attributes.

How to Change a Header or Footer

In Print Layout view, choose Header or Footer from the View menu. Once activated, you can change or delete the text just like regular text. When done, click Close to exit.

To delete a ruling line in the Header or Footer, from the Format menu choose Borders and Shading. Choose None from the Preset section, and click OK.

13

Reports

2

Meeting Minutes

13-15 Purpose and Contents

Minutes are compiled to provide a written record of announcements, reports, significant discussions, and decisions that have taken place during a meeting. Although the degree of formality and extent of coverage may vary, the specific information contained in meeting minutes usually includes the following:

(1) Name of group and meeting

(2) Date, place, and time meeting was called to order; time of adjournment

(3) Names of persons present (if applicable, names of persons absent)

(4) Approval of (or additions to) the agenda

(5) Disposition of any previous minutes

(6) Announcements

(7) Summaries of reports

(8) Motions presented and actions taken on motions

(9) Summaries of significant discussions

(10) Name and signature of person compiling minutes

13-16 Organization and Format of Formal Minutes

a. The organization and format of formal minutes do not follow precise criteria. You may wish, however, to use these guidelines for preparing formal minutes:

(1) Use 8½- by 11-inch white high-quality paper, and set 1.25-inch left and right margins. Count the first page in the pagination, but do not number it. Begin page numbering on the second page, and place the number 0.5 inch from the top and right edge of the page.

(2) Center the name of the group and/or meeting in all capital letters 2 inches from the top edge of the page. Double-space down; then center in capital and lowercase letters the date and scheduled time of the meeting. The place where the meeting was held appears another double space below the time and date. This information, too, is centered in capital and lowercase letters. See page 430 for an illustration of the heading format for meeting minutes.

(3) List those persons attending the meeting after the preliminary information. This listing is placed a triple space below the meeting place. Begin the listing with a phrase such as *Members Present:*, *Managers Present:*, or *Persons Present:*. Then list horizontally or vertically the names in the order of their importance or in alphabetical order.

(4) Note those regular members absent from a meeting, if appropriate. In this case a separate listing appears a double space below the listing of members present. It is usually preceded by *Members Absent:*, *Persons Absent:*, or another such designation. Examples of vertical attendance listings appear on page 430.

(5) Begin the first paragraph of the meeting minutes a triple space below the attendance listing or listings. It generally opens with a statement giving the exact time the meeting was called to order and by whom. This statement is usually followed by ones indicating approval of the agenda and giving the dispensation of any previous minutes.

(6) List any announcements after the opening paragraph. Use a side heading to introduce the announcements, allowing two blank lines above the heading and one blank line below it. Then number and list

each announcement made. If only one announcement occurred, show it in paragraph form without a number.

(7) Separate main ideas with topic headings. Many meeting agendas are organized according to old business and new business. These two categories may be used for topic headings (use side headings) in presenting the motions and discussions that have taken place during short meetings. For lengthy meetings, however, readers can more easily locate information in the minutes if the topic headings describe concretely the subject matter discussed, reported, or voted upon.

(8) Note, and in some cases summarize, reports presented at a meeting. The amount of information provided in the minutes will depend upon their purpose, formality, and use. Include with the reference to the report contents the name of the person giving the report as well as its disposition.

(9) Provide the exact wording of motions in the meeting minutes. Persons making and seconding the motions may be named in the motion statement. Include a brief summary of the discussion for each motion. Finally, indicate whether the motion was passed, defeated, or tabled. The number of yeses, noes, and abstentions for each motion should be recorded.

(10) Indicate the time and by whom the meeting was adjourned, even if the meeting was not concluded with a motion for adjournment. This information is placed in the concluding paragraph of the meeting minutes.

(11) Place the printed or typed signature of the person preparing the minutes on the fourth line below the concluding paragraph. It may be placed at the left margin or begun at the page center. The preparer's signature is placed directly above the printed signature line.

The complimentary closing *Respectfully submitted* may precede the signature line. In this case the entire signature block simulates the signature block of a business letter. Place *Respectfully submitted* a double space below the concluding paragraph, and leave three blank lines for the written signature before displaying the preparer's name. This style of signature block may also begin at the left margin or page center.

b. The major components of formal meeting minutes are illustrated in the following example on pages 430–431.

formal meeting minutes

2-inch top margin

STATE MUTUAL LIFE INSURANCE COMPANY
MONTHLY MEETING OF HOME OFFICE DEPARTMENT MANAGERS
MINUTES

1 blank line ——→

April 11, 2004, 2 p.m.

1 blank line ——→

Room 625, State Mutual Building

2 blank lines ——→

Officers Present: Louise Brannon, Agency Accounting
Anthony Coletta, Claims
David Haberman, Central Records
Phillip Horowitz, Personnel
Vern Knudsen, Vice President, Operations
Robert Miles, Actuarial
Wayne Nugent, Data Processing
George Ross, Treasurer
David Haberman, Central Records
Fred Wyatt, Finance

1 blank line ——→

Officers Absent: Neil Tsutsui, Group Insurance
Diane Zimmerman, Public Relations

2 blank lines ——→

The meeting of the home office department managers was called to order at 2:05 p.m. on April 11, 2004, in Room 625 of the State Mutual Building by Vern Knudsen. The agenda was unanimously approved as distributed. Minutes from the previous meeting held on March 14, 2004, were read and approved unanimously.

2 blank lines ——→

Announcements

1 blank line ——→

1. Effective June 1 Anthony Coletta will assume the position of administrative assistant to the vice president of operations. John Davis, the present assistant manager of the Claims Department, will assume the role of manager on June 1.

1 blank line ——→

2. Two new State Mutual agencies will be opened on July 1. The Chadwick Agency (located in Fort Worth, Texas) will become Agency No. 137, and Graff & Phelps (located in Salem, Oregon) will become Agency No. 138.

2 blank lines ——→

Financial Report for Period Ending March 31, 2004

1 blank line ——→

George Ross distributed copies of the financial report for the first quarter of 2004. He pointed out that overall life insurance sales had increased nearly 8 percent over the same period for last year.

formal meeting minutes (continued)

0.5 inch

1 inch

2

0.5 inch

Claims for the period from January 1 to March 31, 2004, increased 6 percent over the same period for last year. This rise has been assessed to be within the statistical projection based on sales and volume presently carried by the company.

Income from other sources rose 4 percent over the last comparable period. Operational expenses during the first quarter increased 12 percent, mainly because of rising prices due to inflationary factors. Net operations income, consequently, for this period decreased 0.5 percent over the same period for last year.

2 blank lines →

Progress Report, Central Records Microfilm Conversion

1 blank line →

David Haberman reported that a committee had been formed of representatives from those departments that use or store records in the Central Filing Department. These representatives met to discuss which records should be placed on microfilm and which ones should be retained in their present form.

Microfilm readers must be purchased, and the cost of these readers is $738 each. Capital investment in equipment would be reduced considerably by centralizing the viewers in the Central Filing Department; however, additional time would be lost by persons using the equipment if the viewers were isolated there. Louise Brannon moved that a microfilm viewer be placed in those departments that use microfilm records frequently. Viewers should also be placed in the Central Filing Department. The motion was seconded by Robert Miles. The motion was passed 8-2-0.

2 blank lines →

Employment Freeze on Office Personnel

1 blank line →

Phillip Horowitz reported that in February the company established a Document Processing Group to assist all departments with their written communications. Eight clerical employees plus a supervisor were hired to staff this group, which was placed under the direction of the Information Processing Department.

Wayne Nugent moved that a five-person committee be formed to study the work flow generated to the Document Processing Group and the effect of this delegation on the workloads in all affected departments. The committee is to be charged with making recommendations regarding the staff size of the Document Processing Group and the staff size of clerical employees in other departments. The motion was seconded by Fred Wyatt. It was passed 7-2-1.

The meeting was adjourned at 3:45 p.m. by Vern Knudsen. The next meeting of the department managers is scheduled for May 10 at 2 p.m. in Conference Room 621-A.

1 blank line →

Respectfully submitted,

3 blank lines →

Chris Weiser, Secretary

1 blank line →

kc

13

Reports

13–17   Organization and Format of Informal Minutes

The organization and format of informal minutes may vary. The only requisite is that the minutes provide an adequate record of the information needed by the group or organization and that this information be presented in an easy-to-understand fashion. Use the tables feature of your word processing program to simplify the formatting of informal minutes.

informal meeting minutes

COMPUTER APPLICATIONS ADVISORY COMMITTEE
PIERCE COMMUNITY COLLEGE
TUESDAY, APRIL 4, 2004, 2—4 P.M.
BUSINESS 3216

MINUTES

Activity/Discussion	Issues/Relative Information	Resolution
Survey of Classrooms and Laboratories	The faculty familiarized the committee with the equipment presently used for classroom instruction.	Information only.
Language Skills	The faculty described the five departmental courses that meet the requirements for its certificate programs. Two additional courses are required for students completing a degree program in business. The committee emphasized the importance of language skills and how these skills relate to the productive use of a computer.	Information only.
Computer Training: Hardware Issues	The committee discussed the specifications the department should use in ordering replacement computers, printers, and other peripheral components.	**MSP** to replace outdated computers with new computers, ones having these minimum specifications: 2 Ghz, 512 RAM, 40 GB hard drive, network ready.
	A discussion about printer usage in business indicated that laser printers and color printers are used predominantly. Inkjet printers are generally for home use.	**MSP** to replace desktop laser printers with networked laser printers and also acquire a color laser printer.
Computer Training: Software Issues	The committee felt that students should be competent in the use of the Internet and be able to develop and maintain a simple Web site.	**MSP** to offer classes and a certificate program in Web site design and maintenance.
	A discussion about speech-recognition software in the workplace indicated that this tool increased productivity and is being used increasingly in medical offices, legal offices, business, and government.	**MSP** that the department expand its use of voice input into word processing classes.
	A discussion was held concerning the philosophy of upgrading software versions in the business community.	Recommendation: Upgrade software as soon as possible.

informal meeting minutes (continued)

Activity/Discussion	Issues/Relative Information	Resolution
Computer Applications Advisory Committee MINUTES April 4, 2004 Page 2		
	Knowing more than one software program enhances a student s job opportunities. For example, the student has an advantage if he or she has been trained in at least one word processing program as well as in a spreadsheet, presentation, and database program.	Recommendation: Students should be familiar with desktop publishing and graphics software as well.
Job-Related Issues:	Entry-level salaries vary from location to location and from specialization to specialization. Students should be trained to be flexible in their expectations and to study the overall package that an employer offers. In our geographical area entry-level salaries range from $2,000 to $2,450 a month.	Information only.
	Language skills and a knowledge of accounting continue to be requisite skills for entry-level positions and for promotional opportunities. All employers ask for human relations skills at all levels.	Information only.
Recommendations for Future Meetings	Survey technology, software, and business trends by circulating a questionnaire to all advisory committee members prior to the meeting date.	Information only.
Submitted by: Barbara Jacobson, Professor Computer Applications and Administrative Support Department		

Format developed by and used with permission of K. Basil and Associates.

13-18 Meeting Agendas

a. Meeting agendas forecast the items to be considered at a scheduled meeting. Basic information that appears on an agenda includes the following:

(1) Name of committee, name of group, or purpose of meeting

(2) Date, time, and location of meeting

(3) Kind of document—*Meeting Agenda* or *Agenda*

(4) List of items to be considered, along with the names of any persons designated to present the item

b. Use the agenda template or wizard of your word processing program or the following guidelines to create an agenda:

(1) Use a 2-inch top margin and the default left and right margins of your word processing program.

(2) Center and place in all capital letters the name of the committee, the name of the group, or the purpose of the meeting. Double-space.

(3) Center and place in capital and lowercase letters *Meeting Agenda* or *Agenda*. Double-space.

(4) Center and place in capital and lowercase letters the date, time, and location of the meeting. Triple-space.

(5) Number with Arabic numerals the items to be considered at the meeting. Follow the topic with the name of the presenter, if any. Single-space the items and double-space between them.

agenda

2 inches

BENEFITS COMMITTEE MEETING

◄——— 1 blank line

Agenda

◄——— 1 blank line

May 6, 2004, 2 p.m., Room 202

◄——— 2 blank lines

1. Call to order

◄——— 1 blank line

2. Approval of April 3 minutes.............................. Jon Gillman

3. Progress report on investigation of health insurance
   providers for medium-sized companies ....Donna Anderson

4. Unfinished business

   Report to Board of Directors on proposed stock
   option plans .... Barry Logan

   Review of suggestions proposed by subcommittee
   on ergonomics and environment .... Mae Wong

5. New Business

   Projected costs for a comprehensive benefits
   package..Donna Anderson

   Cost sharing of benefits package ....Donna Anderson

6. Announcements

7. Adjournment

modern agenda prepared with a Microsoft Word 2002 Wizard

Agenda

Weekly Sales Meeting

July 20, 2004
3:30 p.m.
Conference Room 16

Meeting called by:	Bill Armstrong
Attendees:	Bill Armstrong, Barbara Berkowitz, Anita Gonzalez, Daniel Ho, Janice Morris, Jerry Phillips, Laura Sullivan, Mark Turbian Charles Urbanek, Tonya Williams, Robert Zimmerman

Agenda topics

1	Approval of Agenda	Bill Armstrong
2	Minutes from July 13 meeting	Janice Morris
3	Announcements	Bill Armstrong
4	Weekly sales summary and report	Bill Armstrong
5	New sales promotions	Anita Gonzalez
6	Discontinued products	Daniel Ho
7	Introduction of new products	Daniel Ho
8	Discussion of problem areas	Bill Armstrong
9	Adjournment	

Special notes:	July 27 meeting room changed to Conference Room 12.

13

Reports

13-19 Itineraries

Itineraries plot out events in a travel plan. Use the tables feature of your word processing program and the following guidelines to prepare an itinerary:

(1) Begin the itinerary with a heading that describes the purpose of travel, the name of the person traveling, and the dates of travel.

(2) Use a table or column format with three columns. Set up *Date, Time,* and *Activity* as columnar headings.

435

(3) Specify all airline flights, hotel reservations, car rental reservations, business appointments, and meal reservations. Include addresses, telephone numbers, and confirmation numbers.

itinerary

	MEETING WITH NationsBank REPRESENTATIVES **Itinerary for Kym Freeman** **March 21–24, 2005**	
Date	**Time**	**Activity**
Monday, March 21	7:11 a.m.	Depart Burbank airport, American Airlines Flight 1502, light breakfast, Seat 23D
	12:13 p.m.	Arrive Dallas-Fort Worth airport
	2:25 p.m.	Depart Dallas-Fort Worth airport, American Airlines Flight 1564, beverage service only, Seat 19D
	5:46 p.m.	Arrive Tampa airport
		Reservations at the Marriott Airport Hotel; hotel located on airport premises; Tel: (813) 879-5151; Confirmation No. 987T385R
Tuesday, March 22	8:00 a.m.	Obtain rental car at Hertz airport booth, Confirmation No. ZBT4314
	10:00 a.m.	Meet with Robin Fielding and Chris Perez, NationsBank downtown offices, 400 North Ashley Drive, Room 450, (813) 555-2236
	12 noon	Lunch with Robin Fielding, Chris Perez, and Michael Morris at the Tampa Club, Barnett Bank Building, 22nd Floor, 437 North Commonwealth Street, (813) 555-8732
	2:30 p.m.– 4:30 p.m.	Conduct orientation session of DLDS computerized loan tracking system for all members of the Loan Department at NationsBank downtown office
	7:30 p.m.	Dinner with Jeff and Janet Spiegel at the Outrigger Steak House, 814 Bayview Drive, (813) 555-7892
Wednesday, March 23	8:30 a.m.– 11:30 a.m.	Conduct training sessions on DLDS computerized loan tracking system for all members of the Loan Department
	1:00 p.m.– 4:00 p.m.	Conduct training sessions on DLDS computerized loan tracking system for all members of the Loan Department
	6:00 p.m.	Dinner with Robin Fielding and Chris Perez at the University Club, 1320 University Avenue, (813) 555-0930
Thursday, March 24	6:57 a.m.	Depart Tampa airport, American Airlines Flight 1573, light breakfast, Seat 20B
	8:42 a.m.	Arrive Dallas-Fort Worth airport
	9:22 a.m.	Depart Dallas-Fort Worth airport, American Airlines Flight 1465, beverage service only, Seat 20B
	10:43 a.m.	Arrive Burbank airport

13-20 Press Releases

Press releases contribute to an organization's visibility and good-will within the community. Important events and occurrences within an organization should be described on a press release and sent to the news media in the area.

Use the press release template of your word processing program and/or the following guidelines to prepare a press release on your word processor:

(1) Label the document in large bold letters *Press Release* or *News Release.*

(2) Specify the date for release or the words *For immediate release.*

(3) Include the name, address, telephone number, and fax number of the contact person.

(4) Provide a headline (centered and in all capital letters) that summarizes the content of the press release.

(5) Begin the opening paragraph with the city, state, and date. State immediately the essence of your news—who, what, when, where, and why. Follow with the details in subsequent paragraphs.

(6) Prepare the press release on letterhead or 8½- by 11-inch white bond paper. Use a 2-inch top margin and the default left and right margins of your word processor. Triple-space before and after the headline and double-space the text.

(7) Number multiple-page press releases with Arabic numbers in the upper right corner beginning with page 2. Center the word *-more-* at the bottom of the first page and all other pages except the last.

(8) Conclude the press release by centering (a double space below the last line) one of the following: *-30-, -# # #-,* or *-end-.*

(9) Place at the left margin a double space below the concluding notation the date (month, day, year) the press release was released.

13

Reports

press release prepared on company letterhead

2 inches

PARAMOUNT TEXTILE COMPANY

170 East Parkland Avenue
Dallas, Texas 75214
(214) 383-5757
(800) 392-5481
Fax: (214) 383-5783

Press Release

From Sandra Dubin
Phone: (214) 383-5726
Fax: (214) 383-5727

For Immediate Release

JEREMY K. COLE NEW PRESIDENT OF PARAMOUNT TEXTILE COMPANY

Dallas, Texas, March 10. The Board of Directors of Paramount Textile Company announced yesterday the appointment of Jeremy K. Cole as its new president, effective June 1.

Mr. Cole, 49, has been with Paramount Textile Company for seven years. He is presently serving as vice president of operations, a position he has held since joining the company in 1997. During this time the company has increased its sales 32 percent and expanded operations into New Mexico, Oklahoma, and Louisiana.

Before joining Paramount, Mr. Cole was vice president of marketing for Dresler Furniture Company, a nationally known furniture manufacturer in South Carolina. Mr. Cole resides with his wife and two children in Dallas.

Mr. Cole will replace William R. Byrd, who will retire on May 31. Mr. Byrd has served as president of Paramount Textile Company for the past nine years.

-30-

March 10, 2004

14

Employment Application Documents

$

Solution Finder for Employment Application Documents

Individuals seeking employment are usually faced with preparing several kinds of documents: a résumé, a letter of application, an application form, reference request letters, and follow-up letters. Candidates may prepare each of these documents or just one or two before obtaining a position.

The initial document prepared by a job seeker is the résumé. A résumé provides the prospective employer with a capsulized visual of an applicant's qualifications. Its chart-like features summarize for the busy executive the attributes a candidate will bring to the position.

Résumés may have various formats and be organized in different ways. Commonly recognized résumé styles are chronological, functional, and a combination of these two. In addition, candidates must take into consideration that their résumés may be subjected to a computer scan before they are ever read by human eyes. Increasingly, too, companies are requiring candidates to submit résumés on-line, and they are providing them with form documents to do so.

Today's job seekers need to prepare their résumés in two formats— one in a traditional format and another suitable for on-line transmission and assessment by an automated applicant tracking system.

The Chronological Résumé

14-1 Information to Include in the Chronological Résumé

The résumé is often the only document an employer will use to screen individuals for an interview; therefore, it must succinctly describe your abilities and present you in a favorable light. The résumé style favored by most employers is the *chronological résumé* because it is easy to follow and assess. Guidelines for preparing this résumé style follow:

(1) Select carefully the information you include in your résumé so that the information can be presented on a single page. Only in those situations where an applicant has considerable experience or other qualifications related specifically to a position should the résumé exceed one page.

(2) Incorporate facts about your education, employment background, abilities, achievements, and awards. Besides the usual name, address, and telephone number, the opening information in a résumé should also designate an employment or career objective. Optional categories include college extracurricular activities, professional memberships, willingness to relocate, and references. Omit from the résumé personal statistics (age, height, weight, gender), marital

14

Employment

status, race, religion, ethnicity, birthplace, high school grades and activities, church responsibilities, hobbies, and interests—unless they relate specifically to the job for which you are applying.

(3) Begin your résumé with a main heading (name, address, telephone number, cell telephone number [if applicable], fax number [if applicable], and E-mail address [if applicable]) followed by your career objective. Whether you begin the presentation of your credentials with a profile of your educational history and performance, special skills and aptitudes, or work experience depends upon where your greatest strengths lie. Launch the display of your abilities with the category that is most likely to get you the job. Follow up with other categories in the order of their importance to the career objective stated initially. Use text headings such as the following for the categories in your résumé:

Objective or *Career Objective*

Education, Educational Background, Academic Preparation, or *Professional Training*

Employment, Experience, or *Employment Experience*

Skills and Abilities

Activities; *Honors and Awards*; or *Honors, Awards, and Activities*

References

14-2 Main Heading

The main heading opens the résumé and displays your name, address, and telephone number. If you have a cell telephone number, a fax number, and/or an E-mail address, include these also. Follow these guidelines for the main heading:

(1) Set up the main heading so that a prospective employer can easily spot your name and where to reach you for an interview.

(2) Include the addresses and telephone numbers for your *temporary* and *permanent* residences if you have both a college and a home residence. If you know an ending date for your temporary residence, indicate it in the heading also.

main heading showing single residence

Morgan D. Schultz
2430 Brockton Drive
Upper Marlboro, Maryland 20772
(301) 555-4374
Cell: (301) 368-5947

main heading showing temporary and permanent residences

Taylor R. Garvey

Temporary Residence:	Permanent Residence:
830 Willow Street, Apt. 6	5460 Roundtree Circle
Columbia, South Carolina 29207	Atlanta, Georgia 30315
(803) 555-7863	(404) 555-9066

14-3 Career or Employment Objective

a. Include in your résumé a career or employment objective so that prospective employers know the kind of position you are seeking. Prepare an objective related to a specific job or one that would make you employable in a number of job categories, depending upon your qualifications and interests.

specific employment objective

> Objective: To obtain a position as a legal office trainee in a medium-size legal office

general employment objective

> *Career Objective*
>
> To begin a career in marketing with exposure to retail sales, customer relations, market research, and advertising. Long-range goal is to become a department manager in a large metropolitan-area department store.

b. Prepare separate résumés if you have more than one employment area in which you wish to apply. Write the career objective to pertain to each of the positions in which you are interested, and tailor the other sections to emphasize the position stated in your objective.

14-4 Educational History and Performance

Résumés furnish the opportunity to provide prospective employers with information substantiating an applicant's academic preparation to perform the job for which he or she is applying. Use these guidelines to present your academic qualifications in the chronological résumé:

(1) Begin this section with the college, university, or other postsecondary institution you attended most recently. Include the name and location of the institution, school or department within the institution, major

14

Employment

and minor fields of study, degrees or diplomas received, and dates of attendance. If you expect to earn a degree, list the degree and include the expected date or a statement such as *to be granted May 2006.*

(2) Provide your grade-point average within this section, but only if it reflects favorably upon you. You may wish to provide your overall grade-point average and/or a grade-point average in your major courses of study. Include the scale on which the grade-point average is based—e.g., 3.65/4.00.

(3) Avoid listings of courses completed. Furnish only those course names and other educational experiences that are directly related to performing successfully in the desired position.

(4) List all collegiate or other postsecondary institutions attended. Include your high school education only if your postsecondary education has not resulted in a degree, an anticipated degree, a diploma, or a certificate.

example of educational background entry in a résumé

Education

- University of Southern California, Los Angeles, Graduate School of Business Administration, Master of Science Degree in Management of Human Resources to be awarded May 2006, 3.9/4.0 grade-point average

  Courses in management of human resources, management-union relations, contract negotiations, and international resource development

- University of Montana, Missoula, Montana, College of Engineering, Bachelor of Science in Mechanical Engineering, June 2002, 3.2/4.0 grade-point average

14-5 Work Experience

Reportings of successful work experiences tell prospective employers that applicants have been productive in the work environment. This section gives you an opportunity to show that you respond positively to supervision, have good work habits, and work well with others.

a. If your work experience is limited, include all the positions you have held—even though they do not relate to the position for which you are applying. They indicate to the employer that you are familiar with the work world and have performed successfully in its environment.

b. If your work experience is vast and varied, include only those positions that are most recent and/or are related to the job for which you are applying.

c. In the chronological résumé, list your work experience in reverse chronological order, that is, your most recent employment first. Provide the following information for each position listed:

(1) *Employer's or company's name and address.* Include only the city and state for the address.

(2) *Dates of employment.* State the month and year you began work and the month and year you terminated. You need not state a reason for leaving or provide salary information.

(3) *Job title.* Supply only the title of the most important or the last position held before leaving the employer.

(4) *Significant duties, activities, accomplishments, and promotions.* Use parallel construction and action verbs to describe succinctly and concretely the activities involved in your employment. Use action verbs such as *composed, conducted, created, designed, initiated, maintained, organized, prepared,* and *upgraded.* For previous employment activities, use the past tense; for ongoing employment activities, use the present tense. As much as possible select those responsibilities and accomplishments that feature your attributes for the position you are seeking.

d. In cases of part-time employment, indicate the part-time status in parentheses after the dates of employment. No notation is necessary for positions held as a full-time employee.

example of work experience entry in a résumé

Work Experience

Freestone Industries, Inc., Portland, Oregon, *Payroll Accountant*, July 2003–present
    Enter and maintain payroll records using a computerized payroll system
    Issue weekly and monthly payroll checks
    Complete payroll and tax reports for local, state, and federal agencies
    Submit withholding and other payroll taxes

Ritter's Clothing Emporium, Eugene, Oregon, *Bookkeeper-Accountant*,
September 2001–March 2003 (part-time)
    Entered daily sales receipts and expense disbursements
    Prepared checks for signature
    Maintained payroll records

Barton-Hagan Ice Cream Parlor, Eugene, Oregon, *Service Representative*,
September 2000–August 2001 (part-time)
    Served and packed ice cream
    Cashiered customer purchases

14

Employment

14-6 Skills and Abilities

a. Your educational background and work experience may not show all the traits and abilities that relate to the job you are seeking. Qualities that fall into the skills and abilities category include knowledge of specific computer programs or the ability to speak a foreign language. In some cases extensive travel in another country or knowledge pertaining to another culture might prove of value. Include here only those skills and abilities that pertain to your job objective. Omit this section in your chronological résumé if the information can be incorporated into another part.

b. Follow these guidelines to list your skills and abilities:

(1) Begin, if possible, each item in the listing with an action verb stated in the present tense.

(2) Use parallel construction to list your special abilities.

example of skills and abilities entry in a résumé

> **Skills and Abilities**
>
> Use proficiently the following computer application programs: Microsoft Word, Excel, PowerPoint, Access, (all MOUS Expert Certified); Microsoft Outlook and FrontPage; Adobe Photoshop; Macromedia Dreamweaver; and Corel WordPerfect
>
> Access and navigate the Internet to retrieve needed information
>
> Speak and write Spanish fluently

14-7 Awards, Honors, and Activities

a. If you have at least three awards and honors and also at least three collegiate extracurricular activities, you may wish to show these items in two categories—*Honors and Awards* and *Activities*.

b. If your career experiences are more important than your education in obtaining the desired position, this category may well be replaced by a listing of your activities in professional and community organizations.

c. Use these guidelines to present any activities, honors, or awards in the chronological résumé:

(1) Begin with the most recent occurrence.

(2) List the names of the honors and awards and the dates they were earned or received.

(3) List the name of the organization, any offices held, and the dates of participation for each activity.

example of honors, awards, and activities entry in a résumé

> **Honors, Awards, and Activities**
>
> *The Wall Street Journal* scholarship award for academic excellence, May 2005
>
> Dean's Honor Roll, Spring 2004, Fall 2004, and Spring 2005 semesters
>
> Fenton College Student Council, Associated Student Body Representative, Business Department, Fall 2004 and Spring 2005 semesters
>
> Alpha Gamma Sigma, honor society, Spring 2004, Fall 2004, and Spring 2005 semesters
>
> Phi Beta Lambda, business fraternity, Fall 2003–Present
> • Treasurer, Spring 2004 semester
> • Vice President, Fall 2004 semester
> • President, Spring 2005 semester

chronological résumé

LORRAINE V. HOOVER

Temporary Address:
3460 S.W. 16th Street, #12
Gainesville, FL 32608
(904) 555-3250, Cell: (904) 387-4470

Permanent Address:
7520 Beachway Drive
Tampa, FL 33609
(813) 555-2840

Objective
To begin a career in accounting with immediate objective to gain experience for certification as a Certified Public Accountant

Education

Master of Accounting (3/2 program)	**May 2003**
Bachelor of Science in Accounting	**May 2002**

Fisher School of Accounting
University of Florida, Gainesville, Florida
GPA 3.53/4.0 (accounting), 3.68/4.0 (overall)

Honors

Beta Alpha Psi	Spring 2001–present
Becker CPA Review Scholarship	Spring 2001
Golden Key Honor Society	Spring 2001
Dean's List	Summer 2000–present
President's Honor Roll	Spring 2000

Activities

Beta Alpha Psi	
Reporting Secretary	Spring 2001–present
Fisher School of Accounting Council	
Vice President	Spring 2001–Spring 2002
Audit Team	Spring 2001
Student Representative to Programs Board	Spring 2001
Class Representative	Fall 2000–Spring 2001
Becker CPA Review	
Student Representative	May 2001–present
Florida Accounting Association	Fall 2001–present
American Marketing Association	
Promotion Cochair	Fall 2000

Work Experience

Alpert, Josey and Grilli, P.A., Tampa, Florida	Summer 1999
Assistant Bookkeeper	

  • Reconciled monthly bank statements and daily deposits
  • Recorded and updated billable time for legal fees
  • Prepared clients' monthly bills
  • Revised clients' financial files

Zudar's Cafe, Server, Tampa, Florida	Summer 1998
Tampa Eye Clinic, Tampa, Florida	August 1997–May 1998
Doctor's Assistant	

  • Updated patients' files
  • Prepared patients for examination

Computer Knowledge
Excel, Access, Microsoft Word, Lotus 1-2-3, WordPerfect

References

Peter Grilli	Dr. Lewis Lauring
Alpert, Josey and Grilli, P.A.	Tampa Eye Clinic
100 Ashley Drive South	3000 Dr. Martin Luther King Jr. West
Tampa, Florida 33601	Tampa, Florida 33601
(813) 555-4131	(813) 555-2020

14-8 References

a. Including references in the chronological résumé is optional. The statement *References furnished upon request* is not necessary if you decide not to furnish references on the résumé itself. Prospective employers assume that at the point of interview you will furnish them from three to five former professors and/or employers who are able to provide firsthand information about you.

b. Select your references carefully. A bad reference is worse than no reference at all. Before giving the name of a reference, check with that person to ensure that he or she is agreeable to giving you a recommendation. Give each reference a copy of your résumé.

c. Use the following guidelines for including references in your résumé:

(1) Limit the number of references to two or three.

(2) Provide the name and title of the individual, the organizational name, the address, and the telephone number for each reference cited.

Examples of references are shown in the chronological résumé on page 447. Examples of chronological résumés are shown below and on page 447.

chronological résumé

DANIEL HO

6201 Rathburn Avenue • Northridge, California 91325 • (818) 555-9770

Objective

To obtain a responsible and challenging position as an administrative assistant where my education and work experience will be of value

Education

Los Angeles Pierce College
Woodland Hills, California
Certificate in Office Administration, General Administrative   May 2003
Associate in Arts degree, Quality Control Engineering   June 2000
Associate in Arts degree, Landscape Maintenance   June 1998

Work Experience

Los Angeles Pierce College   August 2000–
Woodland Hills, California   Present
Computer Laboratory Assistant   (part-time)
    Assist students with computer assignments
    Provide instructional support during evening classes
    Maintain equipment in working order

Nordskog Industries, Inc.   July 1996–
Van Nuys, California   September 2000
CNC Operator
    Assembled and operated CNC (Computerized Numerical
       Control) machine
    Checked and modified CNC program
    Assembled and bonded parts for commercial airplane galleys

Computer Skills

Training in the following computer programs emphasizing the production of documents typically found in business and office applications:
    Microsoft Word for Windows, Excel, Access, PowerPoint, QuickBooks,
    Outlook, PageMaker, FrontPage, Dragon NaturallySpeaking
Ability to access Internet resources and maintain Web sites
Ability to type 60 wpm

The Functional Résumé

14-9 Preparation of the Functional Résumé

The functional résumé, shown on page 450, focuses on an applicant's skills, abilities, and accomplishments. Rather than beginning with an education or employment history, the functional résumé presents competencies and accomplishments in special categories.

a. You may wish to use a functional résumé if you have changed jobs frequently or if there are gaps in your employment history. Applicants with little employment experience also find this form of résumé appealing.

b. Although the functional résumé emphasizes abilities, it should also include information about a candidate's education; previous employment; and any pertinent honors, activities, and affiliations. Use the following guidelines to prepare a functional résumé:

(1) Begin with a main heading that displays your name, address, and telephone number. If you have a cell telephone number, a fax number, and/or an E-mail address, include these also. Follow the main heading with your employment objective.

(2) Continue the functional résumé with a listing of your significant abilities, skills, activities, and accomplishments. As much as possible select items that feature your attributes for the position you are seeking. Group the items into meaningful categories, and use a descriptive heading for each category.

(3) Use parallel construction and action verbs to describe succinctly and concretely the items in your listing. Use action verbs such as *assisted, compiled, coordinated, developed, edited, established, managed, planned,* and *translated*. For previous accomplishments, use the past tense; for present skills and abilities, use the present tense.

(4) Include in the functional résumé a history of your academic preparation (see Section 14-4) and a brief account of your previous employment (see Section 14-5).

(5) Conclude the functional résumé with a listing of any awards, extracurricular activities, or professional affiliations (see Section 14-7).

14
Employment

functional résumé

Rocio Martinez

3221 Nordhoff Street • Northridge, California 91326 • (818) 555-6497 • rmart83@earthlink.net

OBJECTIVE
Obtain a secretarial or an administrative assistant position with opportunity for advancement

SKILLS AND ABILITIES
- *Operate proficiently the following software programs:*
  Microsoft Word for Windows, Excel, Access, FileMaker Pro, PowerPoint, Adobe Photoshop, Windows XP and 2000
- Transcribe and proofread business documents accurately
- Compose and prepare routine correspondence
- Perform computerized accounting functions using QuickBooks
- Use the Internet to obtain information
- Speak and write English and Spanish fluently
- Key 65 words a minute

ACCOMPLISHMENTS
- Trained and supervised student workers
- Performed database entries using FileMaker Pro on a Macintosh computer and Microsoft Access on a personal computer
- Reorganized instructional media for easier access and availability to faculty
- Maintained audio and video equipment
- Filed invoices and catalogs
- Answered telephone inquiries and took reservations for equipment loans
- Duplicated audiocassettes for students

EDUCATION
Los Angeles Pierce College, Woodland Hills, California. Associate in Arts degree, May 2003, Office Administration–General Administrative. Overall GPA 3.9/4.0.

EXPERIENCE
Instructional Media Center, Los Angeles Pierce College, Woodland Hills, California. August 2001 to present (part-time).

HONORS AND AWARDS
- Certificate of Recognition from Alpha Gamma Sigma, the scholastic honor society, for "Outstanding Scholarship and Placement" on the Dean's List each semester
- Frances M. Heinze Memorial Scholarship for outstanding scholastic achievement, May 2002
- Teresa A. Caruana Memorial Award for overall outstanding achievement, May 2003
- Office Administration Department, Highest GPA Award, May 2003

The Combination Résumé

14-10 **Preparation of the Combination Résumé**

The combination résumé, shown on page 452, blends the strongest qualities of the chronological and functional résumés.

a. For candidates who are recent graduates but have some full-time experience, the combination résumé offers the opportunity to highlight both their competencies and their experience.

b. The combination résumé, like the functional résumé, focuses on an applicant's abilities, skills, activities, and accomplishments. It differs from the functional résumé in that the combination résumé provides a complete employment history. Use the following guidelines to prepare a combination résumé:

(1) Begin with a main heading that displays your name, address, and telephone number. If you have a cell telephone number, a fax number, and/or an E-mail address, include these also. Follow the main heading with your employment objective.

(2) Continue the combination résumé with a listing of your significant abilities, skills, activities, and accomplishments. As much as possible select items that feature your attributes for the position you are seeking. Group the items into meaningful categories, and use a descriptive heading for each category.

(3) Use parallel construction and action verbs to describe succinctly and concretely the items in your listing. Use action verbs such as *assisted, compiled, coordinated, developed, edited, established, managed, planned*, and *translated*. For previous accomplishments, use the past tense; for present skills and abilities, use the present tense.

(4) Include in the combination résumé a history of your academic preparation (see Section 14-4) and your previous employment (see Section 14-5). Place first the category that is more likely to qualify you for the job for which you are applying.

(5) Conclude the combination résumé with a listing of any awards, extracurricular activities, or professional affiliations (see Section 14-7).

14

Employment

combination résumé

MARLENE CAPPETTO

6240 Winnetka Avenue • Encino, CA 91371 • (818) 555-4210 • mcappetto213@aol.com

EMPLOYMENT OBJECTIVE	To obtain a paralegal position offering challenge, responsibility, and personal growth
CAPABILITIES AND SKILLS	• Draft complaints/answers • Compose interrogatories/answers • Prepare motions • Conduct legal research • Access and use WESTLAW • Compose and prepare business correspondence • Operate proficiently WordPerfect, Microsoft Word, Excel, Quicken, and Access • Type 70 words per minute • Operate the numeric 10-key pad proficiently • Speak and write English and Spanish fluently
EDUCATION	**University of California, Los Angeles, Extension, Attorney Assistant Training Program**, Certificate in Litigation, November 2001. This program is offered in cooperation with the UCLA School of Law and is approved by the American Bar Association. **Los Angeles Pierce College**, Woodland Hills, Associate in Arts degree, Office Administration—Word Processing, May 1998
EXPERIENCE July 2001–Present	**Litigation Assistant, O'Melveny & Myers, Los Angeles** Perform automated document management on multiple projects Review documents and prepare information for discovery Investigate facts and case law
February 2001– July 2001 (part-time)	**Legal Secretary, Law Offices of Duane Lübbe, Encino** Composed and prepared business correspondence using WordPerfect Managed documents for personal injury cases Transcribed dictation Maintained business calendars
HONORS	Dean's Honor List, 1998–2001 The National Dean's List Award, 2000–2001 Teresa A. Caruana Memorial Award, May 2001 2,000 Notable American Women Award
AFFILIATIONS	Phi Theta Kappa International Honor Society UCLA Extension Attorney Assistant Alumni Association Los Angeles Paralegal Association National Association for Female Executives National Association of Legal Assistants

---

Conventional Résumé Formats

14-11 Formats for the Résumé

The appearance of your résumé creates a first impression, the first impression a prospective employer forms of you. If the résumé is well designed and well written, it is more likely to be read and to lead to an interview. Use the following guidelines to prepare your résumé:

(1) Use 20- or 24-pound high-quality white paper to prepare your résumé. Ensure that the print quality is high density, equal to that of a laser printer.

(2) Strive for optimal top, bottom, left, and right margins—1 inch. Use no less than 0.75 inch for each of these margins.

(3) Select a font with a typeface that is easy to read. Use no smaller than an 11-point font, and do not condense the line spacing so that the copy becomes difficult to read.

(4) Use headings for each of your major categories. Differentiate through size and/or attribute (bold and/or italic) these text headings from the regular text. Use regular second-degree text headings as shown in Section 13-8a and the example résumés on pages 448 and 458–459 or parallel headings as shown in the example résumés on pages 447, 450, and 452.

(5) Use font attributes (bold, italic, bold italic, all capital letters, small capitals) to make your résumé more attractive and easily comprehensible. Be careful, though, not to overuse these attributes and to apply them consistently for the same features.

(6) Single-space the items listed within each section, but double-space between the items. Use parallel construction for all entries within a section, and place a period only at the end of complete sentences. Use no punctuation mark to conclude incomplete word groups unless they are followed by complete sentences or another word group.

Automated Applicant Tracking Systems

14-12 Preparation for Computerized Résumé Searches

a. Large companies are increasingly relying on automated applicant tracking systems to screen candidates. These computers are not programmed to assess personal skills, initiative, motivation, drive, attitude, disposition, or other such attributes. Instead, they look for the marketable skills possessed by a candidate. Automated applicant tracking systems generally operate in the following way:

(1) On-line résumés are loaded directly into the tracking system. A paper résumé is scanned, and its scanned image is sent to a computer equipped with optical character recognition (OCR) software. Here the computer quickly reads, classifies, and stores each résumé.

(2) When a job opening occurs, the employer tells the tracking system the keywords for the position. The computer looks for keywords (nouns that match the candidates' education, experience, skills, abilities, and knowledge with the job requirements).

(3) Applicants' résumés are selected and ranked according to the number of keywords appearing in the résumé. Only applicants whose résumés contain the keywords are candidates for the interview. These

14

Employment

résumés are then subjected to human scrutiny for a decision as to whether the applicant will be invited for an interview.

(4) Automated applicant tracking systems generate response letters to prospective job candidates—interview offers, acknowledgments, and rejections. Most résumés are stored for a stipulated time before they are purged from the system.

b. **Keywords are the core of automated applicant tracking systems. Computers assess what a person can** *do*. **They look for substantiated facts, definitive quantities, and concrete nouns that describe specific, identifiable skills and accomplishments.**

Keywords *differ* **for each job title and each industry. Some companies will use keywords for the specific job opening and other keywords to assess familiarity with terms in the industry. Consider the following examples:**

(1) A company looking for a tax accountant with at least two years' experience with a Big 4 accounting firm might search for the following keywords:

B.A. in Accounting	public accounting
B.S. in Accounting	Excel
Masters of Accounting	computer skills
Masters of Tax Law	communication skills
CPA	years experience
auditing	income tax
tax accounting	Deloitte Touche Tohmatsu
tax law	Ernst & Young
corporate tax	Price WaterhouseCoopers
tax return preparation	KPMG

(2) A major pharmaceutical company posted the following job opening for an "Admin Coordinator II/III, Business Law Group" (July 5, 2002) at its Web site, informing applicants that their résumés would be processed using an "electronic résumé database system":

Works under supervision of Associate Manager, Law Administration, providing administrative support to attorneys and paralegals in the area of corporate law and patent prosecution and litigation. Must possess executive level skills and the ability to interface effectively with internal and external contacts. The ability to deal with sensitive and confidential information with diplomacy and discretion is required, as well as a high degree of accuracy and attention to detail. Typical duties include preparation of contracts, foreign and domestic patent prosecution docket control and assisting with various aspects of filing patent applications, including preparation and coordination of formality documents. Responsibilities include managing calendars with the

ability to use discretion in prioritizing schedules;
making travel arrangements; answering phones and making
proper referrals; processing mail; creating and
maintaining files and databases; and composing routine
correspondence and reports. Prepare and create documents;
i.e. presentations. Provide support in the completion of
projects. Requirements include 3 to 5 years of related
experience in legal and administrative functions in
support of senior legal staff and or executive staff or
equivalent experience. Experience in the area of
intellectual property is preferred. Additional requirements include computer literacy, word processing,
presentation design, spreadsheets and database software
skills. Must demonstrate ability to prioritize and meet
deadlines. Effective written and verbal communication
skills. Independently understand, follow and implement
complex instructions. Associate Degree or equivalent.

Based on the job description provided, an applicant might assume that the employer would suggest the following keywords for the automated applicant tracking system:

Excel	travel coordination
MS Word	legal coordination
PowerPoint	correspondence
corporate law	spreadsheet
litigation	database
associate degree	administrative experience
calendaring	word processing
Outlook	phone
presentations	mail

Additional industry-specific keywords this employer may look for include these:

biology	health industry
medical terminology	research
chemistry	pharmaceutical
life science	anatomy

c. **Check with prospective employers to see if your résumé will be evaluated by an automated applicant tracking system. If so, devise a list of keywords from your qualifications that you think may be used by the employer to select people for the position in which you are interested.**

After the personal information (name, address, and telephone number) in your résumé, begin your listing of qualifications with a keyword summary. Use the following guidelines to prepare this section of your résumé:

14

Employment

(1) Label the section *Keyword Summary*, *Keywords*, or *Keyword Profile*. Use no font attributes such as boldface, italics, or underlining.

(2) Use nouns to feature what you can do or what you have accomplished. Follow each keyword with a period, and list the keywords horizontally across the page.

(3) Begin the listing with the most important qualifications, and follow these keywords with those of lesser significance.

(4) Use variants of the keywords in the main text of your résumé to increase your chances of matching the keyword images of the optical character reading (OCR) software; for example, substitute *Associate Degree* or *Associate in Arts* for *A.A.*, *spreadsheet* for *Excel*, or *administrative assistant* for s*ecretary*.

> Keyword Profile
>
> Microsoft Word. Excel. PowerPoint. Access. Outlook. Internet. E-mail. 3 years' general secretarial experience. Office Administration. Administrative support. A.A. degree. Associate degree. Help Desk. Typing. Filing. Agendas. Meeting minutes. Itineraries. Phones. Scheduling. Mail. Correspondence. Well organized. Good written and oral communication skills. Team-oriented.

d. **Paper résumés submitted to automated applicant tracking systems are scanned and forwarded to computers with optical character reading software (OCR) for reading. Examples of résumés prepared for scanning are shown on pages 457 and 458–459. So that your résumé is read correctly, you need to ensure it meets the following criteria:**

(1) Use black print equal to the quality of a laser or an inkjet printer on 24-pound, 8½- by 11-inch high-quality smooth-surfaced white paper.

(2) Use standard fonts (10 to 14 points in size) in which none of the characters touch each other (Arial, Univers, Helvetica, New Century Schoolbook), and avoid attributes such as underscores, italics, or shadows that are hard for optical scanning equipment to read. Use boldface and/or all capital letters for section headings and emphasis, as long as letters don't touch each other.

(3) Keep your résumé free from graphics, boxed text, and shading; you may use solid bullets or asterisks for a listing, as long as you leave a space after them. Confine your résumé to a single-column format; multiple columns often run together in translations by OCR software.

(4) Place your name on the first line of the résumé. Following lines should include your complete address and telephone number. Include also your cell telephone number, fax number, and E-mail address, if applicable.

(5) Begin your description of qualifications with a keyword summary (nouns used by the computer to match candidates' traits with job requirements).

(6) Continue to employ keywords to describe specifically what you can do in relation to the job for which you are applying. Examples

are (1) perform bookkeeping and accounting functions such as payroll, accounts receivable, and accounts payable; (2) use computer programs such as Microsoft Word, Excel, PowerPoint, Outlook, and Access; (3) work in retail sales and customer relations; and (4) prepare, edit, and proofread reports.

(7) Avoid using abbreviations; use them only if they are common to your profession or after you have spelled them out in full.

(8) Send the résumé in a large envelope, and be sure to include a cover letter. Do not fold or staple the pages; fasten them with a paper clip.

résumé prepared for an automated applicant tracking system

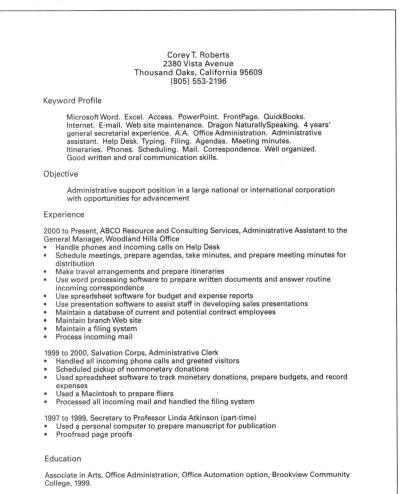

Corey T. Roberts
2380 Vista Avenue
Thousand Oaks, California 95609
(805) 553-2196

Keyword Profile

Microsoft Word. Excel. Access. PowerPoint. FrontPage. QuickBooks. Internet. E-mail. Web site maintenance. Dragon NaturallySpeaking. 4 years' general secretarial experience. A.A. Office Administration. Administrative assistant. Help Desk. Typing. Filing. Agendas. Meeting minutes. Itineraries. Phones. Scheduling. Mail. Correspondence. Well organized. Good written and oral communication skills.

Objective

Administrative support position in a large national or international corporation with opportunities for advancement

Experience

2000 to Present, ABCO Resource and Consulting Services, Administrative Assistant to the General Manager, Woodland Hills Office
- Handle phones and incoming calls on Help Desk
- Schedule meetings, prepare agendas, take minutes, and prepare meeting minutes for distribution
- Make travel arrangements and prepare itineraries
- Use word processing software to prepare written documents and answer routine incoming correspondence
- Use spreadsheet software for budget and expense reports
- Use presentation software to assist staff in developing sales presentations
- Maintain a database of current and potential contract employees
- Maintain branch Web site
- Maintain a filing system
- Process incoming mail

1999 to 2000, Salvation Corps, Administrative Clerk
- Handled all incoming phone calls and greeted visitors
- Scheduled pickup of nonmonetary donations
- Used spreadsheet software to track monetary donations, prepare budgets, and record expenses
- Used a Macintosh to prepare fliers
- Processed all incoming mail and handled the filing system

1997 to 1999, Secretary to Professor Linda Atkinson (part-time)
- Used a personal computer to prepare manuscript for publication
- Proofread page proofs

Education

Associate in Arts, Office Administration, Office Automation option, Brookview Community College, 1999.

High school diploma, Wilson High School, 1996.

two-page résumé—page 1

Shannon Cates

4780 Angus Avenue   Clarkston, MI 48348   (248) 555-8870

Objective

To work in sales or marketing within the automotive industry.

Summary of Qualifications

Background includes practical experience and education, which have provided solid working knowledge of these key areas:

> Sales...new business development...direct/indirect sales...wholesaler responsibility...local marketing and advertising...representative training... new product-line introductions...account management...account service... product support...presentation skills

Relevant Experience

1994–2000   Account Manager, Kraft Foods, Fresno, California
1987–1994   Sales Representative, Kraft Foods, Fresno, California

Managed business for Kraft Foods at wholesale level. Managed Fleming Foods, Fresno, and Market Wholesale, Fresno, for Kraft Foods. Duties and responsibilities:
- Managed from $12 million to $20 million in food sales annually.
- Maintained inventory levels of more than 400 items for wholesalers that served more than 700 grocery stores throughout Central Valley of California.
- Supervised and facilitated all levels of paperwork; that is, invoicing, pricing, billing, terms, price protection, advertising, and promotional dollars.
- Managed $80,000–$100,000 of advertising dollars per year for local marketing at the retail level to increase sales through advertising, new product introductions, presentations, merchandising, and distribution activities.
- Developed unique sales presentations and strategies for selling direct shipments to independent chain stores.
- Assisted independent retail stores with shelf layout of merchandise, and instructed store personnel on consumer shopping and buying patterns.

Accomplishments

- 1994 winner of Award of Excellence for Western Region, most prestigious award.
- 1993 candidate for Award of Excellence.
- Met or exceeded sales target every year since employed.
- Wrote custom computer programs (early 1990s) that increased sales, reduced labor, and provided efficient shipment/delivery system for direct shipments.
- Established and expanded new accounts, which increased direct volume at retail level by 190 percent since 1991.
- Secured extensive competitive information for corporate research and knowledge.

2 page résumé—page 2

Shannon Cates Résumé   Page 2

- Cultivated and maintained effective business relationships while increasing trade and brand franchises over a long-term basis.
- Implemented many creative local-marketing events; for example, sold world's largest cereal display three years in a row. Submitted to *Guinness Book of World Records* (1992–1994).
- Coordinated local Hispanic events, for example, Cinco de Mayo celebration.
- Worked closely with corporate marketing to launch successful air show sponsorship at Lemoore Naval Air Force Base.
- Proficient with computer application programs: Excel, Microsoft Word, PowerPoint, and Access.

Education

Masters of Business Administration—2000
Emphasis: International Marketing
California State University, Fresno
GPA 3.5/4.0

Bachelor of Science—1987
Emphasis: Marketing
California State University, Humboldt
GPA 3.5/4.0

On-Line Career Resources

The Internet is increasingly playing a more dominant role in the job-seeking process. On-line career centers (1) post job openings in organizations throughout the United States, (2) allow applicants to apply for openings on-line, and (3) permit job-seeking candidates to post résumés. Many of these career sites also offer suggestions for preparing résumés and provide general career advice.

Most major corporations that maintain Web sites have established a career center within their site. Here they list job openings within their organization and provide opportunities for interested candidates to submit their résumés on-line.

14-13 Locating Career Centers on the Internet

The Internet furnishes access to a large variety of career centers and services. Career centers usually provide information about employers, post employment opportunities, assist candidates in placing their résumés on-line, and grant employers access to candidates' résumés. Many of these career centers are free of charge to the prospective employee and employer, but others charge the employer or both the employer and employee. Follow these guidelines to locate various career centers on the Internet:

(1) Use a search site (AltaVista, Excite, etc.) to locate a listing of career centers and services for your area of interest and expertise—business, health services, law, entertainment, computing, etc.

14

Employment

(2) Explore a number of the career centers and services your search produces to determine the one or ones suitable for you. Consider job classifications, location of opportunities, kinds of applicants targeted, kinds of employers, scope of coverage, and cost (if any). You may also wish to visit the following Web site that contains links to a large number of career centers and services on the Internet:

Careers.org. <http://www.careers.org/>. This site provides expert job advice, career articles, and nearly 4,000 links organized by topic—including links to Web sites with a significant number of job listings.

(3) Visit well-known, popular career centers that post job openings and candidates' résumés. Some of these are listed here:

America's Job Bank. <http://www.ajb.org>. *America's Job Bank* is the largest and busiest job market on the Internet, providing labor exchange service to employers and job seekers. It is operated under the jurisdiction of the U.S. Department of Labor in partnership with the states and private sector organizations. *America's Job Bank* lists more than 1 million jobs and posts résumés. No fee; registration required for résumé posting.

CareerBuilder. <http://www.careerbuilder.com>. This Web site posts over 400,000 jobs and provides a template for candidates to submit information for on-line résumé posting. In addition, *CareerBuilder* provides a career resource center for job seekers, a newsletter, and links to various departments that provide career advice. This Web site strives to be a valuable source to both the employer and the job seeker. See page 461 to view its template for on-line résumé posting. No fee; registration required for résumé posting.

HotJobs. <http://www.hotjobs.com>. This site is a *Yahoo!* service and provides a nationwide listing of job openings. Categories are refined by state, city, general field, selection of subfields, and keywords. Job seekers may also post their résumé. No fee; registration required for résumé posting.

Monster. <http://www.monster.com>. This is one of the most popular Web sites for job seekers. *Monster* offers a variety of hypertext links to job-search resources and connections to job listings. Maintains separate sites for special fields: Admin/Support, Technology, Healthcare, Finance, Sales, Retail, Legal, Human Resources, and Senior Executives. The Monster Network has more than 1 million job postings and provides a Career Center. No fee; registration required for résumé posting.

MonsterTRAK. <http://www.monstertrak.com/>. *MonsterTRAK* has job listings for full-time jobs, part-time jobs, temporary jobs, and internships. This site provides job search tips, career forums, and a career contact network. Students and alumni from registered colleges and universities may view job listings posted and/or post résumés by obtaining a password from their college or university. No fee; registration required.

TrueCareers. <http://www.truecareers.com>. *TrueCareers* connects entry-level job seekers with employers who want qualified applicants. This Web site is designed to help students and recent college graduates find internships, part-time jobs, or career positions. No fee; registration required.

CareerBuilder on-line résumé template

Step 1 of 2
1. Add your resume.   2. Wrap it up.

Registered users must first login to add a resume. Click here to login.

About You

First Name:		Last Name:	
Email address:		Password:	
Retype email address:		Retype password:	

City List City: ____   State/Prov/Country: ____
Zip: ____   Phone: ____

Job Details

Job Title: ____   What job are you looking for?

Target Pay: $____ Per ○ Year ○ Hour   This value is not displayed to other users. It is only used for searching within salary ranges.

Categories:
Select up to 5 that apply to the job you are looking for. Select more than 1 by holding down the "Ctrl" key while you click. (Mac users: use the "Command" key.)

Accounting
Activism
Administration
Advertising
Aerospace
Agriculture
Air Conditioning
Airlines

Job Type: Full Time
Employment Type: Employee
Degree: None
Experience: Less Than 1 Year
Acceptable Travel: Negligible

Where You Wish To Work

City List   City: ____   Acceptable Relocation: Local Area

State/Province/Country: ____

Citizenship: ☐ I am authorized to work in this country
Security: ☐ I have a government security clearance

Contact Information

Show My:
☑ Name
☑ Phone Number
☑ Email Address

These boxes control the display of your contact information. To conceal your identity while you look for a job, uncheck all of these boxes. Interested users will still be able to contact you anonymously via a "Send Email" button if your email address is not displayed.

Privacy:
☐ Do not allow employers to search this resume. It will be used only to Apply Online.
Find out how to have jobs emailed to you!

Resume Description (10,000 Character Maximum Length)   **Check description length**

Note: Do not include your Social Security number in your Resume. Do not include URLs or HTML.

14 Employment

14-14 Accessing Corporate On-Line Career Centers

a. Major corporations generally include career centers in their Web sites. Here they describe career opportunities and post job openings in their organization. If you are interested in employment with a particular organization, visit its Web site, view its advertised positions, and submit your résumé.

b. Most company Web sites may be accessed by entering *www.[companyname].com* in the address box of your browser. Specific examples are *www.dole.com* and *www.amgen.com*. If this strategy does not produce the desired result, try these procedures:

(1) Use a search site (AltaVista, Excite, etc.) to locate the company Web site you wish to access or to locate an up-to-date directory of company Web sites.

(2) Access the two company Web site directories listed here. Both these directories provide links to major United States corporations.

The 2002 Fortune 500. <http://www.fortune.com/lists/F500/index.html>. This site provides links to capsulized descriptions of Fortune 500 companies; each link contains another link to the respective company's Web site.

Company News. <http://www.fortune.com/companies/>. This page provides links to capsulized descriptions of the "Fortune 1,000 Companies." Each link contains another link to the respective company's Web site.

c. Some companies accept résumés only for the positions that are advertised. Others accept all résumés and store them for a specified time. Should an opening occur that requires the qualifications of an applicant on file, the applicant may then be considered for the position.

Résumés submitted on-line are routed into an automated applicant tracking system. Follow the procedures described in Section 14-12 to prepare your résumé; keywords will be used to determine your qualifications for openings in the organization. In addition, follow the procedures outlined in Section 14-15 to prepare your résumé in ASCII format (text format) for transmission over the Internet.

résumé prepared in ASCII format

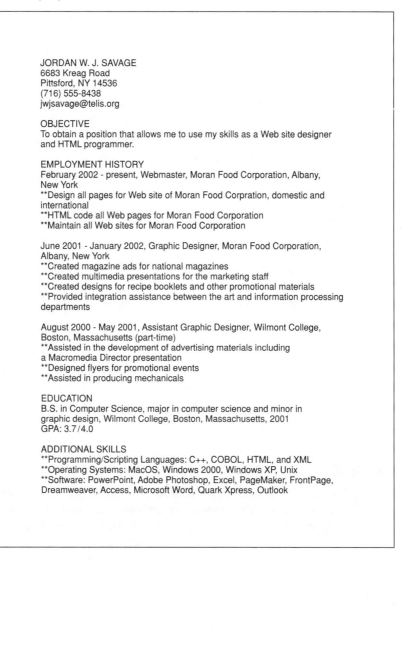

JORDAN W. J. SAVAGE
6683 Kreag Road
Pittsford, NY 14536
(716) 555-8438
jwjsavage@telis.org

OBJECTIVE
To obtain a position that allows me to use my skills as a Web site designer
and HTML programmer.

EMPLOYMENT HISTORY
February 2002 - present, Webmaster, Moran Food Corporation, Albany,
New York
**Design all pages for Web site of Moran Food Corpration, domestic and
international
**HTML code all Web pages for Moran Food Corporation
**Maintain all Web sites for Moran Food Corporation

June 2001 - January 2002, Graphic Designer, Moran Food Corporation,
Albany, New York
**Created magazine ads for national magazines
**Created multimedia presentations for the marketing staff
**Created designs for recipe booklets and other promotional materials
**Provided integration assistance between the art and information processing
departments

August 2000 - May 2001, Assistant Graphic Designer, Wilmont College,
Boston, Massachusetts (part-time)
**Assisted in the development of advertising materials including
a Macromedia Director presentation
**Designed flyers for promotional events
**Assisted in producing mechanicals

EDUCATION
B.S. in Computer Science, major in computer science and minor in
graphic design, Wilmont College, Boston, Massachusetts, 2001
GPA: 3.7 / 4.0

ADDITIONAL SKILLS
**Programming/Scripting Languages: C++, COBOL, HTML, and XML
**Operating Systems: MacOS, Windows 2000, Windows XP, Unix
**Software: PowerPoint, Adobe Photoshop, Excel, PageMaker, FrontPage,
Dreamweaver, Access, Microsoft Word, Quark Xpress, Outlook

14
Employment

14-15 Preparing and Posting an On-Line Résumé

a. Select career centers on which to post your résumé. Use the chronological style résumé described in Section 14-1, and prepare a version of your résumé in ASCII format. Cut and paste from this version to accommodate the templates required by the career centers. A résumé prepared in ASCII format is shown on page 463.

You may also use your prepared résumé as a guide to complete the fill-in blanks of a résumé builder or template provided by a career center or company career site.

b. Use the following guidelines to prepare your résumé for posting at an Internet career center or for on-line transmission to a company career site:

(1) Prepare your résumé in ASCII text. To create an ASCII résumé, key your résumé in a word processing program and save it as a *Text Only* file (if available, use *Text Only With Line Breaks*). This file-type choice should be available in your *Save As Type* option box. You may also use a simple text program to compose your résumé.

(2) Use a 5-inch typing line. Align all text at the left margin. Do not use the tab key; use the space bar for any indentions.

(3) Use hard returns for line breaks; do not rely on the word wrap feature of your word processing program.

(4) Avoid special characters and font attributes such as italics, underlining, and bolding. Fonts will become whatever a computer uses as its default typeface and size.

(5) Use the spelling checker and carefully proofread your résumé before you save it as an ASCII file.

The Application Letter

Although the letter of application functions as a cover letter in the transmittal of your résumé, its importance must not be minimized. This document is your initial introduction to the employer, so care must be taken to make a good first impression. This letter represents you. If it is prepared poorly, there is a good chance that your résumé will not be read.

14-16 Contents of the Application Letter

a. Begin the letter of application with a statement that attracts the interest of the reader and is related to the purpose of the letter. If an opening has been announced and applications are being solicited, use a direct approach. If, on the other hand, you are investigating whether an opening may exist, use a different strategy by approaching your purpose indirectly.

direct opening for solicited application

The opening for an administrative assistant in your Publications Department that you filed with the Loma Vista College Career Center appears to be interesting and challenging. As you can see by the enclosed résumé, my specialty in the office administration/computer applications area has been desktop publishing.

indirect opening for unsolicited application

My high regard for Allerman Corporation and its products has prompted me to inquire whether you could use the services of a knowledgeable administrative assistant who has specialized in desktop publishing.

b. Continue the letter of application with information that explains the purpose of your letter and convinces the reader to consider your qualifications further. Do not summarize your résumé; instead, amplify and briefly explain one or two of your strongest qualifications and relate them to the job for which you are applying. Refer the reader to the enclosed résumé.

body of application letter

My formal study of computer application programs—word processing, desktop publishing, Web page construction, spreadsheet, and database—at Loma Vista College culminated with an internship program at Data Select. Here I was able to use my word processing and desktop publishing skills to produce an instructional manual for one of the company's new software programs.

In addition to my course work and experience in applications software, courses in business English, transcription, and business communication have enabled me to develop the proofreading, editing, and writing skills needed to produce error-free business documents. Information regarding my other qualifications is included in the enclosed résumé.

c. A request for action closes the letter of application. Usually the action requested is an invitation for an interview. It may, however, merely be that the reader mail an employment application or refer your letter and résumé to a local office or representative. Whatever the request may be, preface it with *please* or another such appreciative expression.

In asking for an interview, make it easy for the reader to reply by furnishing your telephone number and the times you may be reached at that number. Serious job seekers, however, invest in answering machines, beepers, and even cellular phones so they are readily reachable when opportunities arise.

Applicants should also furnish E-mail addresses through which they may be contacted, should the prospective employer prefer this method of responding to the letter of application. If you furnish an E-mail address, be sure to check your in box frequently.

14

Employment

465

closing for application letter

> May I have an opportunity to discuss my qualifications with you further? To
> arrange an interview, please call me at (212) 555-5865. I can be reached personally
> before 10 a.m. and after 3 p.m., and my answering machine picks up messages
> between 10 a.m. and 3 p.m. I can arrange to meet with you at any time convenient
> for your schedule.

14–17 Preparation of the Application Letter

Like the résumé, the application letter represents you and forms a first impression. To form a favorable first impression, follow these guidelines:

(1) Use 20- or 24-pound high-quality white paper to prepare your application letter. Ensure that the print quality is high density, equal to that of a laser printer. Select a typeface and font size that complement the ones used in your résumé.

(2) Use one of the three following business letter formats: full block, modified block with blocked paragraphs, or modified block with indented paragraphs. Instructions for preparing letters in these formats are contained in Sections 12-1 and 12-2. An example application letter is shown on page 467.

(3) Limit your application letter to one page. Keep in mind that it is a transmittal letter for your résumé and, in most cases, a request for an interview. Highlight and expand only one or two of your major qualifications. Letters that are too long are less likely to be read. Similarly, letters prepared in fonts smaller than 11 points will receive less attention.

(4) Be sure to begin the application letter with a return address. Although your address and telephone number are prominently displayed in the résumé, your address must also appear on the application letter.

(5) Other parts of a business letter to be used include an inside address, a salutation, the letter body, a complimentary close, a signature line, and an enclosure notation. Specific instructions for the placement and format of letter parts are contained in Sections 12-6 through 12-17.

letter of application

1116 East 59th Street, Apt. 301
Chicago, IL 60615-3022
March 1, 2004

Ms. Denise R. Cueva, Vice President
Human Resources and Development
First National Bank of Arizona
10370 Camelback Road
Phoenix, Arizona 85030-1900

Dear Ms. Cueva:

As a growing bank in the Phoenix area, does First National have a need for a qualified representative in its trust and estate planning area?

In June I will earn a bachelor of science degree in business finance from Chicago State University. Besides fulfilling all the requirements for the regular curriculum in finance, I have completed additional course work in estate planning, trust initiation and management, tax law for trusts, and ethics in trust management.

As you can see by the enclosed résumé, for the past year the knowledge gained in my course work has been applied in a part-time position at Illinois Federal Bank. Here I met with new customers and assisted in setting up trusts to meet their individual needs. I also worked closely with trust officers in establishing and maintaining present clients' trusts.

May I have an opportunity to discuss with you how my education and experience can be put to work for First Federal? I plan to be in Phoenix from April 12 to 16 and would appreciate your scheduling an interview during that time. You may reach me by mail at the above address, by E-mail at rgferreira1531@msn.com, or by telephone at (312) 555-8732. I look forward to hearing from you.

Sincerely,

Robert Ferreira

Robert Ferreira

Enclosure

The Application Form

Many organizations require candidates to complete formal application forms even though they have submitted résumés. Application forms permit employers to obtain and organize standardized information about applicants—and those whom they hire as employees.

14-18 Procedures for Completing Application Forms

Use the following guidelines to assist you in completing application forms efficiently and completely:

(1) Carry with you a copy of your résumé when visiting prospective employers' offices. Much of the information contained in your résumé will be needed to complete the application form.

(2) Write on the reverse side of your résumé copy any information that may be needed for the application form but is not included on your résumé. Such information may include the following:

Social security number

Driver's license number

Beginning and ending dates of *all* employment

Salary history

Name, title, complete address, and telephone number of all former supervisors

Name, title, complete address, and telephone number of all references

(3) Read over all the questions before you begin to answer them. Write neatly and legibly. If you have poor handwriting, print your responses.

(4) Answer all questions on the application form. If a question is not applicable to your situation, respond with a statement such as *Not applicable*.

(5) Write *Negotiable* or *Open* on application forms that contain questions regarding the salary you expect to earn. This strategy is best used when you are uncertain what others in comparable positions are earning.

Reference Request Letters

14-19 Reference Request Letters

a. Prospective employers will undoubtedly ask you to furnish two or three references, persons who can verify your abilities and/or former employment. Provide the names of former professors or employers who will present you in a favorable light. Do not provide "character" references from family friends, personal friends, or relatives.

b. Request permission from potential references to use their names; select people who you feel will enthusiastically endorse you. Remember that a poor recommendation is worse than no recommendation at all.

    c. Solicit the recommendation endorsement in person or by tele-phone, and follow up a *yes* response with an acknowledgment let-ter. Use the following guidelines for writing this letter:

    (1) Express appreciation for the person's willingness to provide you with a recommendation should a prospective employer contact him or her.

    (2) Provide a description of the job for which you are applying. If appro-priate, relate one of your accomplishments or skills (that the person has observed personally) to the qualifications for the job.

    (3) Include and refer to a copy of your résumé.

    (4) Invite the reference to contact you if he or she has any questions.

reference request letter

Dear Professor Simons:

I appreciate your willingness to provide me with a reference for a position as a legal assistant should you be contacted by a prospective employer.

My immediate objective is to obtain a position in a large legal firm where I will have an opportunity for advancement. The courses I took from you—word processing, legal office procedures, and legal transcription—have certainly prepared me well to begin my career in a legal office.

After graduating from Pierce College, I continued my education in the area of legal assisting. As you can see by the enclosed résumé, I enrolled in the Attorney Assistant Training Program at the University of California, Los Angeles, Extension. There I earned a Certificate in Litigation.

Thank you for your support. If you have any questions or wish any additional information, please let me know.

Follow-Up Letters

Follow-up letters may be written when no response is received to an application letter or form. They are also written after an inter-view. The follow-up letter reminds the prospective employer that you are interested in a position with that employer or company.

14-20 Application Follow-Up Letter

If you have not received a response to an application letter or an application form within a reasonable period of time, you may wish to send an application follow-up letter. Such a letter shows serious interest and reminds the personnel officer of your qualifications.

    (1) Begin the application follow-up letter with a statement reaffirming your interest in the job for which you formerly applied. Remind the addressee of your letter or application and mention one of your qual-ifications—or provide any new information that may enhance your likelihood of obtaining the position. Close with a statement express-ing the hope that your application will be kept active.

(2) Use one of the following three business letter formats: full block, modified block with blocked paragraphs, or modified block with indented paragraphs. Instructions for preparing letters in these formats are contained in Sections 12-1 and 12-2. An example application follow-up letter is shown below.

(3) Be sure to begin the application follow-up letter with a return address. Other parts of a business letter to be used include an inside address, a salutation, the letter body, a complimentary close, and a signature line. Specific instructions for the placement and format of these letter parts are contained in Sections 12-6 through 12-17.

application follow-up letter

1116 East 59th Street, Apt. 301
Chicago, IL 60615-3022
March 25, 2004

Ms. Denise R. Cueva, Vice President
Human Resources and Development
First National Bank of Arizona
10370 Camelback Road
Phoenix, Arizona 85030-1900

Dear Ms. Cueva:

I am still very interested in becoming a representative in the Estate Planning and Trust Department of First National Bank of Arizona.

As I mentioned in my March 1 letter, I will be in Phoenix from April 12 through April 16 and would be available for an interview anytime that week. If these dates are not convenient for you, please write me at the above address, e-mail me at rgferreira1531@msn.com, or call me at (312) 555-8732 to set up an appointment to meet with you another time.

If you do not have an opening at the present time, please let me know. I would appreciate, however, your keeping my application in your active file and notifying me when an opportunity with First National arises.

Sincerely,

Robert Ferreira

Robert Ferreira

14-21 Interview Follow-Up Letter

After you have been interviewed, send a brief letter of appreciation to the interviewer. Not only will this courtesy thank the interviewer for his or her time but also it will remind that person of your meeting. Sending a follow-up letter will reaffirm your interest in the position and at the same time distinguish you from the other candidates. More than likely, others will not take this extra step.

(1) Write and send the interview follow-up letter immediately after the interview. A delay will impair its effectiveness. In addition to expressing appreciation and thanks, remind the interviewer of a topic discussed during your conversation and conclude with a positive statement indicating your interest in the position.

(2) Use one of the following three business letter formats: full block, modified block with blocked paragraphs, or modified block with indented paragraphs. Instructions for preparing letters in these formats are contained in Sections 12-1 and 12-2. An example interview follow-up letter is shown on page 472.

(3) Be sure to begin the interview follow-up letter with a return address. Other parts of a business letter to be used include an inside address, a salutation, the letter body, a complimentary close, and a signature line. Specific instructions for the placement and format of these letter parts are contained in Sections 12-6 through 12-17.

14

Employment

interview follow-up letter

1116 East 59th Street, Apt. 301
Chicago, IL 60615-3022
April 19, 2004

Ms. Denise R. Cueva, Vice President
Human Resources and Development
First National Bank of Arizona
10370 Camelback Road
Phoenix, Arizona 85030-1900

Dear Ms. Cueva:

Thank you for meeting with me in Phoenix last week. My interview with you and Mr. Sabian has convinced me even more that I would like to become part of the First National Bank of Arizona staff.

Since there are no openings in your Estate Planning and Trust Department at the present time, I appreciate your suggesting the management training program in the interim. Please consider me for an opening in this program.

Because of my experience at Illinois Federal Bank, I could be a productive member of your staff. I look forward to hearing your decision about my entering the management training program at First National.

Sincerely,

Robert Ferreira

Robert Ferreira

15

Information Sources

Information Sources Solution Finder

Business people often need to consult reference material to gather information for general operations, decision making, and document preparation. Printed reference materials, electronic media, and on-line resources provide access to the information needed by today's fast-paced business environment.

Reference materials are abundant. Numerous kinds and extensive listings are available in libraries, in bookstores, from software vendors, and on the Internet. Some are valuable tools for the business person; others are not. The intent of this chapter is to provide a selective listing of printed materials, electronic media, and on-line resources that may prove valuable for a business person. The sources listed may be (1) purchased from bookstores or software vendors, (2) located at local public or university libraries, or (3) accessed on the Internet.

Published Materials

15-1 Dictionaries

a. Although word processing programs provide a spelling checker, this feature has its limitations. It does not differentiate between words that sound alike but are spelled differently, flag words that are used incorrectly, or assess whether a term should be spelled as one or two words (e.g., *mark down or markdown).* Dictionary entries provide spellings, syllabication, pronunciation guides, definitions, irregular verb and adjective forms, and synonyms—all useful information in preparing business documents.

b. Dictionaries are generally published in paperback-pocket format, collegiate editions, or complete unabridged versions. Collegiate editions—because of their compact, comprehensive nature and more frequent update printings—are considered the best source for office use. Update your office dictionary every three years, and select an authoritative one such as those listed below:

Abate, Frank, and Elizabeth J. Jewell, eds. *The New Oxford American Dictionary.* New York: Oxford University Press, Inc., 2001.
The American Heritage College Dictionary. 4th ed. Boston: Houghton Mifflin Company, 2002.
The American Heritage Dictionary of the English Language. 4th ed. Boston: Houghton Mifflin Company, 2000.
Merriam-Webster's Collegiate Dictionary. 10th ed. Springfield, Mass.: Merriam-Webster, Incorporated, 2002. (Updated annually)
Webster's New World College Dictionary. 4th ed. New York: Macmillan, Inc., 2001.
Webster's Third New International Dictionary, Unabridged. Springfield, Mass.: Merriam-Webster, Incorporated, 2000.

15 Information Sources

c. **Consider whether specialized dictionaries are needed in your office. Besides the regular array of foreign language-English dictionaries, investigate the usefulness of dictionaries that define business terms, computer terms, legal terms, medical terms, and foreign expressions.**

Ammer, Christine. *The American Heritage Dictionary of Idioms*. Boston: Houghton Mifflin Company, 1997.

Black, Henry Campbell. Bryan A. Garner, ed. *Black's Law Dictionary*. 7th ed. St. Paul, Minn.: West Publishing Company, 1999.

Friedman, Jack P. *Dictionary of Business Terms*. 3rd ed. Hauppauge, N.Y.: Barron's Educational Series, Inc., 2000.

Garner, Bryan A., ed. *A Handbook of Business Law Terms*. St. Paul, Minn.: West Publishing Company, 1999.

Gifis, Steven H. *Dictionary of Legal Terms*. 3rd ed. Hauppauge, N.Y.: Barron's Educational Series, Inc., 1998.

Merriam-Webster's Geographical Dictionary. 3rd ed. Springfield, Mass.: Merriam-Webster, Incorporated, 1998.

Microsoft Press Computer Dictionary. 5th ed. Redmond, Wash.: Microsoft Press, 2002.

Newton, Harry. *Newton's Telecom Dictionary*. 18th ed. New York: CMP Books, 2002.

Oxford Essential Dictionary of Foreign Terms in English: The World's Most Trusted Dictionaries. New York: Berkley Publishing Group, 1999.

Stedman, Thomas Lathrop. *Stedman's Medical Dictionary*. 27th ed. Hagerstown, Md.: Lippincott Williams & Wilkins, 2000.

Thomas, Clayton L., and Donald Venus, eds. *Taber's Cyclopedic Medical Dictionary*. 19th ed. Philadelphia: F. A. Davis Company, 2001.

15-2 Thesauri

Use a thesaurus to add variety to your writing style. Locate words with the same meaning to substitute for those words you tend to overuse. A partial listing of thesauri follows:

Bartlett's Roget's Thesaurus. Boston: Little, Brown and Company, 1996.

Kipfer, Barbara Ann, ed. *Roget's International Thesaurus*. 6th ed. New York: HarperCollins Publishers, 2001.

Laird, Charlton, ed. *Webster's New World Roget's A–Z Thesaurus*. New York: Macmillan USA, 1999.

Lindberg, Christine A. *The Oxford American Thesaurus of Current English*. New York: Oxford University Press, Inc., 1999.

Roget's II, The New Thesaurus. 3rd ed. Boston: Houghton Mifflin Company, 1995.

15-3 Encyclopedias and Almanacs

Encyclopedias and almanacs provide answers for questions that might arise concerning events and trends.

Almanacs, published annually, describe significant events of the past year; provide information about government officials, states,

the United States, and other nations; and supply facts on weather and other topics.

For people involved in international communication, encyclopedias furnish background information about countries' political systems, history, and customs. In addition, encyclopedias provide a concise synopsis on virtually thousands of topics.

The following sources may prove valuable in collecting facts and information:

Encyclopaedia Britannica 2002 Print Set and annual yearbook. 32 volumes. Chicago: Encyclopaedia Britannica, Inc., 2001. (Updated annually)

Thomas, Robert B., and Judson D. Hale, ed. *The Old Farmer's 2003 Almanac.* Dublin, N.H.: Yankee Publishing Incorporated, 2002. (Published annually)

Time Almanac 2003. New York: Time, Inc., 2002. (Published annually)

The World Almanac and Book of Facts 2003. Mahwah, N.J.: World Almanac Education, 2002. (Published annually)

Wright, John W., ed. *The New York Times Almanac 2003.* New York: Penguin USA, 2002. (Published annually)

15-4 Atlases

Atlases provide maps of cities, states, countries, continents, and the world. Accompanying a wide variety of maps is often information about population, weather, terrain, agricultural production, and economic orientation. Consult atlases such as the following:

Hammond World Atlas. 4th ed. Maplewood, N.J.: Hammond Incorporated, 2002.

Millennium World Atlas. Skokie, Ill.: Rand McNally and Company, 1999.

Oxford Atlas of the World. 9th ed. New York: Oxford University Press, Inc., 2001.

15-5 Style Manuals

Style manuals govern the presentation style of reports and manuscripts. Three styles dominate the preparation of reports and manuscripts: (1) the Modern Language Association (MLA) style is endorsed by those writing in the fields of language and arts; (2) the American Psychological Association (APA) style is endorsed by those writing in the social sciences; and (3) *The Chicago Manual of Style* prescribes a traditional style usable for business, researchers, and students.

The following listing gives the latest authoritative published sources for preparing manuscripts or reports according to the MLA style, the APA style, or the Chicago Style Manual style. Three other sources—popular among students and business people—have also been included.

15 Information Sources

The AMA Style Guide for Business Writing. New York: American
  Management Association, 1996.
The Chicago Manual of Style. 14th ed. Chicago: The University of
  Chicago Press, 1993.
Gibaldi, Joseph. *MLA Handbook for Writers of Research Papers.* 5th ed.
  New York: The Modern Language Association of America, 1999.
Harnack, Andrew, and Eugene Kleppinger. *Online! A Reference Guide
  to Using Internet Sources.* New York: Bedford/St. Martin's, 2001.
Publication Manual of the American Psychological Association. 5th ed.
  Washington, D.C.: American Psychological Association, 2001.
Turabian, Kate L., John Grossman, and Alice Bennett. *A Manual for
  Writers of Term Papers, Theses, and Dissertations* (Chicago Guides to
  Writing, Editing, and Publishing). 6th ed. Chicago: The University of
  Chicago Press, 1996.

15–6 Quotations

**Books of famous quotations are often useful in preparing speeches,
written presentations, or marketing brochures. Most collections of
famous quotations are organized according to topic so that suitable selections can be made easily. Several books of quotations are
listed below:**

Andrews, Robert, ed. *New Penguin Dictionary of Modern Quotations.*
  New York: Penguin Books, 2001.
Bartlett, John. Justin Kaplan, ed. *Bartlett's Familiar Quotations.* 16th ed.
  Boston: Little, Brown and Company, 1992.
Caruth, Gorton, ed. *American Quotations.* New York: Random House
  Value Publishing, 1999.
Frank, Leonard Roy, ed. *Random House Webster's Quotationary.* New
  York: Random House, 2001.
Peter, Laurence J. *Peter's Quotations: Ideas for Our Time.* New York:
  William Morrow & Company, 1993.
Shanahan, John M., ed. *The Most Brilliant Thoughts of All Time (in Two
  Lines or Less).* New York: Cliff Street Books, HarperCollins Publishers,
  1999.

15–7 Etiquette Standards

**Business etiquette and general etiquette standards are important
in establishing and maintaining business relationships. Etiquette
standards and customs differ throughout the world, so the international business person should be well acquainted with not only
American standards but also standards of other cultures. The following books address a variety of domestic situations and international customs:**

Axtell, Roger E. *Do's and Taboos Around the World.* 3rd ed. Hoboken,
  N.J.: John Wiley & Sons, Inc., 1993.
Axtell, Roger E. *The Do's and Taboos of International Trade: A Small
  Business Primer.* Rev. ed. Hoboken, N.J.: John Wiley & Sons, Inc., 1994.

Axtell, Roger E. *Gestures: The Do's and Taboos of Body Language Around the World.* Rev. and exp. ed. Hoboken, N.J.: John Wiley & Sons, Inc., 1997.

Axtell, Roger E., Tami Briggs, and Margaret Corcoran. *Do's & Taboos Around the World for Women in Business.* Hoboken, N.J.: John Wiley & Sons, Inc., 1997.

Dresser, Norine. *Multicultural Manners: New Rules of Etiquette for a Changing Society.* Hoboken, N.J: John Wiley & Sons, Inc., 1996.

Ford, Charlotte. *21st Century Etiquette.* Guilford, Conn.: Lyons Press, 2001.

Moore, June H. *The Etiquette Advantage: Rules for the Business Professional.* Life at Work Series. Nashville, Tenn.: Broadman & Holman Publishers, 1998.

Morrison, Terri, Wayne A. Conaway, and George A. Borden. *Kiss, Bow, or Shake Hands: How to Do Business in Sixty Countries.* Holbrook, Mass.: Adams Media Corporation, 1995.

Morrison, Terri, Wayne A. Conaway, and Joseph J. Douress. *Dun & Bradstreet's Guide to Doing Business Around the World.* Upper Saddle River, N.J.: Prentice Hall, 2000.

Post, Peggy. *Emily Post's Etiquette.* 16th ed. New York: HarperCollins, 1997.

Post, Peggy, and Peter Post. *Emily Post's The Etiquette Advantage in Business: Personal Skills for Professional Success.* New York: HarperResource, 1999.

Tuckerman, Nancy, and Nancy Dunnan. *The Amy Vanderbilt Complete Book of Etiquette.* Garden City, N.Y.: Doubleday & Company, Inc., 1995.

15-8 Business Information Sources

The following publications contain information that may be used for job seeking, meetings, research, mailings, writing style, or general information:

Atkinson, Toby D. *Merriam-Webster's Guide to International Communication.* Springfield, Mass.: Merriam-Webster, Incorporated, 1999.

Books in Print 2002–2003. 55th ed. New Providence, N.J.: R. R. Bowker, 2002. (Published annually)

Hahn, Harley. *Harley Hahn's Internet Yellow Pages, 2003 Edition.* New York: Osborne/McGraw-Hill, 2002.

The National Job Bank 2003. Holbrook, Mass.: Adams Media Corporation, 2002.

Peck, Terrance W., ed. *Directories in Print.* 21st ed. Farmington Hills, Mich.: Gale Group, 2002. (Published annually)

Robert, Henry M. III, and William J. Evans, Daniel H. Honemann, Henry Martyn Robert, Thomas J. Balch, eds. *Robert's Rules of Order.* 10th ed. Cambridge, Mass.: Perseus Publishing, 2000.

Strunk, William Jr., and E. B. White. *The Elements of Style.* 4th ed. Boston: Allyn & Bacon, 2000.

15 Information Sources

Electronic Media

15-9 Basic Resource Materials

CD-ROM and DVD-ROM drives on computers permit access to volumes of data previously accessible only through printed material.

The following listing of CD-ROMs and DVD-ROMs focuses on dictionaries, thesauri, encyclopedias, atlases, and other such general reference material. Some are single-source references; other packages contain multiple volumes. CD-ROM and DVD-ROM publishers generally maintain Web sites for users to obtain product information and updates. Internet addresses are shown in angle brackets (< >).

2002 Grolier Multimedia Encyclopedia. CD-ROM. Danbury, Conn.: Grolier, 2002. <http://www.scholastic.com/families/gme/>.

Britannica DVD 2001. DVD-ROM. Chicago: Encyclopaedia Britannica, Inc., 2000. <http://www.britannica.com>.

Encarta Reference Library 2003. CD-ROM. DVD-ROM. Redmond, Wash.: Microsoft Corporation, 2002. <http://www.encarta.msn.com/shop/ERL.asp>.

Federer, William J., ed. *American Quotations.* CD-ROM. St. Louis, Mo.: AmeriSearch, Inc., 2002. <http://www.amerisearch.net/store>.

Hammond World Atlas. CD-ROM. Maplewood, N.J.: Hammond World Atlas Corporation, 2002. <http://hammondmap.com>.

Merriam-Webster's Collegiate Dictionary & Thesaurus. 10th ed. Deluxe audio ed. 2.5. CD-ROM. Springfield, Mass.: Merriam-Webster, Incorporated, 2002. <http://www.m-w.com>.

Merriam-Webster's Collegiate Dictionary & Thesaurus. 10th ed. Electronic ed. 2.5. CD-ROM. Springfield, Mass.: Merriam-Webster, Incorporated, 2002. <http://www.m-w.com>.

Simon & Schuster New Millennium Encyclopedia and Home Reference Library. Deluxe ed. CD-ROM. New York: Simon & Schuster Interactive, 2002.

Webster's Millennium 2002 Platinum Encyclopedia Collection. CD-ROM (5). Multimedia 2000, 2002.

Webster's Third New International Dictionary, Unabridged on CD-ROM. CD-ROM. Springfield, Mass.: Merriam-Webster, Incorporated, 2002. <http://www.m-w.com>.

15-10 Directories and Other Locators

Businesses often wish to locate names of individuals and other businesses, addresses, phone numbers, fax numbers, zip codes, Web sites, and other such kinds of information on a nationwide basis. Printed volumes are costly and cumbersome. Inexpensive and easy access to these nationwide lists is available through CD-ROMs, a few of which are listed below:

Microsoft Streets & Trips 2002. CD-ROM. Redmond, Wash.: Microsoft Corporation, 2002. <http://www.microsoft.com/streets/>

*PowerFinder: A Comprehensive Business and Consumer Database
Containing Information on 115 Million Businesses and Residences.*
CD-ROM and DVD-ROM. Omaha, Neb.: infoUSA, Inc., 2002.
<http://www.infoUSA.com>. (Annual subscription with updates) This
resource provides on-line and CD-ROM regularly updated databases
for a large variety of population sectors.

*SelectPhone: The Complete Marketing Solution Database of 115 Million
Businesses and Consumers.* CD-ROM and DVD-ROM. Omaha, Neb.:
infoUSA, Inc., 2002. <http://www.infoUSA.com>. (Annual subscription
with quarterly updates)

Street Atlas 2003 USA. CD-ROM. Yarmouth, Maine: DeLorme, 2002.
<http://www.delorme.com>.

The Thomas Guide Digital Edition for [Local Area]. CD-ROM. Skokie, Ill.:
Rand McNally, 2003. <http://www.randmcnally.com/rmc/search>.
(Updated annually)

On-Line Resources

The wealth of information available on the Internet is overwhelming.[1] Not all of it is valid or reliable—and not all of it is obtainable
free of charge. The Internet user must use good judgment and discretion in selecting sources and decide whether the fees to access
certain sites are justified. The sites recommended here are just a
sampling of the vast resources available on the World Wide Web.

15-11 References

Reference sources such as dictionaries, thesauri, encyclopedias,
almanacs, and atlases are available for access on the Internet. A
number of such sites follow.[2] The dates in parentheses show when
the information at these sites was last confirmed.

Acronym Finder. Mountain Data Systems, 2002. <http://www.
acronymfinder.com/> (21 August 2002). A search site that locates the
meaning of acronyms or locates the acronyms for terms.

Dictionary.com. Lexico LLC, 2002. <http://www.dictionary.com/
dictionary/> (21 August 2002). Provides an English on-line dictionary
and thesaurus as well as links to other English and foreign language
references on the Internet.

Encyclopaedia Britannica Online. Encyclopaedia Britannica, Inc., 2002.
<http://www.eb.com/> (21 August 2002). A subscription Web-based
encyclopedia.

Encyclopedia.com. Alacritude, LLC, 2002. <http://www.encyclopedia.
com> (4 September 2002). A free on-line encyclopedia with more than
57,000 articles.

---

[1]See Chapter 9 for complete information on connecting to the Internet and accessing
World Wide Web sites.

[2]Additional sources may be located through search sites. See Section 9-3d–e.

FindLaw. FindLaw, 2002. <http://www.findlaw.com> (21 August 2002). Links to numerous legal resources including a dictionary of legal terms.

Howe, Denis, ed. *FOLDOC: Free On-line Dictionary of Computing*, 2002. <http://foldoc.doc.ic.ac.uk/> (21 August 2002). A dictionary of computer terms with more than 13,500 entries.

IPL: The Internet Public Library. Ann Arbor, Mich.: University of Michigan, School of Information, 2002. <http://www.ipl.org/> (21 August 2002). Links to almanacs, biographies, census data, dictionaries, encyclopedias, news, quotations, style guides, telephone directories, and many other references on the Internet.

Martindale's: The Reference Desk. Jim Martindale, 2002. <http://www. sci.lib.uci.edu/HSG/Ref.html> (20 September 2002). Links to a vast number of reference resources—from dictionaries to geoscience.

Merriam-Webster OnLine. Springfield, Mass.: Merriam-Webster, Incorporated, 2002. <http://www.m-w.com> (21 August 2002). Provides free access to an on-line version of *Merriam-Webster's Collegiate Dictionary,* 10th ed., and *Merriam-Webster's Collegiate Thesaurus,* along with a number of other valuable language resources.

Moody, H. *Online Resources for Writers.* Professional Training Company, 2001. <http://www.protrainco.com/info/links/gramlink.htm#top> (21 August 2002). Links to dictionaries, thesauri, writing guides, and other language resources on the Internet.

NetLingo. NetLingo Inc., 2002. <http://www.netlingo.com> (21 August 2002). An extensive, comprehensive glossary of Internet terms.

OneLook Dictionaries. n.d. <http://www.onelook.com/> (4 September 2002). A dictionary search site that accesses more than 800 sources to locate words and also allows users to insert wild-card symbols to locate spellings.

Refdesk.com. Refdesk.com, 2002. <http://www.refdesk.com/index.html> (21 August 2002). Links to a comprehensive variety of reference sources, e.g., dictionaries, encyclopedias, atlases, calendars, currency calculations, newspapers, magazines, columns, and movies.

The World Factbook 2001. Washington, D.C.: Central Intelligence Agency, 2001. <http://www.odci.gov/cia/publications/factbook/index.html> (21 August 2002). Links to current information on countries throughout the world.

yourDictionary.com. yourDictionary.com Inc., 2001. <http://www. yourdictionary.com/> (21 August 2002). Provides an on-line English dictionary and thesaurus as well as grammar assistance, vocabulary building, and links to foreign language dictionaries and courses.

15–12 News and Weather Sources

News and weather sources—news channels, weather channels, newspapers, and magazines—are available on-line. Several sites are listed here:

BusinessWeek Online. The McGraw-Hill Companies Inc., 2002. <http:// www.businessweek.com/> (9 September 2002).

CNN.com. Cable News Network, LP, LLLP, 2002. <http://www.cnn.com/> (21 August 2002).

Intellicast.com: Weather for Active Lives. WSI Corporation, 2002. <http://www.intellicast.com/> (21 August 2002).

NBCi. National Broadcasting Company, Inc., 2002. <http://nbci.msnbc.com/nbci.asp> (21 August 2002).

The New York Times on the Web. The New York Times Company, 2002. <http://www.nytimes.com/> (21 August 2002).

Newsweek. MSNBC, 2002. <http://www.msnbc.com/news/NW-front_Front.asp> (4 September 2002).

Sørenson, Søren Isak. *Electronic Newsstand.* 2002. <http://home.worldonline.dk/knud-sor/en/> (21 August 2002). International site that links to newspapers, weather, sports, multimedia, newsletters, e-zines, cartoons, film and music, and computer information.

TIME.com. Time Inc., 2002. <http://www.time.com/time/> (21 August 2002).

USA TODAY. USA TODAY, 2002. <http://www.usatoday.com/> (21 August 2002).

usnews.com. U.S. News & World Report, L.P., 2002. <http://www.usnews.com/usnews/home.htm> (21 August 2002).

The Wall Street Journal Online. Dow Jones & Company, Inc., 2002. <http://online.wsj.com/public/us> (21 August 2002).

The Weather Channel. The Weather Channel Enterprises, Inc., 2002. <http://www.weather.com> (21 August 2002).

15-13 Government Sites

Government offices provide information through the Internet. Mailing, tax, and census information may be obtained at the following sites:

embassy.org. TeleDiplomacy, Inc., 2002. <http://www.embassy.org/> (21 August 2002). A site that provides information about foreign embassies in Washington, D.C.

Fed World.gov. Springfield, Va.: United States Department of Commerce, National Technical Information Service, n.d. <http://www.fedworld.gov/> (21 August 2002). Serves as the on-line locator service for a comprehensive inventory of information disseminated by the federal government.

"Forms and Publications." *Internal Revenue Service.* Washington, D.C.: IRS.gov, 2001. <http://www.irs.ustreas.gov/prod/forms_pubs/index.html> (21 August 2002). Provides access to federal income tax forms.

Statistical Abstract of the United States: 2001. Washington, D.C.: U.S. Census Bureau, 2002. <http://www.census.gov/statab/www/> (21 August 2002).

THOMAS: Legislative Information on the Internet. Washington, D.C.: United States Library of Congress, n.d. <http://thomas.loc.gov/> (21 August 2002). Provides continual legislative updates.

United States Postal Service. Washington, D.C.: USPS, 2002. <http://www.usps.com/> (20 September 2002).

U.S. Census Bureau. Washington, D.C.: United States Department of Commerce, 2002. <http://www.census.gov/> (20 September 2002).

"ZIP Code Lookup." *United States Postal Service.* Washington, D.C.: USPS, 2002. <http://www.usps.com/zip4/> (20 September 2002).

15-14 Private Delivery Services

Private delivery services maintain Web sites that allow package tracking and provide information about their services. Web site addresses for several such providers are listed below:

Airborne Express Home Page. Airborne Express, n.d. <http://www. airborne.com/home/home.asp> (4 September 2002).

DHL Worldwide Express Home Page. DHL International Ltd., 2002. <http://www.dhl.com/main_index.html> (21 August 2002).

FedEx Home Page. FedEx, 2002. <http://www.fedex.com/> (21 August 2002).

UPS Home Page. United Parcel Service of America, Inc., 2002. <http://www.ups.com/> (21 August 2002).

15-15 On-Line Directories

On-line directories provide addresses, telephone numbers, fax numbers, E-mail addresses, Web site addresses (URLs—uniform resource locators), and other similar types of information for individuals, businesses, organizations, and government agencies. A select list of on-line locators follows:

Airline Toll-Free Numbers and Web Sites. Thavery, 2002. <http://www. geocities.com/Thavery2000/> (21 August 2002). Contains toll-free numbers only.

embassy.org. TeleDiplomacy, Inc., 2002. <http://www.embassy.org/> (21 August 2002). Provides information about foreign embassies in Washington, D.C.

Infobel.com. Kapitol, 2002. <http://www.infobel.com/world/default.asp> (21 August 2002). Supports an international telephone directory.

InfoSpace. InfoSpace, Inc., 2002. <http://www.infospace.com/> (21 August 2002). Links to white pages, yellow pages, and general information.

MapQuest. MapQuest.com, Inc., 2002. <http://www.mapquest.com> (21 August 2002). Provides mapping and turn-by-turn directions from one location to another.

Maps On Us. Tele Atlas North American, Inc., 2002. <http://www. mapsonus.com/> (21 August 2002). Provides mapping and turn-by-turn directions from one location to another throughout the United States.

SuperPages.com. Verizon Inc., 2002. <http://www.superpages.com/> (5 September 2002). Provides a lookup service for business addresses as well as links to white pages and a multitude of other services.

Switchboard.com. Switchboard Incorporated, 2002. <http://www. switchboard.com/> (21 August 2002). Offers white pages, yellow pages, driving directions, city guides, an E-mail address locator, and several other locator services.

WhoWhere? Lycos, Inc., 2001. <http://www.whowhere.lycos.com/> (21 August 2002). Offers an address and telephone number locator that contains options for obtaining in-depth information about individuals (for a fee).

15-16 Career Centers

Job searches are no longer dominated by the traditional résumé and letter of application. Most major companies today maintain career centers on their Web sites and accept résumés on-line. In addition, the Internet hosts a large number of career centers that post job openings, post résumés, permit on-line applications for job postings, and offer career advice. The following sites are among the most popular ones on the Internet:

America's Job Bank. <http://www.ajb.org> (21 August 2002). *America's Job Bank* is the largest and busiest job market on the Internet, providing labor exchange service to employers and job seekers. It is operated under the jurisdiction of the U.S. Department of Labor in partnership with the states and private sector organizations. *America's Job Bank* lists more than 1 million jobs and posts résumés. No fee; registration required for résumé posting.

CareerBuilder. <http://www.careerbuilder.com> (21 August 2002). This Web site posts more than 400,000 jobs and provides a template for candidates to submit information for on-line résumé posting. In addition, *CareerBuilder* provides a career resource center for job seekers, a newsletter, and links to various departments that provide career advice. This Web site strives to be a valuable source to both the employer and the job seeker. No fee; registration required for résumé posting.

HotJobs. <http://www.hotjobs.com> (21 August 2002). This site is a *Yahoo!* service and provides a nationwide listing of job openings. Categories are refined by state, city, general field, selection of subfields, and keywords. Job seekers may also post their résumé. No fee; registration required for résumé posting.

Monster. <http://www.monster.com> (8 September 2002). This is one of the most popular Web sites for job seekers. The site offers a variety of hypertext links to job-search resources and connections to job listings. Maintains separate sites for special fields: Admin/Support, Technology, Healthcare, Finance, Sales, Retail, Legal, Human Resources, and Senior Executives. The Monster Network has more than 1 million job postings and provides a Career Center with résumé help, salary data, and industry information. No fee; registration required for résumé posting.

MonsterTRAK. <http://www.monstertrak.com/> (21 August 2002). *MonsterTRAK* has job listings for full-time jobs, part-time jobs, temporary jobs, and internships. This site provides job search tips, career forums, and a career contact network. Students and alumni from registered colleges and universities may view job listings posted and/or post résumés by obtaining a password from their college or university. No fee; registration required.

TrueCareers. <http://www.truecareers.com> (21 August 2002). *TrueCareers* connects entry-level job seekers with employers who want qualified applicants. This Web site is designed to help students and recent college graduates find internships, part-time jobs, or career positions. No fee; registration required.

15-17 **Other Information Sources**

a. Several other kinds of information sources on the Internet that may be of value to persons involved in business, industry, or government are listed below:

all-hotels. All-Hotels, 2002. <http://www.all-hotels.com/> (21 August 2002). Offers worldwide hotel reservations.

Biography.com. A&E Television Networks, 2002. <http://www.biography. com/> (5 September 2002). Provides more than 25,000 biography profiles.

CEOExpress. CEOExpress Company, 2002. <http://www.ceoexpress.com/ default.asp> (21 August 2002). Provides links to hundreds of valuable business resources.

Expedia.com. Expedia, Inc., 2002. <http://www.expedia.msn.com/> (21 August 2002). A popular site for making travel reservations.

Fodors.com. Fodors LLC, 2002. <http://www.fodors.com/> (21 August 2002). Provides information on hotels and restaurants.

HotelsTravel.com. WebScope, 2002. <http://www.hotelstravel.com/> (21 August 2002). A site for making travel reservations.

The List of ISPs. Jupitermedia Corporation, 2002. <http://thelist.internet. com/> (8 September 2002). Functions as a directory of Internet service providers with thousands of listings.

Orbitz. Orbitz, LLC, 2001. <http://www.orbitz.com/> (21 August 2002). A site for making travel reservations.

Smith, Mark J. *Virtual Perpetual Calendars.* 2002. <http://www. vpcalendar.net/> (30 November 2002). Provides calendars from 1901 through 2100 and holidays from 1990 through 2010.

TravelNow.com. Travel Now.com, Inc., 2002. <http://www.travelnow.com/> (21 August 2002). A site for making travel reservations.

Travelocity.com. Travelocity.com L.P., 2002. <http://www.travelocity. com/> (21 August 2002). A popular site for making travel reservations.

xe.com. XE.com., 2002. <http://www.xe.com/> (21 August 2002). Provides international currency rates of exchange and a currency converter.

Yahoo! Yahoo! Inc., 2002. <http://www.yahoo.com/> (21 August 2002). Provides links to a number of valuable resources.

b. Remember that the Internet is still in its infancy. As this information source continues to grow, new Web sites will emerge as others disappear. Some Web sites will be updated almost daily, some periodically, and others not at all. Not every source contains valid information, so evaluate judiciously the contents and origin of each one.

Learn to use search sites to gather the information you need. Bookmark those sites that you use frequently or that you feel will be useful to you sometime in the near future. Continually search out those Web sites that will assist you in carrying out your responsibilities.

16

Manual and Electronic File Management

Manual and Electronic File Management Solution Finder

The Filing Process

16-1 Purpose of Indexing

You may need to set up communication indexes (telephone, fax, E-mail, address), customer files, patient files, vendor files, or some other kind of database involving individual and/or organizational names. To organize names so they can be located easily, you will first need to place the separate words in each name in a sequence to be alphabetized. This process is known as *indexing*. Once placed in the proper order, the units may be alphabetized.

So that filed names may be located easily (retrieved), all names must be indexed and alphabetized in the same manner; that is, you need to follow the same set of guidelines in preparing each name for filing. The most commonly used set of guidelines is called the *Simplified Filing Standard Rules*.

16-2 Simplified Filing Standard Rules

The rules presented here for indexing and alphabetizing individual and organizational names are the Simplified Filing Standard Rules endorsed by ARMA International (The Association for Information Management Professionals).[1]

The ARMA International publication for alphabetic filing explains accepted deviations from the Simplified Filing Standard Rules but cautions that these deviations must be documented for all users. Otherwise, inconsistencies in indexing records for alphabetizing will lead to difficulties in locating and retrieving records.

The following rules and examples are based solely on the Simplified Filing Standard Rules.

Indexing and Alphabetizing

16-3 Indexing and Alphabetizing the Names of Individuals

a. To index the names of individuals, arrange the units (words and initials) in each name in the following order:

(1) Complete last name as written (includes hyphenated last names and *all* prefixes such as *D', Da, De, Del, De La, Della, Den, Des, Di, Du, El, Fitz, L', La, Las, Le, Les, Lo, Los, M', Mac, Mc, O', Saint, San, St., Ste.,*

---

[1] *Alphabetic Filing Rules,* 2nd ed. (Prairie Village, Kans.: ARMA International, 1995), 3–4, 7–9, 17–22. Copies of this publication may be purchased from ARMA International by telephoning (888) 241-0598. Copies are also available at the ARMA International on-line bookstore, which may be accessed through <http://www.arma.org>.

Te, Ten, Ter, Van, Van de, van Der, Von, and *Von der*). Variations in the capitalization of these prefixes are treated the same.

(2) Complete first name or initial (includes two-word first names such as *Jo Ann, Mary Ellen, John Paul,* and *Billy Bob*)

(3) Complete middle name(s) or initial(s)

Do not use suffixes and titles as filing units unless they are needed to distinguish between or among identical names. Titles and suffixes include the following:

(1) Seniority suffix (rank designated by a Roman numeral or the abbreviation *Jr.* or *Sr.*)

(2) Professional suffix (position designated by a certification such as *CPA, Ph.D.,* or *R.N.*)

(3) Title (such as *Mr., Mrs., Ms., Dr., Professor, Sergeant, Dean,* or *Governor*)

Titles followed only by a first name or a last name are indexed in the order they are written. Examples of such names are *Queen Elizabeth, Brother John,* and *Mr. Damico.*

complete names of individuals placed in indexing order

Last (Unit 1)	First (Unit 2)	Middle (Unit 3)	Suffixes and Titles (Unit 4)
Clark	James	L.	Jr.
Clark	James	L.	Sr.
Hoover	Han Nang	Kim	Mrs.
Hoover	Herb	Michael	Mr.
Clark	William	James	Mr.
Clark	William	James	Dr.
Costellano	Maria Elena	Murillo Lopez	
Hoover	Hannah	Kim	Ms.
Clark	Wm.	Bradley	
Clark-Hoover	Karen	Lynelle	Ms.
Clemson	B.	Thomas	II
Ho	Hung		Mr.
Clemson-Clark	Alice	Marie	
Harper	Mary		Sister
Hoover	BettyBruce	Howard	
Hoover	Betty Lou	H.	Ms.
Hertig	Thomas	J.	Major
De Hertog	Thos.	I.	R.N.
De Hertog	Thomas	James	
Hertig	Thomas	J.	Mr.
Clemson	B.	Thomas	III
Hoover	Herbert	Charles Marsh	Mr.
Hoover	Herb	Michael	M.D.
Debrosian	John	T.	
Delano	Marisa	Torti	Mrs.
Hoover	Billy Bob	Scot	

title with first or last name only

Title (Unit 1)	First or Last (Unit 2)
Sister	Mary
Mr.	Hoover
General	Clark

b. Indexed names are alphabetized in indexing order. In alphabetizing names, place (1) nothing before something, (2) numerals before alphabetic letters, and (3) initials before names beginning with that letter.

Compound names (those containing more than one word) in an indexing unit are treated as a single word, whether they are hyphenated or separated by a space. All punctuation marks—such as periods, apostrophes, hyphens, and commas—are disregarded.

Abbreviated and shortened names such as *Wm.* and *Sandy* are alphabetized as they are written.

Unit 1	Unit 2	Unit 3	Unit 4
Clark	James	L.	Jr.
Clark	James	L.	Sr.
Clark	William	James	Dr.
Clark	William	James	Mr.
Clark	Wm.	Bradley	
Clark-Hoover	Karen	Lynelle	Ms.
Clemson	B.	Thomas	II
Clemson	B.	Thomas	III
Clemson-Clark	Alice	Marie	
Costellano	Maria Elena	Murillo Lopez	
Debrosian	John	T.	
De Hertog	Thomas	James	
De Hertog	Thos.	I.	R.N.
Delano	Marisa	Torti	Mrs.
General	Clark		
Harper	Mary		Sister
Hertig	Thomas	J.	Major
Hertig	Thomas	J.	Mr.
Ho	Hung	Mr.	
Hoover	BettyBruce	Howard	
Hoover	Betty Lou	H.	Ms.
Hoover	Billy Bob	Scot	
Hoover	Hannah	Kim	Ms.
Hoover	Han Nang	Kim	Mrs.
Hoover	Herb	Michael	M.D.
Hoover	Herb	Michael	Mr.
Hoover	Herbert	Charles Marsh	Mr.
Mr.	Hoover		
Sister	Mary		

16–4 **Indexing and Alphabetizing the Names of Organizations**

a. Words in organizational names are arranged in the order they are written, even the full names of individuals. Each word—including articles, prepositions, conjunctions, and symbols—is a separate unit. Except for the word *The* appearing as the first word, index the words in the order they are written. When the word *The* begins an organizational name, consider it the last filing unit.

   Spell out any symbols such as & (*and*), $ (*dollar*), or # (*number*). Disregard all punctuation marks such as hyphens, apostrophes, periods, commas, or quotation marks. Close up any letters or words containing hyphens, apostrophes, or periods; index them as a single unit.

organizational names containing articles, lowercase words, and symbols

Organizational Name	Unit 1	Unit 2	Unit 3	Unit 4	Unit 5
Fortune $ Saver	Fortune	Dollar	Saver		
Jane Ryan & Associates	Jane	Ryan	and	Associates	
Jane Ryan and Sons	Jane	Ryan	and	Sons	
The Jane Ryan Realty Company	Jane	Ryan	Realty	Company	The
Rings and Things	Rings	and	Things		

organizational names containing punctuation

Organizational Name	Unit 1	Unit 2	Unit 3	Unit 4	Unit 5
Dr. Ryan's Hospital and Clinic	Dr	Ryans	Hospital	and	Clinic
In-and-Out Burger King	InandOut	Burger	King		
Mark C. Ryan Tires	Mark	C	Ryan	Tires	
Ryan, Irwin, Kirk, and Janns	Ryan	Irwin	Kirk	and	Janns
Ryan-Foreman Furniture	Ryan-Foreman	Furniture			
Ryan's Automotive Repair	Ryans	Automotive	Repair		
R.Y.'s Steakhouse	RYs	Steakhouse			

b. Single letters separated by spaces in business and other organizational names are considered separate indexing units. Single letters written without spaces, letters representing the full organizational name (such as *IBM*, *GM*, and *YMCA*), acronyms (names made from initial letters such as *MADD* and *DARE*), and call letters for radio and television stations are indexed as single units.

letters indexed as separate units

Organizational Name	Unit 1	Unit 2	Unit 3	Unit 4	Unit 5
A B C Linen Service	A	B	C	Linen	Service
A to Z Rentals	A	to	Z	Rentals	
H L T Express	H	L	T	Express	

letters indexed as a single unit

Organizational Name	Unit 1	Unit 2	Unit 3	Unit 4	Unit 5
ABC Learning Systems	ABC	Learning	Systems		
ARMA International	ARMA	International			
A-to-Z Data Systems	AtoZ	Data	Systems		
ITT	ITT				
KABC Radio	KABC	Radio			
KNXT Television	KNXT	Television			
TRW	TRW				
ZZZ Freight Express	ZZZ	Freight	Express		

   c. In business and other organizational names, all abbreviated words such as *Inc., Co.,* and *Mfg.* are indexed as written. Names of cities appearing in business and other organizational names are also indexed as written; however, prefixes (see Section 16-3a) and names appearing together are indexed as one unit.

abbreviations indexed as written

Organizational Name	Unit 1	Unit 2	Unit 3	Unit 4	Unit 5
A & A Paper Co.	A	and	A	Paper	Co
The Clothing Factory, Ltd.	Clothing	Factory	Ltd	The	
Mrs. Ryan's Cookies, Inc.	Mrs	Ryans	Cookies	Inc	

cities indexed as written or combined with prefixes

Organizational Name	Unit 1	Unit 2	Unit 3	Unit 4	Unit 5
El Centro Produce Market	ElCentro	Produce	Market		
Ft. Lauderdale Resorts, Inc.	Ft	Lauderdale	Resorts	Inc	
The Kansas City Inn	Kansas	City	Inn	The	
Las Vegas Credit Bureau	LasVegas	Credit	Bureau		
Los Angeles Flower Exchange	LosAngeles	Flower	Exchange		
New York Stock Exchange	New	York	Stock	Exchange	
Newark Yellow Cab Co.	Newark	Yellow	Cab	Co	
San Diego Gas and Electric Co.	SanDiego	Gas	and	Electric	Co
San Francisco Travel Agency	SanFrancisco	Travel		Agency	
South Pasadena Cleaners	South	Pasadena	Cleaners		
St. Louis Flowers and Gifts	StLouis	Flowers	and	Gifts	
Terre Haute Pharmacy	Terre	Haute	Pharmacy		
West Covina Pet Hospital	West	Covina	Pet	Hospital	
The West Haven Motor Lodge	West	Haven	Motor	Lodge	The
The Westfield Motor Lodge	Westfield	Motor	Lodge	The	

d. Spelled-out numbers in business and other organizational names are treated as any other word in alphabetizing names. Arabic numerals, however, precede all alphabetic letters in arranging indexing units. Roman numerals follow directly after any Arabic numerals—before any alphabetic letters. Arrange the numerals in ascending order, and disregard any ordinal endings such as *st, nd,* or *rd.*

spelled-out numbers

Organizational Name	Unit 1	Unit 2	Unit 3	Unit 4	Unit 5
Twelfth Street Café	Twelfth	Street	Cafe		
Twentieth Century Insurance	Twentieth	Century	Insurance		
Two-for-One Sundries	TwoforOne	Sundries			

Arabic or Roman numerals

Organizational Name	Unit 1	Unit 2	Unit 3	Unit 4	Unit 5
$1 Outlet	1	Dollar	Outlet		
2-for-1 Photos	2for1	Photos			
5 Star Realty	5	Star	Realty		
20th Century Realtors, Inc.	20	Century	Realtors	Inc	
99¢ Store	99	Cent	Store		
A1 Photos	A1	Photos			
Aaron Bros. Art Studios	Aaron	Bros	Art	Studios	
Pier 1 Imports	Pier	1	Imports		
Pier I Food Imports	Pier	I	Food	Imports	
Sixth Avenue Pharmacy	Sixth	Avenue	Pharmacy		
Star 4 Studios	Star	4	Studios		
Star III Studios	Star	III	Studios		

e. Names of domestic government entities are indexed first under the level of government: *United States Government,* (state name) *State of,* (county name) *County of,* (city name) *City of,* or (village name) *Village of.* These levels are a single indexing unit.[2]

Departments and agencies of the federal government are first indexed under *United States Government.* The second indexing unit is the main word that identifies the department, bureau, or office. Terms such as *Bureau of* or *Department of* follow the second indexing unit and are placed in parentheses.

Subdivisions of departments and agencies are subsequently indexed according to their order of authority. Again, use main words for the primary indexing units.

---

[2]*Alphabetic Filing Rules,* 2nd ed. (Prairie Village, Kans.: ARMA International, 1995), 31.

federal government entities

Unit 1	Unit 2	Unit 3	Unit 4	Unit 5
United States Government	Agriculture	(Department of)		
United States Government	Commerce	(Department of) Economic	Development	Administration
		International	Trade	Administration
United States Government	State	(Department of) Passport	Agency	
United States Government	Transportation	(Department of) Coast	Guard	
		Federal	Aviation	Administration
United States Government	Treasury	(Department of) Alcohol	Tobacco (and)	Firearms (Bureau of)
		Customs	Service	
		Internal	Revenue	Service

state and local government entities

Unit 1	Unit 2	Unit 3	Unit 4	Unit 5
California State of	Consumer	Affairs	(Department of)	
California State of	Employment	Development	Department	
Glendale City of	Building	Permits		
Glendale City of	Community	Development (and)	Housing	
Los Angeles County of	Animal	Care (and)	Control	
Los Angeles County of	Disabilities	Commission on		

    f. Index government agencies in foreign countries first by their country. To prevent confusion, use English names. If appropriate, index any additional units in the country name, e.g., *China, Republic of.* States, colonies, provinces, cities, and other such government entities follow, with their names spelled in English.

Unit 1	Unit 2	Unit 3	Unit 4	Unit 5
Belgium	Kingdom of	Taxation	Department of	
China	Republic of	Internal	Affairs	Bureau of
South Korea	Seoul	City of		
Uruguay	Republic of	Public	Education	Secretary of

16-5 Handling Identical and Alternate Names

    a. Use the address to determine the correct filing order of identical individual or organizational names. Compare addresses in the following order: (1) city names, (2) state names, (3) street names (with

File Management

numbered street names appearing first), and (4) house or building numbers. Use these address components in the order listed only until the names are distinguished.

Identical Name	City	State	Street	House No.
John R. Smith	Springfield	Connecticut		
John R. Smith	Springfield	Illinois	23rd Street	
John R. Smith	Springfield	Illinois	Dover Avenue	910
John R. Smith	Springfield	Illinois	Dover Avenue	3640

b. Individuals or organizations that are known by more than one name should be cross-referenced. These second (and even third) names are an additional filing entry indexed in the order of the alternate name. When persons look for the entry under the alternate name, the cross-reference entry refers them to the original record.

Cross-referencing is often used for (1) unusual names, (2) persons or organizations having more than one name, (3) abbreviated names, and (4) foreign business names.

cross-reference entry

IAAP

See: International Association of
      Administrative Professionals

examples of cross-referenced names

Thomas Howard	See: Howard, Thomas
Hung Ho	See: Ho, Hung
Duncan, Thelma R.	See: Nicklin, Thelma R. Duncan
Yama Motors	See: Matsuyama Motor Imports, Inc.
ABC	See: Association for Business Communication
Bonn Chemische Fabrik AG	See: Bonn Chemical Works Inc.

Organizing and Maintaining Computer Data Files

Computer program files and data files are organized into folders for easy access. These folders may be likened to folders you will find in a traditional file cabinet and are sequenced automatically in alphabetical order. A Windows program, Windows Explorer, is used by many to manage the files and folders contained on computer hard drives, removable disks, and CD-ROMs—although most other software applications have data management capabilities too.

16-6 Accessing Windows Explorer[3]

a. Access Windows Explorer by right clicking on the *Start* button in the lower left corner of your screen. Then left click on *Explore* to enter the program. If your computer has a *Windows* key, use the keyboard shortcut—*Windows + E*—to access Windows Explorer.

b. The default configurations for Windows Explorer in Windows 95, Windows 98, Windows 2000, Windows ME, and Windows XP differ, but all these operating systems offer the same options for file management and similar options to change their appearance and configuration.

c. Windows Explorer permits users to display the contents of a computer—*Desktop, My Computer,* all drives (both hard and removable), folders, and files—up to five different ways, depending upon the operating system. These views may be accessed through the *View* menu or through the *Views* icon on the toolbar. Three views are reasonably consistent among Windows 95, 98, 2000, ME, and XP:

(1) *List view.* In the *List* view, Windows Explorer shows the names of files and folders in the open drive or folder. Windows Explorer in earlier operating systems (Windows 95 and 98) may be configured in Web style so that the computer screen looks similar to Windows Explorer in Windows XP. The following illustration shows the open folder *My Documents* in the *List* view in Windows Explorer, Windows XP.

List *view in Windows Explorer, Windows XP*

---

[3]The computer-specific procedures outlined here and in the remaining sections of this chapter are based on Windows Explorer, the versions contained in Windows XP, Windows ME, Windows 2000, Windows 98, and Windows 95.

(2) *Details view.* For the open drive or folder, the *Details* view in Windows Explorer shows the name of any folders within that drive or folder, the type of storage unit (*File Folder*), and the date and time each folder was created. As may be seen in the following illustration created in Windows Explorer, Windows XP, each file in the open folder *My Documents* is displayed by name, size, type, and the date and time it was last saved.

Details *view in Windows Explorer, Windows XP*

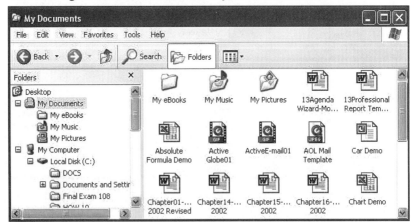

(3) *Icon or Large Icon view.* In the *Icon* or *Large Icon* view, Windows Explorer displays large icons to illustrate the components. Component names are listed below the icons. For example, folders are represented by a standard file folder. The folder name appears directly below the icon. Files within an open folder are represented by icons unique to the program with which the file was created. Directly below each file is the file name. The following illustration of the open *My Documents* folder from Windows Explorer, Windows XP, shows how the *Icon* or *Large Icon* view appears in Windows Explorer versions of Windows 95, 98, 2000, ME, and XP.

Icon *or* Large Icon *view in Windows Explorer, Windows XP*

Windows Explorer in Windows XP offers two additional viewing styles: *Thumbnails* and *Tiles.*

(1) *Thumbnails view.* The *Thumbnails* view is similar to the *Icon* or *Large Icon* view in that document files are represented by the unique icon depicting the program in which they were created. Templates, Excel files, PowerPoint files, and other graphic files, however, are represented by a miniaturized image of their contents. The name of the folder or file appears below the icon or image. A *Thumbnails* view of an open *My Documents* folder from Windows Explorer, Windows XP follows.

Thumbnails *view of* My Documents *folder, Windows Explorer, Windows XP*

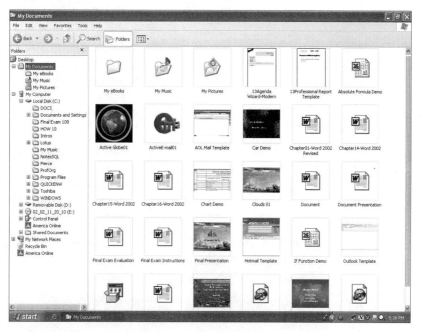

(2) *Tiles view.* The *Tiles* view treats folders the same way as *Icons* or *Large Icons* except the folder name appears to the right of the icon instead of below it. Files within folders showcase in large size the unique icon depicting the program in which the file was created. To the right of each icon is the filename, the name of the program in which the file was created, and the size of the file in terms of bytes or pixels. An illustration of an open *My Documents* folder shown in *Tiles* view in Windows Explorer, Windows XP, appears on page 500.

Tiles *view in Windows Explorer, Windows XP*

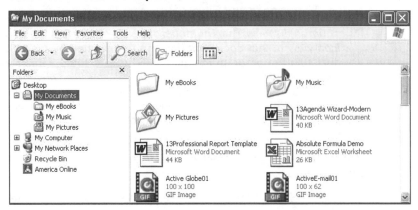

d. **Windows Explorer permits you to change its defaults. You may elect to manage folders and files the same way as you manage Windows applications folders and files—with double and single clicks (the default); or you may elect to manage folders and files in a Web mode—like hyperlinks, with single clicks. Instructions here are based on the defaults for Windows Explorer.**

e. **The screen size of Windows Explorer may be adjusted using the** *Maximize* **or** *Restore (down)* **buttons on the title bar. The size of the viewing area will affect the screen appearance of folders and files. Figure 1, shown below, and Figure 2, page 501, show maximum screen-size illustrations for Windows 98 and Windows 2000.**

Figure 1. *Details* View (Web Style) in Windows Explorer, Windows 98

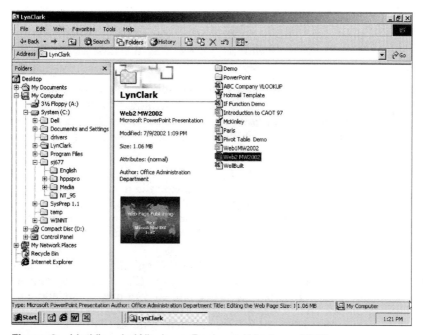

Figure 2. *List* View in Windows Explorer, Windows 2000

16-7 Creating File Folders for Data Files

Program files install automatically with a hierarchy of folders and files. Rarely does the user need to reorganize the structure of program files and folders to use the software.

Windows automatically comes with a folder specifically for the storage of files created by the user—*My Documents.* If you were to use this folder to store all the files you created, it would soon become so full that you would be unable to locate easily files you might need. Therefore, you need to create your own file cabinet—additional folders—to store your data files.

a. Create file folders for the major categories of information that comprise your data files. Use the following procedures to determine the names and the number of folders you will need.

(1) Make a comprehensive list of the major categories of information with which you deal. Your categories may be function based, client based, department based, or a combination of major areas for which you are responsible.

(2) Under each major category list any subcategories that would ultimately contain sufficient files to warrant a separate folder.

(3) List under any subcategories additional subcategories that may be appropriate. Attempt to keep your listing hierarchy to no more than three levels.

16

File Management

501

b. Access Windows Explorer by right clicking on the *Start* button in the lower left corner of your screen. Left click on *Explore* to enter the program. If your computer has a Windows key, use the keyboard shortcut— *Windows + E*—to access Windows Explorer.

Close any open files by left clicking on the drive to which you wish to add new folders for your data files. You should then be in the root directory of your selected drive and ready to create folders to store your data files. Follow these procedures to create new folders in the root directory.

(1) To create a new folder in the root directory, click *File* on the menu bar. Select *New;* then select *Folder*. In the name box that appears next to the new folder, key a name that will describe its contents. Use as few letters as possible, but not so few that you will not be able to recognize easily the subject matter of the folder. Begin the name of each folder with a capital letter.

(2) To create a new folder within a folder that is in the root directory, you must first open the existing parent folder. Do so by double left clicking on it. When the folder is open, you may create additional folders within this major category. Left click *File* on the menu bar, select *New*, then select *Folder*. Name the new folder with a descriptive title.

(3) To create a new folder within a subcategory folder, first open the subcategory folder by double left clicking on it. Follow the usual procedure of left clicking *File* on the menu bar, selecting *New,* and then selecting *Folder* to create any additional folders in this subcategory.

c. As you create files in separate software applications such as Microsoft Word, Excel, PowerPoint, WordPerfect, Lotus, Access, etc., be sure to save your file in the folder that best categorizes the information in the file. To do so, use the *File–Save As* command from the menu bar and make sure the *Save in:* box displays the folder name in which you wish to store the file.

d. You may manage your files from Windows Explorer or from your applications software. In applications software the file management options are available from the menu bar through the *File–Save As* and the *File–Open* dialogue boxes.

16–8 Selecting Folders and Files

a. Selecting a folder permits you to open it, delete it, move it to another location, or copy it to another location. In Windows Explorer and in applications software, select a folder by left clicking on it. Double left clicking on a folder opens the folder and displays its contents.

b. Selecting a file permits you to open it, delete it, move it to another location, or copy it to another location. In Windows Explorer and in applications software, select a file by left clicking on it. Double left clicking on a file in Windows Explorer opens the file in the program in which it was created, provided that program is resident on your computer.

c. **Multiple folders or files may be selected simultaneously. Use the following procedures to select contiguous and noncontiguous files or folders simultaneously.**

(1) Contiguous folders or files, those appearing one after another, may be selected simultaneously by left clicking on the first folder or file, holding down the *Shift* key, and then left clicking on the last folder or file in the series to be selected. Release the *Shift* key. The series of selected items will be highlighted.

(2) Noncontiguous folders or files, those not appearing directly one after another, may be selected simultaneously by left clicking on the first folder or file, holding down the *Ctrl* key, and then left clicking on each folder or file to be selected. Release the *Ctrl* key when your selection has been completed. The selected items will be highlighted.

16–9 Deleting Folders and Files

Folders and files that are no longer needed occupy valuable space on the computer hard disk and slow down its operation. Proper maintenance procedures require that any obsolete folders and files be removed. Follow these procedures to delete any unwanted folders or files:

(1) Select the folders or files to be deleted by following the procedures described in Section 16-8.

(2) Place the mouse pointer anywhere in the highlighted selection and press the *Delete* key on the keyboard. You may, as an alternative, right click the mouse and select the *Delete* option from the drop-down menu.

16–10 Copying Folders and Files

Copying folders or files to another location—in another folder on the hard drive, to a removable disk, or to a CD-ROM—leaves the folders or files in their original location and places a copy in the designated location. Procedures for copying folders and files to another location are not limited to one. The following procedure is just one of several that may be used in Windows Explorer or with applications software:

(1) Select the folders or files to be copied by following the procedures described in Section 16-8.

(2) Place the mouse pointer anywhere in the highlighted selection and press *Ctrl-C* (the keyboard copy command). You may, as an alternative, right click the mouse and select the *Copy* option from the drop-down menu.

16

File Management

(3) **Windows Explorer:** Navigate to the location where the files are to be copied, and double left click on that drive or folder to open it.

Applications software: Use the *Look in:* box (in the *File–Save As* or *File–Open* dialogue box) to navigate to the location where the files are to be copied, and double left click on the drive or folder to open that location.

(4) Place the pointer on the destination drive or folder and press *Ctrl-V* (the keyboard retrieve [paste] command) to place a copy of the folders or files in the opened location. You may, as an alternative, right click the mouse and select the *Paste* option from the drop-down menu.

(5) Copied folders and files will initially appear at the bottom of the listing but will be sorted correctly once a drive or folder has been closed and reopened. A copied folder is copied with all its contents.

16–11 Moving Folders and Files

Moving folders and files to another location removes the folders and files from the original location and places them in a new drive or folder. Procedures for moving folders and files to another location are not limited to one. The following procedure is just one of several that may be used in Windows Explorer or with applications software. It permits folders and files to be moved easily to a designated location.

(1) Select the folders or files to be moved by following the procedures described in Section 16-8.

(2) Place the mouse pointer anywhere in the highlighted selection and press *Ctrl-X* (the keyboard move [cut] command). You may, as an alternative, right click the mouse and select the *Cut* option from the drop-down menu.

(3) **Windows Explorer:** Navigate to the location where the files are to be moved, and double left click on that drive or folder to open it.

Applications software: Use the *Look in:* box (in the *File–Save As* or *File–Open* dialogue box) to navigate to the location where the files are to be moved, and double left click on that drive or folder to open it.

(4) Place the pointer on the destination drive or folder and press *Ctrl-V* (the keyboard retrieve [paste] command) to transfer the folders or files to their new location. You may, as an alternative, right click the mouse and select the *Paste* option from the drop-down menu.

(5) Moved folders and files will initially appear at the bottom of the listing but will be sorted correctly once a drive or folder has been closed and reopened. A moved folder is moved with all its contents.

Glossary A
Grammatical Terms Used in
A Handbook for Office Professionals

Abbreviation
A shortened form of a word or word group. Examples: *in.* for *inches* and *AMA* for *American Medical Association.*

Absolute adjective
An adjective that cannot be compared because it represents a definite and exact state. Examples: *dead, perfect, unique,* and *full.*

Action verb
A verb that shows or represents movement. Examples: *run, talk,* and *breathe.*

Active voice
A method of constructing sentences that identifies who does what. The person or thing performing the action is the subject of the sentence. Examples: The *stockholders* rejected the proposal. *We* signed a one-year lease.

Adj.
Abbreviation of *adjective.*

Adjective
A word or word group that describes a noun or pronoun. It tells what kind, which one, or how many. Examples: *good* investment, *this* bank, and *three* employees.

Adverb
A word that describes a verb, an adjective, or another adverb. It tells when, where, how, or to what degree. Many adverbs end in *ly.* Examples: arrive *early,* come *here,* drive *carefully,* and *too* small.

Adverbial clause
A word group containing a subject and a verb that begins with a subordinating conjunction such as *if, when, since, because,* or *as.* An adverbial clause modifies the verb in the main clause. Example: *If you wish to make an appointment,* please *call* me.

Ampersand
A symbol (&) meaning *and* used mainly in organizational names. Example: We have signed a contract with Robert White *&* Associates.

Animate object
Any person, any living thing, or any group composed of persons or living things. Compare with **Inanimate object**. Examples: *manager, tree, company,* and *flock of sheep.*

Antecedent

A noun or an indefinite pronoun to which a pronoun or any number of pronouns refer. Examples: Our last newsletter asked all *clients who* are interested in bond investment to indicate *their* willingness to attend a free seminar by phoning me. *Anyone* in the office *who* is interested in carpooling should submit *his* or *her* name to our manager.

Apostrophe

A symbol (') used to show noun possession, the omission of letters in contractions, and the beginning and ending of quotations within quotations. Examples: (1) *Carol's* salary; (2) we *haven't*; and (3) He asked, "Have you read my latest article, 'Western Travels'?"

Apposition, Appositive, Appositive expression

A word or word group that renames or explains the noun or pronoun it follows. These descriptive words usually add extra information. Example: Ms. Johnson, *our new manager,* has been with the company for three years.

Article

The words *a, an,* and *the.* These words are used as adjectives. Examples: *a* method, *an* interesting tour, *the* stock market.

Being verb

A form of the verb *to be* when it is used as a main verb, that is, when it appears alone or as the last verb in a verb phrase. These forms are *am, is, are, was, were, be,* and *been.* Examples: (1) Jill *was* here yesterday. (2) He has *been* our client for six years.

Being verb helper

A form of the verb *to be* when it is used in a verb phrase as a helping verb. These forms are *am, is, are, was, were, be,* and *been.* Example: Whitmore appliances *have* not *been sold* in our store for the past three years.

Cardinal number

A number such as 3 (three), 10 (ten), 32 (thirty-two), 541, or 1,856 that is used in simple counting.

Case form

A category used to classify nouns and pronouns in a sentence as subjective, objective, or possessive.

Celestial body

A planet, star, or other heavenly form. Examples: *Mars, North Star,* and *sun.*

Clause

A word group that contains a subject and a verb. Example: before *you leave* the office.

Collective noun

A noun composed of individual persons or things. Examples: *committee, team, jury, herd,* and *class.*

Colon

A punctuation mark (:) used to indicate that the following words explain further the word or word group appearing before the punctuation mark. Example: Our company specializes in the manufacture of the following women's clothing accessories: shoes, boots, handbags, and belts.

Command

A sentence in which the subject *you* is not stated but instead is implied. The sentence directs the understood subject *you* to perform (or refrain from) an action. Examples: (1) (You) Mail this information to me as soon as possible. (2) (You) Do not slam the door as you leave.

Common noun

A noun that does not name a specific person, place, or thing. Examples: *supervisor, building, city council, university,* and *company.*

Common noun element

That part of a proper noun that is not a specific name. Examples: *university* in Rutgers University, *building* in Tishman Building, and *city council* in Miami City Council.

Comparative form

The spelling or form of an adjective or an adverb when it compares two nouns or pronouns or two conditions. Compare with **Superlative form.** Examples: (1) This year's sales are *greater* than last year's. (2) We have progressed *more slowly* in this area than we had hoped.

Complement pronoun

A pronoun that completes a being verb. It follows a form of the verb *to be—am, is, are, was, were, be,* and *been.* Example: The contest winners were *they,* Karen and Bill.

Complete thought

A word group that contains a subject and a verb. The word group must make sense and be able to stand alone as a complete sentence. A complete thought is also known as an *independent clause.* Example: *Mr. Reed agreed to the terms of the contract,* but *his attorney advised him not to sign it.*

Complex sentence

A sentence that contains a dependent clause and an independent clause. Example: As soon as we receive your reply, we will send you a replacement or issue a credit to your account.

Complimentary close

The first closing line of a business letter. Example: *Sincerely yours.*

Compound adjective

Two or more words acting together as a single thought to describe or modify a noun or pronoun. Same as *compound modifier.* Example: *part-time* job.

Compound modifier

See **Compound adjective.**

Compound noun

Two or more words used as a single unit to name a person, place, or thing. Examples: *sister-in-law, notary public, high school, community college, word processing,* and *income tax.*

Compound number

A number requiring more than one word when written in word form. Examples: *twenty-seven, ninety-eight, one hundred, two hundred fifty.*

Compound sentence

A sentence containing two independent clauses (complete thoughts) joined by (1) a semicolon; (2) a transitional expression (such as *therefore, consequently,* or *nevertheless*); or (3) the conjunction *and, but, or,* or *nor.* Examples: (1) Please call me when the shipment arrives; I will pick it up immediately. (2) The Model 432 cart you ordered has been discontinued; *however,* our Model 434 cart has all the features of the cart you ordered. (3) The manufacturer has promised to send us another shipment of these disks by next week, *and* we will fill your order immediately upon its arrival.

Compound subject

A subject that contains two or more nouns or pronouns joined by *and, or,* or *nor.* Example: *Ellen and Jack* have already reached their quotas for this month's sales.

Compound verb

Two or more words combined to produce a single thought unit that functions as a verb. Compound verbs appear as one word, as two words, or hyphenated. Examples: *upgrade, mark up, double-space.*

Compound-complex sentence

A sentence containing two independent clauses (complete thoughts) and a dependent clause. Example: This suite of offices is currently available for occupancy, and we will release the keys to you as soon as you return the signed lease agreement with a certified check for $3,000.

Conjugation

The various forms of a verb that show person. Examples: I *see,* he or she *sees,* we *see,* you *see,* they *see;* I *am,* he or she *is,* we *are,* you *are,* they *are.*

Conjunction

A part of speech that serves as a connector of words or word groups within a sentence. Examples: *and, but, or, nor, either . . . or,* and *not only . . . but also.*

Conjunctive adverb

An adverb—such as *consequently, however,* or *therefore*—that connects the main clauses of a compound sentence. Example: Most of our advertising budget has already been allocated; *therefore,* we are unable to take advantage of your offer.

Conjunctive pair

A class of connecting words—conjunctions—that link contrasting or dependent ideas. These connectors consist of two parts. Examples: *either . . . or, neither . . . nor, if . . . then,* and *not only . . . but also.*

Consonant

Any letter of the alphabet other than *a, e, i, o,* and *u.*

Contingent expression

An expression that depends upon a similar expression for completion. Example: *The sooner* you take advantage of this offer, *the more often* you will be able to enjoy your personal home movie selections.

Contraction

Shortened forms in which an apostrophe is used to show the omission of letters or numbers. These shortened forms may be applied to certain words, verb phrases, and dates. Examples: *internat'l* for *international, doesn't* for *does not,* and *'04* for *2004.*

Coordinating conjunction

A part of speech (conjunction) that joins equal words or word groups. Examples: *and, but, or,* and *nor.*

Courtesy title

A title used to address individuals. Examples: *Mr., Ms., Mrs., Miss, Master,* and *Dr.*

Dash

A mark of punctuation (— or --) used to precede summary statements or for emphasis in setting off words or word groups. The em dash (—) is used in computer-based and printed copy. In E-mail and typewritten copy, the dash is formed by keying two hyphens consecutively (--); no space appears before, between, or after the hyphens. Examples: (1) Sofas, chairs, bedroom suites, dining room sets—we have a large variety of styles and brands from which you may choose. (2) Three employees--Clyde Jones, Janice Lee, and Dennis Martinez--have agreed to work overtime next week.

Decimal

A small dot (.) used in numbers to separate a whole number from a portion of the next number in the sequence. Examples: *12.5, 0.07, 147.38, 6.75 percent,* and *$1.4 million.*

Declarative sentence

A complete sentence that makes a statement. Example: Our company president announced our merger with Cory Industries yesterday.

Dependent adverbial clause

A word group that (1) contains a subject and a verb and (2) begins with a subordinating conjunction such as *if, when, since, because,* or *as.* An adverbial clause modifies the verb in the main clause. Example: *When the shipment arrives,* we will *call* you immediately.

Dependent clause

A word group that contains a subject and a verb but cannot stand alone as a complete sentence. Same as a *subordinate clause.* Example: John told me last week *that he expects to win this month's sales contest.*

Direct address

The act of calling a person by name, title, or classification in written or oral communication *with that person.* Examples: (1) Thank you, *Ms. Burwell,* for responding so promptly. (2) Yes, *Professor,* we will have this textbook available for use during the spring semester. (3) Only you, *fellow citizens,* can prevent a further decline of schools in this city.

Direct object

A noun or pronoun acted upon by the subject and verb of a sentence. Example: Our accountant mailed the *check* yesterday.

Direct quotation

The exact words spoken or written by a person or group. Example: According to the committee's report, "The property was sold in 2002 for $10,950,000."

Ellipsis

A series of three periods (. . .)—with spaces before, between, and after the periods—used to show omissions in quoted material or hesitations in other printed material. Example: According to his latest journal article, Professor Haley concludes, "Social conditions will continue to improve in this area . . . unless the government withdraws its funding commitment."

Essential subordinate clause

A word group that contains a subject and a verb but cannot stand alone as a complete sentence. The word group is needed to complete the main idea of the sentence by furnishing *who, what, which one, when, why, how, whether,* or *to what degree.* An *essential subordinate clause* is the same as a *restrictive clause,* a *restrictive dependent clause,* or a *restrictive subordinate clause.* Example: Dr. Logan is the professor *who is in charge of preparing the accreditation report.*

Exclamation mark

A mark of punctuation (!) used to show strong feeling or emotion. Example: Take advantage of our free offer today—while this letter is in front of you!

First person

I or *we* used as subjects in writing or speaking. Example: After analyzing the specimen, *we* contacted several contagious disease specialists.

Fraction

A part of a whole number expressed in proportion to the whole. Example: The legislature is proposing a ½ percent increase in our state's sales tax.

Future perfect tense

A verb phrase used to express an action that will occur before a certain time in the future. This tense is formed by using the verb helpers *will have* and the past participle of a verb. Example: If donations continue to be made at this same rate, we *will have paid* for this new hospital wing before its completion.

Future progressive tense

A verb phrase used to express an action that will be ongoing in the future. This tense is formed by using the verb helpers *will be* and the present participle of a verb. Example: Our volunteers *will be calling* other alumni during the next month to solicit donations for the newly formed college foundation.

Future tense

A verb phrase used to express an action that will happen in the future. This tense is formed by using the verb helper *will* and the present part of a verb. Example: I *will call* you next week.

Gender

A term used to refer to the sexual classification of nouns, pronouns, and their modifiers. Classifications include *feminine, masculine,* and *neuter.* Examples: (1) *Maria* lost *her* purse. (2) *He* sold all *his* stock. (3) The *company* has just purchased dental insurance for all *its* employees.

Gerund

A verb form ending in *ing* that functions as a noun in a sentence. Example: His *refusing* our offer came as a surprise to all of us.

Helping verb

A verb that appears with the present part, present participle, or past participle of another verb to form tenses. Examples: *will* go, *are* planning, *have been* employed.

Horizontal listing

A listing of items that continue across the page like ordinary text. Compare with **Vertical listing**. Example: Check the following sources for current employment opportunities: *classified ads appearing in your local newspaper, postings in your college or university employment office, and listings provided by career centers on the Internet.*

Hyphen

A mark of punctuation (-) used in some word groups to join two or more words that function as a single idea. In E-mail and typewritten copy, this mark is also used to represent *through* when placed between two numbers. Examples: *mother-in-law, up-to-date,* and pages *34-35.*

Hyphenated compound

A word group joined by hyphens that functions as a single thought unit. Examples: *trade-in, self-employment, well-to-do.*

Imperative sentence, Imperative statement

A complete sentence in which the subject *you* is not stated; it is understood. Example: (You) Please mail your check in the enclosed envelope today.

Implied verb

An intended verb that is not stated. Compare with **Stated verb**. Examples: (1) If possible (If it *is* possible), we would appreciate your shipping this order by July 10. (2) John has more seniority with the firm than I (I *have*).

Inanimate object

A nonliving thing. Compare with **Animate object**. Examples: *computer, lease,* and *pen.*

Indefinite pronoun

A pronoun that does not represent a specific person, place, or thing. Examples: *everybody, anyone,* and *something.*

Independent adjective

An adjective that describes a noun without relying on other adjectives to enhance its meaning. Two or more independent adjectives modifying a noun are separated by commas. Examples: an *intelligent, conscientious* student. Note that in the phrase "... printed in *large bold* print ... " the adjectives are not independent and therefore are not separated by commas.

Independent clause

A word group that (1) contains a subject and a verb and (2) can stand alone as a complete sentence. An *independent clause* is the same as a *main clause*. Example: Although he was at first reluctant, *Senator Richards has agreed to seek reelection for a third term.*

Independent phrase

A word group that represents a complete sentence although it is not. Example: *Now to the point.*

Independent question

A word group stated in question format that stands alone as a complete sentence. Example: Who is responsible for closing the office on Friday evenings?

Indirect object

A noun or pronoun acted upon by a subject, a verb, and a direct object. Example: Chris gave *him* the check yesterday.

Indirect question

A statement that describes the content of a question or questions. Example: Several customers have asked whether we will extend our shopping hours during the holiday season.

Indirect quotation

A statement that describes written or spoken words of another person or source but does not employ the exact words used by that person or source. Example: Sharon said that if she is not promoted within the next three months, she will begin to look for another position.

Infinitive

The present part of a verb preceded by the word *to*. Example: You will probably need *to work* overtime *to finish* this project by its deadline date.

Infinitive phrase

A word group beginning with an infinitive and ending with a noun or pronoun. Example: *To obtain more information,* just mail the enclosed card.

Inside address

The part of a business letter that lists the addressee's name, professional title (if any), company name (if any), street address, city, state, and zip code.

Intransitive verb

A verb that does not have a direct or an indirect object. Compare with **Transitive verb**. Examples: (1) The governor will *campaign* heavily in the southern part of the state next week. (2) Responsibility for the success of this project *lies* with the project manager. (3) Prices *rise* when manufacturers encounter increased costs.

Introductory clause, Introductory dependent clause

A word group that (1) contains a subject and a verb and (2) starts with a subordinating conjunction such as *if, when, since, because,* or *as*. The word group begins the sentence, ends with a comma, and is followed by the main clause. Example: *Because we are unable to obtain this merchandise,* we are returning your check.

Introductory phrase

A word group without a subject and corresponding verb that starts with a preposition, an infinitive, or a participle. Such word groups that begin a sentence and appear directly before the main clause are introductory. Examples: (1) *By this time next year,* we will have moved our home office to Louisville. (2) *To receive your free copy,* simply sign and mail the enclosed card. (3) *Lured by the promise of large profits,* investors poured millions of dollars into this fraudulent development project.

Introductory prepositional phrase

A word group that starts with a preposition but does not contain a subject or a verb. The word group begins the sentence and is followed directly by the main clause. Example: *During this time* we will need to gather more information about the economic conditions of this area.

Irregular verb

A verb that does not form its parts in the usual way, that is, by adding *ed* to the present part to form the past part and the past participle. Examples: *eat, ate, eaten; go, went, gone;* and *sing, sang, sung.*

Limiting adverb

A word or word group that restrains, confines, or negates the meaning of a verb. Examples: *not, barely, scarcely,* and *hardly.*

Limiting expression

A word group that restrains or confines another word group. Example: You may petition for a grade change, *but only for a valid reason.*

Linking verb

A form of the verb *to be* used as a main verb or a form of another nonaction verb. Examples: (1) She *is* a conscientious employee. (2) I *feel* bad that our manager is being transferred.

Lowercase

Refers to the format of alphabetic characters; letters that are not capitalized. Examples: *a, d, m,* and *u.*

Main clause

A word group that (1) contains a subject and a verb and (2) can stand alone as a complete sentence. A *main clause* is the same as an *independent clause.* Example: When we receive your signed contract, *we will order the equipment needed for your installation.*

Main verb

A single verb or the last verb in a verb phrase. Examples: (1) Please *call* me tomorrow. (2) The display *was* too large to fit into a suitcase. (3) Only three candidates have been *called.* (4) Our manager was *disappointed* with the results of the advertising campaign.

Main word

The most descriptive or definitive word in a compound noun. Examples: *mother*-in-law, personnel *manager, notary* public, and vice *president.*

Main words in a heading or title to be capitalized

All words except the articles *a, an,* and *the*; the conjunctions *and, but, or,* or *nor;* and prepositions with three or fewer letters such as *of, for, to, in,* or *out* UNLESS any of these words appear as the first or last word. Examples: (1) Normal Climate Conditions in the Northeastern Part of the United States, (2) Corporate Goals and Strategies for 2002, (3) An Analysis of Marketing Strategies Used by an Independent Mail-Order House.

Modifier

An *adjective* that describes a noun or pronoun. An *adverb* that describes or limits a verb, an adjective, or another adverb.

N.

An abbreviation for *noun.*

Nominative case, Nominative case form

A noun or pronoun used as the subject of a sentence, the complement of a *being* verb, or the object of the infinitive *to be* when this infinitive has no subject. Nouns always maintain the same form; pronouns require a specific form: *I, he, she, you, we, they, who, whoever.* Same as *subjective case, subjective case form.* Examples: (1) *We* called you yesterday. (2) The winner was *she,* Joyce Moore. (3) I would not want to be *he* when the mistake is discovered.

Nonaction verb

A verb that does not demonstrate action. Examples: *am, is, was,* and *were.*

Nonessential subordinate clause

A word group that (1) contains a subject and a verb and (2) starts with a subordinating conjunction such as *if, when, as, after,* or *although* or a relative pronoun such as *who* or *which.* This word group provides an additional thought unit that does not change or modify the main clause of the sentence. It is the same as a *nonrestrictive clause* or a *nonrestrictive subordinate clause.* Examples: (1) Our major advertising campaign will begin on November 1, *after all our dealers nationwide have the new product line in their stores.* (2) Jan Davidson, *who has been with our company for four years,* has been placed in charge of the project.

Nonrestrictive

A word or word group that is not essential to the meaning of the main idea.

Nonrestrictive clause

A word group that (1) contains a subject and a verb and (2) appears with a main clause. This word group is subordinate to the main idea and does not alter its meaning. It complements the main idea by adding additional information. A *nonrestrictive clause* is the same as a *nonessential subordinate clause* or a *nonrestrictive subordinate clause.* Examples: (1) This proposal, *as I explained to you earlier,* has not yet been approved by the Board of Directors. (2) The profit and loss statement for this project was shown in our last annual report, *which was distributed to the stockholders on March 1.*

Nonrestrictive phrase

A word group that begins with a preposition, an infinitive, or a participle, does not contain a subject with a corresponding verb; and ends with a noun or pronoun. This word group does not affect the meaning of the main clause; it adds an additional idea that does not modify the main idea. Examples: (1) You cannot, *in my estimation,* expect a greater return on your investment at this time. (2) Susan and Randy, *to name at least two people,* were among those staff members in our department who were affected by the abolishment of our child care center. (3) Our president, *concerned about the steady sales decline,* has decided to invest more heavily in research and development.

Nonrestrictive subordinate clause
See **nonessential subordinate clause**.

Noun
A person, place, thing, animal, quality, concept, feeling, action, measure, or state. Examples: *employee, city, chair, cat, sincerity, democracy, love, swimming, inch,* and *happiness.*

Object
A noun or pronoun acted upon by another part of speech, e.g., a verb or a preposition. Examples: (1) Scott sent *me* the *check* yesterday. (2) For the next three *months,* you will receive a free trial *subscription.*

Object of a preposition
The noun or pronoun that follows a preposition. Examples: of our *clients,* for the last few *months,* from *her,* and through your *efforts.*

Objective case, Objective case form
A noun or pronoun used as the object of a verb, the object of a preposition, the subject or object of an infinitive other than *to be,* or the object of the infinitive *to be* when this infinitive has a subject. Nouns always maintain the same form; pronouns require a specific form: *me, him, her, you, us, them.* Examples: (1) You may *contact me* at this number after 3 p.m. (2) Please send this information *to me* directly. (3) I do not want *to give her* too much information about our new product. (4) I would not want our new *supervisor to be him.*

Open compound
Two or more words used to represent a single idea. The words appear as separate words and are not hyphenated. Examples: *information processing, golf club,* and *vice president.*

Ordinal number
A number form that indicates order in a series. Cardinal numbers such as *3, 10,* and *246* are numbers used in counting; ordinal numbers such as *first (1st), second (2nd),* and *twenty-fourth (24th)* indicate order or position in a series. Example: Our sales report for the *fourth* quarter must be ready by January 15.

Parallel structure
Words or word groups used in a similar fashion that are expressed in the same format. Parallel structure applies to words joined by a conjunction, joined by a conjunctive pair, appearing in a series, and appearing in a listing. Examples: (1) Our receptionist's main duties are to *answer the telephone* and *greet office visitors.* (2) You may order supplies from not only *our standard supply catalog* but also *Kalleen's*

Computer Supply Catalog. (3) The whole day was spent *returning phone calls, reading the mail,* and *responding to E-mail messages.*

Parenthesis

A mark of punctuation signifying the beginning [(] of a side thought and the ending [)] of a side thought. Example: Please request copies of any ancillary materials (at least an instructor's manual and key) that may accompany the text.

Parenthetical element, Parenthetical expression, Parenthetical remark

A word or word group that does not contribute to the meaning of the main clause but merely acts as a transitional thought or provides an additional idea. Examples: (1) *Therefore,* we are returning this order for credit. (2) The meeting scheduled for October 24, *as you probably already know,* has been canceled.

Participial phrase

A word group beginning with a past or present participle. Examples: (1) *Encouraged by last month's increased sales,* our Advertising Department has decided to extend the present campaign another month. (2) *Hoping to sell the property immediately,* Mr. Rice agreed to drop the price $10,000.

Parts of a verb

The forms of a verb that are used to construct tenses, that is, those spellings of a verb used in expressing time periods. The parts of a verb include the *infinitive, present part, past part, present participle,* and *past participle.* Examples: *to send, send, sent, sending, sent.*

Passive voice

A form of sentence construction in which the doer of the action is not the subject of the sentence. This form is used primarily to deemphasize the person performing the action by focusing instead on the results. The passive voice is constructed by using a form of the verb *to be* as a helper and the past participle of the main verb. Example: These reports *were mailed* last week. The back gate *was left* unlocked last night.

Past part

One of the five verb parts used in constructing tenses. For most verbs this part is formed by adding *ed* to the present part, the form listed in the dictionary. Examples: *called* (call), *discussed* (discuss), and *answered* (answer). The past part for verbs not following this pattern is shown in the dictionary directly after the main entry. Examples: *saw* (see), *wrote* (write), and *went* (go).

Past participle

One of the five verb parts used in constructing tenses. The past participle is always used with a helping verb. For most verbs this part is formed by adding *ed* to the present part, the form listed in the dictionary. Examples: *called* (call), *discussed* (discuss), and *answered* (answer). The past participle for verbs not following this pattern is shown in the dictionary directly after the main entry. Examples: *seen* (see), *written* (write), and *gone* (go).

Past perfect tense

Used to describe a past action that has taken place before another past action. This tense is formed by using the helping verb *had* and the past participle of the main verb. Example: The applicant *had accepted* another position before he *received* our offer.

Past progressive tense

Used to describe an ongoing action that took place in the past. This tense is formed by using the helping verb *was* or *were* with the present participle of the main verb. Example: Last year our company *was hiring* additional personnel; this year the company is reducing its staff in all departments.

Past tense

Used to report a single past action or occurrence. This tense is formed by using the past part of a verb. Example: We *finished* the report last Friday.

Perfect tense

Describes the present, past, or future by using a form of *have* as a helping verb and the past participle of the main verb. Examples: *have completed, had completed,* and *will have completed.*

Permanent compound

A dictionary entry consisting of more than one word to represent a single idea. Examples: *air-conditioning, high school, community college, up-to-date,* and *full-time.*

Personal pronoun

A word that substitutes for the name of a person or thing. Examples: *I, he, she, it, we, they, you, me, him, her, us,* and *them.*

Phrase

A group of two or more grammatically related words that act upon one another in a modifying, coordinating, or composite relationship. The word group does not have a subject and a verb. Examples: (1) Our sales have increased *during the past few months.* (2) Mr. Lee requested the custodial crew *to wash the windows, vacuum the carpeting,* and *set up the chairs.* (3) Our supply *of printer toner cartridges* is diminishing rapidly.

Plural

More than one. Nouns, pronouns, and verbs have plural forms.

Plural noun

More than one person, place, or thing. These nouns usually require a special form and appear with a plural verb. Examples: *disks* (disk), *losses* (loss), *companies* (company), *curricula* (curriculum), and *potatoes* (potato). The examples in this entry show different formats for forming plural nouns.

Polite request

A command worded like a question that requests the reader or listener to perform a specific action. Example: Will you please send us your remaining application materials by November 16.

Possessive

A noun or pronoun that shows ownership. Examples: (1) The *company's* liability has not yet been determined. (2) The company awarded all *its* employees a bonus.

Possessive case, Possessive case form

The spelling of a noun or pronoun that shows ownership. Examples: *Sally's* desk, an *accountants'* convention, *his* books, *your* paycheck, and *their* tickets.

Predicate

That part of the sentence that includes the verb or verb phrase and all its modifiers—all parts of the sentence except the complete subject. Example: All parts in this assembly *will need to be replaced within the next few months.*

Prefix

A syllable attached to the beginning of a word that forms a derivative word or an inflectional form. Compare with **Suffix.** Examples: *un*able, *dis*cover, *mis*pronounce, and *ful*fill.

Preposition

A part of speech that links a noun or pronoun to another word in the sentence. Examples: *of, for, behind, in, through, during, around, above, between,* and *except.*

Prepositional phrase

A word group that begins with a preposition and ends with a noun or pronoun. The phrase modifies another noun or pronoun or a verb in the sentence. Examples: (1) Our new line *of office equipment* will be on display at the convention. (2) Do not park your car *between these posts.*

Present part

One of the five verb parts used in constructing tenses. This part is the form shown as the main dictionary entry of the verb. Examples: *call, discuss, answer, see, write,* and *go.*

Present participle

One of the five verb parts used in constructing tenses. For most verbs this part is formed by adding *ing* to the present part, the form listed in the dictionary. Examples: *calling* (call), *discussing* (discuss), and *answering* (answer). The present participle for verbs not following this pattern is shown in the dictionary directly after the main entry. Examples: *omitting* (omit), *writing* (write), and *starring* (star).

Present perfect tense

Used to describe an action that began in the past but has continued during the time leading to the present. This tense is formed by using the helping verb *has* or *have* and the past participle of the main verb. Example: We *have sent* this client at least three reminders about his past-due account.

Present progressive tense

Used to describe an action in progress during the present time. This tense is formed by using the helping verb *am, is,* or *are* and the present participle of the main verb. Example: We *are* now *taking* applications for this position.

Present tense

Used to describe an ongoing action or an existing condition. This tense is formed by using the present part of the verb. Examples: (1) Lisa *drives* 20 miles each day to work. (2) Your company *has* too many employees.

Principal parts of a verb

See **Parts of a verb.**

Principal word

The word in a compound noun that describes or defines the noun most explicitly. Examples: *brother*-in-law, *sergeant* at arms, lieutenant *colonel,* and high *school.*

Principal words in a heading or title to be capitalized

See **Main words in a heading or title to be capitalized**.

Professional title

A title related to a person's employment. Examples: *Professor* Scot Ober, *Governor* Joyce Arntson, *Dean* Dolores Denova, *Vice President* Norlund, *General* Rodriguez, and *Mayor* Bradley.

Progressive tenses

Used to describe actions in progress during various time periods. Describes the present, past, or future by using a form of *to be* as a helping verb and the present participle of the main verb. Examples: *are processing, were processing,* and *will be processing.*

Pronoun

A word that functions as the substitute for a noun. Examples: *I, her,* and *they*; *that* and *who*; and *this, each,* and *everyone.*

Proper noun

The name of a specific person, place, or thing. Examples: *Jane Thompson, San Francisco Bay Bridge,* and the *Empire State Building.*

Question mark

A mark of punctuation (?) used to end a word group or complete sentence that is a direct question. Example: Have you received any further information about the proposed project?

Quotation mark

A mark of punctuation (") used primarily to set off the exact words spoken or written by another person. Example: The author stated in his article, "As interest rates decline, investments in the municipal bond market become less attractive."

Reflexive pronoun

A pronoun ending with *self* or *selves* that refers back to or is acted upon by another noun or pronoun in the sentence. Examples: *Tom himself* was unsure of the date when the property was sold. *We* can certainly give *ourselves* a pat on the back for this major accomplishment.

Regular verb

A verb that forms its parts by adding standard endings to the present form; that is, by adding *ed* for the past part, *ed* for the past participle, and *ing* for the present participle. Example: *check, checked, checked, checking.*

Relative clause

A word group (containing a subject and a verb) introduced by a pronoun that refers back and relates to a noun or pronoun in the main clause. Relative clauses are introduced by *who, whoever, whom, whomever, that,* or *which.* Same as *relative pronoun clause.* Example: Dr. Williams is the physician *who will handle your case.*

519

Relative pronoun

The noun substitutes *who, whoever, whom, whomever, that,* and *which* used to introduce a clause that refers back and relates to a noun or pronoun in the main clause. Example: The *subsidiary* of our company *that* handles this product is Belegrath Tool & Die.

Relative pronoun clause

A word group containing a subject and a verb that appears with a main clause; it begins with *who, whom, whoever, whomever, that,* or *which*. Same as *relative clause*. Example: Heritage Inc. is the real estate agency *that is handling the sale of our Springfield warehouse.*

Restrictive

A word or word group that contributes substantially to the main idea of the sentence and is needed for it to convey the same meaning. Without the word or word group, the meaning of the sentence would be changed or incomplete.

Restrictive appositive

A word or word group used to rename or describe a previous noun or pronoun. The word or word group is needed to identify *which one*. Example: The *book The Pentagon Heroes* has been on the best-seller list for the past eight weeks.

Restrictive clause

A word group that (1) contains a subject and a verb and (2) appears with a main clause. Although this word group is subordinate to the main idea, it does clarify, limit, or otherwise affect its meaning. A *restrictive clause* is the same as an *essential subordinate clause,* a *restrictive dependent clause,* or a *restrictive subordinate clause*. Examples: (1) This order will be shipped *as soon as I receive approval from our Credit Department*. (2) The only person *who can approve this request* is the vice president of financial services.

Restrictive dependent clause

See **Restrictive clause**.

Restrictive phrase

A word group beginning with a preposition, an infinitive, or a participle and ending with a noun or pronoun. This word group affects the meaning of the main clause by answering such questions as *who, what, which one, when, why, how, whether,* or *to what degree*. Examples: (1) The auction will be held *on Saturday, December 4*. (2) Please mail the enclosed postcard *to obtain further information*. (3) We increased our advertising budget *hoping to increase sales*.

Restrictive subordinate clause

See **Restrictive clause**.

Return address

The complete address of the person writing a business letter that is not prepared on letterhead stationery. On envelopes prepared for mailing, the complete address of the person mailing the envelope and its contents.

Roman numeral

One of a sequence of numbering based on the ancient Roman system. In business this system is used primarily for numbering the major divisions in an outline, the chapters in a report, and the preliminary pages of a report. Examples: *I, II, III, IV, V* and *i, ii, iii, iv, v.*

Salutation

The opening greeting in a business letter. Examples: *Gentlemen, Ladies and Gentlemen, Dear Dr. Gates, Dear Ms. Howell,* and *Dear Bob.*

Semicolon

A mark of punctuation (;) used primarily to join two complete thoughts in a sentence. Example: We have not received any responses to our advertisement for an administrative assistant; therefore, please do not renew our ad in the *Valley Star.*

Sentence fragment

A word group ending with a period, question mark, or exclamation mark that is not a complete sentence or does not represent a complete thought. Example: We are interested in sponsoring a number of spot announcements. *That describe how our services and employees benefit the community.*

Series

Three or more words or word groups that have the same structure within a sentence. Items in a series consist of words, phrases, or clauses. The last item is joined to the others with a coordinating conjunction: *and, or,* or *nor.* Example: You may *telephone, fax, or mail* your orders.

Signature block

In a business letter, the lines that contain the signature of the writer, the typewritten name of the writer, and the title of the writer, if any.

Simple fraction

Any portion of a whole number that is less than *one.* Examples: 1/4 or *one fourth,* 2/3 or *two thirds,* and 3/5 or *three fifths.*

Simple noun

The name of a person, place, or thing that consists of one word. Examples: *Mary, desk, computer,* and *manager.*

Simple sentence

A word group that contains only one subject and one verb (or verb phrase) and makes sense. Example: I received the package of materials yesterday.

Simple subject

The single word in the main clause of a sentence that answers *who* or *what* in relation to the verb. Example: All *employees* in our division *have received* copies of the employee newsletter.

Simple tenses

The present, past, and future tenses. Examples: (1) He *writes* well. (2) He *wrote* this letter yesterday. (3) He *will write* the letter tomorrow.

Singular

A mode or form of nouns, pronouns, and verbs signifying *one*. Examples: *truck* (vs. *trucks*), *she* (vs. *they*), and *drives* (vs. *drive*).

Singular noun

The form used to name a person, place, or thing that signifies *one*. Examples: *supervisor, country,* and *bank*.

Slash

A symbol (/) used primarily for expressing fractions and certain expressions. Same as a *solidus* and a *virgule*. Examples: *3¾, c/o* (in care of), and *and/or*.

Solidus

See **Slash.**

Stated verb

A verb expressed orally or in written format. Compare with **Implied verb**. Examples: (1) If this *is* so, please *call* me. (2) He *is* older than I *am*.

Statement

A word group that presents facts or ideas. It is concluded with a period. Example: Our company was established in 1973.

Subject

The word or word group in the main or subordinate clause of a sentence that answers *who* or *what* in relation to the verb. Examples: (1) The *stockholders* of the corporation *approved* the merger last month. (2) Both *answers and explanations* for this test *are contained* in the instructor's manual. (3) *We will notify* you when your *order arrives.*

Subject complement

The noun, pronoun, or adjective following a being verb (*am, is, are, was, were, be, been*) that either renames or describes the subject. Examples: (1) The former *supervisor* of our department *is* the new *vice president*. (2) The *paintings* in this exhibition *are* exceptionally *valuable*.

Subject of a clause

The word or word group in the subordinate clause of a sentence that answers *who* or *what* in relation to the verb. Example: If *you are interested* in this position, please send us your résumé.

Subject of a sentence

The word or word group in the main clause of a sentence that answers *who* or *what* in relation to the verb. Example: As I mentioned in my previous memorandum, any further *delays* in the completion of this contract *will cost* the company thousands of dollars.

Subject of an infinitive

A noun or pronoun that appears directly before an infinitive. Example: I did not expect *him to have* the authority to release this kind of information.

Subjective case, Subjective case form

A noun or pronoun used as the subject of a sentence, the complement of a *being* verb, or the object of the infinitive *to be* when this infinitive has no subject. Nouns always maintain the same form; pronouns require a specific form: *I, he, she, you, we, they, who, whoever.* Same as *nominative case, nominative case form.* Examples: (1) *They* signed the contract this morning. (2) The only person who responded was *he.* (3) I would not want to be *she* when our manager discovers her errors.

Subjunctive mood

Used to describe events that cannot or probably will not happen and conditions that are not true or highly unlikely. The plural form *were* is used with *if, as if, as though,* or *wish* for singular subjects when the situation described is not true or is unlikely. Examples: (1) *If* I *were* you, I would refer this letter to my attorney. (2) During the meeting Tina acted *as if* she, not Ms. Elliott, *were* the department manager.

Subordinate clause

A word group that contains a subject and a verb but cannot stand alone as a complete sentence. Same as a *dependent clause.* Example: Please notify our office *if you need any additional sales literature.*

Subordinating conjunction

A specific kind of conjunction used to introduce a dependent or subordinate word group that contains a subject and a verb. Examples: *if, as, when, because,* and *since.*

Suffix

A syllable attached to the ending of a word or word root that forms a derivative word or an inflectional form. Compare with **Prefix**. Examples: invest*ment,* account*ing,* and fruit*ful.*

Superlative form

The spelling or form of an adjective or an adverb when it compares more than two nouns or pronouns or more conditions than two. Compare with **Comparative form**. Examples: (1) Your firm is the *most* highly *respected* one in the industry. (2) Sales figures for this year are the *highest* in our company's history.

Suspending hyphen

A hyphen following the first word (or multiple words) of a compound adjective in which the last word of the compound adjective appears later. Examples: (1) This carpeting may be purchased in *10-, 12-,* and 15-foot widths. (2) Most of our automobile loans extend over a *four-* or five-year period.

Syllable

A unit of spoken language used to make up words. Syllables are marked off in main dictionary entries; a small dot separates each syllable. Written words may be divided at the end of a line only between syllables. Examples: *syl•la•ble, di•vi•sion,* and *ir•re•vo•ca•ble.*

Temporary compound

A compound adjective not appearing in the dictionary. This compound is hyphenated only when it precedes the noun it modifies. Examples: (1) These *easy-to-follow instructions* were written by one of our staff members. (2) These *instructions* are *easy to follow.*

Tense
The form of a verb that places an action or a condition in a time frame.

Transitional expression, Transitional word
A word or phrase that does not contribute to the meaning of a sentence but takes the listener or reader smoothly from one concept to another by bridging two ideas or signaling a turn in thought. Examples: (1) Our supplier is unable to obtain any additional pieces of Harwood china by Lexington; *therefore,* we are returning your deposit. (2) You may, *on the other hand,* wish to upgrade the memory of your computer to 512 megabytes.

Transitive verb
A verb that has an object. Compare with **Intransitive verb**. Examples: (1) Mr. Morris *called me* yesterday. (2) Please *place the book* on the table. (3) Our supervisor *gave her* an excellent *rating.*

Uppercase
Capital letters. Examples: *A, M,* and *IBM.*

Verb
A part of speech that shows action or movement or describes a situation or condition. Examples: *write, listen, send, be, appear,* and *look.*

Verb phrase
A verb part combined with helpers such as *was, have, did,* and *will* to form tenses. Examples: *were divided, had reached, does work, will have finished,* and *may be reached.*

Vertical listing
A listing of items in which each item begins a new line on the page. Compare with **Horizontal listing**. The following entries are an example of a vertical listing:

First entry in the listing
Second entry in the listing
Third entry in the listing
Fourth entry in the listing
Last entry in the listing

Virgule
See **Slash.**

Vowel
Letters of the alphabet *a, e, i, o,* and *u.*

524

Glossary B
Glossary of Computer and Internet Terms

The following listing of terms is only a sampling of words and phrases peculiar to computer applications, computer technology, and the Internet. Specialized dictionaries dealing with computer and Internet terms are available in printed form (see Section 15-1c) and on-line (see Section 15-11). Two additional on-line sources for obtaining definitions and detailed explanations of computer and Internet terminology are *Webopaedia* (a search site that locates definitions and explanations of computer and Internet terms)[1] and *Walt's Internet Glossary* (an extensive, up-to-date listing of Internet terms and their definitions).[2]

Access point
A network device that interconnects a wireless network to a wired local area network.

Access time
The amount of time the computer takes to locate (retrieve) a piece of data in its storage system. See also **Megahertz** and **Gigahertz**.

American Standard Code for Information Interchange (ASCII)
A seven-bit code used for transferring information asynchronously on local and long-distance telecommunications lines.

Animated GIF
A GIF (Graphical Interchange Format) graphic file, which consists of two or more images shown in a timed sequence that gives the illusion of motion.

Applet
A miniprogram that may be downloaded quickly from a Web page and deployed by any computer with a Java-capable browser.

Applications software
Computer programs developed for a specific purpose such as word processing, desktop publishing, graphics, spreadsheets, presentations, database management, accounting, Web page design, and other related functions.

ASCII
See **American Standard Code for Information Interchange**.

---

[1]*Webopedia,* INT Media Group Incorporated, 2002, <http://www.pcwebopaedia.com/> (21 August 2002).

[2]Howe, Walt, *Walt's Internet Glossary,* 2002, <http://www.walthowe.com/glossary/> (21 August 2002).

Backup

A copy of computer data on an external storage medium, such as a floppy disk or tape, to preserve that information in case the primary storage device fails.

Binary numbering system

A numbering system with a base of 2 that uses either 0 or 1 to represent values.

Bit

A binary digit (either 0 or 1).

Bookmark

The process of marking a Web page so that it may be located easily again at a later time. Web browsers contain a bookmarking feature that permits the user to save the address (URL) of a Web page so that the page can easily be retrieved and revisited.

Boolean operators

Phrases and words such as *AND, OR,* and *NOT* that may be used in a search string at some Internet search sites to refine or limit a search.

Boot

The process of loading the operating system program into the computer, enabling it to accept and run applications software.

Browser

A graphic interface program that provides user-friendly techniques for searching and viewing World Wide Web Internet sites.

Buffer

The area within a computer or printer memory into which information is read and held until the data are recorded or printed.

Bulletin board system (BBS)

An on-line message system where information on a topic is posted electronically. Once a message is posted, anyone having access to that board may read and respond to the posting.

Byte

A group of eight bits used as a measure of the storage capacity of computers, e.g., 32K = 32,000 bytes of data that can be stored in memory. One byte may be equated to a single letter or space.

Cable Internet

Internet access via traditional cable television networks through a cable modem that permits users to transmit and receive data over their cable television line approximately 20 times faster than through a standard telephone modem. Cable Internet does not interfere with television viewing.

Cache

The storage area within a browser that houses the URLs, text, images, and sounds of Web pages that have been accessed. If the sites are revisited, the pages do not have to be downloaded if they are still resident in the cache.

Cathode-ray tube (CRT)

A television-like screen used with a computer or terminal for displaying data.

CD-R

See **Compact disc recordable**.

CD-ROM

See **Compact disc read-only memory**.

CD-RW

See **Compact disc rewritable**.

Cell

A specific point in a spreadsheet or table where both the row and column intersect.

Cell address

The code designation such as *A2, C4,* or *G9* that identifies the column and row location of a specific cell in a spreadsheet or table. Columns are labeled with alphabetic characters; rows are numbered.

Central processing unit (CPU)

Components of computer systems that enable processing to occur by controlling the input and output functions.

Chip

A tiny electronic component that enables computers to process and store data.

Communicating computer

A computer that is connected through a modem (or other transmission means) to other computers so that data may be exchanged between or among the terminals.

Compact disc read-only memory (CD or CD-ROM)

A disc that can store up to 650 MB of data, all of which can be made available interactively on the computer's display screen. A CD-ROM disc can be used, for example, to access an entire set of encyclopedias, Merriam-Webster's collegiate dictionary, and large numbers of fonts or clip art images for desktop publishing and Web page design.

Compact disc recordable (CD-R)

A technology that permits computer users to write to and read from a standard, initially blank compact disc but not erase or change what has been recorded.

Compact disc rewritable (CD-RW)

A compact disc that is erasable and may be used again and again in the same manner as an audiocassette.

Compatible

The ability of one computer to accept and process data from another computer without conversion or code modification.

Cookie

Cookie technology allows the storage of personal preferences for Internet use through a message given to a Web browser by a Web server. The browser stores the message in a text file called a *cookie file*. Each time the browser requests a page from the server, the message is sent back to the server. Cookie files may be used to (1) personalize Web sites and (2) record information accessed, ads viewed, purchases made, files downloaded, and other preferences. Individuals who view cookies as a privacy problem may purchase *cookie munchers,* software that deletes cookies upon logging off.

CPU
See **Central processing unit**.

CRT
See **Cathode-ray tube**.

CRT screen
See **Monitor**.

Cursor
A highlighted mark on a computer display screen that shows where the next character will appear.

Cut
A command used to move (1) a section of text, a display of values, or an image from a document; (2) a file or array of files; or (3) a folder or array of folders to a temporary buffer from where they may be deleted or moved to another location. (See also **Paste**.) The process of moving selected items from one place to another is often called *cut and paste.*

Data processing (DP)
The process of employing computers to store, manipulate, and report on data used by an organization.

Database
A collection of interrelated data composed of fields and records that may be accessed in a nonsequential manner. Information may be sorted, extracted, and summarized.

Default
A setting in a computer, printer, or program that is automatically implemented if no other choice is designated.

Desktop
The opening screen of the operating system that displays shortcuts to frequently used software applications, functions, folders, or files.

Desktop computer
A computer designed to fit on top of a desk. Typically the monitor sits on top of the desk, and the keyboard is in front of the monitor. The tower may sit on the floor or be housed in a special compartment in the desk.

Desktop publishing
Combines a laser printer or inkjet printer with a microcomputer and software application programs to create documents that appear as though they have been professionally printed. Desktop publishing permits the use of graphics and a variety of fonts to achieve print quality.

Dialog box
A temporary box that appears on the screen to display information or request input.

Digital camera
A camera that stores images digitally instead of on film. Pictures are stored in image files and may be downloaded to the computer where they may be edited and printed through various software applications.

Digital subscriber line (DSL)
Refers to several new digital technologies for fast two-way data connections over ordinary telephone lines. Consumer DSL is purported to offer speeds up to 1 MB per second.

Digital video disc or digital versatile disc (DVD)
Similar to a CD-ROM, but different because it can hold up to 17 GB of data instead of 650 MB. One DVD can play up to 133 minutes of a Hollywood full-featured film, which encompasses about 92 percent of the films ever made. DVD technology, however, is not restricted to recording Hollywood films.

Directory
A list of files stored on a disk.

Disk
A magnetic storage device on which information may be stored. Disks may be either floppy or hard. Hard disks are internal and have considerably more storage capacity than do floppy disks. See also **Floppy disk**; **Hard disk**.

Disk drive
A computer device that reads data from and writes data to a disk.

Documentation
A set of instructions that enable an operator to run a computer or program.

Domain name
The unique name that identifies an Internet site. Domain names have at least two parts, each separated by a dot (.); e.g., *amgen.com, cbeaonline.org,* and *census.gov.*

Download
The process of transmitting a file from one computer to another, e.g., the process of transferring a file or files from the Internet (or a file attached to an E-mail message) to the user's computer.

DP
See **Data processing**.

DSL
See **Digital subscriber line**.

DVD
See **Digital video disc**.

E-commerce
The sale and purchase of goods and services through the Internet.

Electronic mail (E-mail)
A system for the transmission of computer-generated messages and documents from one point to another through the use of telephone lines, satellite, microwaves, or direct cable.

Emoticon
See **Smiley**.

Ergonomics
The science of designing office systems to meet the needs of the human body.

Execute
To carry out an instruction, perform an operation, or run a program on a computer.

External storage
A device that stores information separate from the computer.

Facsimile (fax)
A device used to scan printed pages—including text, tables, charts, diagrams, photographs, and any other graphic data—and transmit copies of these pages electronically through a similar device at another location.

Fiber optics
A technology that uses hair-like glass fibers to enable telecommunications systems to transmit data at high rates of speed.

Field
A defined group or block of data within a record in a database, for example, *Patient Name*.

File
A named location within a computer disk in which data has been placed and stored; for example, *Glossary B.doc, 2004 Sales.xls,* and *Model 83 Sales Presentation.ppt.*

File transfer protocol (FTP)
A system that enables one computer to transfer files to another without distorting the data during the transfer process.

Floppy disk
A removable, magnetically sensitive disk used as a secondary storage device.

Folder
An organizational storage unit, similar to paper filing systems, in the Windows and Macintosh environments that contains multiple files related to the same topic.

Font
A complete set of characters for a single typeface in one size and one type style.

Footer

Information automatically printed at the bottom of each page of a document.

Format

The organized layout or appearance of data, usually when the data is printed on paper.

FTP

See **File transfer protocol**.

Function keys

The *F1* through *F12* keys on a computer keyboard, which are programmable. Their function depends on the program being used.

Gigabyte (GB)

A unit of capacity or memory measurement equal to approximately 1 billion bytes or 1,000 megabytes. For desktop and laptop computers, this measurement is usually applied to the size of the hard drive installed in the computer.

Gigahertz (GHz)

A measure used to assess the speed of a computer processor. A computer with a processing speed of 1 GHz is processing data at 1 billion bytes or 1,000 megabytes per second.

Global search

A computer search throughout an entire document for words, characters, or other data that need to be located or changed.

Graphical user interface (GUI)

A program component that uses the graphics capabilities of the computer to make the program easier to use; e.g., icons, dialog boxes, and drop-down menus.

Graphics

Information entered into a computer and formatted as graphs, charts, illustrations, and images. These forms may be displayed on the screen or printed on paper.

GUI

See **Graphical user interface**.

Hard copy

A document printed on paper that has been transferred from the document displayed on a computer monitor or a file stored on a computer disk.

Hard disk

A magnetic storage device that has a large data storage capacity. Typical contemporary microcomputers have a permanently installed hard disk that holds from 20 gigabytes (20 billion bytes) to 80 gigabytes (80 billion bytes) of data.

Hardware

A term used to describe the actual equipment, as distinguished from the programs, used in the computing process. (See also **Software**.)

Header
Information automatically printed at the top of each page of a document.

High-capacity disk
A magnetic storage disk that stores from 100 to 250 megabytes of data.

High-density disk
A magnetic storage disk that stores 1.44 megabytes of data.

Home page
An opener that usually outlines the contents of a Web site and provides links to other pages on the site.

HTML
See **Hypertext markup language**.

HTTP
See **Hypertext transfer protocol**.

Hyperlink
On the World Wide Web, graphic images or words appearing in a different color and/or underlined that transport the viewer with a mouse click to a related site.

Hypertext markup language (HTML)
The programming language used to create pages for sites on the World Wide Web of the Internet.

Hypertext transfer protocol (HTTP)
A protocol used to transfer information within the World Wide Web. It prescribes how messages are to be formatted and transmitted and how Web servers and browsers should interact.

Icon
An on-screen graphic symbol that represents a program file, data file, or some other computer entity or function.

Information processing
The movement of words, symbols, or numbers from the origination of an idea to its destination.

Inkjet printer
A nonimpact printer that forms an image by spraying ink from tiny jets.

Input
Data entered into a computer for processing.

Insert mode
Inserted text pushes existing text to the right as information is keyboarded at the point of insertion. (See also **Typeover mode**.)

Interface
The process that connects one component of the computer with another or connects one computer with another.

Internet
An extensive system of connected computers that comprise a vast number of networks made up of millions of host computers. This on-line global network, which is accessible in more than 170 countries, has promoted information exchange among virtually all segments of our society.

Internet service provider (ISP)
A company or organization that provides a dial-up, cable, or digital subscriber line (DSL) connection to the Internet and an E-mail account.

Intranet
An organizational network (usually corporate) based on Internet protocols that look and act like Web pages. An intranet is accessible only to members of the organization and those others given access.

ISP
See **Internet service provider**.

Java
A high-level programming language that permits miniprograms, known as *applets,* to be downloaded and run on Web pages.

Justification
Distributing letters, numbers, symbols, and spaces within lines of text so that the right margin ends evenly.

KB
See **Kilobyte**.

Keyboarding
Using a keyboard to enter data into a computer.

Kilobyte (KB)
A term used to describe the storage capacity of computer memory and storage devices. One *KB* equals 1,024 bytes of memory.

LAN
See **Local area network**.

Landscape orientation
Repositioning the printed page so that text and graphics are printed across the length (the longer dimension) of the page instead of the width. (See also **Portrait orientation**.)

Laptop computer
A portable computer.

Laser printer

A high-speed, high-quality nonimpact printer that employs a narrow beam of electromagnetic light to enable it to print at speeds over 20,000 lines per minute.

Liquid crystal display (LCD)

A type of monitor used with many portable computers.

Listserv

A mailing list server that automatically distributes a prepared E-mail to all those addresses on a specified list.

Local area network (LAN)

A computer network that is in one physical location—a building or a group of buildings.

Macro

A recorded set of computer instructions that may be executed with a minimum number of keystrokes or mouse clicks.

MB

See **Megabyte**.

Medium

The material on which information is recorded, e.g., magnetic tape or disks.

Megabyte (MB)

A term used to describe the storage capacity of computer memory and storage devices. One megabyte equals 1,024,000 bytes of memory or storage capacity.

Megahertz (MHz)

A measure to describe the speed at which a computer operates to execute commands and process data.

Memory

That part of the computer that holds information for use.

Memory, random access (RAM)

Temporary memory within the computer that is used primarily for loading programs from disk or tape or holding data until it is stored to disk. Data in RAM memory is lost when the computer is turned off.

Memory, read only (ROM)

Stores permanent programs that may not be altered. They include the programs that instruct the computer what to do when the power is turned on and how to do various jobs such as loading the operating system and application programs from disk or tape. ROM will not lose its information when the power is turned off.

Menu

A listing on the screen of possible commands an operator may choose to perform tasks on a computer.

Merge
A word processing function that allows the data in two prefiled locations to be combined—on screen or during the printing process.

MHz
See **Megahertz**.

Modem
A device attached to computer terminals that allows the transmission of data between terminals over telephone wires by converting digital signals to analog signals at one end and reconverting the analog signals back to digital signals at the other end.

Monitor
A television-like screen that connects to a computer and displays data. The monitor is also referred to as the *CRT screen*.

Mouse
A small device that moves an on-screen arrow to select functions. Clicking a control button on the mouse enables the operator to activate a selected function such as opening or closing a file, displaying a menu on the screen, or performing another operation.

Multimedia
The integration of text, graphics, sound, animation, and video in computer applications.

Network
A group of computers (or other devices) connected into a planned system to enable the exchange of files and resources among the members of the system.

OCR
See **Optical character recognition**.

On-line
Connected to the Internet through an Internet service provider with the computer and peripherals turned on and ready to send and receive data.

Operating system (OS)
An integrated collection of service routines for supervising the sequencing and processing of programs by a computer. Operating systems may perform debugging, input-output, machine accounting, compilation, and storage-assignment tasks. Computers will perform no functions until an operating system has been loaded. The most popular operating systems for personal computers include Windows and Macintosh System.

Optical character recognition (OCR)
Text read into a computer by scanning a document electronically.

OS
See **Operating system**.

Overstrike mode
See **Typeover mode**.

Paste
A command used to retrieve (1) a section of text, a display of values, or an image from a document; (2) a file or array of files; or (3) a folder or array of folders from a temporary buffer and place the selection in another location. The process of moving selected items from one place to another is often called *cut and paste*. The process of copying selected items from one place to another is often called *copy and paste*.

PDA
See **Personal digital assistant**.

Peripherals
Equipment such as printers, monitors, scanners, and external disk drives that work in conjunction with the computer but are not part of the computer itself.

Personal digital assistant (PDA)
A handheld device that functions as a personal organizer and provides computing, telephone/fax, and networking features.

Pointer
An on-screen symbol, usually an arrow, that shows the current position of a mouse.

Points
A font-size measurement method that measures the height of a character; 72 points equals 1 inch. A 12-point font is $12/72$ or $1/6$ inch high, and a 24-point font is $24/72$ or $1/3$ inch high. The higher the number in this method of measuring font size, the taller the font.

Port
An entry/exit opening in the computer that connects the central processing unit (CPU) with external devices such as the printer or scanner.

Portrait orientation
Positioning the printed page so that text and graphics are printed across the width (the shorter dimension) of the page. (See also **Landscape orientation**.)

Processing
The transformation of computer input to a final product through the execution of program instructions.

Program
Instructions given to a computer to perform certain tasks. Commercial programs (software) are available for word processing, spreadsheets, databases, presentations, desktop publishing, and many other areas.

Programming
The process of writing instructions to direct a computer to perform certain tasks.

Protocol
A set of conventions for the electronic transmission of data including modes, speed, character length, and code.

RAM
See **Memory, random access**.

Record
Represents all the related fields for a single person, company, or thing in a database.

Replace mode
See **Typeover mode**.

Reprographics
The duplication of hard copy usually by employing a photocopier.

ROM
See **Memory, read only**.

Sans serif
A typeface without small cross strokes at the top and bottom of the characters.

Scanner
A computer peripheral that copies pages of text, artwork, and photographs in digital format for use in applications software.

Screen capture
The process of copying the current screen display to a file or to the printer.

Scrolling
The process of moving text up or down on a computer screen.

Search and replace
A word processing command that directs a computer to locate a piece of information wherever it occurs in a document and replace it with another piece of information.

Search site
A World Wide Web site that contains software for searching and locating a given topic of information on the Internet.

Serif
A typeface with small cross strokes at the top and bottom of the characters.

Shouting
In E-mail messages, placing a series of words in all capital letters.

Smiley
An icon used in E-mail messages that is made up of punctuation marks to indicate the writer's mood; e.g., :-) [smile], ;-) [wink], and :-([sad]. Also known as *emoticons,* an acronym for e*motion icons.*

Soft copy
Information or data shown on the screen.

Software
Programs written to direct the operations of a computer. (See also **Hardware**.)

Sorting
Process of directing the computer to organize information or data in a specific order.

Spam
Unsolicited E-mail, e.g., advertisements.

Split screen
The ability of some software programs to display two or more documents on the screen simultaneously.

Spreadsheet
A computer program similar to an accounting worksheet that displays columns and rows in the form of cells on the screen. When values in the cells are changed, the result may be calculated automatically throughout the worksheet.

Strikeover mode
See **Typeover mode**.

Template
A document or spreadsheet that includes only the identical text and/or formulas needed for an application that are repeated continually. For each repetition of the application, the preparer needs only to insert the variable information.

Terminal
A configuration connected to the computer for the purpose of entering and retrieving data. The most common computer terminal consists of a monitor and a keyboard.

Tilde
An accent mark produced by the keyboard that is a small horizontal wavy line (~).

Toggle
The process of switching back and forth between two modes by pressing a key. For example, once the *Caps Lock* key is pressed, the keyboard will remain in the all-capital-letter mode until the *Caps Lock* key is pressed again.

Toolbar
A set of navigational buttons—icons—used in graphical user interface (GUI) applications that perform frequently used related commands.

Typeface
The design of a set of type characters. Examples of typefaces are Times Roman, Arial, CG Times, and Univers.

Typeover mode
Inserted text replaces existing text from the point of insertion; also known as *overstrike mode, replace mode,* or *strikeover mode.* (See also **Insert mode**.)

Type style
The treatment of typeface characters; such as, regular, bold, italic, underline, shadow, outline, and bold italic.

Uniform resource locator (URL)
The unique address of each Web page. A World Wide Web address locator that enables the World Wide Web system to search for, locate, and open a page.

Universal serial bus (USB)
An external bus standard for microcomputers that supports data transfer rates up to 12 megabits per second. A single port may be used to connect up to 127 peripheral devices such as printers, mice, joysticks, scanners, modems, keyboards, and tablets.

UNIX
An operating system for a wide variety of computers (from mainframes to personal computers) that is suited for multitasking and multiuser operations.

Upload
To transmit data from a computer to a mainframe or a network.

URL
See **Uniform resource locator**.

USB
See **Universal serial bus**.

User friendly
The degree to which the operations of a computer or software program are made relatively easy to learn through the use of menus, function keys, and documentation.

VGA
See **Video graphics array**.

Video display terminal (VDT)
A television-like screen used with a computer or terminal for displaying data. Same as *monitor*.

Video graphics array (VGA)
A color bit-mapped graphics display standard developed by IBM and supported by all microcomputers manufactured today.

Virus
A command or program hidden in an executable file that can cause computer damage or data loss.

Voice-recognition software
An applications software program that recognizes spoken words and prints them on the computer screen as they are spoken.

Wi-Fi
See **Wireless fidelity**.

Windows

(1) A series of Microsoft operating systems. (2) Divisions on a computer screen that enable an operator to view parts of a document or different documents simultaneously. Windows are created on a computer screen through software application programs.

Wireless fidelity (Wi-Fi)

A wireless network installed primarily in offices, coffee shops, airports, and homes. Wireless fidelity is another name for a wireless network running under the 802.11b standard, which is now the most common wireless local area network.

Word processing

The use of computerized equipment and software programs to keyboard, edit, produce, and store business documents.

Word wrap

A process by which a word at the end of a line is automatically dropped to the next line if it extends beyond the right margin.

World Wide Web (WWW)

A vast network of computers on the Internet that host documents formatted with graphics, sound, and other media. These documents may be accessed with an on-line connection and appropriate software (a browser).

WYSIWYG

A term used to describe on-screen displays that show the appearance of the printed text. This acrynom for the phrase *What you see is what you get* is pronounced "wizzy wig."

Zip drive

A high-capacity floppy disk drive. Zip disks can hold 100 MB or 250 MB of data and are often used for backing up hard drives.

Index

541

Q

T

Abbreviations of States and Territories

State or Territory	Two-Letter Postal Designation	Standard Abbreviation
Alabama	AL	Ala.
Alaska	AK	—
Arizona	AZ	Ariz.
Arkansas	AR	Ark.
California	CA	Calif., Cal.
Colorado	CO	Colo., Col.
Connecticut	CT	Conn.
Delaware	DE	Del.
District of Columbia	DC	D.C.
Florida	FL	Fla.
Georgia	GA	Ga.
Guam	GU	—
Hawaii	HI	—
Idaho	ID	—
Illinois	IL	Ill.
Indiana	IN	Ind.
Iowa	IA	—
Kansas	KS	Kans., Kan.
Kentucky	KY	Ky.
Louisiana	LA	La.
Maine	ME	—
Maryland	MD	Md.
Massachusetts	MA	Mass.
Michigan	MI	Mich.
Minnesota	MN	Minn.
Mississippi	MS	Miss.
Missouri	MO	Mo.
Montana	MT	Mont.
Nebraska	NE	Nebr., Neb.
Nevada	NV	Nev.
New Hampshire	NH	N.H.
New Jersey	NJ	N.J.
New Mexico	NM	N. Mex.
New York	NY	N.Y.
North Carolina	NC	N.C.
North Dakota	ND	N. Dak.
Ohio	OH	—
Oklahoma	OK	Okla.
Oregon	OR	Oreg., Ore.
Pennsylvania	PA	Pa., Penn., Penna.
Puerto Rico	PR	P.R.
Rhode Island	RI	R.I.
South Carolina	SC	S.C.
South Dakota	SD	S. Dak.
Tennessee	TN	Tenn.
Texas	TX	Tex.
Utah	UT	—
Vermont	VT	Vt.
Virgin Islands	VI	V.I.
Virginia	VA	Va.
Washington	WA	Wash.
West Virginia	WV	W. Va.
Wisconsin	WI	Wis., Wisc.
Wyoming	WY	Wyo.